M000227269

Deliberation, Democracy, and Civic Forums

Innovative forums that integrate citizen deliberation into policy making are revitalizing democracy in many places around the world. Yet controversy abounds over whether these forums ought to be seen as authentic sources of public opinion and how they should fit with existing political institutions. How can civic forums include less powerful citizens and ensure that their perspectives are heard on equal terms with more privileged citizens, officials, and policy experts? How can these fragile institutions communicate citizens' policy preferences effectively and legitimately to the rest of the political system? *Deliberation, Democracy, and Civic Forums* proposes creative solutions for improving equality and publicity, which are grounded in new theories about democratic deliberation, a careful review of research and practice in the field, and several original studies. This book speaks to scholars, practitioners, and sponsors of civic engagement, public management and consultation, and deliberative and participatory democracy.

Christopher F. Karpowitz is an associate professor of political science and the co-director of the Center for the Study of Elections and Democracy at Brigham Young University. He is a coauthor of *The Silent Sex: Gender, Deliberation, and Institutions* (2014) and of *Democracy at Risk: How Political Choices Undermine Citizen Participation, and What We Can Do about It* (2005). He has published in a variety of journals, including the *American Political Science Review*, the *American Journal of Political Science*, the *Journal of Politics, Public Opinion Quarterly*, the *British Journal of Political Science, Perspectives on Politics, Political Communication, Politics & Society, PS: Political Science and Politics*, and the *Journal of Public Deliberation*. Prior to joining BYU, he was a postdoctoral fellow in democracy and human values at Princeton University's Center for Human Values.

Chad Raphael is a professor of communication at Santa Clara University. He is the author of *Investigated Reporting: Muckrakers, Regulators, and the Struggle over Television Documentary* (2005), which won the Frank Luther Mott–Kappa Tau Alpha Research Award for the best book on journalism and mass communication, the Donald McGannon Award for social and ethical relevance in communications policy research, and the Association for Education in Journalism and Mass Communication History Division Award for best book. He has published in many journals, including *Political Communication, Politics and Society, Communication Law and Policy, Journalism Studies*, the *Journal of Educational Computing Research*, the *Journal of Computer-Mediated Communication*, and *Games and Culture*, and in many edited volumes. He consults for non-profit organizations on their communication strategies and is former chair of the board at the Jessie Smith Noyes Foundation and the Silicon Valley Toxics Coalition. Before entering academia, he was a community organizer on affordable housing and environmental issues.

Deliberation, Democracy, and Civic Forums

Improving Equality and Publicity

CHRISTOPHER F. KARPOWITZ

Brigham Young University

CHAD RAPHAEL

Santa Clara University

CAMBRIDGE
UNIVERSITY PRESS

CAMBRIDGE
UNIVERSITY PRESS

32 Avenue of the Americas, New York, NY 10013-2473, USA

Cambridge University Press is part of the University of Cambridge.

It furthers the University's mission by disseminating knowledge in the pursuit of education, learning, and research at the highest international levels of excellence.

www.cambridge.org
Information on this title: www.cambridge.org/9781107046436

© Cambridge University Press 2014

First published 2014

Printed in the United Kingdom by Clays, St Ives plc

A catalog record for this publication is available from the British Library.

Library of Congress Cataloging in Publication Data
Karpowitz, Christopher F., 1969–
Deliberation, democracy, and civic forums : improving equality and publicity / Christopher F. Karpowitz, Chad Raphael.
    pages   cm
Includes bibliographical references and index.
ISBN 978-1-107-04643-6 (hardback)
1. Political participation.   2. Political planning – Citizen participation.
3. Democratization.   I. Raphael, Chad.   II. Title.
JF799.K37   2014
323'.042 – dc23   2014018611

ISBN 978-1-107-04643-6 Hardback

For Betty and Adin and
for Jordan, Caleb, Quinn, Cami, and Zachary

Contents

Tables and figures

Acknowledgments

Unlike Athena, the Greek goddess and protector of Athenian democracy who sprang from Zeus' head fully grown, this book did not leap from the authors' brains in its finished form. Instead, it was the product of much deliberation with colleagues, research assistants, and each other, and a great deal of support from our funders, publishers, and families.

Our thinking about democratic deliberation benefitted from good advice offered by our academic colleagues, including Betty Achinstein, Jane Mansbridge, Tali Mendelberg, Seeta Peña Gangadharan, and Kathy Cramer. We especially appreciate the thoughtful and helpful feedback on drafts of the book manuscript from Archon Fung, John Gastil, Peter Levine, and Kenneth Manaster. Allen Hammond IV coauthored the research reported in Chapter 3. We also benefitted from the support of colleagues in our home departments, Brigham Young University's Department of Political Science and Santa Clara University's Department of Communication.

Our analysis of how civic forums practice publicity depended upon the research assistance of several terrific undergraduate students who assisted us with content analysis, including Etmae Brinkers, Sarina Caragan, Channing Hancock Christensen, Alicia Gessell, Kyla Moran, and Amanda Waldron. Kathleen Lynn conducted interviews with participants for the study reported in Chapter 3.

We are grateful to the Community Technology Foundation of California and the California Consumer Protection Foundation for funding the civic forum that introduced us to one another, which we discuss throughout this book. Our research and writing were also supported by Santa Clara University's Center for Science, Technology, and Society and the university's Markkula Center for Applied Ethics as well as Brigham

Young University's Department of Political Science and Center for the Study of Elections and Democracy.

Several chapters expand considerably upon previously published journal articles, which we thank the publishers for permission to use:

> Chapter 3: Christopher F. Karpowitz, Chad Raphael, and Allen S. Hammond IV. 2009. Deliberative Democracy and Inequality: Two Cheers for Enclave Deliberation among the Disempowered. *Politics & Society 37*: 576–615, by permission of Sage Publishers.

> Chapters 5 and 6: Chad Raphael and Christopher F. Karpowitz. 2013. Good Publicity: The Legitimacy of Public Communication of Deliberation. *Political Communication 30*: 17–41, by permission of Taylor & Francis Publishers.

Figure 6.5 is used with permission of By the People-MacNeil/Lehrer Productions and the Center for Deliberative Democracy.

We thank Robert Dreesen, our editor at Cambridge University Press, and Elizabeth Janetschek at Cambridge, for shepherding this book to completion. The anonymous reviewers for the Press offered insightful and critical feedback that improved the work. Many thanks also to Sara Barnes for copyediting the book, Ariel O. Tuplano for indexing it, Chloe Harries for designing the cover, and Nitesh Sharma for managing production.

Each of us is also thankful for the opportunity we have had to collaborate with one another. Like all good partnerships, ours involved both shared and complementary contributions. We designed and performed this research together. Chris was primarily responsible for conducting and drafting the data analyses we report in Chapters 3 through 6. Chad took the lead on drafting the theoretical material. However, we passed our drafts back and forth many times, editing and improving each other's thinking, so that both of us have shaped each section of the final manuscript. In the process, we learned a great deal from one another about the theory, research, and practice of civic deliberation, and about scholarly collaboration.

We are most grateful to our families for supporting us in countless ways and for forgiving us the hours we spent writing. We dedicate this book to them.

Introduction

In 2010, a year after many US congressional representatives' "town hall meetings" on health care policy erupted in shouting matches between some legislators and conservative activists, a bipartisan commission charged by President Barack Obama with proposing a plan to reduce the national deficit tried a different way of consulting public opinion. The commission turned to America*Speaks*, a non-partisan organization that convenes public deliberations on policy issues, called 21st Century Town Meetings. America*Speaks* held a series of innovative forums, entitled "Our Budget, Our Economy," in which citizens conferred about fiscal reform. While the 2009 health care town halls were open meetings that mainly attracted conservatives mobilized by interest groups to oppose Democrats' health care proposals, the America*Speaks* forums required participants to apply to participate and affirmatively recruited some participants, in hopes of assembling a more diverse, representative, and open-minded sample of Americans. Also in contrast to the health care meetings, the "Our Budget, Our Economy" forums primarily focused citizens on deliberating with each other, rather than in engaging in highly controlled questioning and debate with their congressional representative.

On one day in June, over 3000 individuals in 19 communities took part in the forums. Participants read briefing materials drafted in partnership with a committee of 30 ideologically diverse budget experts, heard brief presentations from Republican and Democratic officials, and sat down to discuss the issues in small groups. Each group was asked to select from a menu of over 40 possible tax increases or budget cuts and come to agreement on a plan to reduce the federal budget deficit by half within 15 years. Each individual was then given the choice to construct her or his own package of tax hikes and spending cuts that would accomplish the same goal.

However, even before the forums were held, some policy advocates and bloggers publicly attacked "Our Budget, Our Economy" as an illegitimate attempt to manipulate participants into supporting draconian budget cuts in the midst of a global recession, when, critics argued, fiscal stimulus was most needed. One commentator predicted that the agenda and briefing materials were so biased that they "virtually guarantee[d] that most of the participants will opt for big cuts to Social Security and Medicare. The results of this song-and-dance will then be presented to President Obama's...commission which will use it as further ammunition...to gut these programs."[1] Another commentator warned that "America*Speaks* is part of a well-coordinated media campaign" aimed at "slashing government programs."[2]

Political scientists Benjamin Page and Lawrence Jacobs also wrote a pre-emptive paper critiquing the forums. Interest advocates often criticize a civic forum when they fear it will arrive at different conclusions than their own.[3] But when two respected political scientists who have authored important books on the value of civic deliberation raise warnings, extra attention is warranted.[4] Page and Jacobs expressed concern that the deliberators would not be a representative sample of Americans, which would violate the principle that all citizens' voices should count equally in assessments of public opinion, and called on the organizers to disclose the details of how participants were selected. They worried that one sponsor of the event, the economically conservative Peter G. Peterson Foundation, would exert undue influence over the briefing materials and agenda, priming participants to prioritize deficit reduction over social spending, and especially Social Security. Jacobs and Page therefore cautioned that the forum should not be weighed as heavily in public decision making as long-term, stable support for social programs demonstrated in public opinion polls over many decades.[5]

On the whole, these fears were not borne out. Post-event evaluations found that "Our Budget, Our Economy" attracted a fairly representative sample of Americans, and of the communities in which the forums were held, by income, age, ethnicity, and partisan identification.[6] Rather than growing more supportive of cutting Social Security benefits, participants overwhelmingly opted to shore up the program through more

---

[1] Baker 2010.   [2] Eskow 2010.   [3] Hendriks 2011.
[4] Jacobs, Cook, and Delli Carpini, 2009; Page 1996.   [5] Page and Jacobs 2010.
[6] Esterling, Fung, and Lee 2010, 7; Lukensmeyer 2010.

progressive taxation of high earners.[7] Citizens moderated their other positions somewhat: conservatives and moderates grew much more supportive of defense cuts and liberals became more willing to agree to a 5 percent cut in the projected growth of health care spending. While participants' individual budget preferences corresponded closely to their political ideology, the group agreements on deficit reduction packages were less driven by the liberal or conservative leanings of individual group members. This pattern suggests that deliberation allowed citizens to forge agreement across ideological divides, despite the highly polarized national debate at the time.[8] Certainly, the majority of the "Our Budget, Our Economy" deliberators found more common ground on specific steps to reduce the deficit than Congress was able to find in the coming three years, when congressional gridlock on these issues led to the downgrading of the nation's credit rating, and, eventually, to deep across-the-board spending cuts to defense and social programs that few citizens or political leaders of either party publicly professed to want.

While reasonable people may disagree with how the participants as a whole chose to balance spending, taxation, and deficit reduction, we do not see good evidence that participants' views were manipulated or poorly informed, especially in comparison with public opinion polls. Although forum organizers set a restrictive goal for deliberators of halving the deficit, rather than reducing it by more or less, and provided a limited menu of possible taxes or cuts, many participants showed themselves quite capable of challenging these restrictions. A majority supported more government spending in the short term to stimulate the economy even if it raised the deficit, and some participants successfully demanded to add another policy option: adopting single-payer national health insurance as a way to cut health care spending without decreasing benefits.[9] Despite being primed by the briefing materials to consider the deficit an important problem, over half of the groups agreed to cut the deficit by less than 50 percent,[10] which suggests to us that they did not feel bound to meet the target set by the organizers, perhaps because they had higher priorities. While 89 percent of forum participants said they were dissatisfied or very dissatisfied with the quality of political discussion in the United States, 91 percent of participants were satisfied or very satisfied with the discussions

---

[7] At present, Social Security taxes are only applied to the first $106,800 dollars of an individual's income.

[8] Esterling, Fung, and Lee 2010, 44–6.   [9] Hickey 2010.   [10] Lukensmeyer 2010.

at "Our Budget, Our Economy."[11] Seventy-three percent somewhat or strongly agreed the meeting was fair and unbiased, and over 80 percent agreed that "decision makers should incorporate the conclusions of this town meeting into federal budget policy."[12]

There are many reasons that the "Our Budget, Our Economy" forum should have been expected to enjoy widespread acceptance as one legitimate input into the policy-making process, which is all that it aimed to be. It might have appeared as an attractive way of soliciting more thoughtful public input on policy making than traditional ways of consulting citizens, such as the acrimonious town hall meetings on health care a year earlier, ritualized public hearings, or a blizzard of individual public comments submitted online and through the mail. The forum included a more representative sample of Americans than one would find in most public consultations or elections. This was a well-funded effort, and the sponsors included organizations not only from the right but also from the left and center (funding came also from the MacArthur and Kellogg foundations, a fact that many critics failed to note). The forum was organized by an independent organization with a good track record of convening civic deliberation on high-profile issues, such as the redevelopment of the former World Trade Center site in lower Manhattan after the September 11, 2001, attacks.[13] It had the ear of a presidential commission on a high-profile issue, and therefore more potential to influence policy than many exercises in civic deliberation. Yet the forum's legitimacy was undercut before it even began.

"Our Budget, Our Economy" is just one example of the growing number of forums that aim to incorporate citizen deliberation in policy making and that are becoming a significant feature of the global political landscape.[14] Deliberative civic forums have helped to shape many policy proposals and processes, including the state of Oregon's health care reforms, the annual budgets of Latin American cities, energy policy in Texas and Nebraska, Chicago's community policing and school boards, Danish regulations on genetically modified foods, development projects in India and Indonesia, and proposals for electoral reform in two Canadian provinces.[15] Some of these forums have been adopted as

---

[11] Lukensmeyer 2010.   [12] Esterling, Fung, and Lee 2010, 42.

[13] Lukensmeyer, Goldman, and Brigham 2005.

[14] Throughout this book, we use the term "citizens" broadly; we have in mind all people who are taking responsibility for public matters and for governing themselves collectively, regardless of their official citizenship status.

[15] Baiochi 2005; Dryzek and Tucker 2008; Gibson and Woolcock 2008; Isaac and Heller 2003; Fishkin 2009, 152–3; Fung 2003; Fung 2004; Warren and Pearse 2008.

ongoing institutions within the political system, with their own decision-making power. As experiments in civic deliberation have become more consequential, they have sparked criticisms from some officials, interest advocates, and scholars who question the legitimacy of these forums and their proper contribution to democracy.[16] As with "Our Budget, Our Economy," disparagement of deliberative forums' shortcomings, whether real or perceived, can undermine their ability to influence public opinion and policy, and their continued existence.

Our aim in this book is to explore how these new public forums might come to be seen as more legitimate aspects of our democratic system. Part of the reason the "Our Budget, Our Economy" forum and others like it have been undercut is that despite considerable effort on the part of scholars and practitioners of deliberation, there is still much uncertainty about how such forums should fit into the larger system of democratic governance. In this book, we will take on two important challenges forums tend to face.

In our view, these challenges are best understood as doubts about whether the new civic forums can practice equality and publicity, broadly defined. The first challenge has to do with whether citizens can form their preferences autonomously by participating on equal terms. Civic forums must respond to concerns about how multiple power inequalities can affect who is included, how they participate, and the influence they wield within and outside the forum. Do citizens participate fully and freely, or are their views manipulated or ignored by the sponsors who commission and fund these forums; by the organizers who frame the issues and moderate the discussion; and by the experts, advocates, and public officials who often provide information? Are the least powerful elements of the public able to participate as influentially as more privileged citizens?

The second challenge has to do with how organizers of civic forums practice publicity by communicating their goals, process, and conclusions to other elements of the political system. Not everyone wants, or is available, to participate in a given forum. Even if all who are affected by the issues under consideration wanted to take part, deliberation must happen in small groups to allow each member to contribute her or his views and to consider the views of others, so it is often the case that not everyone who is affected by an issue can participate.[17] If a civic forum aims to influence policy or public opinion legitimately, it must involve

---

[16] For summaries of these criticisms, see Barisione 2012; Collingwood and Reedy 2012; Hendriks 2011, especially Chapters 4 and 8; Levine and Nierras 2007; Parkinson 2006a, especially Chapter 1; Tucker 2008.

[17] Parkinson 2006a.

good internal deliberation, but it must also persuade those who did not take part in it of its legitimacy. How can organizers and participants hold themselves accountable for considering the perspectives, opinions, and interests of all who are affected by the issue? How can forums practice transparency about the deliberative process, the conclusions reached, and participants' reasons and evidence for those conclusions? How can other citizens and decision makers evaluate the credibility of deliberative forums and whether they should be seen as authentic expressions of public opinion or the public will? After all, deliberation must ultimately be integrated with other features of the political system, including other measures of public opinion, the claims of elected officials, and the perspectives of interest advocates and other civil society actors. How can civic deliberation establish its legitimacy in a polarized political environment in which other political actors are less willing to deliberate?

We will argue that these new civic forums can make unique and indispensable contributions to democracy. Therefore, our aim in this book will be to strengthen civic forums, not to bury them. We see them as offering an important corrective to the problems of contemporary democracies, in which citizens' voices are too often expressed through uneven electoral participation, unequal interest groups and campaign contributions, unaccountable political parties and leaders, unbalanced media coverage, unreflective public opinion polls, and unattended or unruly public meetings. Civic forums can help to create a healthier democracy, in which citizens develop better informed and more thoughtful political preferences and exercise greater control over the decisions that affect their lives. At the same time, we suggest that these forums can best fulfill their promise by improving how they engage the least powerful on more equal terms and by practicing publicity that better realizes the aims of deliberative democracy outside the forum.

One of our main arguments will be that political equality in the deliberative system as a whole can sometimes be served best by asking the least powerful citizens to deliberate among themselves in their own forums, or as one stage in forums that are more representative of the larger public. This runs counter to the approach of many organizers of civic forums, who often address the challenge of achieving equality by engaging representative or random samples of participants in discussion across social differences. We see deliberation as an activity that ought to be distributed across the political system, rather than as an ideal that must be perfected within a single forum. This should allow us to address some problems of inequality differently. It can free us from the strictures of trying to make every forum representative of the whole, or every small group within the forum as internally diverse as possible, in ways that enhance rather than diminish the forum's contribution to political equality. Integrating "enclave" deliberation among the least powerful participants in civic forums can motivate the marginalized to participate, develop their civic capacities, and create productive tension between identifying their shared interests and considering how these interests relate to a larger common good. This could contribute a broader range of arguments to the public sphere beyond the forum and can even be perceived as legitimate by observers. We offer recommendations for how organizers of civic forums could make space for enclave deliberation of the disempowered while avoiding its potential pitfalls.

Our second major argument will be that deliberative forums must improve how they communicate their work publicly if they are to strengthen the role of civic deliberation across the political system. We define a set of fundamental criteria for the legitimate practice of publicity and use them to assess the final reports of a small but diverse array of civic forums. This is the first sustained examination of how these forums communicate the fruits of their labors to the public and policy makers. We find that all of the reports in our sample slight at least some important principles of deliberative publicity. In response, we show how forums can pay greater attention to reporting deliberators' conclusions as a form of public argumentation and how forums can practice greater transparency about the deliberative process. We also consider some ways of institutionalizing channels of communication between forums and other decision-making arenas.

Deepening democracy will depend on many of the communities to whom this book is addressed. We hope that it prompts academics interested in civic engagement and democratic reform to open up new lines of research that illuminate how thoughtful public opinion can better inform public policy. We hope that the book helps the growing network of practitioners of public consultation and civic engagement to discover new ways to include the least advantaged as full participants and to communicate what happens within civic forums more effectively to government agencies, political leaders, the news media, and the public. And we hope that the book assists the tens of thousands of public officials, non-profit leaders, and other private sector organizations around the world who seek more effective and legitimate ways to respond to the public's expectations that it should be consulted on matters that affect it. Each of these communities has a critical role to play in enhancing the legitimacy of civic forums as meaningful institutions of democratic governance.

In the remainder of this introduction, we explain the growth and define the types of civic forums that are our focus. We go on to root our rationale for these forums in theory and research on civic deliberation, preparing the ground for our arguments about how equality and publicity in civic forums might be improved, and conclude with an overview of the plan of the book.

The rise of civic forums

The spread of civic forums has been inspired by growing interest in citizen deliberation, but also by broader efforts to boost civic engagement and participation, community organizing, and new means of public consultation more broadly.[18] In many cases, these forums are attempts to revive a more authentic and authoritative role for citizens than is provided by the constellation of institutions that defines democracy today. The contemporary state's large scale, the growing complexity of the issues it must address, the increasing diversity of its peoples, and the rise of supra-national institutions and actors that challenge the state's power to regulate economic and political activity all raise questions about whether it can govern effectively and responsively.[19] Public satisfaction with traditional democratic institutions has declined considerably, as seen in waning electoral participation, decreased willingness to identify with political parties, and plummeting trust and confidence in political leaders and institutions.[20] By January 2013, for example, less than 10 percent of Americans approved of Congress, which, according to one waggish poll, was less popular than head lice, cockroaches, traffic jams, root canals, and colonoscopies.[21] Public discontent is not necessarily unhealthy if it spurs experimentation with new means of reconnecting citizens to political engagement and power that revivify democracy. Civic forums have been one kind of experiment in revitalization.

These experiments have been organized by a myriad of institutions for a host of reasons. Churches, schools, academic institutions, and civic organizations have convened citizens to deepen public consultation on specific issues or to help imagine how the public might be more fully

---

[18] Nabatchi 2012; Smith 2009, 4–6.
[19] See, e.g., Bohman 2012; Dryzek 2010, chapters 6 and 9.
[20] Hetherington and Husser 2012; Hetherington 2005; Dalton 2004.
[21] Public Policy Polling 2013.

engaged in democracy in general. Health care providers and social service agencies have held forums to better understand their clients' needs and how institutional and public policy might serve them better. Advocacy organizations have also organized civic forums when traditional methods of researching, lobbying, and organizing seem insufficient. While these forums frequently aim to recruit greater numbers and more diverse publics to help move advocates' issues up the policy agenda and build public support for action, there is often a good deal of room for debating competing policy preferences and strategies.[22] Governments at every level have organized civic forums too. Sometimes, the aim is to gather deeper and more thoughtful citizen feedback on proposed policies, seek input on policy development on emerging issues, or implement policies that depend on widespread citizen compliance or efforts. Other forums are designed to help break legislative deadlocks, enlisting the public in helping to make difficult and potentially unpopular choices (such as the question of how to balance budgets in lean times). Still other forums address problems that cannot be solved by legislation alone because they require broad behavioral or cultural changes (such as improving relations between racial or ethnic groups).[23]

Many of these forums have been sincere attempts to improve public consultation by people who are frustrated with traditional ways of soliciting public input. As John Nalbandian, the former mayor of Lawrence, Kansas, explains, "What drove me to try structured, planned public engagement was my awful experience with unstructured, unplanned public engagement."[24] Politics being politics, some conveners have also tried to use civic forums to co-opt potential critics, make symbolic gestures to listen to the public, and attempt to orchestrate citizen approval of decisions that have already been made.[25] But civic forums are not more vulnerable to manipulation than other means of gathering public opinion. Some public hearings suffer from efforts to pack the room with like-minded speakers, some opinion polls are "push polls" designed to lead respondents to support one side of a controversy, and some "grassroots organizations" are astro-turf groups organized by powerful political or economic interests. Any means by which the public can express its voice will attract some political ventriloquists.

[22] Fagotto and Fung 2006; Leighninger 2012.
[23] This summary of governments' reasons for convening forums is indebted to Leighninger 2012.
[24] Quoted in Leighninger 2012, 19.
[25] See, e.g., Dryzek et al. 2009; Cooper and Smith 2012; Talpin 2011.

In this book, we examine three broad kinds of civic forums, which have been called popular assemblies, mini-publics, and co-governance institutions. Many popular assemblies look for inspiration to ancient Athenian democracy, in which citizens chosen by lot deliberated and decided the laws that governed them, and to New England town meetings – open forums where citizens have debated and enacted laws on local matters and elected their town officials since the seventeenth century.[26] The limitations of both of these paradigmatic examples of deliberative democracy are well known. Most community members were denied standing as citizens and excluded from the deliberative bodies of the state, and these kinds of face-to-face popular assemblies are less well suited to today's large and complex societies, in which the scope of local control over politics has narrowed considerably. Still, the deliberative and direct democracy of town meetings survives in some rural New England towns.[27]

Contemporary extensions of popular assemblies include the Citizens Assemblies that developed proposals for new electoral systems in British Columbia and Ontario, Canada, which were then put to a popular vote.[28] These kinds of assemblies supplement direct democracy with civic deliberation in innovative ways, assigning diverse groups of citizens to develop policy proposals that are voted on by the electorate as a whole. A more limited role is accorded to the state of Oregon's Citizens Initiative Review panels, which have been convened by the state each year since 2010 to review proposed ballot initiatives and advise the electorate on whether to support or oppose them. The panels' recommendations and their reasoning are included in official state voter pamphlets distributed to every household before Election Day, thereby promoting a deliberative citizen perspective on ballot initiatives.[29]

The other kinds of civic forums developed since the 1970s are attempts to recreate space for citizen deliberation that can affect politics, even if citizens do not enact policy directly or exclusively. Robert Dahl provided an influential early conception of a new type of citizen body when he proposed the creation of a representative sample of the public, or "minipopulus," which would deliberate about an issue for up to a year

---

[26] Fishkin 2009, 11–13; Smith 2009, 30.

[27] Bryan 2004; Mansbridge 1983. There are other traditions of deliberative direct democracy, including the Swiss *Landsgemeinde*, an open-air popular assembly developed in the Middle Ages, which survives in a few cantons and localities (Hansen 2008).

[28] Fournier et al. 2011; Warren and Pearse 2008.

[29] Gastil and Richards 2013; Knobloch et al. 2013.

and offer advice to the legislature.[30] Others who have taken up this idea of creating representative or quasi-representative microcosms of reflective public opinion that play an advisory role have renamed them "mini-publics."[31] These include National Issues Forums, Consensus Conferences, Citizens Juries, Deliberative Polls, Planning Cells, and 21st Century Town Meetings (like "Our Budget, Our Economy.")

On a spectrum of citizen empowerment, the third model of civic forums, co-governance institutions, sits between the direct democracy exercised by the popular assemblies of Athens and New England and the new advisory mini-publics. In co-governance forums, citizens and officials develop and implement policy together.[32] Contemporary examples include the Participatory Budget, developed in Porto Alegre, Brazil, which involves citizens helping to determine municipal spending priorities each year, and the People's Campaign for Decentralized Planning of Kerala, India, in which local civic forums, development experts, and officials shape regional development projects.[33] The city of Chicago's community policing meetings, in which neighborhood residents and police work together to identify crime prevention priorities and strategies, provide another example.[34]

These three kinds of forums share a number of common features. First, each enlists people more in their capacity as lay citizens than as organized members of interest groups. Civic forums tend to draw their legitimacy more from discussion among everyday citizens than from negotiations among the most interested or expert parties on an issue. While this distinction can be blurred in practice, if we imagine a continuum from deliberation among everyday citizens to discussion among more expert and activist citizens, most civic forums are on the grassroots end of the spectrum. At the other end, one finds stakeholder mediations, which aim to craft compromises among more organized competing interests, and blue ribbon commissions of leaders and experts convened by government to offer policy advice.[35]

---

[30] Dahl 1989, 340.   [31] E.g., Goodin and Dryzek 2006.

[32] These have also been conceived of as examples of "empowered participatory governance" (Fung and Wright 2003).

[33] On Participatory Budgets, see Abers 2000; Baiocchi 2003; Baiocchi 2005; Wampler 2012. On the Kerala People's Campaign, see Heller 2005; Isaac and Heller 2003.

[34] Fung 2004.

[35] A handful of forums integrate stakeholder and citizen involvement. For example, the Brazilian Participatory Budget includes citizens as representatives of their neighborhoods and representatives from voluntary associations in making annual city budgets.

Second, civic forums emphasize citizen *deliberation*. Unlike other forms of public consultation, such as public hearings, public comments solicited by administrative agencies, or most public meetings in which political representatives face their constituents, civic forums engage citizens, at least in part, in reasoning and seeking agreement among themselves, rather than exclusively in expressing their individual opinions to officials. Once again, this should be seen as a continuum rather than a sharp opposition, with mini-publics in which citizens confer mainly with each other on one side and co-governance forums in which citizens and officials collaborate to make policy on the other side.

Third, in contrast to most public consultations, citizens are often the main objects of persuasion, or share the spotlight with officials. Officials may help to shape briefing materials, testify at hearings, or be held to account for their performance, but in the civic forums that are our focus there is a greater emphasis than in most public meetings on *developing* the lay public's views, not just offering a forum for the public to express its pre-existing preferences. In addition, while most forms of public participation involve citizens petitioning their government, many civic forums involve officials consulting citizens, who offer their policy decisions or recommendations.

Fourth, unlike everyday political discussion or the typical committee meeting, most forums employ facilitators and procedures to promote participants' ability to speak on equal terms and to consider diverse views. Forums involve highly structured group deliberation. Finally, forums typically conclude with some public report of the participants' conclusions about policy issues. In this way, civic forums differ from American juries, which are asked to rule on more narrow questions about individual defendants, rather than more expansive public policy matters, and which do not publicize members' reasons for arriving at decisions.

Despite these commonalities, there is a great deal of diversity among forums. Table I.1 compares and contrasts ten forum designs. Because there is much adaptation and intermingling of designs, these should be considered as ideal types. While this list is by no means exhaustive, most of these designs are included because they are widely used and have been employed longest. We also include two kinds of forums that are rare but especially significant because they influence politics in unique ways – Citizens Assemblies and the Citizens Initiative Review panels – both of which supplement direct democracy with civic deliberation.

As Table I.1 indicates, forums employ different ways of including citizens. Most forums limit access to participate in order to provide

Table I.1 *Types of civic forums*

Design	Access and recruitment	Number of participants	Length of deliberation	Agenda	Decision rule	Output and influence
National Issues Forum	• Open or limited • Convenience sample	10–1000+ in multiple small groups	90 minutes to one day	Closed	Synthesis by organizers, some polling	• Representation of public opinion • Educative and advisory
Consensus Conference	• Limited • Random, quota sample	12–24 in one group	Three weekends	Open	Consensus	• Policy recommendations • Advisory
Citizens Jury	• Limited • Random, quota sample	12–24 in one group	Five days	Closed	Consensus or voting	• Policy recommendations • Advisory
Deliberative Poll	• Limited • Random or stratified random sample	100–500 in small groups and plenary	Two days	Closed	Polling	• Representation of public opinion • Advisory
Planning Cell	• Limited • Random or stratified random sample	100–500 in small groups	Four days	Closed	Synthesis by organizers, some polling	• Policy recommendations • Advisory

(cont.)

Table I.1 (*cont.*)

Design	Access and recruitment	Number of participants	Length of deliberation	Agenda	Decision rule	Output and influence
21st Century Town Meetings	• Limited • Aims for stratified random sample	100–1000+ in small groups and plenary	One day	Open or closed	Consensus of small groups and polling	• Policy recommendations • Advisory
Citizens Initiative Review Panel	• Limited • Random, quota sampling	18–24 in one group	Five days	Closed	Voting	• Voting recommendations • Advisory
Citizens Assembly	• Limited • Random or stratified random sample	100–200 in small groups and plenary	Several months	Open	Voting	• Policy development • Ballot initiative for public referendum
Participatory Budget	Open invitation and network recruiting	100–1000+ in plenary and elected small groups	Several months	Open	Voting	• Policy development and implementation • Advisory or direct authority
New England Town Meeting	Open invitation	100–1000+ in full group	One day	Open	Voting	• Policy development and elections • Direct authority

opportunities for small-group deliberation or to include a sample that approximates representativeness of the larger polity. While a few designs are open to all who want to deliberate, some employ voluntary associations to help recruit members of groups that would be under-represented without additional efforts, such as less educated, lower income, less politically interested, and younger citizens, and many forums practice some version of random sampling to include a more diverse and representative group. In addition, many organizers use quota sampling to attract members of particular groups that should be included in some critical mass, because either the issue touches especially on their interests or their participation is seen as important to the legitimacy of the forum. Although the number of participants varies dramatically in forums that include multiple groups of deliberators, all forums typically limit the size of each discussion group to allow each member to participate. Several kinds of forums mix small-group discussion with plenary sessions, in which experts testify or a synthesis of participants' comments is shared with the full group. Some designs can be as brief as 90 minutes, while others involve multiple meetings that can extend across several months.

Forums also offer deliberators different degrees of control over the agenda, decision-making processes, and political influence. Some deliberations adopt a closed agenda, restricting participants to select from among a menu of policy options determined by the organizers, often to meet demands for specific inputs from government agencies that commission the forums. Other designs have a more open agenda that allows citizens to generate their own policy preferences. Some forums put greater weight on group decision making by consensus, while most conclude with individual voting or polling on policy choices.

The output and intended influence of forums can also vary considerably.[36] A few are primarily educative. For example, some National Issues Forums are intended mainly to develop participants' political understanding and capacities, and secondarily to provide officials or civil society associations with a picture of public opinion that might inform policy making.[37] Most forums are advisory, generating a representation of well-informed public opinion (as in most Deliberative Polls) or specific policy recommendations (as in Citizens Juries and Planning Cells) that aim to influence officials and others. Advisory forums may also aim to persuade the broader public, as the Citizens Initiative Review

---

[36] This typology of influence draws on Carcasson 2009; see also Fung 2003.
[37] Melville, Willingham, and Dedrick 2005.

panel does by issuing recommendations on whether to vote for ballot initiatives. Co-governance partnerships, in which authority is shared among citizens and officials, have resulted in a range of policy outputs, including Participatory Budgets at the municipal level, but also state development plans and local crime fighting measures. Popular assemblies allow citizens alone to exert direct authority over public resources and decisions, as in New England Town Meetings, or indirect authority, as in the Canadian Citizens Assemblies, which set the electoral agenda by developing ballot initiatives on electoral reform.

Civic forums in a deliberative system

What role should these forums play in a larger theory of democracy? While many of the new civic forums pre-date the renewal of scholarly interest in deliberative democracy since the 1990s, or have mushroomed since then without requiring much inspiration from political theory, academics and practitioners have increasingly worked together to design, evaluate, and reflect on civic forums and their contribution to building a more deliberative politics.[38] Therefore, the development of scholarly theory and research on deliberation is also one history of civic forums. At the heart of the theory of deliberative democracy is a normative claim that politics is most legitimate when citizens come together as political equals to engage in public reasoning in a search for agreement about how to rule themselves.[39]

In the first phase of academic interest in deliberation, theorists focused on articulating the deliberative ideal against models of democracy

---

[38] Fishkin 2009; Gastil and Levine 2005; Nabatchi et al. 2012; Steiner 2012; Warren and Pearse 2008.

[39] Despite differences among theorists of deliberation, we see reasoning, publicity, equality, and the aim to draw conclusions about civic life as central to the major theories offered by Cohen 1989; Dryzek 2000; Gutmann and Thompson 1996; and Habermas 1996. Similarly, Mark Button and David Ryfe see the "essential meaning of democracy [as involving] free and equal citizens with an equal opportunity to participate in a shared public life and to shape decisions that affect their lives" (2005, 30). Simone Chambers writes, "Deliberation is democratic when it is undertaken by a group of equals faced with a collective decision. So the question is how do – or ought – a group of equals reason together?" (2012, 60). And, as eight leading theorists of deliberation have recently written, Above all, any conception of deliberative democracy must be organized around an ideal of political justification requiring free public reasoning of equal citizens" (Mansbridge et al. 2012, 25). We develop this definition of deliberative democracy more fully in Chapter 1.

variously described as "thin,"[40] "aggregative,"[41] or "adversary"[42] democracy. These models tend to assume and accept that citizens come to politics with preferences and interests already formed; that people are mainly self-interested and that their interests inevitably conflict; that the essential acts of citizenship are to join groups and parties or to cast votes that will advance one's individual preferences and interests; that political communication is mostly instrumental and strategic; and that democracy's chief purpose is to referee the competitive scrum of private interests.

In response, advocates of deliberative democracy contended that it is both possible and desirable for citizens to form their interests and preferences in reasoned discussion with other citizens and officials; for this kind of interaction to deepen participants' understanding of their views and transform them into preferences that take greater account of the facts, the future, and their fellow citizens; for citizens to resolve conflicting preferences through the give-and-take of arguments, when possible, or for deliberation to inform more authentic and fair-minded compromises or votes, if necessary; for political communication to focus on mutual justification and understanding; and for democracy's main purpose to be the forging of agreements among a public that is capable of self-rule.[43] Theorists devoted their attention to identifying the ideal conditions required for legitimate deliberation, such as Jürgen Habermas' ideal speech situation, an inclusive site in which all speakers are competent, free from coercion, equal in status, and rational, and Joshua Cohen's ideal deliberative procedure, which required similar elements of freedom, reasoning, equality, and consensus.[44] Theorists nominated a host of sectors and institutions in which deliberation might be best achieved, including legislatures,[45] courts,[46] civil society,[47] the media,[48] and, of course, civic forums.

The second phase of scholarly attention to deliberation brought theory and practice into closer contact, as scholars studied experimental deliberations, moved out into the world to study civic forums, and began

---

[40] Barber 1984, 4.   [41] Dryzek 2000, 1; Young 2000, 19–21.

[42] Mansbridge 1983, 5. On the three phases of deliberative theory and research, see Mansbridge et al. 2012, 24–6.

[43] Especially in its original formulations, the deliberative ideal was contrasted strongly with elite, technocratic, interest group pluralist, and social choice theories of democracy. Benhabib 1996, Bohman and Rehg 1997, Cohen 1989; Elster 1998, Fishkin and Laslett 2003, Habermas 1996; Macedo 1999; Rawls 1993.

[44] Cohen 1989; Habermas 1984, 25.   [45] Bessette 1994.   [46] Rawls 1993.

[47] Dryzek 2000; Habermas 1996.   [48] Page 1996.

organizing a few of their own. Some early exchanges between theorists and empirical researchers were fraught with misunderstandings and produced frustration on both sides. Some researchers found that deliberation did not always produce the salutary outcomes envisioned by theorists – indeed, sometimes precisely the opposite.[49] Theorists responded that these negative findings hardly meant that the theory as a whole had been debunked. Moreover, the theorists claimed, many of these studies treated aspirational claims about how politics *ought* to be conducted as assertions about how it *is* conducted.[50] This confused a normative political theory with a descriptive social scientific theory. In response, empirical researchers argued that the theory of deliberative democracy also makes empirical claims and that testable hypotheses were needed in order to evaluate those claims.[51]

In light of these initial challenges, a more productive line of research began to elucidate the circumstances in which political deliberation is most and least likely to be achieved. This approach does not aspire to show that the normative theory as a whole has been proven or disproven, but rather to understand better *the conditions under which* group deliberation comes closer to or departs from some of the discrete goals articulated by theorists. At its best, this work has applied theory to deepen our understanding of the contexts for legitimate civic deliberation in the world, while also reflecting on what the empirical findings suggest for practical improvements to forums and normative refinements to the theory.[52]

While the research is nascent and the findings are mixed, there is evidence that under the right conditions, well-designed civic forums can deliver some of the benefits that theorists desire. Forums can develop participants' individual civic capacities, such as political knowledge, interest, and efficacy; understanding of diverse viewpoints and experiences; consistency and coherence of opinions; and ability to withstand symbolic or manipulative political claims.[53] Deliberative forums can strengthen group reasoning, generating policy proposals that are seen as well informed and convincing by experts, officials, and researchers, and leave participants

---

[49] See, e.g., Hibbing and Theiss-Morse 2002; Jackman and Sniderman 2006.
[50] See, e.g.,Thompson 2008, 498–99.   [51] See, e.g., Mutz 2008.
[52] Examples include Dryzek 2010; Fishkin 2009; Fung 2004; Fung and Olin Wright 2003; Gastil 2008; Hendriks 2011; Levine and Gastil 2005; Nabatchi et al. 2012; Rosenberg 2007; Smith 2009; Steiner 2012; Thompson 2008; Warren and Pearse 2008.
[53] For summaries of the literature on civic capacities, see Dryzek 2010, 158–9; Pincock 2012; Ryfe and Stalsburg 2012.

feeling that they have had an equal voice in the process.[54] Depending on the external context, forums may also contribute positively to the larger political system, strengthening communities' capacities to address political problems by creating new institutions and revitalizing old ones, loosening political gridlock among officials, and improving citizens' perceptions of the legitimacy of political decision making.[55]

However, another important outcome of this research has been a greater appreciation for the difficult trade-offs between deliberation and other democratic values, and among the values prized by deliberative democrats themselves. For example, based in part on his experience in creating and studying Deliberative Polls, James Fishkin has discussed a "trilemma of democratic reform," which describes the tensions between maximizing citizen deliberation, universal political participation, and equality.[56] Fishkin concludes that practical constraints on all democratic institutions, including civic forums, mean that institutions that attempt to realize any two of these important values will struggle to achieve the third. He argues that Deliberative Polls offer especially good conditions for citizens to practice deliberation as equals, but at the price of limiting participation to a closed group of randomly selected citizens that aims to be representative of a political unit. In contrast, forums that encourage broader participation by throwing open their doors to all comers typically do so at the cost of equality because they especially draw the most politically interested and privileged citizens. Similarly, Graham Smith's comparative study of civic forums finds that they make very different contributions to six democratic goods – inclusiveness, popular control, political judgment, transparency, efficiency, and accountability – not all of which are easily achieved in a single forum.[57]

The institutionalization of civic forums, and the increasingly realistic understanding of their strengths and limitations, has taken some of the sting out of the criticism that deliberative democracy is inspired by utopian dreams about citizens' virtues or quaint nostalgia for small-scale democracy. While there is much left to learn, there is ample evidence that under the right conditions citizens are indeed capable of deliberating without halos or togas. Other forms of civic expression and action – including

---

[54] For relevant literature summaries, see Black 2012; Callon, Lascoumes, and Barthe 2009; Collingwood and Reedy 2012; Fishkin and Luskin 2005; Mercier and Landemore 2012.

[55] Goodin and Dryzek 2006; Leighninger 2012; Kinney 2012.

[56] Fishkin 2009, 32–64.

[57] Recognition of these trade-offs has promoted useful thinking about further institutional reforms. See, for example, Ackerman and Fishkin 2004; Smith 2009.

elections, interest group participation, and social movement activism – also involve much theoretical idealism and difficult trade-offs among democratic goods and values in practice. The notions that democracy is best realized through universal participation in free and fair elections, or through the equilibrium achieved among a plurality of competitive interest groups, or through emancipatory social movement activism, are based on hopes that are often as far from standard political practice as the ideals of deliberative democracy.[58] Of course, we cannot imagine a thriving democracy without elections, interest advocates, or social movements. But the fact that each of these institutions fails to meet ideal standards in practice means that deliberative forums should not be held to unrealistic standards either. The question is whether civic deliberation adds something valuable to the mosaic of democratic institutions.

Continuing in this pragmatic direction, the third phase of deliberative theory takes a more systemic approach. Rather than seeking out or trying to design a civic forum that can render perfectly legitimate decisions, many theorists recognize that "no single institution can meet all of the demands of deliberative democracy at once."[59] Still, they maintain that we can achieve more widespread, higher quality, and more consequential civic deliberation that informs all levels of government and civil society.[60] Like these scholars, we do not assume that deliberation is the *only* legitimate means of practicing democracy, but we see it as a desirable and often necessary component of any democratic institution. Thus, we focus on how theory can help improve citizens' opportunities for democratic deliberation throughout the political system, and how deliberative civic

[58] Elections in the United States and around the world are routinely undermined by practices such as corruption that gives outsized influence to certain interests at the expense of others; the narrowing of the electorate due to uneven turnout and laws that exclude large swaths of the polity; and the manipulation or restriction of political information in the mass media (Bjornlund 2004; Blais 2013; Thompson 2013). Similarly, participation in interest groups is notoriously uneven, with more privileged citizens most likely to join and lead, and groups representing business and government interests far more numerous, well-resourced, and powerful than other groups (Schattschneider 1960; Schlozman, Verba, and Brady 2012). Compromises reached between interest groups are often at the expense of the interests of the unorganized and are not clearly authorized through the democratic process (Lowi 1969). Broad-based social movements thrive intermittently, face significant barriers to mobilizing collective action (such as limits to participants' time and money, free rider problems, and the like), struggle with the dilemma of political irrelevancy or co-optation by the state, are not always internally democratic, and sometimes pursue anti-democratic goals (McVeigh 2009; Melucci 1996; Olson 1965).

[59] Mansbridge et al. 2010, 25.

[60] Dryzek 2010, 7–8; Goodin 2008, Chapter 9; Hendriks 2006; Mansbridge 1999; Parkinson 2006a, 166–73.

forums can communicate more effectively with the wide variety of institutions, both deliberative and non-deliberative, that are likely to be found in any diverse democracy.[61]

The systemic turn is both pragmatic and constitutional. It recognizes that no single element of the political system, including a civic forum, is likely to offer perfect conditions for deliberation, so the inevitable shortcomings in the deliberative quality of any one element of the system should be checked and balanced by other elements. Similarly, the US Constitution sought "to form a more perfect Union" rather than staking a claim to perfecting the state. The Constitution did this by establishing the separation of powers among the legislative, executive, and judicial branches, as well as the relationship of state and federal power. We see the need for similarly systemic thinking about the role of deliberation today, and considering the contributions of civic forums is one small contribution to that much larger goal. In addition, as Cass Sunstein has argued persuasively, the Constitution was not merely the product of elite deliberation; many of the rights it has established over the centuries are aimed in part at allowing all citizens to deliberate in a common political structure as equals.[62] We think that a more deliberative politics, even if it can never be perfected, would be a more desirable politics than we have today.

Theorizing about deliberation at a systemic level opens up several promising perspectives, as described by Jane Mansbridge and her coauthors.[63] One advantage of a systemic lens is that it helps us think about how to scale deliberative forums up and out into an expanded political structure with a complex and dynamic division of deliberative labor. While the state continues to have many crucial functions, it is not the central agent to which all political discussion and opinion must be oriented. Informal or binding decisions on matters of common concern made outside the state – in social, cultural, and economic institutions, and in transnational or supranational bodies – are also part of a deliberative political system. In addition, a systemic approach draws attention to the division of labor among different elements of the system, encouraging us to think about how civic forums might complement deliberation in

---

[61] On the distinction between theory about democratic deliberation as one especially valuable kind of discourse within all political institutions and theory about how deliberative democracy is the most important or only source of legitimacy in politics, see Gastil 2008, Chapter 10; Mansbridge 2007.

[62] Sunstein 1993.   [63] Mansbridge et al. 2012.

other locations, such as legislatures or the public sphere. A systemic perspective also suggests the need to consider how civic forums can avoid displacing other legitimate forms of public opinion, as critics feared the "Our Budget, Our Economy" event would divert attention from long-term and widespread support for Social Security expressed in opinion polls. This approach also draws attention to how other institutions need to be reformed to be more receptive and responsive to citizen deliberation. One reason the deficit forum failed to gain a hearing is that the federal government in the United States has well-established channels for interest groups to influence fiscal and tax policy – especially through lobbying and campaign contributions – but no clear channels for civic deliberation to affect the issue. A more democratic political system would have redundant sites of deliberation, as well as checks and balances among them, so that no one institution is entrusted or burdened with the sole responsibility for fostering civic or official deliberation. These sites of deliberation would be connected to many direct and indirect decision-making mechanisms (legislatures, administrative agencies, referenda, and the like).[64] Envisioning the role of civic forums in such a system is an increasingly important task.

Deliberative equality and publicity

What do we mean by equality and publicity in deliberation, and why are they the most important elements of the new civic forums that need strengthening? For now, let us say that in ideal terms, equality means that all who are affected by a decision have an equal opportunity to be included in making it, an equal capacity to participate in deliberation, and an equal chance of influencing a collective decision based on the merits of their views.[65]

Publicity also has multiple meanings in the theory of deliberation. First, publicity refers to the kind of reasoning that deliberation ought to elicit. As we will see, there is much debate over how citizens should link their self-interest and the common good, but we think most theorists would accept that deliberation should challenge citizens to consider their own

---

[64] See also Parkinson 2012a, 168.

[65] While theorists have proposed multiple definitions of deliberative equality, the elements of inclusion, participation, and influence can be found in many of the major treatments of the issue, especially Bohman 1996, Chapter 3; Knight and Johnson 1997; Young 2000.

interests in relation to the interests of others, and to exchange arguments that are not *only* narrowly self-interested or group-interested.[66] Public reasoning does not demand that people, especially the least powerful, should put aside or transcend their interests, but involves translating and enlarging personal consideration into claims about justice, social goods, or truths. Publicity also encompasses the topics appropriate to democratic deliberation, which are matters of common concern, questions of politics, or "issues the public ought to discuss," which can include the definition of what is "public" or "political" itself.[67] In addition, publicity can be conceived of as defining what James Bohman calls the "social space in which deliberation occurs."[68] This social context sets a series of expectations for participants which, when they are met, can foster more respectful discussion, in which citizens consider one anothers' needs and wants, and frame arguments in terms that others are more likely to accept.[69] In this sense, publicity also can hold deliberators accountable to the larger public who are not present in the forum.[70]

The idea of accountability suggests a fourth meaning of publicity, which concerns the way in which those inside the forum communicate to those outside it. This is the kind of publicity with which we are most concerned in this book. Practicing transparency about how forums are organized and revealing participants' rationales for their conclusions can check potential manipulation of deliberators by organizers and sponsors, as well as unfounded suspicions that citizen participants have been dominated or co-opted. Transparency and the presentation of arguments to the public allow outsiders to make more authentic judgments about the legitimacy of a forum's process and decisions, and to decide whether or not to trust the forum's conclusions. How forums should communicate to the rest of the political system is the element of publicity that has been least fully considered in deliberative theory and research. It becomes ever more important to consider when imagining a deliberative system, rather than a single best forum. Aspirations for a high-functioning deliberative

[66] On this debate, see especially Bächtiger et al. 2010; Mansbridge et al. 2010.
[67] Mansbridge 1999, 217. See also Mansbridge et al. 2012, 9.
[68] Bohman 1996, 37. One can also consider how the physical spaces in which deliberation occurs can shape power and discourse, as Parkinson (2012b, 113ff) does for committee rooms or Hannigan (2006, 188ff) does for public hearing rooms.
[69] Elster 1998; Gutmann and Thompson 1996, 52, 128.
[70] Fung and Wright 2003, 37; Levine and Nierras 2007, 6; Parkinson 2006a, 17, 119–20; Smith 2009, 101–105, 110.

system depend on the quality of communication between its parts. Pub-licity forms the institutional channels that connect the parts and what flows through those channels.

We focus on strengthening equality and publicity in civic forums for several reasons. First, these concepts are central to the theory of deliber-ative democracy, and they are interdependent. Deliberation is often justi-fied in part because it allows participants to develop fully their abilities to exercise autonomy in ways that can only be realized in concert with oth-ers. While deliberative theorists are not of one mind about how to define and prioritize conceptions of autonomy, most see it as emerging from the public exchange of reasons among equals.[71] As Christian Røstboll points out, this is quite different from approaches that see autonomy pri-marily as "the negative liberty to live according to one's own ideas."[72] In Habermas' formulation, "no one is truly free until all citizens enjoy liberties under laws that they have given themselves after a reasonable deliberation."[73] We can choose preferences autonomously only if we are aware of, and have reflected on, our own and others' preferences, and the reasons that justify those preferences. We can engage in this reflection only if others treat us as equals in deliberation and we see them as our equals. If some people or arguments are excluded or slighted, everyone's autonomy is the poorer for it. As Stephen Elstub puts it, "for the auton-omy of all to be cultivated . . . equal agency of all must be preserved."[74]

Equality and publicity are also interdependent in arguments for the epistemic advantages of deliberation. In this view, compared with individ-ual decision making or the aggregation of individual preferences, delib-eration often produces better decisions because they are informed by consideration of the widest possible array of perspectives, beliefs, values, and interests.[75] Deliberation can allow individuals and groups to over-come their bounded rationality when they reason together about matters of common concern, exchanging public-minded arguments that can be understood and potentially accepted by others, including those outside

---

[71] Major statements on the role of autonomy in deliberative democracy include Elster 1983; Habermas 1996; Elstub 2008; Rostbøll 2008; Warren 2001.

[72] Rostbøll 2008, 710.

[73] Habermas 2006, 120. Habermas recognizes that citizens in large complex democra-cies can and must delegate the task of lawmaking to representatives, which is legiti-mate as long as citizens themselves validate the laws through deliberation in the public sphere, and democratic and politically accountable legislatures recognize public opinion in "revisable majority decisions as well as compromises" (Habermas 1996, 186).

[74] Elstub 2008, 68.   [75] Estlund 1997; Martí 2006.

the forum. Yet these epistemic benefits also depend on each person's arguments being considered equally on the merits, rather than according to speakers' power or status. Jack Knight and James Johnson link public reasoning to equality when they argue that transparency helps to ensure that decisions

> are actually informed by and result from debate rather than being simply imposed by one or a few well-placed parties. To this end deliberative procedures rely on public contest of reasons as a way of checking power and, thereby, ensuring that participants are treated equally.[76]

The prospect of making an account of citizen deliberation to a wider public after the forum can be a powerful incentive for sponsors and organizers to ensure consideration for all within the forum and to report citizens' conclusions without fear or favor. For example, the pre-emptive criticism of the "Our Budget, Our Economy" forum may have encouraged its organizers to begin the forum by emphasizing that they were not necessarily asking citizens to prioritize long-term deficit reduction over short-term economic stimulus, and to allow participants to add single-payer health insurance to the forum's predefined list of policy options for reducing the federal deficit.[77]

Second, we focus on strengthening equality and publicity because concerns about both stem from common sources unique to deliberative democracy. It is difficult to include all citizens in deliberation, and it is not easy for them to participate on equal terms. As we have noted, the limits to inclusion arise either from background inequalities that make the least powerful the hardest to recruit to open forums, or because numbers must be limited to construct a more representative sample of a larger population or a group small enough to deliberate effectively. In addition, critics of the first phase of deliberative theory raised important concerns about whether disempowered citizens can participate on equal terms within the forum. Historically, the marginalized have often asserted their public claims most powerfully by mobilizing themselves in large numbers to withdraw their political acquiescence, their labor, or their consumption by demonstrating, striking, or boycotting. In contrast, power in deliberation is exercised in small groups by exchanging discursive claims. Critics objected that these conditions favor the interests of the educated and privileged, who are better prepared to engage in this kind of talk, especially if the emphasis is on reaching consensus, using

[76] Knight and Johnson 1997, 288 (footnote omitted).   [77] Hickey 2010.

abstract reasoning, and excluding appeals to group interests in favor of claims oriented toward the common good, which is likely to be defined outside the forum in hegemonic terms that favor the most powerful.[78]

Full inclusion and participation of disempowered citizens are integral to civic forums' legitimacy, not only in theory but also in practice. Recall that two of the main criticisms of the deficit forum were that it would not include all Americans' views and that it presented deficit reduction as a more important need than economic stimulus aimed at helping the poor and unemployed. As this same example suggests, potential barriers to inclusion and participation also create an urgent need for valid publicity to foster civic forums' accountability and transparency in ways that would increase their standing in the eyes of the public and decision makers who are not directly part of the deliberation. In most cases, civic forums will involve relatively few citizens speaking to a multitude outside the meeting room. If the world outside is highly polarized and suspicious of attempts to reconcile conflicting views, the forum will suffer.

Third, the changing status of the field of citizen deliberation poses new questions about practitioners' ability to practice publicity and equality. The spread of civic forums has engendered a new market for firms and organizations that conduct deliberative public consultations, especially on behalf of government agencies. As Carolyn Hendriks and Lyn Carson observe, this new professional infrastructure can enrich the field by raising standards for practitioners' training and accreditation, encouraging independent evaluations of forums, developing and sharing best practices, and establishing standards for the legitimate conduct of civic forums, including ones that preserve citizens' independence and that foster better communication to those outside the forum.[79] For example, through their professional associations, practitioners have developed codes of conduct that advocate equal inclusion of peoples and viewpoints in forums and minimal standards for publicity.[80] But, as Hendriks and Carson also note, changes in the field also raise potentially troubling questions. Will professional organizers build valuable experience in practicing transparency about the deliberative process or will their commercial interest in building a client base render them less willing to challenge sponsors who want to control the outcomes of citizen deliberation? Will professionalization lead

---

[78] Sanders 1997; Young 2000.   [79] Hendriks and Carson 2008. See also Lee 2011.

[80] For a discussion of these codes of practice, see Cooper and Smith 2012. For examples, see International Association for Public Participation ND; Involve and National Consumer Council 2008; National Coalition for Dialogue & Deliberation, International Association for Public Participation, and the Co-Intelligence Institute 2009.

to ongoing information sharing and collective learning or to competitive hoarding of "trade secrets" and unwillingness to admit failures if this might tarnish practitioners' brand names? Will a system in which private firms organize deliberation under contract for government agencies seek out disempowered and unpopular views and participants?

Finally, it seems to us that any form of democracy, including deliberative democracy, ought to be judged in part by how well it addresses the most important problems of the time, many of which seem, at least from the vantage point of the United States and at this historical moment, to stem from a system in which economic and political inequalities are widening and politicians are increasingly polarized.[81] The ability of those who control wealth to convert it into disproportionate political power, which has always bedeviled capitalist democracies, has grown especially entrenched in the United States over the past four decades.[82] Reversing these trends has proved extremely difficult in an age of insufficient party competition, increasingly homogeneous partisan districts, the shift to a permanent campaign mentality that rewards extreme position taking and militates against legislative compromise, and ever more partisan news media that allow citizens and their representatives to retreat to their own echo chambers.[83] As a result, American democracy seems less capable than in the past of responding to significant crises that demand timely working agreements – on federal budgets, the situation of over ten million undocumented immigrants, the growing threats posed by climate change, and the like.

Our point is not to reduce deliberation to an instrumental good in service to equality or efficiency, but it is to say that the ability of citizen deliberation to include all citizens' perspectives and to affect political choices depends on creating more political equality within the system, and building institutional and communicative channels that transform deliberative citizen opinion into political decisions. This should be a concern of anyone committed to deliberation, because the power of citizens' voices cannot circulate without better receptors in the political system.

While a single book cannot resolve all of these problems, even on paper, our goal is to redirect the conversation about them with some fresh arguments and evidence, and to suggest how civic deliberation can be better integrated into the wider landscape of political decision

---

[81] McCarty, Poole, and Rosenthal 2006.

[82] Bartels 2008; Jacobs and Skocpol 2005; Schlozman, Verba, and Brady 2012; Gilens 2012.

[83] Gutmann and Thompson 2012.

making. Most forums have been episodic experiments and projects. One important goal is to embed deliberative forums more firmly in governing routines, comparable to the American jury system and Brazilian Participatory Budgets.[84] We will argue that judicious incorporation of enclave discussions among marginalized citizens and improving how all forums are communicated publicly should help to multiply the range of civic forums that are incorporated within routine democratic politics, rather than existing as experiments that depend on the kindness of political strangers for acceptance. These forums could inspire greater trust among foundations, governments, and other potential sponsors, as well as among the citizens, officials, and advocacy organizations that comprise the typical audiences for forums' policy recommendations. Because they will be more equal and transparent, forums will deserve that trust. While better forums that are better communicated will not please everyone, observers will be able to make more informed judgments about how to incorporate civic deliberation in governance.

To summarize, equality and publicity lie at the heart of deliberative democracy. Achieving one of these values often depends upon achieving the other. Both can be undermined by the necessity for deliberation to occur in small groups, which requires forums to mitigate the background inequalities that citizens bring to the table and to explain what happened there in ways that demonstrate accountability and transparency to the forum's audiences. The emerging market for professional practitioners of citizen consultation may build expertise in fostering equality and publicity, but might undermine commitments to these important values if they conflict with sponsors' demands and organizers' needs to protect their brands. Growing efforts to institutionalize civic deliberation in everyday politics are at a crossroads. The success of these efforts will be judged in large part by whether they can provide better arenas for addressing conflict in unequal and divided democracies than other means by which the public has traditionally expressed itself. This demands attention to how citizens communicate within forums and to how forums communicate what participants have to say to other elements of the democratic system.

The plan of the book

In Chapter 1, we begin by working out a more complete theoretical definition of what political equality, public reasoning, and decision making

---

[84] Leighninger 2012.

should look like in civic forums. We address debates among theorists of deliberative democracy about the value of different kinds of forums, as well as criticisms of deliberative ideals as utopian, elitist, or incoherent. We are particularly attentive to the need for a practical and realistic theory of citizen deliberation. Therefore, we differentiate some basic descriptive conditions for deliberation, which are regularly met by civic forums, from ideal standards by which forums might be evaluated, which are more ambitious yet can still be observed in practice. We also identify a few illustrative empirical conditions that may affect deliberative equality and publicity in forums. This discussion establishes some grounds for our proposals later in the book.

Thereafter, our argument proceeds in two parts. In the first section, we present normative arguments and empirical evidence for the value of incorporating enclave deliberation among the least powerful citizens into the deliberative landscape. In Chapter 2, we specify what we mean by enclaves of disempowered individuals and groups, who may suffer from pervasive and enduring political inequalities, or who are situationally disempowered relative to a particular issue under deliberation, or who may be disadvantaged by the act of deliberation itself. We argue that it would often advance equality in the deliberative system if these marginalized citizens had opportunities to confer among themselves in civic forums and political processes. This can occur as part of a larger deliberation that takes place within representative civic forums, between enclave forums and more representative forums, or in ongoing processes that allow enclaves of the weak to engage directly with officials who can represent the larger public. At the same time, we review evidence that suggests how forums can avoid some well-known dangers of enclave deliberation, including social pressures to conform to dominant views within groups, unreflective extremism, and sectarian pursuit of group interests.

There are few studies of enclave deliberation in civic forums, so we begin to fill this void in Chapter 3. We present our own case study of a forum that convened members of social groups with least access to broadband Internet service to develop policy proposals for bridging the digital divide in Silicon Valley. In this case, an established format for cross-cutting deliberation among social groups – the Consensus Conference – was modified to foster deliberation among the disempowered about their interests. Instead of falling prey to social pressures within the group or failing to consider a broad range of arguments, participants perceived a greater diversity of views among themselves the longer they deliberated, yet were still able to agree upon a long list of policy recommendations. These recommendations contributed new perspectives to the larger policy debate, addressing issues that extended beyond the agenda outlined by conference organizers. By deliberating together, members of groups who were among the least powerful in relation to the issue were able to articulate a distinct set of values, experiences, and policy preferences about the digital divide. The participants and a panel of outside telecommunications experts in government, advocacy groups, and business perceived the deliberative process and outcomes as legitimate. Thus, the case study shows how enclave deliberation among the marginalized can contribute constructively to a larger policy debate.

In the second part of the book, we turn our attention to publicity. We argue that successfully integrating civic forums into the political system will depend in part on establishing broadly shared standards for organizing and reporting forums. While comparable institutions, such as public hearings and opinion polls, are not always conducted legitimately, there are widely accepted criteria for how these kinds of public consultation ought to be practiced and how they should be communicated to the public.

In Chapter 4, we propose a set of benchmarks for assessing whether forums should be seen as more or less valid expressions of public opinion, which should help observers make good decisions about whether to trust a particular forum. We derive standards for evaluating publicity about forums by translating widely accepted criteria for good deliberation *within* forums. One set of criteria concerns deliberative *argumentation*, which includes clarifying the group's conclusions; revealing the reasons, evidence, and norms upon which the group's conclusions are based; and discussing the opposing views considered by deliberators. Because good deliberation is expected to include each of these kinds of talk, it is important that they be shared with those outside the group to advance deliberation in the public sphere and official arenas. A second set of standards addresses *transparency* about the control, design, intended influence, and evaluation of the deliberative process, as well as the fidelity of the publicity to the underlying deliberation. Transparency is important because the particular designs and conditions of deliberative forums can significantly affect their perceived legitimacy and policy proposals. Transparency can also hold the authors of publicity accountable to deliberators and the larger public, ensuring that the kinds of coercion that some skeptics fear can happen *within* deliberative groups are not committed *against* the group after the fact by those who report the forum.

In Chapter 5, we begin to analyze an illustrative sample of final reports that emerged from a diverse sample of forums. Using quantitative content analysis and close qualitative readings of the reports, we identify their different emphases on conclusions, reasons, evidence, and other aspects of argumentation. We find that *decisional* reports emphasize deliberators' conclusions at the expense of revealing their reasoning, while *dialogic* publicity focuses on reasoning over conclusions, and other documents offer a rough balance between the two. This relationship between conclusions and reasons can be influenced by factors such as the design of the deliberative forum and its relationship to formal policy-making processes, but is not wholly reducible to these factors. Deliberative publicity can be shaped as well by several dominant genres of political discourse – policy analytic, academic, populist, and activist – that can exhibit biases toward abstract and systematic argumentation, or experiential and particularistic reasoning. Moreover, we find that across all types of reports in our sample, authors often neglect to reveal other important elements of deliberation, such as the opposing views considered by the group and the values that motivated participants' policy preferences. We find that deliberative publicity is not a mere function of other aspects of a civic forum, but an independent variable in its own right, and that authors can attend more consciously to the ways in which publicity is authentically deliberative.

Returning to our sample of final reports of civic forums in Chapter 6, we explore the extent to which each report practiced transparency about important details of the deliberative process. We find that these reports devoted most attention to revealing the control, design, and intended influence of forums, yet many authors divulge these aspects of forums only partially. Very few reports include evaluation data – either a systematic assessment of how participants or others perceived the fairness of the deliberative process or an evaluation of the participants' knowledge, attitudes, or dispositions. There is little reporting of the criteria used to decide how elements of the group's argumentation were included in publicity, whether these criteria were agreed to by the group as a whole, or whether group members perceived the final report as an accurate expression of their views. Overall, no reports addressed all the elements of transparency in a comprehensive way. Some of the variance in transparency is rooted in similar factors as differences in argumentation, especially the forum design. Yet compared with argumentation, transparency seems more independent of the underlying deliberation, and more dependent on authorial discretion.

In Chapter 7, we offer recommendations for practicing and evaluating equality and publicity in civic forums. We suggest practical steps for organizing enclave deliberation among the least powerful and linking it to discussion with other citizens, experts, and officials in ways that could reap the benefits of enclave deliberation among the marginalized, while avoiding its perils. Certain issues and forum designs may be especially optimal for this kind of deliberation among the disempowered. We also suggest principles and methods for improving the publicity of deliberative forums in ways that contribute to the larger political system. We conclude by outlining a research agenda on the effects of publicity on the perceived legitimacy and persuasiveness of deliberative groups. There is much more to be learned about how policy makers, activists, and the public view different types of argumentation and transparency. This work could illuminate how civic forums can maximize both their independence from external power and their policy impacts by communicating well to other actors in the deliberative system.

Throughout the book, our perspectives on civic deliberation are shaped and limited by several factors. As academics, we have observed and studied deliberation in many public consultation processes and lab experiments, but we have done so at an early stage in the development of deliberative theory and practice. We are also influenced by our own experiences as citizens in the late twentieth-century and early twenty-first-century United States, who have attended many public meetings, some deliberative but most not, and participated in expert panels that advise officials, on the boards of voluntary associations, in demonstrations, and in union–management negotiations. We have been struck by the unequal conditions in so many of these civic processes in which we have taken part and by how much their legitimacy depended upon how they were communicated publicly. In some of them, we occupied privileged positions because of our educational training, credentials, gender, or race. In others, we were marginalized because of our views, although never as much or in the same ways as the most disempowered people among us are excluded or humiliated by the political process. We also come to this work as an organizer (Raphael) and an evaluator (Karpowitz) of one of the civic forums we study in this book. This experience deepened our appreciation of the difficulty and the importance of practicing and publicizing civic deliberation under conditions of social inequality. Our admiration for the citizens who took part in this forum and our desire to learn from this experience, including from our novice mistakes, were our first inspirations to write this book. In doing so, we have tried to arrive at conclusions about deliberative democracy that take seriously the perspectives of academics, practitioners of civic forums, advocates, and citizens. We hope that they will help to find and fill in our blind spots of theory and method, historical and geographical contexts, social positions and personal experiences. That is something that deliberation does best.

1

Democratic deliberation in civic forums

Democratic deliberation is often presented as a regulative ideal, one that sets a standard for political discourse that is unlikely to be met in practice, but toward which we can aim, and by which we can judge the relative legitimacy of actually existing politics.[1] It is primarily a normative theory about how democracy ought to work most legitimately, rather than a social scientific theory about how democracy works most of the time. But normative theories of democracy are more persuasive to the extent that they also describe recognizable empirical conditions (even if they are rare or difficult to achieve) and offer plausible accounts of how politics might be transformed for the better (regardless of how challenging that may be or how long it may take).[2] Therefore, we should expect the theory of democratic deliberation to be primarily normative, but also descriptive and practical.

As Dennis Thompson has observed, there is a good deal of confusion and disagreement about the descriptive, normative, and practical aspects of the theory of deliberation.[3] We agree with Thompson that these three elements need to be distinguished more clearly, although in this chapter we will distinguish them somewhat differently than he does. Thompson notes that a descriptive definition should identify only what is necessary to distinguish deliberation from other kinds of political discourse, so that we can identify and analyze it, especially in contrast with other kinds of communication. Citizen discourse should be able to meet the threshold definition of deliberation, or the theory becomes utopian. Evaluative

---

[1] E.g., Mansbridge et al. 2012, 25; Steiner 2012, 3.
[2] Bohman 1996, 10–11; Horkheimer 1982, 244.   [3] Thompson 2008.

criteria should help us to judge how well a given deliberation meets the normative ideals of deliberation. These criteria are more expansive and aspirational, so it is unlikely that any one civic forum will meet all of them fully or simultaneously. This means that a forum does not need to fulfill every criterion in order to be legitimate enough to conduct. But if the ideals are clear, they are useful for understanding the trade-offs among them, and for assessing and guiding political action. The perfect need not be the enemy of the good, but the good should not be the enemy of the better. Empirical conditions are the contextual factors that can affect the dynamics and quality of deliberation in practice. We need to separate these conditions clearly if we are to understand what contributes to better and worse deliberation, the potential trade-offs between the elements of deliberation, and the trade-offs between deliberation and other kinds of political discourse.

In the Introduction, we wrote that democratic deliberation occurs in civic forums when *political equals engage in public reasoning in a search for agreement about how to rule themselves.* In this chapter, we will work backward through the parts of this definition, at the same time distinguishing them from more ideal criteria by which civic forums can be evaluated, and from a few illustrative conditions that may affect the practice of deliberation in forums. Many conditions have been discussed in theory, but empirical research on deliberative forums is in its infancy, so we should be careful about making hasty generalizations about the circumstances that favor good deliberation. We address the research on conditions and potential trade-offs more fully in later chapters, especially Chapters 2 and 5.

We cannot offer a comprehensive review of all versions of deliberative theory, which involve too many views to summarize here, much less a grand synthesis. Instead, our goals in this chapter are fourfold. First, we want to offer a fuller rationale for considering the kinds of civic forums addressed in this book as relevant to the theory of democratic deliberation. Second, we aim to explain our understanding of the central aspects of deliberative theory that motivate our proposals for advancing equality and publicity in civic forums, presented later in the book. Therefore, our account of deliberation may not apply as well to legislatures, juries, everyday political discourse, and other political contexts in which deliberation can occur. Third, we want to offer a practical theory of citizen deliberation, especially to address criticisms that it is based on unrealistic hopes that citizens can treat each other as equals, exchange in public-minded reasoning, and draw conclusions based on good judgment.[4] We do so by distinguishing basic descriptive conditions for deliberation, which are not so difficult to meet, from ideal evaluative standards, which are more ambitious. Fourth, because we want to suggest feasible steps that civic forums might take, we also need to articulate evaluative standards that are amenable to observation. As Thompson argues, in the end, the normative ideals of deliberation cannot be "disproved" by empirical evidence because they are claims about how politics *ought* to be conducted, rather than how it *is* conducted.[5] But we also agree with Diana Mutz that research and evaluation that aim to improve deliberation in practice should pay attention to social scientific standards, employing concepts that are clear and measurable, and empirical claims that could be falsified.[6]

Table 1.1 outlines the elements of deliberation we will present in this chapter. The first column states threshold definitions of political equality, public reasoning, and agreement seeking for self-rule that we see as necessary for any forum to meet if it is to be considered democratic deliberation. The second column expands on these bare bones definitions to articulate ideal but achievable standards for equality, publicity, and decision making in forums. The third column highlights a few example empirical conditions that may especially affect whether forums can meet each standard in practice.

Seeking agreements for self-rule

Definition
We begin by defining decision-making conditions because they are central to identifying deliberative civic forums as a distinct object of study. In the introduction, we argued that one of the central rationales for democratic deliberation is that it enables autonomy, because individuals can only make authentic choices for themselves and the polity if they are fully informed about other citizens' views. We noted that individual and collective autonomy both arise through the process of public deliberation among political equals. We see deliberation as defined by a *search* for agreement about what is to be done about public issues. It begins with a state of non-agreement, but not necessarily with disagreement. Before deliberation, many participants may not have clearly defined

---

[4] See, e.g., Hibbing and Theiss-Morse 2002; Jackman and Sniderman 2006. For a summary and response to criticisms of deliberative democratic theory, see Collingwood and Reedy 2012.

[5] Thompson 2008, 499–500.   [6] Mutz 2008.

Table 1.1 *Elements of democratic deliberation in civic forums*

Definition (descriptive)	Evaluative standards (ideal)	Example conditions (empirical)
Political equality • Inclusion – in a group discussing multiple arguments and conclusions • Participation – in common language, without domination of speaking opportunities on any issue • Influence – over one's own reasons and conclusions	*Political equality* • Inclusion – of a well-justified sample of all affected by the issue • Participation – in initiating discussion of topics and commanding attention to one's claims • Influence – over one's own and others' reasons and conclusions	*Political equality* • Inclusion – open invitation and recruitment of critical mass of under represented and most affected perspectives; subsidies for participants • Participation – open forum design • Influence – background political, economic, and educational equality
Public reasoning • Mutual justification	*Public reasoning* • Public-mindedness • Respect • Clarification of values • Knowledge • Accountability and transparency – of argumentation and process	*Public reasoning* • Access to relevant and accurate information • Access to diversity of competing arguments • Time
Self-rule • Seeking agreement on decisions or recommendations • Informed consent to procedures	*Self-rule* • Structuring of views – group meta-consensus and individual coherence • Autonomy – procedural and substantive • Authorization – of process and conclusions	*Self-rule* • Conditions for political equality and public reasoning • Clear chain of authorization • Well-functioning deliberative system

policy preferences or know how to align them with their values, beliefs, and interests, especially when confronting complex or emerging issues.[7] However, deliberation is not limited to situations in which participants reach a formal collective agreement. When deliberation concludes by surfacing substantive conflicts without resolving them it may be a failed deliberation. But it may also be a sign of healthy deliberation that contributes to political autonomy if the alternative is to ignore deep conflicts or force a decision.[8] It may even be a collective decision to "resolve" the argument by settling for the status quo.[9] Regardless, it is the pursuit of agreement, rather than its achievement, that defines whether people deliberated. The kinds of agreements that democratic deliberation seeks may be ones that directly bind a larger community or advisory recommendations aimed at influencing public opinion, government, corporations, or civil society organizations.

There is much at stake in this definition for what counts as deliberation and, therefore, whether the theory of deliberation applies to many of the civic forums we consider in this book. Not all theorists would agree with us. For example, Thompson would limit the definition of deliberative democracy to a group decision "to which all members are bound whether they agree with it or not." For him, the "fundamental problem deliberative theory is intended to address" lies in this question. "In a state of disagreement, how can citizens reach a collective decision that is legitimate?" Elsewhere, Thompson says deliberation can be "decision-oriented," which seems to hold the door open a bit wider, but he still would not admit Deliberative Polls because participants do not come to a collective agreement. Rather, "they may be seen as taking part in an early phase of a process that leads to a deliberative decision." But he also acknowledges that some Deliberative Polls "have involved groups that make decisions or advise decision makers."[10] He argues that people behave differently when faced with making decisions under which they must live, rather than offering recommendations, because participants may either invest themselves more fully in the hard work of deliberating and arriving at mutual agreements, or become more strategic and extreme in their positions.

---

[7] Zaller (1992) shows that in many public opinion polls, citizens have no meaningful positions on public issues. In addition, some civic forums are convened to create "anticipatory publics," which can signal potential problems and develop policy on emerging issues, when publics have not yet formed around topics that may be contentious in the future (Mackenzie and Warren 2012, 96).

[8] Karpowitz and Mansbridge 2005.   [9] Mansbridge et al. 2010, 65.

[10] Thompson 2008, 502–3. See also Mansbridge et al. 2010, 65.

Were we to accept this definition, few of the civic forums we analyze in this book would count as instances of democratic deliberation. Perhaps only the popular assemblies and some of the co-governance forums we mentioned in the Introduction would merit attention, but none of the advisory forums. However, we think that Thompson is mixing the definition of deliberation with empirical circumstances that can affect it. First, the extent of deliberators' empowerment is more conditional than descriptive. As Simone Chambers argues, Thompson's view would likely restrict democratic deliberation to the existing power structure, especially the state or bodies directly authorized by the state to make decisions on its behalf, which narrows the institutional field of democracy unnecessarily.[11] One of the important aims of theorizing about a more democratic political system is to understand and judiciously expand the role of citizen deliberation in many arenas, including voluntary associations, interest groups, the public sphere, and civic forums.[12] Second, Chambers also points out that it is often unclear whether anyone in politics wields the ultimate power to make decisions that will be enforceable on all, or knows whether such decisions will be binding. For example, legislators often pass laws without knowing whether a second chamber or an executive will approve them, how bureaucracies will implement them, or whether courts will strike them down.

We would add that whether people think they are making a *collective* decision is also conditional. Legislators often disavow a law they did not support, challenging not only the outcome but also the procedures by which the law was brought to a vote. It is not clear whether legislative minorities think that they have participated in a collective decision rather than thinking that they have lost an unfair vote to the majority, which is now wholly responsible for a decision that should be resisted immediately.[13] Fourth, the fact that people may behave differently when

---

[11] Chambers 2012, 60–2.

[12] "The systemic approach does not dictate that we take a nation or large polity as our object of study. Schools and universities, hospitals, media, and other organizations can be understood along the lines offered by a deliberative system approach" (Mansbridge et al. 2012, 2).

[13] For example, here is US Senator John Barrasso speaking about the Independent Payment Advisory Board, created to recommend ways to control Medicare spending, by President Obama's 2010 health care reform legislation:

> Congress gave this board its authority to manage Medicare spending. I didn't vote for it. Members of my side of the aisle didn't vote for it. But this is part of the health care law that was crammed down the throats of the American people... Let's take a look at what happens when this board actually makes a recommendation... The recommendation becomes law. How can we prevent that from becoming

they think they are empowered to make enforceable decisions seems to us to be an open empirical question, one that demands considerable further exploration of both the dynamics of the decision-making group and the decisions that participants make. While more work to understand these differences is needed, we agree with Chambers that citizens can see themselves as affected by or responsible for their choices, commit fully to deliberating about them, and very much intend for these decisions to be enforced on others, even if people are acting in an advisory capacity to decision makers. Research on advisory civic forums often finds that participants feel that they have the attention of officials or the public, that deliberators express a sense of self-efficacy and accountability to the wider public interest, and take the deliberative process quite seriously.[14]

Rather than drawing a bright line between forums that make binding and advisory decisions, it makes more sense to envision forums along a spectrum of empowerment to influence an ongoing policy-making process. In the Introduction, we outlined several ways in which civic forums can influence political change, including the kind of direct authority over the political agenda or public decisions exercised by popular assemblies, the shared power of citizens and officials in co-governance institutions, and the power of public opinion and recommendations generated in advisory mini-publics.

Robert Goodin and John Dryzek elucidate several more specific ways in which mini-publics have influenced policy indirectly. Some mini-publics have issued recommendations that were taken up in the policy process by other actors, informing and influencing public debates. Other advisory forums have market-tested policy by evaluating specific proposals and plans. Others have built citizen confidence and policy constituencies among participants, who have gone on to advocate for their preferred

---

law? The recommendation will become law unless the House and the Senate each adopt – not by simple majority – each adopt by a three-fifths majority a resolution to block them. That is not enough... Then the House and Senate have to pass legislation to achieve equivalent savings of what this board claims to be saving by the care they deny. This is an incredible concentration of power that should belong in Congress to a board of unelected – unelected – individuals who are appointed by the President. Is there concern about this? In the House of Representatives, there is. There has been a repeal provision created that would repeal this board, and I will tell my colleagues it is a bipartisanly cosponsored attempt to repeal this provision. (US Congress 2011, S2472–3)

In the two years after the 2010 health care reform law was enacted, the US House of Representatives held 40 votes to repeal some or all of the law.

[14] Collingwood and Reedy 2012, 237; Parkinson 2006, 80; Smith 2009, 82.

solutions through associations and further public consultations. Many forums have increased official accountability by subjecting officials to citizen inquiry. Some forums have exerted influence by legitimating existing or proposed policies, strengthening their status in political debates. In some mini-publics, citizens have actively resisted government sponsors' attempts at using the forums to co-opt potential critics they would have to face in traditional consultation processes, such as adversarial public hearings. Goodin and Dryzek's analysis of multiple cases suggests that advisory forums that have exerted greater influence have done so because they are appointed by government, attract official attention, or garner media attention. These forums may influence officials, but also private institutions, the news media, and public opinion.[15]

The question of what kind of decisions count is motivated by the understandable desire to distinguish deliberation from other types of political discourse. We think that an emphasis on seeking agreements for self-rule can still differentiate deliberation from structured political dialogue, which focuses on achieving greater mutual understanding or tolerance among participants from divided social groups, and from organized political discussions that aim only to improve participants' civic capacities.[16] Discussion and dialogue are democratically valuable, but in different ways than deliberation. Political discussions that occur in group settings, such as civic education classes in schools or churches, can develop a taste for all forms of political engagement, including deliberation, and can prepare people to deliberate knowledgably, skillfully, and productively.[17] Dialogue is sometimes a necessary first step, especially among highly polarized social groups, to understand and bridge profoundly different views before participants can even consider whether to deliberate over solutions.[18]

Yet we agree with those who distinguish deliberation from these other kinds of talk because each has different goals and should be judged by different standards of equality and publicity. Political discussion may aim to educate, illuminate, ascertain, or even entertain. But if discussion does not endeavor to influence broader public opinion or pursue decisions to

---

[15] Goodin and Dryzek 2006.

[16] These three kinds of communication can be separated even if people move between deliberation, dialogue, and discussion at different moments in a civic forum, and even if some members of the group are engaged in deliberating, while others are not in the same moment.

[17] Colby, Beaumont, Ehrlich, and Corngold 2007, 156–74.

[18] Saunders 2011; Walsh 2007.

be applied to those outside the discussion, it need not be expected to be public in the senses we discuss below and it is not necessarily harmed by some inequalities of status and roles, such as in a teacher–student relationship. Dialogue often "seeks accommodation, reconciliation, mutual understanding, or at the very least, informed tolerance."[19] Given its goals, dialogue is better when participants have equal standing, so they can recognize and reciprocate with others across deep divisions, but dialogue may legitimately confine itself to reconciling only those who participate in it, rather than trying to establish policy prescriptions that extend to people outside the dialogue. While dialogue may try to inspire participants to act as ambassadors of tolerance to their own communities, it typically does not involve asking the *full* group to pursue a joint decision or issue a common set of public recommendations to others outside the group. We see these prescriptive aims as key to the kinds of forums we will explore.

The quest for self-rule also requires that participants consent to the deliberative process used in a civic forum. Like all forms of structured democratic action, citizen forums require an organizing entity that constructs a public and offers it an opportunity to express itself through some rules of engagement and publicity. Many of the criticisms of civic forums are aimed at the power of sponsors and organizers, especially when governments strategically deploy civic forums not to consult the public but to co-opt policy critics, to displace the voices of a larger public, or to legitimate policies decided in advance. For example, Aviezer Tucker assails the "oligarchic tendencies in deliberative democracy," which he defines as "changes in the preferences of a majority to match those of an interested minority that manages the deliberation and uses the selection of voters, control of the flow of information to them and the rules of deliberation to manipulate the results."[20] This degree of manipulation undermines citizens' autonomy so greatly that we cannot say that they are engaged in a search for self-rule. To avoid deception, the offer to deliberate should not promise a benefit it cannot deliver, such as an independent voice rather than an exercise in ventriloquism, and should not put citizens at risk of unanticipated harm, including wasting their time and effort.

[19] Levine, Fung, and Gastil 2005, 282.
[20] Tucker 2008, 128. Many organizers of public consultations raise concerns about government sponsors imposing narrow limits on the issues and framings that citizens are permitted to discuss in government-commissioned forums (Cooper and Smith 2012, 24–5).

At a minimum, we can say that citizens make independent decisions about whether and how to participate in deliberation when they give informed consent to a forum's procedures. We borrow the notion of informed consent from the system of peer review that researchers must undergo before conducting studies of human subjects, which is regulated by broad principles that overlap with deliberative theory.[21] Translated to civic forums, these principles include:

- Disclosure: forum organizers provide citizens with sufficient information to make an autonomous decision about whether to participate in plain language that participants can understand, and ensure that citizens understand that information well enough to decide.
- Capacity: citizens are able to form reasonable judgments about the possible consequences of participating.
- Voluntariness: citizens can decide freely whether to participate, without coercion or manipulation.

To give informed consent, citizens need to be aware of the purpose for convening the forum, how empowered it is to give advice or to enact policy, the initial issue agenda, the identity of the sponsors and organizers, the principles used to select participants, who will control the flow of information to them, the role of facilitators in managing deliberation, the decision rule that will be used to resolve differences, and how the deliberation and its outcomes will be made public.

As we discuss in more detail below, each of these features will shape participants' freedom to exchange reasons and the conclusions they can consider in deliberation. Some arrangements may expose participants to unnecessary risks.[22] Citizens can still deliberate even if the agenda,

---

[21] The classic treatment of informed consent in academic research is Faden, Beauchamp, and King 1986. The notion of informed consent is also important, if articulated somewhat differently, in many areas of law (such as medical decision making).

[22] Just as in research settings, so in civic forums it is important for participants to know in advance whether what they say will be reported to others and with what level of confidentiality. For example, there are many forums organized by public and private social service agencies, which convene their clients to give input on the organization's policies or performance. Participants need to know before speaking whether their comments may be used to deny their benefits or will be attached to their names publicly in ways that may harm their reputations. There may be a good case for extending a legal privilege to all comments that citizens make in such forums, comparable to the protection that representatives have in the United States against being sued for libel for comments made in legislative debates. And there may be good reason to extend privileges to conveners of these forums, similar to privileges that offer reporters, doctors, and lawyers some protection against revealing information that clients share with them.

information, and decision rule are defined in advance by a forum's organizers, even in very restrictive terms, as long as participants know what
they are getting into and freely agree to get into it. Civic forums typically
meet standards for informed consent by notifying participants at the outset about the process through recruitment materials, briefing papers, and
norm-setting presentations, sometimes asking explicitly for participants'
consent to these procedures.[23]

Evaluative standards

What makes the pursuit of agreements on matters of self-rule more and
less legitimate? We will propose three ideal criteria, including participants' ability to arrive at well-structured views, their autonomy, and
their authorization of the deliberative process and conclusions. Taken
as a whole, these criteria address the procedural and substantive components of decision making. Our motivation is to bridge as much as possible
competing views that see deliberation as best justified by the quality of
its process or by the quality of its outcomes, over whether deliberation is
best thought of as an intrinsic good or merely instrumental to some other
good. We also aim to incorporate responses by theorists of democratic
deliberation to important criticisms made by liberal democrats, difference
democrats, and social choice theorists. We are by no means the first to do
so, and because this is well-traveled theoretical ground, we will traverse
it briefly and from an altitude that obscures some of its contours, touch-
ing down on the points that seem most important for clarifying our own
evaluative criteria and for our argument later in the book. Let us turn to
these criticisms first.

Foundational statements of deliberative democracy posited a rational
consensus as the ideal outcome, which was seen as guaranteed by a perfect
procedure. Jürgen Habermas and Joshua Cohen each grounded deliberation's legitimacy in an ideal discursive process, in which speakers are
free from coercion, equal in status, inclusive, and rational.[24] In this ideal
situation, it is said that participants would be able to converge on self-
evident reasons for a common position, forming a rationally motivated
consensus. This view has not aged well, for several reasons.

First, the ideal of consensus seems untenable given the irresolvable plurality of worldviews in contemporary democracies. Even Habermas and

---

[23] Lee 2011, 21.
[24] Cohen 1989, 24–5; Habermas 1990, 88–9. Other proceduralist statements include Benhabib 1994; Sunstein 1999.

Cohen now seem to question whether a perfect procedure oriented toward consensus is a defensible political goal. Both have taken stock of what John Rawls called the "pluralism of incompatible yet reasonable comprehensive doctrines" among citizens of modern democracies.[25] Cohen acknowledges that "there are distinct, incompatible understandings of value, each one reasonable, to which people are drawn under favorable conditions for the exercise of their practical reason," and this pluralism needs to be accommodated in democratic deliberation when it cannot be resolved.[26] Habermas, who once saw all discourse as inherently oriented toward rational consensus, has recognized a paradox in his way of thinking: "This entropic state of a definitive consensus, which would make all further communication superfluous, cannot be represented as a meaningful goal because it would engender paradoxes (an ultimate language, a final interpretation, a nonrevisable knowledge, etc.)."[27] In his democratic theory, he accepts that compromise, fair bargaining, and elections are features of a plural political landscape, although he continues to argue that legitimate laws must "meet with the assent of all citizens in a discursive process of legislation that in turn has been legally constituted."[28] Both Cohen and Habermas have squared the ideal of consensus with the practical necessity of recourse to majority rule, each in his own way.[29] Others have bridged deliberation and pluralism somewhat differently by arguing that voting and negotiation of competing interests, including in lawmaking, can be legitimate if the procedures are justified in advance by deliberation among citizens or their representatives.[30]

---

[25] Rawls 1993, xviii.   [26] Cohen 1997, 408.

[27] Habermas 1996b, 15–18.   [28] Habermas 1996a, 110.

[29] Habermas, drawing on Fröbel, contends that a legitimate "majority decision may come about only in such a way that its content is regarded as the rationally motivated but *fallible* result of an attempt to determine what is right through a discussion that has been brought to a *provisional* close under the pressure to decide" (Habermas 1997, 47). Joshua Cohen accepts a necessary dependence on majority rule when consensus cannot be obtained, but argues that this "does not, however, eliminate the distinction between deliberative forms of collective choice and forms that aggregate nondeliberative preferences. The institutional consequences are likely to be different in the two cases, and the results of voting among those who are committed to finding reasons that are persuasive to all are likely to differ from the results of an aggregation that proceeds in the absence of this commitment" (Cohen 1989, 23).

[30] E.g., Mansbridge et al. (2010, 93) argue:

Although we want to stress the importance of seeking a genuinely common good, we argue that deliberation can and should in certain conditions include both self-interest and the negotiation of conflicting interests... Voting and the negotiation of cooperative antagonists are not themselves deliberative acts but, when they are

Second, a liberal democratic critique of proceduralism contends that deliberation must also be judged by whether resulting decisions protect conditions for practicing individual and collective autonomy, especially the status of rights that support equal and public political participation in deliberation and other forms of democratic politics. This critique has also gained traction. As Cohen now acknowledges, "some democratic collective choices are too execrable to be legitimate, however attractive the procedures that generate them," especially when they issue from tyrannous majorities that deprive minorities of their political voices.[31] Liberal democrats are not willing to gamble that an ideal deliberative procedure will always respect individual rights, which are seen as needing independent protection in constitutions or more restrictive discursive rules in deliberation. Liberal theorists integrate constitutionalism with deliberation by arguing that the latter can be used to derive individual rights such as free expression and association,[32] that constitutions can create conditions for democratic deliberation within the state (in legislatures, courts, and juries)[33] and in the broader civil society,[34] and that the process of making and amending constitutions can itself be democratically deliberative.[35] Some theorists in this tradition would also constrain deliberation by limiting the kinds of reasoning that could be introduced, disallowing arguments that violate core principles of political equality (such as racism) or reciprocity (such as sectarian religious claims that could not be accepted by others).[36] Some would limit the domain of citizen deliberation to constitutional issues or the fundamental aims of society, rather than the means by which citizens' goals are pursued in everyday policy making.[37]

Third, theorists influenced by difference democracy have pointed out that the kind of rational agreement proposed especially by Habermas risks systematic coercion of the least powerful social groups. In this view, a vision of rational discourse in which speakers must give logical reasons and evidence for their positions favors the most educated and privileged, who are best prepared to engage in this kind of discussion. If the ideal of rational consensus is too narrowly restricted to formal argumentation, it excludes other potentially valuable forms of democratic

justified through deliberative procedures and preceded in practice by such procedures, can be accepted by deliberative theorists as legitimate components of democracy complementary to and in some cases integrated with deliberation.

[31] Cohen 1997, 409–10.   [32] Rawls 1993.   [33] Bessette 1994; Rawls 1993.
[34] Sunstein 1997; Walzer 1991.   [35] Ackerman 1991; Estlund 1992; Rawls 1993.
[36] Gutmann and Thompson 1996; Rawls 1993.   [37] Christiano 2012; Rawls 1993.

discourse that may be more available to less educated and empowered groups, such as personal testimony, storytelling, rhetoric, and greeting (or recognition).[38] In addition, insistence on consensus can suppress discussion of marginalized groups' perspectives in ways that "narrow the possible agenda for deliberation and thereby effectively silence some points of view."[39] To expect that deliberators of rationally incompatible perspectives and unequal power should arrive at agreement on preferences can enforce censorship and self-censorship of less powerful speakers and perspectives.[40] If the object of consensus must be a shared vision of the common good, this too can be a subtle means of domination because "definitions of the common good are likely to express the interests and perspectives of the dominant groups in generalized terms."[41]

Theorists who bridge deliberative and difference democracy suggest that it may be more just for deliberation to expose and even heighten fundamental conflicts that are masked by hegemonic views, so that weaker parties can challenge those views in further deliberation, or mobilize themselves to vote or bargain for fairer conditions for deliberation.[42] These theorists do not want to dispense with notions of the common good and public reason, but to expand them. For example, Iris Marion Young argues for "explicitly acknowledging social differentiations and divisions and encouraging differently situated groups to give voice to their needs, interests, and perspectives on the society in ways that meet conditions of reasonableness and publicity."[43] For her, storytelling and other alternative modes of reasoning are valuable not simply because they allow the least powerful to express themselves, and not because the marginalized are epistemically privileged, but because these ways of speaking allow the disempowered to connect their claims to broader notions of a good society and to enlarge the range of perspectives in deliberation.[44]

---

[38] On testimony, see Sanders 1997. On storytelling, rhetoric, and greeting, see Young 2000.

[39] Young 2000, 43.

[40] This insight highlights the importance of institutional rules and other group-level conditions of deliberation, which can affect the extent to which disempowered groups speak up (Karpowitz, Mendelberg, and Shaker 2012) and articulate their distinctive views (Mendelberg, Karpowitz, and Goedert 2014).

[41] Young 2000, 43.   [42] E.g., Mansbridge 1999.   [43] Young 2000, 119.

[44] "Inclusion of differentiated groups is important not only as a means of demonstrating equal respect and to ensure that all legitimate interests in the polity receive expression . . . Inclusion has two additional functions. First, it motivates participants in political debate to transform their claims from mere expressions of self-regarding interest to appeals to justice. Secondly, it maximizes the social knowledge available to a democratic public, such that citizens are more likely to make just and wise decisions" (Young 2000, 115).

Another response to proceduralism suggests that deliberation is valuable because it arrives at the best agreements according to an independent standard of justice or the common good.[45] In its strongest formulation, this epistemic rationale contends that deliberation has instrumental value for producing better decisions because it fosters consideration of the widest possible array of relevant facts, values, and interests. Deliberation can correct falsehoods and individual biases, increase the pool of available information and arguments, optimize chances for identifying mutually beneficial solutions, and enhance the legitimacy of political decisions even in the eyes of those who disagree. While this argument can lead to elitist visions of protecting deliberation by restricting it to experts – whether philosopher kings or social scientists – let us take it in its most democratic form and assume it extends to all citizens. Many theorists suspect that deliberation often does result in better decisions the more that citizens engage in public reasoning as political equals. But even if civic deliberation meets those ideal criteria for equality and publicity, few theorists are prepared to say that citizens will always make the *best* decisions, especially if this involves adopting a standpoint that claims to be objective, transcendent, or neutral. As we have seen, some would argue that the plurality of visions of justice and the common good that can be arrived at through reason means that it is unlikely that a single vision of any of them can be identified in actual deliberation. More importantly, even if such a vision were attained, we would need an objective standpoint from which to judge with certainty whether it is best. As Stephen Elstub writes, "If we could test this justification, it would mean that there is another method for identifying the common good and therefore deliberative democracy would not be required."[46] We think these matters are best discovered through the search for agreement in civic deliberation, rather than outside it.

A final set of theoretical concerns are raised by social choice theorists, who cast doubt on whether deliberation, or any other means of democratic decision making, can arrive at rational collective decisions. While these are ancient worries, the modern argument begins with Kenneth Arrow's theorem, which demonstrated that no single procedure for aggregating individual preferences can satisfy the criteria for a rational collective choice if there are more than two voters and more than two

---

[45] For discussions of different versions of the epistemic argument, see Estlund 1997; Martí 2006.

[46] Elstub 2008, 62. See also Festenstein 2002, 99–100.

options.[47] Arrow noted that one solution was to limit the range of permissible preferences to two, which he acknowledged was an unacceptable restriction on voters' autonomy. William Riker expanded on Arrow's theorem to argue that there is no way of ascertaining group preferences that is independent of the voting procedure.[48] How we vote can determine the decision because the order and grouping of votes can be manipulated to arrive at a variety of decisions derived from the same distribution of individual preferences. In place of stable majority rule, we get ambiguous and cyclical decision making. Riker concluded that no voting procedure was better than any other at aggregating individuals' preferences and therefore that the idea of collective decisions reflecting an underlying popular will was absurd.

But this problem can be mitigated when multiple preferences are ordered on a spectrum according to a single underlying dimension. For example, if the issue is energy policy, a group could order its preferences for multiple energy sources (oil, gas, nuclear, and coal) on a spectrum of best to worst according to a single dimension, such as environmental benefits, short-term economic needs, or long-term economic advantage. Theorists of deliberation argue that it can help citizens to narrow the dimensions of a decision or split complex decisions into multiple choices, each decided according to one or two key dimensions.[49] Under such conditions, preferences become "single-peaked," meaning that each individual has a favorite preference and a decreasing preference for other alternatives arrayed along a continuum. The median individual's favorite option carries the day, and majority decisions can be collectively consistent and stable. While the kinds of problems that social choice theorists raise may be rare in practice, they draw attention to the concern that in

---

[47] The first criterion for rational collective decision is unanimity: if everyone ranks choice X above Y and Z, then X should win. Second, there is non-dictatorship: if the majority prefer Y to X, while the minority opts for X to Y, the group decision should not be for X. Third, there is transitivity: if the group prefers X to Y, and Y to Z, then X should beat Z. Fourth, there is no restriction on the domain of preferences that group members can endorse: X, Y, and Z are all options. Fifth, irrelevant alternatives are independent: if all individuals' preferences are X or Y, then the group's choice should not be changed by introducing option Z. See Arrow 1963 [1951].

[48] Riker 1982.

[49] The argument that deliberation can focus the dimensions of a choice is from Miller 1992, from whom we also borrow the energy policy example. Deliberation's ability to split decisions into more tractable sets of choices is suggested by Dryzek and Niemeyer 2010. Other accessible discussions of deliberation and social choice theory include Dryzek 2000 and Elstub 2008. List et al. (2013) offer empirical evidence that Deliberative Polls can structure participants' preferences to make them more single-peaked.

the absence of consensus, the mechanism used to add up votes can decide the issue.[50]

Structuring of views

The epistemic rationale and appreciation of difference suggest that we should want deliberators to consider a broad variety of views, including the views of the least powerful. The need to accommodate pluralism suggests that the ideal of consensus on preferences could give way to another standard for arriving at preferences. The social choice problem suggests the need to structure those preferences rationally in the absence of unanimous consent.

These considerations prompt John Dryzek and Simon Niemeyer to suggest that an ideal outcome of deliberation is a meta-consensus on the range of reasons and preferences acceptable to the group. Dryzek and Niemeyer suggest that groups can seek meta-agreements on the range of disputed values (norms), beliefs (about facts), and discourses (such as market liberalism, environmental justice, and the like) that could focus the array of acceptable preferences.[51] The last dimension, preferences, delineates the acceptable range of decisions. The first three dimensions – values, beliefs, and discourses – refer to agreement on the scope of reasoning the group considers legitimate. We would add that groups can agree upon their perceived *interests*, which are staples of democratic theory. We would subtract discourses, which seem too all-encompassing and complicated to win all group members' consent, or even to distinguish cleanly as dimensions of group decision making.[52]

---

[50] On the rarity of majority cycles, see Mackie 2004; Regenwetter et al. 2006.

[51] Dryzek and Niemeyer 2010, 85–118. The authors also suggest another dimension of meta-consensus – agreement over how to order the agenda in deliberation – which we discuss below as an element of equal participation.

[52] In Dryzek's (2010) view, a discourse defines entities that are existing and relevant to a decision (such as individuals, social classes, technology, or nature), endows these entities with varying degrees of agency (e.g., to make history), ascribes motives to these entities (e.g., selfishness or altruism), interprets the relationships among entities (e.g., as competitive, cooperative, or symbiotic), and is tied to specific metaphors and other rhetorical devices (e.g., "survival of the fittest" or "the selfish gene.") Getting deliberative groups to agree on something as comprehensive, complex, and potentially diffuse as a discourse seems less realistic than achieving concord on some basic beliefs, values, and ascribed interests, which may be all that is necessary to make a dispute tractable. For example, in another context, Dryzek (1997) has identified nine major discourses of environmentalism, which he has more recently reduced to four (Dryzek 2013), each of which has multiple variants. Other scholars have characterized and classified environmental discourses in additional ways (see, e.g., Clapp and Dauvergne 2005; Eckersley 1992). Getting a

In civic forums, any of these kinds of agreements should make it more likely for individuals to reason autonomously, reducing the danger of coercion or manipulation of participants' thinking by each other or by the forum's organizers, and increasing the likelihood of a meaningful collective choice. Therefore, we can say that the search for collective agreement is more legitimate to the extent that it achieves a meta-consensus that structures the scope of views (of values, beliefs, and interests) that could reasonably shape the group's preferences.[53] In short, better deliberation focuses the range of reasons and conclusions that is acceptable to the group. This is legitimate whether deliberation narrows options to the point of a genuine consensus on reasons or preferences, or enough for members to engage in a rational vote on the remaining alternatives.

More legitimate deliberation would go further to develop the coherence of each participant's values, beliefs, perceived interests, and political preferences.[54] While any of these may be transformed in deliberation, all of them should be better aligned afterward.[55] All should be more durable when tested by elite manipulation or symbolic politics.[56] Some other standards used to judge opinion quality in the empirical literature do not square well with theoretical ideals. Opinion quality does not depend on ideological consistency, especially if measured on the traditional

---

diverse group of environmentalists to agree on one approach to environmentalism seems daunting. Coming to agreement on a single environmental discourse among a group of lay citizens, who are likely to have more inchoate and self-contradictory visions of nature and humanity, seems even harder.

[53] Of course, meta-consensus alone does not guarantee that preferences are ideal. As Dryzek and Niemeyer note, we also need to ask whether meta-consensus is arrived at freely and equally (and we address those criteria below). We also need to apply some substantive standard for judging the preferences (which we address in the discussion of authenticity below). For their part, Dryzek and Niemeyer argue that this judgment depends on the political context. They contend that meta-agreement on the range of acceptable discourses is especially important in societies deeply divided over identity, agreement on the scope of acceptable values is most important in situations of heightened moral conflict, agreement on the spectrum of acceptable beliefs is most important when elite actors make questionable and manipulative empirical claims, and agreement on preferences is most important when one or more actors can manipulate the decision-making process (e.g., by limiting the scope of issues under discussion or the order in which votes on alternatives are held) (Dryzek and Niemeyer 2010, 115).

[54] The criteria suggested in this sentence and the previous one are widely used in empirical research on civic forums. For recent summaries of the research, see Pincock 2012; Fishkin 2009, Chapters 4–5; Steiner 2012, Chapters 2–7.

[55] For summaries of the literature on civic forums' effects on opinion consistency, see Fishkin 2009, 135–9; Pincock 2012, 146.

[56] Chong and Druckman 2007; Druckman and Nelson 2003; Niemeyer 2004; Niemeyer, Ayirtman, and Hartz-Karp 2008.

liberal-left to conservative-right spectrum.[57] The goal of democratic deliberation is to develop our capacities for independent and reflective decision making, not necessarily to fit ourselves into conventional political categories by making better progressives or conservatives of us. Opinion quality also does not necessarily mean preference change. While deliberation should transform individuals' views – by making them more other-regarding or well-informed by good evidence, for example – this does not necessarily mean that deliberation is better when it alters people's policy preferences. If people engage in public reasoning as equals, it can be as legitimate for their discussion to reinforce or strengthen their preexisting positions as to change them.

Autonomy

Concerns that are raised by social choice theorists about whether deliberative decisions are rational or manipulable, by difference democrats about whether these decisions are non-coercive or hegemonic, and by liberal democrats about whether these decisions respect or violate the basic rights of others all point in different ways to the question of whether deliberative agreements can integrate individual and collective autonomy. Civic forums do this best when they extend greater control over procedures to participants and when the substance of deliberators' conclusions preserves or expands the ability of all citizens to reconcile their individual and collective autonomy.

Even if participants give informed consent to the procedures in a civic forum, ideally we would want citizens themselves to help shape these procedures through their deliberation. Of course, practical politics requires some way to narrow the range of problems and solutions in order to focus inquiry and decision making, so there will always be some authority over the agenda. In deliberation, some authority is also inevitable for applying rules of order to ensure that all can speak, none dominate the floor, major themes in discussion can be identified, and the discussion is sequenced productively.[58] Often, the net effect of these interventions is to increase

---

[57] Studies that confuse ideological consistency with the goal of deliberation include Jackman and Sniderman 2006; Sturgis, Roberts, and Allum 2005. In contrast, Neblo (2010) argues that opinion quality is better measured by the *weakening* of ideological consistency after deliberation.

[58] Kuyper 2012; Moore 2011a. Jane Mansbridge and her coauthors offer a hypothetical rationale for this:

citizens' political equality rather than to diminish it. Holding a forum often involves creating an opportunity for civic speech that would not exist otherwise, thereby expanding the range of legitimate speakers in the public sphere by authorizing citizens to question and advise experts and officials. Peter Levine and his colleagues are correct that "[o]rganizers' decisions can never be perfectly democratic and deliberative [so] there is a danger that deliberation will be overly influenced by skilled organizers, but the greater danger is having no competent organization at all."[59]

Yet many theorists agree that deliberation is better when citizens have a more equal voice, with organizers and each other, in devising procedures for seeking agreement, as long as political equality and public reasoning are not sacrificed.[60] The initial issue agenda, information, facilitation, and the decision rule all shape the forum, with profound implications for citizens' autonomy. Moreover, the fairness of how a decision is made is often the substance of a conflict, as in disputes within groups over whether to decide by consensus or majority rule, or within states over alternative electoral systems and how the drawing of political districts affects minorities' voting power. As Amy Gutmann and Dennis Thompson argue, often "citizens have to deliberate about the substantive value of alternative procedures" and "[t]here is no substitute for substantive moral deliberation in resolving conflicts over procedures."[61]

Ideally, civic forums can grant participants some power to devise their own agenda, or at least to reflect on the agenda that is given to them and revise it if it seems *unnecessarily* constraining.[62] Deliberation can

> In a context of preexisting inequality, some coercive power may also be necessary to maintain basic rights, equal opportunity, and the other conditions that help participants approach the deliberative ideal. In a metadeliberation over the conditions of deliberation free and equal participants would be likely to adopt these mutually justifiable rules not only as a guard against others but also to curtail their own future weaknesses of the will. (Mansbridge et al. 2010, 82; see also Bächtiger et al. 2010, 46–7)

> Clearly, there is a role for organizers in structuring deliberation in ways that are more likely to bring in the voices of those who are disempowered. The key is to find rules that are likely to help all deliberators recognize their fellow discussants as authoritative speakers and to engage in public reasoning.

[59] Levine, Fung, and Gastil 2005, 275.
[60] E.g., Barber 1984; Fung and Wright 2003; Gastil 1993; Lang 2008.
[61] Gutmann and Thompson 1996, 32.
[62] While we acknowledge the power of agenda setting (Bachrach and Baratz 1962), we also note that not every meeting can take up every subject. A reasonable set of issues to discuss can make meetings more focused and productive, so the key is the power of participants to revise agendas that are, in their view, *needlessly* constraining.

call attention to competing ways of framing issues and ask participants to develop their own framings.[63] It can ask deliberators about what background information or experts they want to consult. It can seek participants' ongoing impressions of facilitation and solicit suggestions for how it can be improved. It can identify acceptable ways of arriving at decisions, including specifying when to resort to non-consensual decision making, such as the use of majority rule. It can employ decision methods that maximize participants' freedom to introduce their own preferred reasons and conclusions, and to prioritize their conclusions rather than choosing only one. Each of these strategies has been employed in one civic forum or another.

The choice of a decision method deserves additional attention because it can shape the entire forum and because of the long debate among theorists over the value of consensus in deliberation. Most civic forums require participants to come to consensus on a single group decision or to produce a collective decision by aggregating deliberators' individual votes.[64] Consensus and majority rule each offer a unique set of benefits and risks for integrating individual and collective autonomy (see Table 1.2). While other ways of arriving at decisions can be used, these two are sufficient for now to illustrate two important implications: first, decision methods

---

[63] For example, as we discuss further in Chapter 6, National Issues Forums organize discussion around competing frames of an issue, asking participants to explore the strengths and weaknesses of each frame without requiring citizens to choose one of them exclusively. Alison Kadlec and Will Friedman (2007, 11) call this *"nonpartisan framing-for-deliberation,"* which involves clarifying the range of positions surrounding an issue so that citizens can better decide what they want to do. They distinguish this from *"partisan framing-to-persuade,"* in which political actors define an issue to their advantage to mobilize support. The kind of framing advocated by Kadlec and Friedman is an attractive solution, but especially if forums also give participants an option to discuss additional frames that emerge in deliberation and are embraced by many participants. Few organizers can anticipate all frames that may arise in discussion. Another alternative is to develop frames through wide consultation with citizens before the forum (Lezaun and Soneryd 2007, 283).

[64] We distinguish here between the decision *method*, which is a broader category that includes many different aspects of the process of decision making, and the decision *rule*, which involves the specific threshold for settling on an outcome. For example, a decision rule might be unanimity, super-majority, majority rule, or some other, more complex threshold. In the discussion that follows, we explore alternative decision *methods*. For example, we take consensus to mean arriving at a single group decision during the process of discussion, in contrast to individual voting, which may end up unanimous but does not require participants to decide as one during the discussion. Other forums, such as Deliberative Polls, which aim to generate a representation of public opinion rather than a decision, do so by aggregating participants' individual opinions after deliberation.

Table 1.2 *Decision methods and autonomy in civic forums*

	Consensus	Voting and polling
Potential benefits	*Individual autonomy* • Public reasoning: knowledge, public-mindedness, respect, and clarification of norms • Each member's preference is reflected in the group preference.	*Individual autonomy* • Each member expresses her final preference without compromise.
	Collective autonomy • Strong group acceptance of conclusions • Clarity of conclusions • Strong capacity to influence others outside the group	*Collective autonomy* • Fair aggregation of views: each member's vote counts equally • Tractability of reaching conclusions
Potential risks	*Individual autonomy* • Majority coercion	*Individual autonomy* • Strategic reasoning: concealing information and reasons • Self-regarding reasoning, unresponsiveness, and disrespect
	Collective autonomy • Minority veto	*Collective autonomy* • Weak group acceptance of conclusions • Ambiguity of conclusions • Weak capacity to influence others outside of the group

can influence the quality of deliberation if participants know the expectations at the outset; and, second, each method offers its own mix of advantages and disadvantages for autonomy. This means that majority rule is not always a practical but normatively "second best" alternative to consensus.

Forums that end by issuing unanimous group statements, such as Consensus Conferences, can contribute to individual autonomy especially by promoting public reasoning. The group psychology literature offers evidence that consensus can create non-coercive and inclusive communication. Some studies of groups find that unanimous decision making can foster cooperative behavior[65] and increase information sharing among the group.[66] The research shows that minorities can influence majorities to reconsider their positions and sometimes to change them. Minorities can be most persuasive in some ways that comport fairly well with deliberative ideals, such as presenting their positions clearly and consistently, and demonstrating that they share similar values or principles with the majority before recommending divergent decisions.[67] These findings suggest that seeking consensus can contribute to many of the aspects of public reasoning. While there are different kinds of consensus, in unanimous decisions each member's preference is reflected in the group preference.[68] This too serves individual autonomy. Because the final decision must be acceptable to all, every voice is valuable; no one can be overlooked. Consensus strengthens collective autonomy by increasing participants' perceptions that the group's decision is legitimate and acceptable[69] and by expressing a clear collective verdict on the issues, which may be more likely than a split decision to influence others outside the group. This is no small consideration for civic forums, which typically depend on others outside the forum to take up their recommendations.

However, consensus may also increase the risk of two kinds of coercion found in experimental research on groups and studies of organizations. The demand for consensus may increase social pressure on those who hold minority views to agree with the majority.[70] This is the fear of many difference democrats, who tend to assume that more privileged citizens

---

[65] Bouas and Komorita 1996.   [66] Mathis 2011.   [67] Smith and Mackie 2000, 363–8.

[68] Mansbridge identified three kinds of consensus: "the search for a correct solution (overlapping private interests), the independent value of unity (identifying one's own good with the good of the whole), and empathy (identifying one's own good with the good of other individual members)" (1983, 255). In addition, Mansbridge et al. (2010, 70) identify four types of agreements that involve "a kind of consensus, that is, a genuine agreement among participants that the outcomes are right or fair." These include convergence, in which participants begin without conflict and agree on an outcome for the same reasons; incompletely theorized agreements (Sunstein 1999), in which people start from conflict and agree on an outcome for different reasons; integrative negotiations, in which conflicting parties resolve a conflict by reframing it or seeing it from a new perspective; and fully cooperative distributive negotiations, in which participants relinquish part of what they originally wanted to arrive at an agreement that they perceive as fair.

[69] Kameda 1991; Kaplan and Miller 1987; Nemeth 1977.

[70] Devine et al. 2001; Mendelberg 2002.

will form the majority.[71] It is also a concern of theorists of group polarization, who predict that discussion leads groups to adopt more extreme
positions to which the group's members are initially inclined.[72] Of course,
the consensus requirement can also allow minorities to coerce majorities by threatening to veto decisions. Mansbridge's classic study of New
England Town Hall meetings and democratic workplace collectives found
that some communities use consensus "not only to affirm the existence of
common interests but also to give every member a self-protective veto,"
which can lead to social coercion or a deadlock that preserves status quo
arrangements that no one prefers most.[73] Because every deliberator matters in consensus decision making, this approach empowers minorities,
for better or worse. Whether it is better or worse depends, in part, on
who comprises the minority and how the minority uses its power.

Forums that end in non-unanimous individual voting on recommendations (such as Citizens Assemblies and some Citizens Juries) or polling
(such as Deliberative Polls and Planning Cells) reduce pressure on participants to agree with the majority or to bend to minority vetoes.[74]
After deliberation, each participant can express an individual preference
without having to worry about compromising with others. Collective
autonomy can take the form of a fair aggregation of views, in which
each person's preference counts equally. The group's conclusions are far
easier to reach than forming consensus during the discussion, especially
if majority rule is used to interpret the meaning of the results. The trade-
offs for individual autonomy are that when people know that they do
not have to reach unanimity, it is more tempting to act strategically by
withholding information and concealing reasons for one's position that
are unlikely to survive public scrutiny. One need not consider others'
interests, respond to their arguments, or treat their views with the same
respect as when one must come to consensus with others. This can undermine the individual autonomy of all participants because majority views
are less reflective and minorities go unheeded. Group autonomy may be
weakened if minorities do not accept the majority position. If there is no
large majority in support of a single option, the forum transmits a more

---

[71] Of course, under majority rule, the more privileged citizens can simply ignore the minority (if those privileged citizens form the majority).

[72] In Chapter 2, we address this theory and its limitations more fully with regard to enclave
deliberation.

[73] Mansbridge 1983, 255–6.

[74] We recognize that a forum might choose post-discussion voting but require unanimity as
a decision rule. In practice, this would be very similar to the consensus decision making
we have described above.

ambiguous message about the group's preference, which can undermine its ability to influence those outside the forum.

How should the choice of decision methods be decided to serve autonomy best? The answer to that question depends in large part on the forum's goals.[75] Forums can have multiple legitimate aims and benefits, including "political education, social solidarity, political critique, or popular control," as well as advancing "public accountability, social justice, effective governance, and popular mobilization."[76] Forums also can have different practical aims: a clear decision or recommendation in favor of one policy or another may be needed to break a logjam, ranking of multiple options may be needed to help prioritize allocation of resources, generating multiple solutions to emerging problems may be needed to anticipate change, and so on. Typically, the forum's charge is defined by the sponsors in government agencies, associations, or academia, often in consultation with an advisory committee of stakeholders or experts on the issue. Because the quality of deliberation and the decision are always influenced by the decision method, it is ideally chosen through deliberation by participants themselves. In most civic forums, however, this is impractical because of time limitations or the demands of the sponsors or organizers.

Nonetheless, we see at least two ways in which procedural deliberation can occur. In well-funded and more empowered forums, we can imagine a two-step process in which a first group of citizens deliberates to set fair procedures, while a second group follows those procedures to discuss the content of the issue and seek agreement. Of course, the first group would need to be briefed well about the implications of different decision methods in civic forums. A two-step arrangement might protect the task of procedural design from strategic thinking about how to game the process to obtain a desired result because it takes the choice out of the organizers' hands, and the citizens choosing the decision rule would not be the same ones making the decision.

While this ideal cannot be met within each forum, it can be approached over time through institutional deliberation. This can occur within and among organizers, in consultation with citizens who have taken part in civic forums. For example, as Participatory Budgeting was developed in

---

[75] As we discuss in Chapter 2, creating conditions for citizens to speak on *equal* terms also requires attention to the composition of the deliberative group, which recent research shows can interact with decision methods to influence whether all group members can participate equally (Karpowitz and Mendelberg 2014).

[76] Fung 2003, 339–40.

Porto Alegre, Brazil, the city government adopted significant changes in the charge and decision rule in the first few years in response to discussion with citizens and associations who took part in crafting the initial budgets. Initially, citizens from each district pooled their budget requests, which were winnowed by a city-wide budget council of citizens elected from each district. However, after a few years, officials and the city-wide council agreed to move certain issues onto the permanent agenda by supplementing neighborhood representation with issue-oriented representatives (on health and welfare, education, and so on) chosen from city-wide associations, and they adopted a redistributive formula for allocating more resources to low-income districts with the worst infrastructure.[77] This illustrates the possibility for institutional deliberation about procedural designs.

Substantive principles for assessing civic forums' decisions are difficult to articulate in the face of pluralism, but necessary. It seems reasonable to say that a forum's conclusions are more legitimate to the extent that they preserve conditions for all citizens to deliberate about public issues in the future. Otherwise, the theory of deliberation itself would be incoherent. More specifically, we could say that better decisions facilitate all citizens' ability to realize and reconcile their autonomy, or at least do not harm this ability. Regardless of its deliberative virtues, a civic forum that recommended curtailing basic rights, for example by narrowing the definition of eligible voters in elections to those who are literate, should arouse skepticism about its democratic virtues.

Conversely, this does not mean that any conclusion that *expands* some group's political rights necessarily serves the goal of reconciling individual and collective autonomy. For example, it might be argued that a recommendation to extend the vote to children as young as 12 years old would not be legitimate because children lack the necessary judgment, experience, and material independence to exercise their political autonomy, and therefore children's interests are best represented by their parents' votes.[78] A more difficult proposal to evaluate would be that all voters should have to pass the test administered orally to immigrants who apply for US citizenship, which measures basic knowledge of American political institutions, history, and English language proficiency. Presumably, many native-born children could pass this test easily, but many adult citizens

---

[77] Wampler 2012.
[78] These are indeed a few of the common arguments for denying children the same citizenship rights as adults (Papandrea 2008).

could not. This test, or some expanded version of it, could dispel concerns about whether some children lack the political knowledge and judgment to vote legitimately, yet raise new worries about whether some adult voters have the capacities that children are assumed to lack and immigrants are required to prove. The effect of requiring such a test might be to improve some citizens' political capacities and enfranchise some children, but it would likely dissuade even more citizens from registering to vote and would certainly disenfranchise many existing voters. Therefore, from the standpoint of preserving individual and collective autonomy, it should not be hard to reject such a recommendation, especially if one considered alternatives, such as giving children the opportunity to take an "advanced placement" test that allowed them to vote earlier, while maintaining existing voting rights for adults.

Authorization

Another criterion for assessing deliberation's legitimacy is the extent to which it is authorized to represent the views of a larger group to which its recommendations or decisions apply.[79] In theories of representative democracy, citizens' votes authorize their political representatives to enact laws, appoint an administration to implement and execute them, and select a judiciary to interpret them. In civic forums, the chains of authorization from citizens to deliberators are less clear. Authorization may be granted before deliberation, as when ballot initiatives, legislation, or administrative agencies create and empower civic forums. Examples include the British Columbia Citizens Assembly, which was empowered by the provincial government to propose revisions to the province's electoral system; the Oregon Citizens' Initiative Review Commission, which was created by the state legislature to advise citizens on whether to vote for proposed ballot initiatives; and the California Citizens Redistricting Commission, which was created by popular referendum to draw the state's political districts. But authorization can also be extended afterward, as when a forum's conclusions are put to a popular or legislative vote, or undergo review by courts, administrative agencies, relevant voluntary associations, or even a diverse group of experts or stakeholders. For example, the British Columbia Assembly's proposed electoral system was eventually submitted to a popular referendum and the California commission's electoral maps underwent judicial review.

---

[79] On the importance of authorization for forums, see Bohman 2012, 87–93; Dryzek 2010, 59–60; Young 2000, 128–33, 142–3.

Whether deliberative forums are approved before or after they convene, we can devise several dimensions of authorization. A strong version of authorization would say that deliberative agreements better serve civic self-governance the more they survive further deliberation within other parts of a democratic system. If a legitimate process cannot guarantee a legitimate conclusion, then there is a crucial role for public judgment of claims that emerge from deliberation. This challenge is especially acute for conclusions drawn in civic forums that can only include a sample of the whole. Even if they are empowered to make binding decisions for others, forums still depend upon recognition and validation of their claims by a broader citizenry or their representatives.[80] If forums are only authorized to make recommendations, then civic deliberation is even more dependent on other sources of political authority. Of course, not every source is unimpeachable. In keeping with the theory's normative thrust, the most significant evaluations of a forum's conclusions are assessments from other sources that are most deliberative, such as the collective judgment of well-functioning legislatures or administrative agencies, voluntary associations, or public spheres. One example would be the way in which Participatory Budgeting subjects district-level spending priorities to further review in a city-wide body of citizens, who deliberate to set final spending priorities. District priorities that are adopted in the final budget can be seen as authorized by the additional round of deliberation among citizen representatives from across the city.

A weak version of authorization would be the extent that other political actors see a civic deliberation as a trusted proxy for public judgment. In this version, citizens, officials, or others accept a civic forum's authority because they trust in the composition of the group, its deliberative process, or its expertise. This kind of authorization stems from public acceptance that a representative group, or a "good enough speech situation," or well-informed and thoughtful judgment, is sufficient to underwrite a forum's conclusions. It does not require that observers examine the

---

[80] Habermas addresses this issue in his later work, when he roots the validity of political judgments not simply in the reasoning process of the people who produce them, but in their acceptance by public opinion:

> The political influence that actors gain through public communication must *ultimately* rest on the resonance and indeed the approval of a lay public whose composition is egalitarian. The public of citizens must be *convinced* by comprehensible and broadly interesting contributions to issues it finds relevant. The public audience possesses final authority, because it is *constitutive* for the internal structure and reproduction of the public sphere. (1996b, 364)

forum's arguments and conclusions closely. For example, in the popular referendum held in 2005 on the political redistricting proposal generated by the British Columbia Citizens' Assembly, many citizens who lacked information about the details of the proposal based their vote on whether they saw the Assembly as including people like themselves or on whether they perceived the Assembly as having developed expert knowledge.[81] When citizens face issues that are complex, or information is difficult or time-consuming to obtain, there is a legitimate place in democracy for trusting other citizens' political judgments, if one has good reasons to trust them.[82] Similarly, some evidence shows that in elections, voters can use heuristics or information short cuts – such as basing their votes on the endorsements of parties, interest groups, or others – to make a kind of rational decision in the absence of political information.[83] But trusting proxies does not encourage as much autonomous judgment as when citizens deliberate over the substance of the matter themselves. From the standpoint of democratic deliberation, proxy-based decisions are less reflective and authentic than the choices one would make if one evaluated the question of which endorsers to trust, or, better yet, discussed the details of proposals with others.[84]

---

[81] Cutler et al. 2008. However, as Cutler and his colleagues show, the proposal narrowly failed to garner the required 60 percent supermajority of voters needed for passage in part because less than 60 percent of the public knew anything about the Assembly or its proposal. This is another reminder of how important publicity can be for the impact of a civic forum.

[82] Mackenzie and Warren (2012) argue that trust is necessary to "allocate or maximize the scarce political resources of citizens" (97). They contend that democratic institutions should enable people not just to participate actively, but also to make good judgments about when not to engage and to trust that others will act in citizens' interests. There is bad citizen passivity, but also good and necessary passivity, when a citizen makes "active choices to remain passive" because she or he has warranted trust in others to act on her behalf (99). Mackenzie and Warren suggest that trust in a civic forum's conclusions can be warranted by its members' representativeness of a larger public, the absence of conflicts of interest on the issue, the quality of their deliberation, and the extent of agreement on conclusions (not because consensus is necessary, but because more disagreement signals that the larger public needs to deliberate about the issue). For a discussion of trust and information short cuts in political decision making more generally, see Lupia and McCubbins 1994.

[83] Popkin 1991. Research has shown that voters who know little about the details of ballot propositions can use these kinds of shortcuts to make decisions that emulate those of well-informed voters (Lupia 1994). For evidence of the limitations of such shortcuts, see Lau and Redlawsk 2001 and Kuklinski and Quirk 2000.

[84] Smith 2009, 126–9. See also Chambers (2004, 397), who argues, "The approval or disapproval of other people's deliberations reduces democracy to voting. This is a far cry from the participatory ideals found in much deliberative democratic theory."

There is a third form of authorization which may be strong or weak, but which is more diffuse. This form is suggested by studies of deliberation's effects on communities' political capacities, rather than on individual participants' abilities, or on discrete public choices.[85] These studies suggest that forums can inspire individual or organizational participants to develop communal capacities for deliberative and participatory self-governance, such as creating mechanisms for dispersing information and expertise more widely among citizens, increasing and coordinating civic activity, developing or strengthening organizations that increase government responsiveness to citizens, and the like. These actions can retrospectively authorize forums as participants apply what they have learned about the deliberative process or its conclusions, going on to create or transform local institutions in ways that strengthen collective autonomy.

Example conditions
What are some example conditions that may foster autonomous agreement seeking in civic forums? The formation of well-structured views likely depends on the interplay of many factors, but especially on high-quality public reasoning as we have defined it (such as the degree of individual participants' issue knowledge and the coherence of their views) and the extent that the forum is designed to focus participants on identifying facts, values, and interests that they can all reasonably accept as valid. Forum design is an obvious condition favoring citizens' ability to affect the process. For example, Consensus Conferences tend to give participants more power than in many other kinds of forums to transform the agenda by adding new dimensions of issues. Citizens can also request their own information, sometimes give input on which experts testify, and generate their own lists of policy recommendations rather than choosing from among a handful of options prescribed by the organizers.[86]

External autonomy, or the ability to foster agreements that are taken up by other democratic institutions, depends upon the degree to which a forum is clearly and broadly authorized by other elements of the political system. In the Introduction, we saw that a long and possibly ambiguous chain of authorization undermined the reception of the "Our Economy, Our Budget" forum. Deliberation's ability to resonate beyond the forum depends also on whether it is integrated within a well-functioning democratic system, in which deliberation is valued and practiced in many sites.

---

[85] Fagotto and Fung 2006; Goodin and Dryzek 2006; Leighninger 2012; Kinney 2012.
[86] Hendriks 2005.

"Our Budget, Our Economy" could not affect budget debates because the issue polarized Congress and no other political actors championed the forum. In contrast, for many years the reports of consensus conferences organized by the Danish Board of Technology were regularly reported to members of parliament and the national media at press conferences in which legislators and others responded directly to the citizens' report. Because these consensus conferences were authorized by the legislature and received by a deliberative political system, they had greater impact on public opinion and policy making than "Our Budget, Our Economy" did.[87] External autonomy is also promoted by background conditions that favor political equality and public reasoning, such as Denmark's consensus-oriented political culture, egalitarian distribution of wealth and educational opportunities, and relatively homogeneous social and cultural traditions.[88]

Public reasoning

Definition

Deliberation is most clearly distinguished from other kinds of democratic action by its emphasis on the act of mutual justification, in which people give and respond to reasons in pursuit of agreements that result from persuasion rather than coercive threats or inducements.[89] While most theorists acknowledge that deliberation can and must be integrated with other kinds of political communication, we are not aware of any theory that would say that deliberation can be *reduced* to pure bargaining, negotiation, organizing, protesting, or voting. Although there is much debate over what sorts of reasons are better and worse, most theorists agree that deliberation involves exchanging reasons that could be understandable and acceptable (or at least tolerable) to others, even if others end up rejecting those reasons.[90] Civic forums aim to create spaces for this kind of reasoning.

---

[87] Joss (1998) finds that some Danish consensus conferences influenced legislation, sparked regional debates, and initiated public discussion through the news media.

[88] Dryzek and Tucker, 2008.

[89] Cohen 1997, 412–14; Gutmann and Thompson 2004, 3; Mansbridge et al. 2010, 67.

[90] Bächtiger et al. 2010, 36; Mansbridge et al. 2010, 80–2; Thompson 2008, 504. Bohman and Richardson (2009) critique the idea of basing deliberation on reasons that all can accept because we cannot know what others will accept until we deliberate with them. While we agree that we cannot know this, we see the effort to offer arguments that others can accept as a threshold definition of deliberation and succeeding at giving such arguments as the ideal.

Evaluative standards

Public mindedness

We agree with theorists who accept that, even in its ideal form, reasoning need not be restricted to appeals to the common good and that it should admit a role for arguing from self-interest and group interests. Mansbridge and her colleagues have made this argument most fully. For them, exploring how policy options affect self-interest promotes respect for pluralism, equality, and autonomy: "deliberative democracy must include self-interest and conflicts among interests in order to recognize and celebrate in the ideal itself the diversity of free and equal human beings."[91] In addition, they argue that the epistemic value of deliberation depends on people's ability to discuss their own interests, which makes a necessary contribution to understanding the common good by providing information about how policies would affect people differently.[92] These authors also incorporate the criticisms of difference democrats, who argue that restricting reasoning to the good of all means that "the understandings of the common good of the more powerful in the polity may dominate, even without ill will or the intent to exercise power."[93] However, they would still restrict the expression and pursuit of self-interest "both by the *universal constraints* of moral behavior and human rights and by the particularly *deliberative constraints* of mutual respect, equality, reciprocity, fairness and mutual justification."[94] We would agree, but would add that such deliberative aims also can be furthered, rather than inhibited, when individuals raise and openly negotiate a collective path through their differing interests.

How can this ideal be applied to civic forums? It suggests that forums should not ask participants to be wholly impartial and should not discourage all talk of participants' self-interest, as some facilitators apparently do.[95] We can say that forums are better when organizers and facilitators challenge authors of briefing materials, witnesses, and citizens to discuss the effects of policy options on specific interests, while also challenging citizens to question their own interests and to enlarge their arguments into ones that are not *merely* self-interested or group-interested. In this process, participants consider and justify their own interests in a wide variety of terms that others might recognize as claims to some tolerable and generalizable notion of truth, justice, or the collective good. In

---

[91] Mansbridge et al. 2010, 69.   [92] See also Røstboll 2008, 29, 156.
[93] Mansbridge et al. 2010, 74.   [94] Mansbridge et al. 2010, 76.
[95] Mansbridge et al. 2006, 22.

practice, that may mean a facilitator or deliberator responding to my self-focused assertions about the facts of my situation by asking, "Who else is in your situation?"; or to my self-interested assertions about what would be best for me by asking, "Who else would benefit?" and "How would that make the world more fair?" When such questions achieve their aim, deliberators consider how to present reasons, including reasons about their own interests, to other citizens in terms they might comprehend and accept.

This shift is what makes deliberation public-minded, in its most basic sense. In a more public-minded forum, more participants would consider their interests in light of others' interests, and offer enlarged reasoning that links participants' transformed sense of what is best for them to ideas of what is accurate, fair, or good for others who are affected by the issue. Participants would not simply change their opinions because they acquired new information, better logic, or a long-term view of their own self-interest, but because citizens incorporate others' perspectives or interests into their own.[96] Research on opinion change in civic forums has not measured this process well, and we need to develop better ways of observing these changes in discourse and pre- and post-deliberation thinking.

Respect

The ideal of respect encompasses several concepts. It suggests that deliberators practice reciprocity by giving arguments in terms that others can understand and by responding to others' arguments, positively or negatively, rather than ignoring them.[97] It acknowledges others as authoritative contributors to the group discussion, with ideas and perspectives worth engaging (even if they are very different from other members of the group). It may involve empathy, in which participants try to take the perspective of others in order to weigh their arguments.[98] Respect can also involve "civic magnanimity," by acknowledging the moral status of

---

[96] Mansbridge et al. 2010, 78.

[97] Gutmann and Thompson 1996, 52, 128. Christian Kock (2007, 11) articulates a "principle of explicitness" in practical argumentation, which means that "any assumption on which there is dissensus should be made explicit and supported by reasons. And the same principle also dictates that any reasons given by opponents should be answered – either rebutted or acknowledged, and if acknowledged, compared and 'weighed,' all on the assumption that in conductive reasoning there may be non-rebuttable reasons on both sides."

[98] Mansbridge et al. 2010, 67–8.

others' arguments rather than dismissing them as strategic, demonstrating openness to considering others' views, and making arguments that state one's own position in ways that minimize unnecessary rejection of elements of opposing positions.[99] Similarly, it can include a kind of discursive rapport and group solidarity, in which participants feel encouraged to raise their views in a collegial conversational atmosphere.[100] It can even involve offering minor concessions to opponents in order to allow them to save face by saying that they won some part of the argument. If both sides understand the purpose of these concessions, this can be a sign of respect for the minority rather than of manipulation.

Civic forums are more legitimate when participants engage in reciprocity, empathy, and magnanimity, all of which can be observed in discourse and triangulated with participants' and facilitators' interpretations.[101] Confronting opposing views can be the most difficult aspect of deliberation for many participants. Research on citizens' political discourse has found that the ability to articulate and refute arguments against one's own position is rare.[102] Individuals may seek to avoid cognitive dissonance by focusing on sources and views that reinforce rather than challenge their beliefs through processes of selective exposure, selective interpretation, and selective recall.[103] Nonetheless, group psychology research suggests that exposure to opposing viewpoints can stimulate more thorough information searching and evaluation of views, and can prompt groups to generate solutions that are more numerous, original, and creative, although these outcomes are often context-dependent.[104] Therefore, groups in which members can offer more arguments for and against the group's final position might be considered to have deliberated more legitimately than those who are familiar with fewer counter-arguments. However, this is an open question because those with higher

---

[99] Gutmann and Thompson 1996, 82–5.

[100] Mendelberg, Karpowitz, and Oliphant 2014.

[101] For example, respectful treatment of others' demands and counter-arguments has been studied in citizen deliberation by Talpin 2011; Steiner 2012, 114–21; and Wesolowska 2007.

[102] Rhee and Cappella 1997.

[103] On cognitive dissonance, see Festinger 1957. On selective exposure, see Lazarsfeld, Berelson, and Gaudet 1944. On selective interpretation, see Taber and Lodge 2006. On selective interpretation and recall, see Nickerson 1998. For an overview of the process of motivated reasoning through which individuals reach conclusions that justify their prior beliefs, see Kunda 1990.

[104] For summaries, see Delli Carpini, Cook, and Jacobs 2004; Mendelberg 2002; Nemeth and Goncalo 2011.

"argument repertoire" scores have also been found to have stronger partisan and ideological commitments. People may learn arguments against their position for the narrow purpose of refuting those arguments rather than considering them fully.[105]

Clarification of values

Deliberative theory's demand that citizens provide reasons that can be justified to others also requires what Amy Gutmann and Dennis Thompson call "the integration of substantive moral argument into democratic processes."[106] At its best, deliberation addresses not only the strategic effectiveness of law and policy but also their underlying values. Deliberation is a theory about not only how to handle disagreement, but how to address *moral* disagreement as well. Habermas also grounds his democratic theory in the position that law and democracy must be justified by and for each citizen in moral terms, not simply in instrumental terms as the most efficient or effective means to pre-given ends, such as political stability.[107] Others have argued that a special strength of citizen deliberation is that it is more likely than discussion among technical and policy experts to consider the ethical impacts of policy proposals.[108] Many civic forums ask participants to identify and prioritize the values at stake in public choices before taking positions on the issue at hand.[109] Some forums use briefing materials that take special care to draw connections between values and policy options.[110]

A forum that is framed exclusively as an exercise in technical problem-solving would be less legitimate than one in which citizens also discuss, reconsider, and apply their values to their conclusions. This can be observed in discussion and in reports of the forum. In our discussion of substantive standards for judging conclusions, we argued that decisions are better when they facilitate future civic deliberation. Therefore, in an ideal forum, not only would participants' preferences be informed clearly

---

[105] Cappella, Price, and Nir (2002) develop the concept of argument repertoires and find the connection between them and ideological-partisan commitments. For summaries of the empirical literature demonstrating civic deliberation's contribution to increasing participants' knowledge of evidence for and against their positions, see Barabas 2004; Fishkin 2009, 135–9; Pincock 2012, 145.

[106] Gutmann and Thompson 2004, 50; see also Gutmann and Thompson 1996, 43–51.

[107] Habermas 1996, Chapter 1 and 104–18.

[108] Sclove 1996; Tickner 2001.   [109] Black 2012, 68–9; Lee 2011, 21.

[110] For example, National Issues Forums' briefing booklets and discussions are typically organized around three major framings of an issue, which are presented as distinct packages of values and policy choices. Melville, Willingham, and Dedrick 2005.

by their values, but also their reasons and conclusions would be judged as morally legitimate by deliberative institutions outside the forum. This too can be studied through interviews, surveys, and observation of reactions to forums in a range of institutions most relevant to the issue.

Knowledge

Ideal public reasoning is based in part on weighing the best available knowledge relevant to the issue at hand. Gutmann and Thompson ground the importance of information quality in the principle of mutual justification. In regard to factual claims, they maintain that

> reciprocity requires that they be consistent with relatively reliable methods of inquiry. Such methods are our best hope for carrying on discussion on mutually acceptable terms. The claims need not be completely verifiable, but they should not conflict with claims that have been confirmed by the most reliable of available methods.[111]

The notion that legitimate deliberation depends in part on the quality of information that informs participants is implicit in several claims and findings about the epistemic benefits of deliberation – that, through exposure to the arguments of others, deliberative talk can help participants overcome their bounded rationality, enlarging their knowledge of issues and perspectives;[112] that deliberating can correct false beliefs;[113] and that it can help participants to arrive at more sophisticated, considered, and consistent views.[114] It is also implicit in Habermas' claim that deliberators should be swayed only by "the unforced force of the better argument," which requires unrestricted flows of information.[115]

Civic forums best foster public reasoning on equal terms when welcoming a broad spectrum of ways of reasoning. The way a statement contributes to group knowledge in discussion is far more important than the form it takes. Like almost all theorists of deliberation, we value many possible forms of reasoning that are increasingly recognized as valid additions to early deliberative theory's narrow focus on rational argumentation. These include affective reasoning, personal testimony, storytelling, recognition, and certain kinds of rhetoric, as long as they contribute to

---

[111] Gutmann and Thompson 1996, 56.
[112] Bohman, 1996, 16; Fearon 1998, 49–52; Manin 1987, 349.
[113] Smith and Wales 2000, 53; see also Fishkin 2009, 34.
[114] Gastil and Dillard 1999.   [115] Habermas 1996, 306.

mutual justification in ways that meet the other standards for public reasoning outlined here.[116] Because these modes of reasoning can be more accessible to the least educated, enabling them to speak from their perspectives more easily, the choice of ideal modes is not a neutral one.

At the same time, the *effect* of a particular statement in deliberation is what matters most. People can give personal testimony that raises important values and contributes useful experiential knowledge to the discussion, but testimony can also silence others when speakers assert that their personal experience could not possibly be understood by others, or that others have no right to interpret it for themselves. In addition, all forms of reasoning serve many masters, rather than aligning neatly and exclusively with the interests of disadvantaged or privileged citizens. One can tell stories about "welfare queens" aimed at demonizing the poor for taking advantage of public programs to live the high life.[117] One can also offer facts and statistics about the conditions of the impoverished in an effort to compel recognition of their situation, create empathy with them, and justify public investment in anti-poverty programs.[118] In

---

[116] On the value of testimony, see Sanders 1997. The major theoretical case for storytelling can be found in Young 2000, Chapter 2. For a review of the growing empirical literature on the potential benefits of storytelling, see Steiner 2012, Chapter 2. On rhetoric and recognition (or greeting), see Young 2000, Chapter 2; Dryzek 2010, Chapter 4. Other theorists who offer similarly broad definitions of deliberative discourse include Bohman 1996, 7, 45; Dryzek 2000, 64–70; Chambers 2003, 322; Gastil 2008, 20–1; Ryfe 2005; Thompson 2008, 503–5.

[117] During his 1976 presidential campaign, Ronald Reagan repeatedly told a story, later disconfirmed, about a Chicago woman who "has 80 names, 30 addresses, 12 Social Security cards . . . She's got Medicaid, getting food stamps and she is collecting welfare under each of her names. Her tax-free cash income alone is over $150,000" (Blake 2012). This image of the "welfare queen" has lodged itself in campaign discourse ever since.

[118] Contemporary justifications for public spending to alleviate poverty typically use stories and statistics to appeal to empathy and efficiency, the good of the poor and the common good, and mutual obligation as well as personal responsibility. Here, for example, is Barack Obama's (2007) argument for providing prenatal care to the poor, made in a speech announcing his presidential candidacy in 2007:

> We can diminish poverty if we approach it in two ways: by taking mutual responsibility for each other as a society, and also by asking for some more individual responsibility to strengthen our families . . . If we want to stop the cycle of poverty, then we need to start with our families. We need to start supporting parents with young children. There is a pioneering Nurse-Family Partnership program right now that offers home visits by trained registered nurses to low-income mothers and mothers-to-be. They learn how to care for themselves before the baby is born and what to do after. It's common sense to reach out to a young mother. Teach her about changing the baby. Help her understand what all that crying means, and when to get vaccines and check-ups. This program saves money. It raises healthy babies and creates better parents. It reduced childhood injuries and unintended pregnancies,

real-world discourse, political arguments mix multiple modes of reasoning: statistics are embedded in stories, facts in testimony, affective appeals within rational argumentation, and so on.

Adopting an expansive definition of ideal ways of reasoning in deliberation does not eliminate the need for reliable forms of knowledge or mean that every contribution to knowledge is equally valuable. It is vital and inevitable for collective judgment to try to distinguish better and worse knowledge through deliberation, even amidst a plurality of beliefs and some necessary reliance on expert knowledge of complex matters. Civic forums confront this question in developing briefing materials, choosing expert witnesses to testify, and facilitating discussion in which experts and participants often make conflicting empirical claims.

Sifting expert knowledge presents one set of challenges. Thomas Christiano points out that there are several kinds of expertise that are especially important in public deliberation.[119] Witnesses tend to have natural and social scientific expertise, but also expertise in politics and policy analysis. Scientists' and policy experts' understanding can be limited by their commitment to particular theories, methods, models, and findings; by their ties to corporate, foundation, or state research funders or employers; and by their tendency to undervalue the knowledge of citizens, especially the marginalized. For their part, citizen participants often possess valuable local knowledge of problems and how policy options might affect their circumstances, but their situated knowledge can be limited to a partial understanding or view, from which it is difficult to generalize to the whole.

Given these challenges, how can we evaluate the quality of knowledge in civic forums? Most evaluation studies of civic forums measure participants' knowledge gains through before and after responses to a handful of factual questions related to the issues.[120] Another approach, developed recently by Katherine Knobloch and her colleagues, is to rely on a mix of researchers' observations and participants' self-reports to rate deliberators' command of knowledge during deliberation, supplemented by fact-checking of the claims in the forum's final report.[121] While we would not dismiss the value of these approaches, relying on them alone

increased father involvement and women's employment, reduced use of welfare and food stamps, and increased children's school readiness. And it produced more than $28,000 in net savings for every high-risk family enrolled in the program.

[119] Christiano 2012, 28.

[120] This approach is used in many Deliberative Polls (Fishkin 2009).

[121] Knobloch et al. 2013. This study also rates several other aspects of deliberation, which we address as other elements of public reasoning, such as depth of exploration of policy options' pros and cons (akin to argument repertoire) and discussion of values.

seems insufficient. They can tell us whether citizens can identify factual claims that are supported by an expert's testimony or by the briefing materials. They can tell us whether citizens felt they comprehended the facts well. And they can tell us whether citizens used facts that researchers have tried to verify independently. But they cannot tell us much about whether those facts really are uncontroversial from the standpoint of wider communities of experts or citizens. And they cannot say much about how those facts were produced and why citizens should trust them.

We can say that forums are better when citizens' judgments are informed by knowledge that is least disputed among relevant experts *and* among citizens who have direct experience relevant to the issue. It seems important to consider the degree of expert consensus and experienced citizen consensus because they often conflict internally and with each other. Consider the example of chemical risk assessment as conducted in the United States.[122] In the 1980s, this developed as a distinct form of regulatory science charged with determining the probability of additional harm from exposure to a chemical at a particular dosage. These estimates were employed to decide acceptable levels of exposure and whether to restrict or ban the use of some chemicals. Like prescription drug trials, many chemical assessments were funded by the manufacturers themselves. But unlike the regulatory process used to evaluate pharmaceuticals, risk assessment calculated the health threats posed by an individual chemical, not the cumulative or interactive effects of introducing the chemical into the environment. This is a bit like measuring how many sleeping pills are safe for a person to take and how much alcohol is safe to drink, without asking how many sleeping pills and drinks are safe in combination. Risk assessors often evaluated the effect of a chemical on the "average person," who was assumed to be a healthy adult, rather than on the most vulnerable people, such as children, fetuses, and people with weakened immune systems. The burden of proof that a chemical posed unacceptable health risks fell on the critic; chemicals were innocent until proven guilty, which is very challenging for epidemiology to prove, given the difficulty of tracing diseases such as cancer to any one risk factor.[123] Little weight was

---

[122] Our account of chemical risk assessment draws on O'Brien 2000.

[123] In contrast, many European regulators employ some version of the "precautionary principle," which states, "When an activity raises threats of harm to human health or the environment, precautionary measures should be taken even if some cause and effect relationships are not fully established scientifically. In this context the proponent of an activity, rather than the public, should bear the burden of proof" (Montague 1998, 1).

given to local, experiential knowledge – such as farm workers' testimony about the effects of pesticides on their health or neighborhood residents' evidence of abnormal rates of cancer – even if it strongly conflicted with risk assessors' estimates. Many citizens who were most affected by chemical risks and even some risk assessors criticized this system as designed to protect chemicals rather than the public. Change has been slow.

Like risk assessments, much of the knowledge that is presented in civic forums, and in public discourse more generally, is *interested* knowledge. This suggests a second principle: deliberators make better judgments the more they know about the supply chain of the knowledge presented to them, including its source, its funder, its methods, how it has been received in peer review processes in its profession, and how it is viewed by other knowledgeable sources outside the profession, including by citizens most familiar with the issue from their own experience. Evaluations of civic forums should measure this kind of meta-knowledge as well. Our point is not that citizen deliberation should look like an idealized version of an academic seminar, but that experts' and citizens' knowledge claims should be cross-examined the way they are in a courtroom.[124] This is not simply to realize the epistemic benefits of deliberation. Citizens are most empowered to exercise their autonomy when they can weigh information with an understanding of who produced it, how it was produced, and how it is viewed by others.

One of the most valuable contributions that civic forums can make is to create a rational process through which expert and citizen knowledge can be compared and their differences resolved.[125] When grappling with issues such as risk assessment, the best forums will equip participants to make decisions not just about evidence but also about *rules* of evidence, such as standards of certainty, who should bear the burden of proof, and what methods of inquiry are reliable. To make these kinds of decisions, citizens need to be able to weigh competing claims with a deep understanding of how the evidence that supports them was produced and by whom.

Accountability and transparency

In this book, we are most interested in the kind of public reasoning that extends beyond the forum, as it makes public its process and conclusions to others. This element of publicity has been least carefully considered

---

[124] On the value of legal thinking as one model for citizen thinking, see Manaster 2013.
[125] On this point, we are indebted to Archon Fung's comments on a draft of this manuscript.

in theories of deliberation. While we develop our rationale and measures for ideal external publicity more fully in Chapter 4, for now let us say that the legitimacy of a forum depends upon giving an adequate account of participants' arguments and conclusions, as well as practicing transparency about deliberative procedures. Scholars and practitioners of *civic* deliberation especially value publicity because it can hold deliberators accountable to the larger public as they weigh arguments and can also act as a check on manipulation or co-optation of deliberators by officials and powerful stakeholders.[126] Knowing that their deliberations will be communicated to a wider public can encourage participants to respect and consider others' arguments more fully and clarify how the group's decisions relate to others' positions. Transparency can also check the power of publicity's authors, who are rarely identical with the deliberators themselves. Accountability and transparency allow outsiders to make more informed and authentic decisions about whether to accept the forum's process and decisions.

Example conditions

Knowledge and public-mindedness are especially enhanced by conditions summarized by James Fishkin, including participants' access to relevant and accurate information and to a substantive balance of competing arguments, the diversity of perspectives that participants bring to the forum, the conscientiousness with which participants weigh arguments, and the consideration of arguments on their merits.[127]

Facilitation can influence all aspects of public reasoning, including the extent to which participants are encouraged to give reasons and evidence for their positions, to examine their values, to respect others' views, and to come to individual or group judgment. For example, David Ryfe's research on civic forums distinguishes strong and weak facilitators. Strong facilitators intervene often to direct the conversation by posing questions, providing missing information, summarizing themes in the discussion, and raising opposing views that the group has not yet considered. This kind of active moderation can push participants to consider alternative views and trade-offs between positions, or to bring groups to agreement more quickly. Yet this style also runs the risk of short-circuiting participants' ability to work through issues fully by thinking out loud, to make

---

[126] Fung and Wright 2003, 37; Levine and Nierras 2007, 6; Parkinson 2006a, 17, 119–20; Smith 2009, 101–5, 110.

[127] Fishkin 2009, 34. For a similar summary, see also Gastil 2008, 20.

personal connections with issues by telling stories about their lives, and therefore to invest themselves fully in deliberating. Weak facilitators can create an environment in which deliberators take more responsibility for the quality of their talk, yet may also allow a group to gravitate toward self-congratulatory consensus in order to avoid conflict or to struggle with uncertainty in the absence of information.[128] These findings underscore that the mere presence or absence of facilitation is less crucial for eliciting public reasoning than the *quality* of facilitation. Depending on the group dynamics and the particular moment in the discussion, strong or weak moderation may be most successful.

All aspects of public reasoning likely benefit from deliberators having more time to talk, either in longer forums or in iterative series of forums. Time allows deliberators to work through competing knowledge claims, identify values and interests, and consider a wider array of policy preferences.

Political equality

According to the theory of democratic deliberation we have sketched out, we can engage in autonomous reflection only if others treat us as equals and we see them as our equals. Therefore, "for the autonomy of all to be cultivated...equal agency of all must be preserved."[129] Equal agency is affected by opportunities for inclusion, participation, and influence in deliberation. It is grounded in the extent to which each deliberator regards himself or herself as well as his or her fellow discussants as authoritative contributors, worthy of full standing in the discussion and capable of influencing the group's decisions. These are probably the most difficult ideals for any theory of democracy to meet in a world of extreme and persistent economic, political, and cultural inequities. We think it is possible to settle on minimal criteria that can define deliberative equality, while expecting more from the standards by which we evaluate it.

Definition

By inclusion, we refer to who gets to sit at the deliberative table. There are many thoughtful treatments of the ideal standards for inclusion in deliberation, but almost no definitions of who, or how many, must have access to a discussion for it to be called deliberation at all. Robert Goodin's argument that democratic deliberation may be best achieved in each of our

---

[128] Ryfe 2006.   [129] Elstub 2008, 68.

heads, as we consider the interests of others and weigh reasons for and against preferences, suggests that one person is enough to deliberate.[130] But, as Goodin notes, a *political* deliberation conducted only in our heads would still lack "the ratification by others required for it to count as fully democratic."[131] Some studies of deliberation in everyday political conversation assume that it only takes two to tango.[132] We see the theory of democratic deliberation as addressing a fundamentally social process that occurs in groups and among a demos. This is suggested by the main rationales for deliberation, which emphasize the epistemic value of considering multiple perspectives, deliberation's ability to develop civic capacities that are oriented toward engaging in political groups, and its ability to co-constitute individual and collective autonomy through the exchange of reasons. Thus, we will say that democratic deliberation requires a group that is discussing multiple arguments. All civic forums surpass this threshold definition.

At a minimum, equality of participation requires that all participants understand the language(s) in which the forum will be held or have access to translators, that speaking opportunities are divided fairly evenly among the group, and that all participants are able to speak to each of the major issues under consideration if they choose. Individual speaking turns do not have to be precisely equal by the stopwatch, but no one person or subgroup dominates discussion as a whole or any of the main topics on the agenda.

Minimal equality of influence involves each participant having a formal opportunity to choose one's own reasons and conclusions for oneself, even if she or he is selecting from among a limited menu of options provided by organizers or winnowed in discussion with other participants. In addition, each person has a formally equal opportunity to influence the outcome, and no one is dismissed as unworthy of full standing. If deliberation ends with a consensus decision, it cannot do so unless each participant agrees to the conclusions, and each can agree with the outcome for his or her own diverse reasons. If talk concludes with voting or polling, each person's vote or opinion counts equally. But because some

---

[130] Goodin 2003, Chapter 9.   [131] Goodin 2003, 171.

[132] For example, on the basis of survey research on mainly dyadic political conversation in personal networks, Diana Mutz (2006) concludes that deliberation with conversation partners who hold different views reduces one's political participation. But these conversations are political discussions, as we define them in this chapter. They are a far cry from organized, facilitated deliberation in civic forums focused on agreement seeking among groups of citizens.

people may make better arguments than others, equal opportunity does not necessarily require that each person must be equally persuasive to others. The key, in our view, is that deliberators must not be dismissed *a priori* because of their background or ascriptive characteristics. Most civic forums attempt to meet these criteria by establishing speaking rules and employing facilitators to protect each participant's formal right to share their views and participate in decision making.[133] Of course, while these steps are helpful and perhaps even necessary, to avoid blatant coercion in the search for agreement with others, they certainly do not guarantee that deliberation will meet theoreticians' hopes for deliberative equality.

Evaluative standards

Inclusion
Standards for inclusion in deliberation are among the most difficult to establish. Many theories of democracy, some deliberative and some not, maintain that all who are affected by a decision should have an equal opportunity to influence it.[134] Unfortunately, no one has devised a very specific explanation of how any form of democracy can do this. The principle that all affected should decide is intended as a corrective to much classical democratic theory. Fashioned to account for the practice of democracy in nation-states, classical theory tended to assume that a people constitutes itself, and, curiously enough, agrees to form a nation-state.[135] This was convenient because it drew the original boundaries of the demos without requiring much justification for how they were drawn, so theorists could get on with the business of justifying the state's relationship to the people. Much original and unpleasant bloodletting at the formation of peoples and states could recede into the mists of time. In addition, the power of non-state actors – corporations, non-governmental organizations, and others – was yet to be theorized. By extending the decision-making franchise to people across established territorial jurisdictions, and applying it to non-state actors, the "all affected" principle

---

[133] Lee 2011, 21.

[134] The "all affected" principle is accepted by many theorists of deliberation (e.g., Cohen 1989, 22; Dryzek 2000, 172; Habermas 1996, 107; Manin 1987, 352; Young 2000, 23) and also by other democratic theorists (such as Dahl 1989, 184, 208; Held 1996, 324).

[135] Robert Dahl writes, "How a people accomplishes this mysterious transformation is therefore treated as a purely hypothetical event that has already occurred in prehistory or in a state of nature. The polis is what it is; the nation-state is what history has made it. Athenians are Athenians, Corinthians are Corinthians, and Greeks are Greeks" (1970, 60–1).

offers a broader principle of inclusion that is not based on the historical uses of force that drew our contemporary maps or an antiquated notion of the state as shaping all significant decisions. That is commendable.

Unfortunately, this raises a new problem of identifying all who will, or might possibly, be affected by a decision. Determining the legitimate boundaries of the community that experiences the impacts of a decision becomes ever more complicated in an age of heightened global inter-dependence, privatization of state functions, and proliferating forms of representation by non-state actors. More of us are affected by laws and policies enacted by bodies that do not formally or directly represent us, especially in matters of trade, diplomacy, war, and the environment. More of us are represented by non-governmental organizations which we join to advance our views on these matters or which represent our views without our knowledge. More conflicts are in part over who or what should have jurisdiction. As James Bohman observes, uncritically accepting dominant definitions of our political communities based on territoriality increasingly risks forcing decisions on unrepresented people and externalizing the costs of decisions on those who are deemed out-side the polity. This situation calls forth new constituencies and creates new forms of political representation. Bohman writes that "[a]s polit-ical communities become more transnational, pluralistic, and complex, democratization requires both various formal and informal intermedi-aries, emerging publics to generate communicative power across borders, and transnational institutions in which publics can elaborate constituen-cies with decisional statuses."[136]

How should we draw the lines of these constituencies and institutions? As Goodin argues, we cannot know who will or might be affected by a

---

[136] Bohman 2012, 93. Theorists have proposed a number of deliberative intermediaries and institutions that could represent perspectives that are not well-represented by terri-torially based representative governments. Leib (2004) proposed a popular, randomly selected deliberative branch of government that would operate much like civic forums to review and enact legislation. Thompson (1999) suggests that legislatures should have a tribune to represent the interests of people outside the polity and future generations, exercising a veto over laws that would unduly harm their interests. Dryzek (2000, 2010) has argued for creating a parliamentary chamber to represent the diversity of discourses at the level of the state. Dryzek (2010) also argues that global governance networks made up of non-governmental organizations, social movement activists, academics, and others can engage in consequential deliberation across borders. Dryzek, Bächtiger, and Milewicz (2011) suggest that a Deliberative Global Citizens Assembly, with partici-pants randomly selected from around the world, would bring citizens' voices into the United Nations.

decision until it is made, but who gets to participate in making the decision will likely affect the outcome, so the question of who is affected
and who gets to decide are inseparable.[137] To offer our own example,
many governments at all levels make decisions that affect climate change,
either directly by setting targets for greenhouse gas emissions in their
jurisdictions, or indirectly through their transportation, industrial, and
urban planning. It is evident that climate change poses real and serious
risks to all living people and to future generations, and that identifiable
regions and people are especially at risk from sea level rise, droughts,
and more frequent and intense storms. Responsibility for and influence
over climate change are similarly uneven. Regions that have historically
emitted greater levels of greenhouse gases, and that do so today, have
imposed the effects of their decisions far beyond their borders. Given
the disparities in who will be most affected, and the disparities of influence, who should participate in decisions about all policies that affect
climate change enacted by the city of Los Angeles, the state of California,
the United States, or the World Trade Organization? Goodin offers a
provocative *reductio ad absurdum* to this kind of problem: by arguing
that there is no logically or normatively attractive way to draw limits on
those who might be affected, he concludes that this "would mean giving virtually everyone everywhere a vote on virtually everything decided
anywhere."[138] The same could be said of the opportunity to deliberate.

We can say that whoever draws the lines of the demos is obligated to
justify that they are drawn to include as many people who are affected by
a potential decision on the issue as is possible for deliberation to occur
among them or their freely chosen representatives. Legitimacy increases
the more that deliberation's organizers can offer a normatively and logically strong justification for their conception of all who are affected by

---

[137] Goodin 2008, 137. Even if we try to narrow the definition to those who are *most*
affected or who must *obey* a decision, the same problem arises.

[138] He continues, one imagines with tongue at least halfway in cheek, "Maybe that is not
practical, for one reason or another." If so, and it is difficult to imagine it not being
so, he contends that "the price of not enfranchising everyone we ideally should is that
we would have to pay them off for any harms we inflict upon them and accede to their
demands for recompense for any benefits we derive from the wrongfully disenfranchised" (2008, 153–4). But who counts as the "we" who should decide who is wrongly
excluded and how to calculate what is owed to people who are denied something as
inestimable as the franchise or their ancestral homeland? Goodin's other conclusion
is to propose institutions of world government that represent all who are affected. Of
course, the trade-off is that the larger the demos that is represented by any government,
the less any individual can influence that government, so expanding the scope of all
included diminishes each one's power to decide.

the decisions under consideration and all who can be included without rendering deliberation impossible. That may sound like weak theoretical tea, but it includes a useful distinction. It pegs legitimacy to the *justification* for each deliberative forum's principle of inclusion, rather than to more abstract, unjustified, or reductive assumptions about the demos and how it should be represented. That should push us to think more reflectively and expansively about who is included in civic forums, which typically recruit from among an established political community's residents, registered voters, or eligible voters.[139] In Chapter 2, we argue for a broader range of principles of inclusion, one that is better suited to deliberative systems thinking, which would justify different ways of representing the social whole throughout a deliberative process, rather than only in a single forum.

Participation

Equality of participation inside the forum involves different standards. If the threshold definition of equal participation requires linguistic bridges among all participants and lack of domination over speaking opportunities, ideal standards revolve around four additional elements.

First, participation is more legitimate when deliberators share the speaking time equally. In deliberation, speaking time is a valuable resource that can translate into influence over the group's reasoning and conclusions. A recent experimental study that offers the most rigorous test of this connection finds that "[p]articipants who held the floor for a greater percentage of the group's deliberation were more likely to be seen as influential by the other members of the group" in follow-up surveys.[140]

Second, participation is more equal when each participant is capable of speaking on each major issue in the forum. Participants do not defer to others on some topics because of their perceived expertise or out of fear for how others will respond. Deliberators do not adopt a division of labor in which groups of participants take control of separate issues and present their reasons and conclusions to the forum as a *fait accompli*. That may be efficient, but it is not the best kind of deliberation, which involves each participant weighing reasons and conclusions oneself and with the group.

Third, participation is better when each deliberator has an equal capacity to introduce material into deliberation. James Bohman notes that, in

---

[139] Fishkin 2009, 117; Smith 2009, 80.
[140] Karpowitz, Mendelberg, and Shaker 2012, 542.

the public sphere, deliberative inequality can create a vicious cycle of exclusion of some groups from initiating public debate, and therefore exclusion from public debate. Others assume that the group's silence indicates consent.[141] In contrast, facilitators in civic forums typically work to involve all participants. When facilitators succeed, all participants should have a similar ability to introduce new evidence, reasons, and potential conclusions into discussion. People can initiate this kind of material through many forms of speech, such as making assertions, posing questions, or seeking clarifications.

Fourth, each participant should be able to command others' attention equally. When a person introduces a claim or question, others respond, whether positively or negatively.[142] All group members are regarded as worthy of full standing, with views and perspectives that command the attention of others in the group.

We can get a good sense of whether deliberators share speaking time, are capable of speaking to each issue, have an equal capacity to initiate discussion, and can compel attention by triangulating observations of speaking patterns, participants' perceptions of whether they feel inhibited or empowered to speak, and facilitators' impressions of participants' willingness to contribute and ability to be heard.

Influence

Because democratic deliberation values citizens' reasoning and deciding *together*, it increases in legitimacy as each participant attains more equal influence over others' reasoning and agreements. This also depends on being able to choose one's own reasons and conclusions freely because one cannot exercise equal agency by advocating views that are not truly one's own. We defined equality of influence in minimal terms as involving each participant having a formal opportunity to choose one's own reasons and conclusions for oneself and to affect the group's conclusions by having an equal vote or opinion, or the ability to withhold one's consent to a consensus decision. Clearly, the notion of influence is another dimension of autonomy, which therefore could be considered just as well as a standard for seeking agreements for self-rule. We discuss it here to emphasize its inseparability from equality.

---

[141] Bohman 1996, 125–6.
[142] Sunstein (2002, 155) agrees, "If people are not heard, and if they do not speak, both democracy and deliberation are at risk. And if members of certain groups receive less respectful attention, both liberty and equality are at risk."

In its ideal form, equal capacity for influence depends on evaluating each person's reasoning on its merits, rather than judging arguments according to speakers' status or by whether arguments comport with prior commitments to a particular outcome imposed by organizers or powerful groups outside the forum. But because deliberation should be resolved by what Habermas famously called the "forceless force of the better argument," it is not necessarily ideal that outcomes reflect each participant's views in equal measure.[143] Rather, equality implies that each deliberator should have comparable capacities to influence one's own and others' conclusions, shaping one's views autonomously by giving a fair hearing to others' views and obtaining a fair hearing from others.[144]

At the end of a civic forum, each individual's preferences and underlying reasons should be authentic. Authentic choices are made by competent actors, well-informed about their options, exerting real rather than symbolic control over their preferences.[145] Non-authentic preferences include the products of coercion, in which another forces his or her judgment upon me, or manipulation, in which "another's judgment has been substituted for mine without my knowing it."[146] But preferences can also be subject to more subtle forms of inauthenticity. What Jon Elster calls "adaptive preferences" are formed by the unconscious adjustment of people's wants to the range of possibilities offered to them.[147] Cohen offers the example of "instinctive centrists who move to the median position in the political distribution, wherever it happens to be."[148] What Cohen calls "accommodationist preferences" are more conscious "psychological adjustments to conditions of subordination in which individuals are not recognized as having the capacity for self-government."[149] His example is of Stoic slaves, who knowingly restrict their own wants to fit the limitations imposed by their enslavement in order to minimize their frustration, rather than forming preferences that include changing their situation. Others have argued that inequalities borne of contemporary poverty and gender relations impose similarly adaptive or accommodationist preferences on the poor and women.[150] One of our main points in this book

---

[143] Habermas 1984, 25.   [144] Bohman 1996, Chapter 3; Knight and Johnson 1997.

[145] Dryzek 2007, 270. See also Sunstein's (1991, 11) argument: "The notion of autonomy should refer instead to decisions reached with a full and vivid awareness of available opportunities, with reference to all relevant information, and without illegitimate or excessive constraints on the process of preference formation."

[146] Røstboll 2005, 385.   [147] Elster 1983, 25.

[148] Cohen 1989, 25.   [149] Cohen 1989, 25.

[150] On the poor's preferences, see Bohman 1996, Chapter 3. On women's preferences, see Nussbaum 2000. Both authors draw from Amartya Sen's theory of human capabilities and development as a form of freedom (see, e.g., Sen 1999).

will be that the people who are in the least powerful position relative to an issue under deliberation outside a civic forum might legitimately develop their capacities by discussing the issue together inside the forum, before or alongside discussion with more powerful citizens, and that this can enhance equality of influence.

Ideally, deliberation transforms inauthentic preferences into authentic ones as citizens develop equal capacities to exercise their agency to shape their own preferences in light of others' wants and reasons. As Christian Røstboll puts it,

> what makes a preference autonomous is that it has survived a certain process. And this process is not merely an internal and subjective one; it is one in which you can check your preferences against the arguments of others. My preference is autonomous if I still find reasons to hold it after I have heard the relevant arguments and considered the relevant information . . . [In deliberation,] there is a substitution of one judgment for another, but it is not of mine for yours, rather of what results from deliberation for both of them.[151]

However, in civic forums, there is often a tension between the group's ability to reason authentically with one another and its anticipation of how unconventional arguments will be received by political leaders or the public. This dilemma surfaces in questions about whether the group is permitted to consider alternatives that are not widely supported outside the forum or assertions that the group should not waste its time discussing options that are unlikely to be considered in the wider political system.[152] This is a tension within deliberative theory, which also expects that people should give reasons that others could accept, including others outside the forum. We can maintain that forums serve equality best when people exert authentic influence over their own and others' thinking, while recognizing that there can be trade-offs in practice between this ideal and the ideal of mutually respectful public reasoning.

Clearly, it is no easy task to know whether this interplay of authentic and equal influence occurs on civic forums. While acknowledging the danger of measuring a complex idea in a reductive manner, we can still try to learn whether people influence themselves and others equally through

---

[151] Røstboll 2005, 377, 385. See also Cohen (1989, 25): "While preferences are 'formed' by the deliberative procedure, this type of preference formation is consistent with autonomy, since preferences that are shaped by public deliberation are not simply given by external circumstances. Instead they are the result of 'the power of reason as applied through public discussion'."

[152] Smith 2009, 100.

multiple measures. We can begin by examining the distribution of speaking time, which, as noted above, can be one indication of equality of influence. We can go on to ask participants questions about whether each felt that others considered her or his reasons and preferences, and whether the group or majority choice reflects some part of what each participant wanted. We can ask about the extent to which each deliberator accepts the consensus or majority choice as the legitimate product of the group's discussion ("our decision") rather than as something that a participant decided alone ("my decision") or that others imposed on the participant ("their decision"). We can also examine whether the range of information provided and discussed in deliberation, the initial framing of the issues for deliberators, and the spectrum of policy choices that citizens considered were reflective of the range of information, frames, and preferences in the larger political environment.

Example conditions

We have argued that inclusion means aiming to incorporate the perspectives of all affected by the decision, but because this is often unclear, legitimacy depends greatly on organizers' justifications for defining who is affected. Multiple principles of representation can be tailored to civic forums' goals and ability to admit all affected without making deliberation impossible. Forums can justifiably use a number of approaches, including random sampling and stratified sampling to include members of groups who are especially hard to recruit otherwise or whose perspectives on the issues discussed in the forum are especially important to include. Often, including members of under represented groups requires subsidizing their ability to participate by paying stipends, and recruiting must be done through associations that serve the least powerful, such as social service agencies, adult education programs, and churches.[153] Forums can also include the disadvantaged by addressing topics of greatest importance to them and by offering them a clear opportunity to reach policy makers or effect change directly.[154]

Equal participation and influence are especially shaped by facilitation, the format of the forum, and background conditions in the larger society. Facilitators can allow some participants to dominate or can actively moderate the conversation to engage all in deliberation and to draw attention to participants' claims that might otherwise be ignored. Open forum designs, such as Consensus Conferences, which give citizens leeway to

---

[153] Lee 2011; Leighninger 2012.   [154] Fung 2003, 351.

contribute to the agenda and generate their own list of conclusions, allow deliberators to participate on more equal terms with organizers than forums that focus discussion more narrowly. Many theorists suggest that higher levels of political, economic, and educational equality in the larger society are likely to mitigate inequality of status in the forum.[155]

Conclusion

In this chapter, we have aimed to outline a practical theory of deliberation in civic forums. We have argued that a broad range of forums are worthy of considering as instances of democratic deliberation, including forums that can influence politics indirectly through many of the complex ways in which public opinion functions in a democracy. Our basic definitions of the requirements of agreement seeking, equality, and publicity are ones that can be met in many contexts. Forums need only to obtain participants' consent to the deliberative process and orient them toward arriving at agreements on policy decisions or recommendations. Organizers can create necessary conditions for public reasoning by engaging citizens in justifying positions to one another. These forums can offer basic opportunities for political equality in the way they include citizens, foster their participation, and protect their abilities to influence their own reasoning and conclusions. In this light, democratic citizen deliberation is more feasible than many of its critics recognize.

We have also tried to clarify the ideal standards that deliberative theory can hope forums might meet and that organizers can aim to achieve. These standards will motivate our proposals for enhancing equality and publicity. Agreements for self-rule gain in legitimacy when the group's preferences are more clearly structured and its members' views are more coherent, when participants enjoy greater autonomy over deliberative procedures and the content of conclusions, and when the forum is more clearly authorized by other citizens or their representatives, beforehand or afterward. The quality of publicity increases as participants engage in deliberation that is more public-minded, respectful, normative, accountable, and transparent. Equality is best served when forums include a well-justified sample of all who are affected by the issues under consideration, with special attention to including the least powerful and most affected people with regard to the topic of the forum. All participants have equal standing to initiate discussion about their concerns and to draw the

---

[155] Bohman 1996; Gutmann & Thompson 1996; Knight and Johnson 1997.

group's attention to their claims. Each citizen has equal opportunity to influence others' conclusions and the reasons that motivate these views.

Many forums that make important contributions to democracy will not meet all of these ideals fully. Some of these ideals will be in tension, such that achieving one makes it harder to reach another. However, these trade-offs arise in any form of democratic consultation of public opinion or political decision making, even if they manifest themselves differently. Deliberation does not deliver us from the constraints of politics, but it improves the authenticity of citizens' voices in democracy.

Part I

Equality

2

Enclave deliberation of the disempowered

Creating conditions of equality in civic deliberation has never been easy. In classical Athens, professional rhetors with greater education and political knowledge took the most active role in addressing the citizen Assembly.[1] In the New England Town Meetings of the 1700s, the poorest citizens who were eligible to attend often did so in smaller numbers than their wealthier counterparts. Consensus was often achieved by discounting the interests of low-status citizens and deferring to the leadership of the affluent, who were also more likely to be elected to official posts.[2] Of course, in both of these paradigmatic examples of democratic deliberation, most community members were denied standing as citizens and excluded from the deliberative bodies of the state. Thus, neither body resolved the problems of how to provide all community members with equal access to deliberative forums, equal capacities to participate in deliberation, and an equal opportunity to influence others with the merits of one's arguments. Some observers fear that if today's civic forums cannot create better conditions for equality, they may end up simply reinforcing the power of the most politically active and privileged citizens.[3] How might we address these difficult challenges?

One answer would be to devote our attention to reducing background inequalities of wealth, power, education, and status that undermine democratic deliberation. Indeed, many theorists have argued that the greater informational and communicative demands of democratic deliberation relative to other kinds of democracy require us to raise threshold provisions of primary goods – education, income, and the like – so that

[1] Ober 1989.   [2] Mansbridge 1983, 130–35.   [3] See, e.g., Geissel 2012, 211.

all are prepared to participate effectively in deliberation.[4] Whether theorists call for a more equitable distribution of resources, opportunities, or capacities for effective deliberation among individuals or social groups, each approach can suggest dramatic changes in public investment and institutions.[5]

We agree that more egalitarian conditions would enhance deliberation and justice. However, as Archon Fung observes, theorists have offered few specific details about how existing institutions would commit to redistribution under current conditions of stark political, economic, and social inequalities.[6] Institutional reform and improving background conditions of equality need to go hand in hand, rather than one before the other. It is difficult to see how deliberative theory would justify reallocating power and resources unless this is agreed upon through a process that involves all sectors of society, including the privileged, given the principle that all who are affected by a decision should have an opportunity to deliberate about it. Advancing background equality typically involves shifting power and resources from those who have more to those who have less. If the powerful feel that their interests are excluded from deliberation over redistribution, they are likely to resist by using the non-deliberative means that give them their current advantages, including "authority, status, numbers, money, or muscle."[7] Therefore, addressing background inequalities may depend in part on finding better ways of enhancing equal deliberation, including deliberation about inequality itself.

Most of the civic forums that are the focus of this book employ several common strategies aimed at achieving equality of inclusion, participation, and influence. In open forums, all have an equal opportunity to attend and speak, and, where applicable, an equal vote. Because these are formal rights, some citizens will participate and influence decisions more than others. Closed forums practice equality in different ways. In the interest of incorporating the least powerful in numbers proportional to their presence in a larger population, forum organizers recruit random representative samples or quasi-representative microcosms of a polity, or recruit participants in part through networks of organizations that work with the least powerful.[8] Some forums subsidize the costs of

---

[4] See, e.g., Cohen and Rogers 1983; Dryzek, 2000, 172; Fung 2005, 397–8; Gutmann and Thompson, 1996; Knight and Johnson 1997.
[5] For a discussion of these different approaches and the policies they suggest, see Bohman 1996, Chapter 3.
[6] Fung 2005, 398.   [7] Fung 2003, 344.
[8] Leighninger 2012; Levine and Nierras, 2007.

participation – including information acquisition, time, and money – by providing background materials about the issues, providing translation services, paying stipends to participants, and the like.[9] To create conditions for equal participation and influence, facilitators set ground rules that aim to allow all deliberators to talk on equal and respectful terms, and that are open to a broad range of communication styles.[10] Each of these strategies seeks inclusion of the disempowered on more equal discursive terms than are often found in traditional public forums. The latter can be dominated by self-selected citizens who are often more privileged than the norm, or by officials or policy experts, and generally do not offer opportunities for cooperative dialogue between community members as equals.[11]

Nonetheless, in this chapter we contend that achieving equality in civic forums and in the larger deliberative system can require more than throwing open the doors to all or engaging proportional numbers of the disempowered in cross-cutting talk with members of more powerful groups. Several democratic theorists have argued that the marginalized sometimes need to confer among themselves in civil society associations if the least powerful are to contribute autonomously and effectively to deliberation in the wider public sphere.[12] We extend this argument to civic forums, maintaining that it would be better for equality, and therefore for the quality of deliberation, to create opportunities within and among forums for enclave deliberation among the least powerful. Our aims are to counteract extreme background inequalities among participants and perspectives, the sometimes problematic dynamics of small-group discussion among people of different statuses, and the weakness of associations of the least powerful and the ideas they espouse in the larger political system.

We also want to recognize the reality that enclave discussion, sanctioned or not, is a feature of all political institutions. Many civic forums draw metaphorical legitimacy and some design features from established institutions of democracy, even as they try to improve upon them. We have "Citizens Assemblies," "21st Century Town Meetings," "Deliberative Polls," "Citizens Juries," "National Issues Forums," and the like. Enclaves influence each of the traditional institutions that give these forums their names. In legislative assemblies, members form caucuses based on common issue priorities and interests. Citizens who want to bring proposals to Town Meetings meet to plan their

---

[9] Lee 2011.   [10] Black 2012.   [11] Gastil 2008, 177–212.
[12] See, e.g., Fraser 1992; Mansbridge 1996; Sunstein 2002.

strategy beforehand.[13] Polls reflect the individual views of respondents, which are shaped by their networks of family, friends, and others with whom they discuss politics. Citizens who care deeply about political issues join together in voluntary associations and advocacy groups, which are networked into social movements. Side conversations among small groups of jurors, and between jurors and their families, occur inside and outside jury rooms.[14] And, as we will see, participants in many civic forums also talk in enclaves, either by design or despite the best efforts of some forums to convene people only in cross-cutting conversation among a microcosm of the public. To be sure, talking in enclaves presents some real dangers for equal and public reasoning, but this kind of talk also presents opportunities that we explore in this chapter.

We think that the advantages of enclave deliberation may be realized, and its risks minimized, if it is part of a larger process of democratic deliberation. For example, enclaves could be convened within large cross-cutting civic forums, such as 21st Century Town Meetings. Exchanges can occur *between* enclave forums and cross-cutting forums, such as in the Deliberative Poll, discussed later in this chapter, about conditions faced by indigenous Australians, in which regional meetings among indigenous citizens informed policy proposals that were considered in a subsequent forum that was representative of all Australians. Enclaves can also interact with officials who represent the larger public, either in a single forum or as part of an ongoing political process, as in the Brazilian Participatory Budgets and Chicago Community Policing meetings discussed below. Figure 2.1 illustrates these three ways of incorporating enclaves within broader and more representative forums or political processes. Of course, these are just a few possible ways of institutionalizing enclave deliberation, not an exhaustive list.

Rethinking democratic deliberation as part of a systemic *process*, rather than as something that happens at a single *event* that convenes a representation of the whole polity, allows us to imagine enclave deliberation of the least powerful in a civic forum as one moment in a larger

---

[13] Mansbridge 1983, 62–3.

[14] We are not advocating that jurors should be encouraged to discuss cases with their families or that enclaves should be formed among juries. Both practices present greater risks than enclaves in civic forums. Family members may expose jurors to prejudicial pre-trial publicity, pressure them to decide cases based on incorrect understandings of the law and facts of the case, and so on. Jurors who cluster together in cliques can isolate their peers and exert unequal influence over deliberation. On jurors' discussing cases with family and friends during trials, see Hannaford-Agor, Hans, and Munsterman 2000. On juror clustering, see SunWolf 2007, 309–10, 594–6.

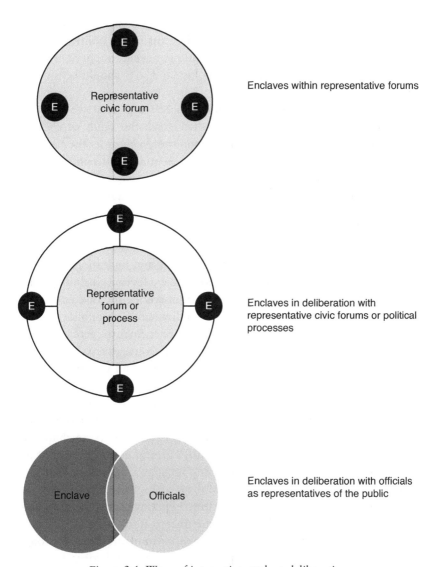

Enclaves within representative forums

Enclaves in deliberation with representative civic forums or political processes

Enclaves in deliberation with officials as representatives of the public

Figure 2.1 Ways of integrating enclave deliberation

political conversation. This approach should enable us to advance equality through deliberation that can stretch across forums and other institutions for representing public opinion or making decisions, rather than assuming that each forum should be designed as if it were solely responsible for these tasks. In this light, forums may not always need to strive for convening a proportional microcosm or representation of the whole polity, or of all who are affected by an issue under consideration, as long as the forum is connected well to other elements of the political system. Democracies rarely expect a single institution or event to represent public opinion or the decision of the whole polity, and so it should be for civic forums.

To make this argument, we begin by specifying what we mean by disempowered groups. We go on to distinguish the kinds of enclaves of the disadvantaged we would and would not suggest as the basis for some deliberations. Then we examine the potential pitfalls and promises of our proposal for deliberative equality, public reasoning, and agreement seeking – each of the elements of deliberation that we discussed in Chapter 1. We discuss more detailed proposals for institutional reform in Chapter 7.

In making our argument, we draw on four strands of theoretical and empirical research, each with its own strengths and limitations. The primary strand emerges from the literature on civic forums, including some that already incorporate enclave deliberation among the disempowered. This research comprises case studies of individual mini-publics and co-governance forums, which mainly rely on participants' perceptions of equality and some direct observation. We find diverse dynamics and outcomes, owing to the variety of designs, durations, and purposes of civic forums, and the different concepts and methodologies used to study them. While there is much more to learn about what kinds of forum designs and contexts can best create conditions of equality for the marginalized, we see enough evidence from a wide variety of forums to conclude that civic deliberation is by no means inherently harmful to the interests of the least powerful. At the same time, equality remains a significant challenge and might be improved by enclaves of the disempowered.

Another strand of research comes from experimental studies of deliberation in small groups. These lab experiments allow for precise examination of factors such as equal participation and influence. Through the random assignment of participants to treatment and control groups, experiments also allow for greater isolation of cause and effect, and can therefore especially illuminate the impact of deliberators' individual attributes, group composition, and decision rules on equality in the deliberative process and its outcomes. Careful lab experiments can greatly expand scholars' understanding of the micro-foundations of successful (or unsuccessful) deliberation. Yet some experimental findings can be limited in their application to complex, real-world forums, where conditions are less easily controlled, potential causes and outcomes multiply and intermix, or key conditions might differ from those found in the lab.[15] Field experiments in civic forums can provide greater external validity, but most of these have been conducted on a single forum design, Deliberative Polls.[16] In general, we treat experimental studies of group deliberation as offering valuable insights into some of the problems that can arise in deliberation as well as into the conditions under which deliberation comes closer to theorists' ideals. The problems uncovered by lab experiments are not insurmountable, but they must be considered carefully by anyone committed to realizing political equality in forums.

A third research thread emerges from surveys that inquire into people's deliberative attitudes and behaviors. These can help illuminate the distribution of deliberation outside civic forums in the wider political system, including who deliberates, how, why, and relationships between deliberation and other political behaviors. Yet these surveys offer weaker evidence of causal links between deliberation, its antecedents, and its consequences. Surveys also offer less powerful evidence of group dynamics in civic forums and how forums affect the political system because this kind of research measures people's self-reports about deliberation rather than observing it directly. One important question raised about survey research is whether respondents are liable to give socially desirable answers, especially by over estimating how often and how well they engage in political discussion.[17]

Fourth, we also look to the literature on deliberation in relevant civil society organizations of marginalized groups to help shed light on the possibilities for enclave deliberation. Some theorists draw strong contrasts between deliberative and participatory democracy, associating the former with the search for consensus about the common good and the latter with activist contestation.[18] Other theorists see civic deliberation as most authentic when it is held within civil society institutions because they are relatively independent from market and state pressures.[19] The research on how citizens deliberate in associations is the most methodologically

[15] Karpowitz and Mendelberg 2011. For example, in real-world forums, discussion is most often led by facilitators who employ egalitarian speaking rules, people tend to deliberate longer, participants may perceive that their choices have greater consequences for real-world politics, and deliberators sometimes interact with experts and officials.

[16] For a summary of the research on Deliberative Polls, see Fishkin 2009.

[17] Steiner 2012, 39–40. For a high-quality example of a survey approach to the study of deliberation, see Jacobs, Cook, and Delli Carpini 2009.

[18] Treatments of deliberative and participatory democracy as distinct, even competing visions, include Mouffe 1999; Mutz 2006; Young 2001.

[19] Dryzek 2000; Habermas 1996a; Cohen 1989.

heterogeneous of the four strands we draw together, as it employs a mix of historical analysis, participant observation, interviews, and surveys. While this literature can offer insights into how people confer in enclaves that are less politically powerful, we will argue that civic forums should involve some different goals and conditions than associations and movements. Therefore, even if civil society enclaves can tell us some things about what may happen in civic forums, we should be careful when drawing comparisons between these different political contexts.

The disempowered

Political power can be complicated, multifaceted, and historically fluid.[20] Yet we can still identify three kinds of citizens who may be disempowered in civic forums, if compensatory measures are not taken or do not work. One group, which we will call the politically disempowered, includes people who are systematically disadvantaged in the larger political system outside the forum. Another group, the situationally disempowered, may be in a weaker position in regard to the issues on the agenda in a particular forum. A third group, the deliberatively disempowered, may be disadvantaged by the conditions of deliberation itself. Of course, these groups often overlap in practice.

Political disempowerment

Who are the politically disempowered? At any given time and place, there are identifiable groups that are "more difficult to organize, articulate, mobilize, and integrate into policy discussions."[21] These groups may be formally excluded from aspects of the political system, for example because they are denied voting rights or legal standing in judicial or administrative arenas. Such groups may be hampered by the lingering effects of past exclusion, or may lack the same access to resources for effective organization and action enjoyed by more privileged groups. Members of disempowered groups typically have a weaker political voice, participating at lower rates than others in efforts to influence institutional and public policy making through organized lobbying, campaign contributions, legal advocacy, voting, direct action campaigns, and other methods of affecting policy.[22] As a result, government serves these groups'

---

[20] Bachrach and Baratz 1962; Gaventa 1982.   [21] Hendriks 2006b, 587.

[22] Sidney Verba and his colleagues define political voice as including any individual or organizational activities that have "the intent or effect of influencing government action –

interests or preferences less well when they conflict with those of better organized groups who have greater resources to press their case. In sum, a group is disempowered if political or economic conditions are tilted against its ability to participate equally in political life, the group has a weaker political voice, or government is consistently less responsive to the group's policy preferences or interests. Many groups may be hindered by one or more of these kinds of political marginalization, based on their gender, race, ethnicity, language, religion, sexual orientation, income, level of education, citizenship status, and other characteristics. In the interest of brevity, we will illustrate our point with just a few examples of politically disempowered groups.

Two of the clearest and most durable markers of disempowerment in the United States are educational attainment and income, which are often combined into a single measure of socio-economic status (SES). Since the 1960s, income mobility and equality have declined as the poor have seen their economic conditions stagnate or erode by most measures of real wages, health insurance, and social welfare benefits.[23] Political conditions have also increasingly disfavored the poor as candidates for office have relied more heavily on large donors and political action committees to fund increasingly expensive campaigns, lobbying by businesses and trade groups has grown, and the political influence of unions has declined.[24] The individual and collective political voices of the poor are a whisper compared with the relative shouts of more privileged citizens and organizations. Low-SES Americans participate far less than members of higher income groups in the political system through traditional means such as voting, joining interest groups, and contributing to campaigns, but also through alternative forms of expression such as boycotting products and engaging in political discussion with others.[25] Interest group activity is

either directly by affecting the making or implementation of public policy or indirectly by influencing the selection of people who make those policies" (Verba, Schlozman, and Brady 1995, 38). We would expand this definition to include efforts to influence the policies and practices of private institutions as they affect the public, including direct actions that do not involve government, such as public campaigns, boycotts, and the like. We would also include forms of "discursive participation" (Jacobs, Cook, and Delli Carpini 2009, 24–6, 35–6), which aim to influence others' views of political issues. This includes participation in the kinds of civic forums discussed in this book and informal conversations about politics.

[23] Piketty and Saez 2003: 1–39; Bartels 2008, Chapter 1; Wolff 2009, Chapter 1; Schlozman, Verba, and Brady 2012, Chapter 3.

[24] Hays 2001, 59–62; Bartels 2008, 2.

[25] Taking into consideration multiple factors that can influence political voice – including gender, race, ethnicity, religion, ideology, and party identification – Kay Schlozman and

even more unequal than individual political expression. The major barriers to organized political participation – lack of resources and free rider problems – are especially high for low-SES people.[26] Kay Schlozman, Sidney Verba, and Henry Brady's recent encyclopedic study of national interest groups finds that 0.8 percent of all groups active in Washington, DC, politics consistently represent the interests of the poor or advocate for investment in social welfare programs. This figure has remained fairly stable over the past 50 years, at a time when organized political participation by interest groups has mushroomed, mainly on behalf of corporations, large institutions, and state and local governments.[27] Low-SES Americans are less likely than the more affluent and educated to join, lead, and feel that they are represented by interest groups of any kind.[28]

In addition, there is growing evidence that the American political system is less responsive to the policy preferences of low-income citizens than those of higher-income constituents. Several studies indicate that when state and local voting rates among low-income citizens decline, officials at these levels of government spend less on programs to aid the poor.[29] Larry Bartels' research comparing public opinion by income level with US senators' voting patterns finds that "senators consistently appear to pay

---

her colleagues find that SES is at the root of most observed differences in political voice, with age playing a secondary role. The authors find that the top-quintile of Americans "is responsible for 1.8 times the number of votes, more than 2.6 times the number of hours [devoted to political action], and 76 times the number of dollars [in campaign contributions] of the lowest quintile." Top quintile Americans are more than twice as likely to engage in daily political discussion than lowest-quintile Americans. Of all of the authors' measures of voice, the least advantaged are only as likely as the more advantaged to engage in political protest, which is often called the "weapon of the weak" (Schlozman, Verba, and Brady 2012, 14, 22, 124, 136). See also Verba, Schlozman, and Brady 1995; Jacobs and Skocpol 2005; Berry and Wilcox 2009; Gilens 2012.

[26] While all social groups possess unequal resources to devote to politics – including time, money, information, and political expertise – the poor typically have the fewest of these resources (Schattschneider 1960; Hays 2001, Chapters 2, 6). On the problem of free ridership, see Olson 1965.

[27] See also Skocpol 2003.

[28] Schlozman, Verba, and Brady 2012, Chapters 12, 13. Summarizing their findings about participation in multiple kinds of political activity, the authors conclude,

> In no domain of organized interest activity does activity by organizations that provide services to or political representation of the poor register more than a trace. Activity on their own behalf by recipients of means-tested benefits barely exists at all. Unless nonprofessional, nonmanagerial workers are union members, their economic interests receive very little representation in any arena of organized interest activity. The interests of unskilled workers receive none at all. (442)

[29] Hill and Leighley, 1992; Hill, Leighley, and Hinton-Andersson 1995; Hajnal 2010, Chapter 5; Osberg, Smeeding, and Schwabish 2004; Brady 2003.

no attention to the views of millions of their constituents in the bottom third of the income distribution."[30] Senators are especially likely to vote according to the views of their most affluent constituents and against the more egalitarian policy preferences of low-income citizens on economic issues such as the minimum wage and tax cuts for the wealthy. In a broader study of thousands of policy proposals and the level of support for each expressed in public opinion surveys between 1981 and 2002, Martin Gilens arrives at similar findings: across multiple issue domains and periods, policies that were enacted reflected the preferences of the affluent, but not the poor when their views conflicted with those of more privileged citizens.[31]

Among the poor, undocumented immigrants are especially disempowered politically. Despite being tightly integrated into the American labor force, these immigrants cannot exercise full economic rights or basic citizenship rights. Historically, the fortunes of the undocumented have depended less on their own political voices than on the balance of power between anti-immigration and pro-immigration blocs, led by employers, labor unions, and nativists pursuing their own interests first and foremost.[32] To the extent that government responds to the preferences and interests of the undocumented, it mainly does so indirectly by heeding the voices of documented citizens and their organizations.

Situational disempowerment

Some groups may also be situationally disempowered in relation to particular issues or contexts, regardless of their status in the political system as a whole, or of their socio-demographic attributes or privileges. These groups may find themselves in disadvantaged positions in the social, economic, or cultural realms, not only in politics oriented toward the state. In any of these spheres, the situationally disadvantaged encounter conditions

---

[30] Bartels 2008, 282, and Chapters 6 and 8. For a similar study of class bias in economic policy making in the Reagan White House, see Druckman and Jacobs 2011, Chapter 6.

[31] Gilens 2012. Unlike Bartels (2008), Gilens finds that upper-class bias in policy making is less strong on economic issues than in some other policy areas, perhaps because Gilens examines policy outcomes rather than only Senate votes, and because his study includes economic issues in which the middle class also had a strong stake and on which broad-based interest groups countered the preferences of the affluent. For example, while Bartels examined views on issues such as the minimum wage, which most affects the working poor, Gilens looked at opinions on issues such as employer health care requirements, Medicare spending, and Social Security reform. For similar findings of unresponsiveness to the preferences of poor constituents in state-level policy making, see Rigby and Wright 2011.

[32] Gimple and Edwards 1999; Mapes 2009.

that limit their ability to participate, speak, and be heard on equal terms. For example, in relation to freedom of speech, even the most affluent American youth are relatively disempowered by laws and customs that give schools great leeway to limit and sanction their students' speech, both on and off campus, in the interest of maintaining discipline, curbing bullying or hate speech, and the like.[33] While journalists appear to have a good deal of power over representing political events, many reporters are also disempowered citizens in that they are prohibited by their employers and discouraged by professional norms of objectivity from expressing their own political views in public. Many news organizations forbid their journalists from attending political demonstrations or playing leadership roles in political organizations, a situation that journalists' unions and professional associations have not significantly challenged.[34]

As the examples of students and journalists suggest, there are many groups who are disempowered by legal, organizational, professional, or cultural constraints. While this certainly does not mean that everyone is *equally* disadvantaged in life, it suggests that there are enclaves of situationally disempowered people with regard to particular contexts and issues that might be discussed in civic forums, such as student speech or journalistic ethics. These groups might benefit from discussing their shared situation and their discussion might add important perspectives to public deliberation.

Deliberative disempowerment

A third kind of disadvantage may accompany and compound political or situational disempowerment. As we noted in Chapter 1, theorists influenced by difference democracy have argued that political deliberation itself may be a daunting arena for some citizens, especially if it is restricted to a style of reasoning that is combative, abstract, dispassionate, or impartial, or that presumes specialist knowledge; or if it is conducted in an unfamiliar language. People who are less educated, or of lower social status, immigrants deliberating in their second tongue, and others may be penalized by these narrow expectations. Like political and situational disempowerment, deliberative disadvantage can be mitigated or exacerbated by conditions in the forum. As we will discuss below, recent experimental research presents ongoing and troubling evidence that in some contexts women continue to be less likely to speak and to be perceived as influential in deliberation, compared with men.

---

[33] Papandrea 2008.   [34] Smith 2008, 275–95.

Enclaves

Cass Sunstein, who coined the term "enclave deliberation," warns against the potential dangers of discussion within groups of "like-minded people who talk or even live, much of the time, in isolated enclaves."[35] While we will address his concerns more extensively below, the first question to ask is what exactly "like-minded" means. As Sunstein observes, "Any judgments about enclave deliberation are hard to make without a sense of the underlying substance – of what it is that divides the enclave from the rest of society."[36]

Of the many kinds of affinities that citizens may share in civic forums, we see shared *perspectives* as the most legitimate basis for the kind of enclave deliberation of the disempowered that we are advocating. Iris Marion Young defines perspectives as including the "experience, history, and social knowledge" derived from individuals' locations in social groups. Perspectives are not necessarily identical with ascriptive or descriptive identities. Young cautions against a crude essentialism that would define a group by these kinds of attributes, such as race or gender, and assume that this attribute consistently confers a common identity on the group's members, much less common interests. Considerable diversity of views and identities can be found within people of the same race, ethnicity, gender, and so on. Yet Young also rejects a simplistic view of persons as free agents unencumbered by social structures. In her view, individuals are "positioned in social group structures rather than having their identity determined by them." For Young, "social perspective consists in a set of questions, kinds of experience, and assumptions with which reasoning begins, rather than the conclusions drawn." Because a "perspective is a way of looking at social processes without determining what one sees," it does not include the perception of one's most important interests, the content of one's beliefs, or the formation of one's policy preferences.[37] Yet, "especially in so far as people are situated on different sides of relations of structural inequality, they understand those relations and their consequences differently."[38]

To exemplify this notion of a perspective as a way of looking that does not determine what one sees, Young discusses the *Pittsburgh Courier*, a longstanding newspaper for African-Americans. The newspaper embodies an African-American perspective on the world by focusing on

---

[35] Sunstein 2002, 177. [36] Sunstein 2000, 112.
[37] Young 2000, 136–7. [38] Young 2000, 136.

events and institutions in which blacks are the main actors. The *Courier* approaches local and national stories, including ones that are not only associated with African-Americans, from angles informed by issues and experiences of special importance to black Americans. Yet, within this shared perspective, the *Courier* also reports on controversies that dramatize blacks' conflicting views of what is in their best interests and what values they should embrace. Likewise, the opinion pages of the *Courier* include articles from a wide range of ideological positions, from libertarian to socialist, and from advocacy of economic separatism to integration.

Returning to our examples of political disempowerment, we can speak of a diverse but coherent perspective of the poor or of undocumented immigrants. We can identify situationally disempowered perspectives of youth on student speech rights or journalists on reporters' rights to political expression. We can consider deliberatively disempowered perspectives shared by those whose acculturation can make them less comfortable with public argumentation as it occurs in civic forums. Our argument is that the deliberative system is enhanced by offering opportunities for those who are disempowered in these ways to deliberate amongst themselves in civic forums. Of course, we do not assume that any individual's views are defined solely by a single perspective. And we do not have to assume that people cannot understand or embrace the views of others from different perspectives, even if they cannot fully inhabit those perspectives. We need only recognize that some people come to civic forums with common experiences of political, situational, or deliberative disadvantage.

While our perspectives, rooted in our social locations, endure in deliberation, other aspects of our views can and should be open to transformation in discussion with other citizens, including our interests, beliefs, values, and policy preferences. Therefore, we do not suggest that civic forums should decide in advance that disempowered people do or ought to share these kinds of characteristics and group them accordingly in enclaves. Following Young, we call *interests* the means that individuals and organizations see as necessary for pursuing their chosen ends, including "both material resources and the ability to exercise capacities – e.g. for cultural expression, political influence, economic decision-making power, and so on."[39] Yet, as Young points out, each of us often has multiple conflicting interests, which might be prioritized differently in any given decision. In deliberative theory, interests are most legitimately identified and

[39] Young 2000, 134.

prioritized through deliberation, rather than beforehand.[40] This makes it very difficult to form enclaves based on common interests without defining people's interests in advance for them in rather specific ways, including which of their interests should be most important to them. This sort of paternalism would fail to respect citizens' autonomy.

Moreover, we often have additional things at stake in politics that go beyond interests. Some deliberators may be motivated chiefly by their *beliefs*, by which we mean their understanding of what sorts of knowledge, facts, and causal relations can be considered true. Other citizens may reason mainly from their *values*, which consist of normative commitments to what people consider just, fair, beautiful, desirable, sacred, and the like. Still other citizens may be focused mainly on their *preferences* for the particular policy actions they think should be taken. One job of deliberation is to help participants re-examine, prioritize, and align their interests, beliefs, and values with specific preferences, all of which should be open to discussion in civic deliberation, and none of which should be defined on their behalf by others beforehand.[41]

However, perspectives are easier to identify before deliberation and more legitimately durable within it. Therefore, it is not necessarily a threat to the legitimacy or coherence of deliberative democratic theory if marginalized people who deliberate in civic forums begin to think differently than others in their communities.[42] These deliberators retain their perspectives, which enrich political discussion with their experience of

---

[40] Jane Mansbridge and her colleagues (2010, 68), using a somewhat broader definition of interests than we have, also see them as best formed in deliberation, not beforehand: "We use the word 'interest' here to mean an 'enlightened' preference, that is, what hypothetically one would conclude after ideal deliberation was one's own good or one's policy preference, including other-regarding and ideal-regarding commitments."

[41] We do not argue that citizens must give up their most closely held values and beliefs to participate fully in deliberative discussion, but rather the opposite: binding agreements about political outcomes are most defensible when citizens have deliberated together in ways that help clarify and prioritize the relationships between their values and collective political decisions.

[42] Our concern should not be that the disempowered will lose some aspect of their *identity* in deliberation (for summaries of these worries, see Ryfe 2005; Newton 2012a). A better way of thinking about the problem is that there is a trade-off between the value of citizens accruing expertise by participating in a forum over time, for example by being elected to a Participatory Budgeting District Council, and the entrenchment of a "sub-elite" of citizen participants who take control of forum procedures, exclude newcomers, or grow less accountable to their fellow citizens (Fagotto and Fung 2006; Talpin 2012). To curb this danger, many forums that continue over longer periods of time enforce rotation of representatives. For example, many Participatory Budgeting processes around the world ban citizen delegates from standing for election two years in a row (Talpin 2012).

inequality and can help to resist co-optation of the views of the weak by the powerful, as all participants consider whether to realign their interests, beliefs, and values through discussion. When people share a disempowered perspective, we should ask whether it would advance equality of inclusion, participation, and influence if they deliberate together in civic forums, as well as with others.

We are advocating for the value of deliberation among people who are disempowered because of their *social position in relation* to an issue, which may or may not align with their *political position on* the issue. In contrast, it may be argued that anyone who advocates unpopular or innovative ideas is situationally disadvantaged in deliberation, regardless of their position in society. For example, in most contexts it will be harder to convince others to accept collective sacrifices or to embrace policies that would disrupt the status quo.[43] However, this line of reasoning may lead to forming enclaves of people based solely on their shared political preferences, which should be open to reconsideration in deliberation. In civil society organizations, deliberation in enclaves of shared preferences is valuable for helping to develop and expand the range of arguments in the public sphere by advocating for unfamiliar ideas. But grouping deliberators primarily by their existing political preferences poses significant challenges to the deliberative ideals of most civic forums, which involve creating conditions in which all participants can consider or reconsider their views fully and freely.

In contrast, forming enclaves of students, as in the above example, does not presume that all students will begin or end their discussion in agreement over how to regulate their own speech. Nor do we assume that student enclaves *ought* to arrive at policy agreements among themselves before deliberating with others of different perspectives. For example, some students may emerge from enclave deliberation in favor of restrictions on hate speech based on personal experience of its effects on their classmates, while others may prioritize counter-speech or mediation as the best response to racist or sexist epithets because they have seen these techniques used effectively in schools. Our proposal is simply that students can make these decisions more autonomously if they deliberate with each other *and* in mixed groups with parents, teachers, school principals, and so on.[44]

---

[43] We are obliged to Peter Levine for raising this argument in comments on an earlier draft.

[44] It might also be argued that anyone who has a diffuse interest in a policy decision, rather than a specific stake, is situationally disempowered. Local school board meetings, for example, tend to draw parents and teachers more than citizens who have no

Inclusion

Can forming enclaves of the disempowered be integrated within a legitimate account of how civic forums should practice equal inclusion of all citizens? In particular, would enclave deliberation involve excluding the perspectives of the broader public, including the privileged? In Chapter 1, we argued that whether forums practice legitimate inclusion depends greatly on organizers' justifications for defining who is affected by the issues on the agenda. Depending on the forum's relationship to the deliberative system, multiple principles of representation might serve equality best, and all of them can involve enclaves of the least powerful. We can now fill in more detail about these principles and how enclave deliberation can be compatible with them in many kinds of forums.

Four ideals of inclusion with enclaves

With regard to inclusion, once again we would distinguish attributes that exist before deliberation and that we should want to preserve from other attributes that we should most want people to remain open to rethinking during deliberation. Especially when a forum must be limited to a group that is smaller than all affected by the decision, a preexisting attribute that does not need reconsidering could be used to select participants who are diverse and representative according to that attribute. Once again, that attribute is one's perspective. Because one's perspective is based on one's life experience in a social location, it cannot be divorced easily from the actual person in the world who bears that perspective and represented by someone who has not shared the same experience. Therefore, it makes sense to think of the population of all affected by a decision as a collection of perspective bearers most relevant to the issue at hand.[45]

---

direct connection to schools. However, we are not suggesting enclaves of the "less interested," because their interests can be represented by citizens in broader forums, as well as by officials and experts. We thank Archon Fung for drawing this example to our attention.

[45] Bohman (2012) makes a similar argument for representing perspectives first and foremost in deliberation. But he objects to Young's argument for defining perspectives based on people's structural locations because he fears that the variety of potential topics of deliberation makes it "not possible to decide in advance which among the potential candidate perspectives ought to be included" (83). However, we think that the example forums discussed in this section show that the most affected perspectives can be identified with regard to the specific issue and goal of the forum.

When a civic forum cannot accommodate all perspective holders, often it should represent them descriptively.[46] This kind of representation is more important in civic deliberation than in electoral politics. As Jane Mansbridge argues,

> In deliberation, perspectives are less easily represented by nondescriptive representatives... [especially] in the contexts of communicative mistrust and uncrystallized interests this vicarious portrayal of the experience of others by those who have not themselves had those experiences is often not enough to promote effective deliberation.[47]

While we can and should empathize with others of different perspectives, we are less likely to know their experience than they are, and often less likely to attend to it if they are absent. Imagine a hypothetical forum on the proposed Development, Relief, and Education for Alien Minors (DREAM) Act, which would extend citizenship rights to many undocumented immigrants brought to the United States as children, most of them from Mexico.[48] It is unlikely that these young immigrants' perspectives could be represented fully by immigrants who arrived as adults from Europe and obtained legal citizenship. Members of the latter group made more autonomous decisions to emigrate as adults, and are more likely to have qualified for citizenship by virtue of having immediate family ties to legalized citizens, having advanced educational degrees, or possessing skills that employers demand.

---

[46] Descriptive representation has a bad name among many theorists of electoral democracy, who fear that it would undermine the performance of legislatures by electing less talented representatives, or that it fosters divisive and essentialist approaches to politics that undermine pursuit of the common good (Pennock 1979, 314; Pitkin, 1967, Chapter 4). Many of these criticisms are aimed at what Mansbridge (1999) calls microcosmic descriptive representation, which aims to recreate all aspects of the polity in miniature within the legislature. In contrast, we are arguing for representation of the most salient perspectives on the issue under deliberation, a more focused version, which Mansbridge calls selective descriptive representation (see also Phillips 1995 on the "politics of presence" and Williams 1998 on "self-representation.) With regard to performance, the benefits of this kind of targeted descriptive representation are that it seeks a breadth of perspectives that help to overcome individuals' bounded rationality, enriching the range of arguments and conclusions under consideration. Divisiveness based on good cause, such as resistance to discrimination or exploitation, is not necessarily to be avoided. Essentialism is, as we discuss below.

[47] Mansbridge 1999, 635.

[48] The most reliable estimate at the time of this writing is that over 70 percent of potential beneficiaries of the DREAM Act were brought to the United States from Mexico (Immigration Policy Center 2012).

In general, forums should include the least powerful perspective bearers on the issue at hand at least in proportion to their numbers in the larger demos, however that political population is defined. Proportional representation, as Mansbridge has argued in relation to legislatures, meets four goals of deliberation in civic forums as well. First, greater representation of disempowered perspective holders allows them to contribute more, and perhaps better, evidence and arguments to the larger discussion. Second, the disempowered often need a critical mass to develop the courage to suggest minority views and to persuade others to consider those views seriously. Third, even in large forums much deliberation happens in small breakout groups, so disadvantaged perspective bearers need to be present in sufficient numbers for their views to be heard in each group. Finally, broader representation of less privileged perspectives acts as a check on any one participant or subset of the marginalized who might impose a singular definition of the group's preferences based on an essentialist view of who its members are or what they should want. This increases the chances for incorporating into the forum the internal diversity of disadvantaged groups' perceived interests, beliefs, and values. Mansbridge raises other benefits of proportional representation that we see as enhancing the external legitimacy of a civic forum. Proportional inclusion communicates to the polity as a whole that members of disadvantaged groups are equally capable of participating in collective self-rule. It enhances the legitimacy of the forum in the eyes of disempowered people who do not participate by communicating that their perspectives were included.

A multiplicity of ideal standards for inclusion of the disempowered in microcosmic forums can be based on the goals of each forum, the kinds of issues it considers, its degree of empowerment, and its openness to all who want to deliberate.[49] Deliberation within enclaves of the least powerful can be incorporated in each of these ideal standards. Some forums have *holistic* goals to make decisions for, or represent the collective opinion

---

[49] Our thinking on this point is influenced by Archon Fung (2006), who presents a more complex model of institutional designs for civic forums, adding the dimension of communicative mode to participant selection and empowerment of the forum. We focus on a simpler two-dimensional model because our focus is only on inclusion here. In addition, we do not address forums that aim only to build citizens' civic capacities, which may not be obligated to practice broad inclusion, in our view. Our discussion of the regularity and depth of influence of an issue's effect on citizens borrows from Fung's (2013) rethinking of the "all affected" principle, although our application to civic forums differs from his theorizing about citizens' rights to influence organizations' decisions in a broader array of settings.

of, the entire demos. These kinds of forums are especially appropriate for considering the provision of public goods, management of the commons, and the design of the democratic system within existing jurisdictions.[50] Examples of these kinds of issues include public budgeting, infrastructure, management of public lands, public safety, and the design of electoral systems or political districts. These are issues that affect all members of the demos regularly and deeply.

Other forums aim to influence *relational* matters that more clearly concern the relationship of one sector of the public to another, or to the demos as a whole, or the relationship of one demos to another. These forums address matters such as social problems that especially affect some members of the public (such as alcohol abuse or domestic violence), reconciliation between religious or ethnic groups, the conditions and status of minorities and diasporas, and issues that are explicitly addressed at a transnational level. These issues often touch all people to some extent, but some people far more deeply than others.

A second factor concerns whether the forum is empowered to enact policy directly. At present, the few forums that are more empowered tend to be popular assemblies and co-governance bodies that have holistic goals, such as the New England Town Meeting and some Participatory Budgeting forums.

The openness of the forum to all citizens who want to attend is a third key factor. Here, the question is whether all citizens could potentially influence the forum through their presence or whether some must be represented by other citizens in order to make deliberation possible. For each type of forum, we sketch out a standard for recruiting an inclusive sample of the public, and an example forum that approaches each standard (see Table 2.1). Each of these examples also incorporates some element of enclave deliberation of the least powerful. Of course, these forums are examples only of good inclusion, not necessarily paragons of other aspects of equality or public reasoning or agreement seeking.

Quadrant I articulates a standard for forums with holistic goals that can accommodate all who want to attend without making deliberation

---

[50] Public goods are nonrivalrous (once produced, they can be consumed by an indefinite number of people at no marginal cost) and nonexcludable (consumption cannot be limited to one consumer without limiting consumption to all). Because private production of public goods is rarely profitable, governments tend to produce them. Examples include national defense and public infrastructure. The commons refers to economic, political, cultural, natural, and knowledge resources that are accessible to all members of a society and are held in common rather than privately owned.

Table 2.1 *Inclusion and enclaves in civic forums*

	Holistic goals (demos)	Relational goals (sector–sector, sector–demos, demos–demos)
Characteristic issues	Management of the commons, public goods, and democratic system	Social problems, conditions of minorities and diasporas, reconciliation between communities, and transnational issues
Current extent of influence	Empowered or advisory	Advisory
Open access	I. *Sample* • Equal access for *all* affected *Recruitment* • *Open* invitation and affirmative recruitment of *under-represented* *Example* • Chicago Community Policing Beat Meetings	II. *Sample* • Equal access for *all* affected and proportional or over representation of *most* affected *Recruitment* • *Open* invitation and affirmative recruitment of *most* affected *Example* • West Virginia Domestic Violence Forums
Limited access	III. *Sample* • Stratified random sample of *all* affected and critical mass of *under-represented* *Recruitment* • By selection or election *Example* • Porto Alegre Participatory Budgeting	IV. *Sample* • Stratified random sample of *all* affected and proportional or over representation of *most* affected *Recruitment* • By selection or election *Example* • Bulgarian Roma and Australian Reconciliation Deliberative Polls

impossible. In these circumstances, the best response is to open the doors to everyone, while making special efforts to recruit people who are least likely to attend to ensure that enough relevant and diverse perspective holders walk through the doors. If the forum is open, then every citizen has a *formally* equal opportunity to participate, even if not all do. Of course, if these forums recruit only through participant self-selection, they will likely over represent people who have more time, money, political motivation, and information. In practice, this means over inclusion of more privileged and civically active citizens, who tend to be more educated, more affluent, older, male, and members of more privileged racial or ethnic groups.[51] Therefore, under represented citizens are affirmatively recruited to these forums, either through networks of associations that can mobilize the least powerful or by offering a chance to affect policy on issues of greatest importance to the least privileged, which can be a powerful incentive to attend.[52] If there is a good rationale for why the under represented perspectives recruited are indeed affected by the issue, and the recruiters do their jobs well, then the resulting sample is one in which all relevant perspective bearers on the issue have a *substantively* equal opportunity for inclusion. In the past, this kind of forum has been possible only at the local level in a small polity, such as a neighborhood or town, although online participation could make it more feasible to scale up these kinds of forums as Internet access and computer skills diffuse throughout society.

For example, Chicago Community Policing meetings, designed in the 1990s, brought together citizens and police officials to make collaborative decisions about how to strengthen neighborhood crime prevention.[53] These co-governance forums were empowered to shape local policing strategies and priorities. The meetings were open to all residents of the city's 280 neighborhood beats. Beat meetings in poor neighborhoods attracted enclaves of low-income residents most victimized by street crime – people who were both situationally disempowered by the issue and politically disempowered in the political system. Because low-income residents were overrepresented as crime victims, and therefore had the biggest stake in curbing crime, the issue offered a structural incentive that

---

[51] Lee 2011; Ryfe and Stalsburg 2012, 50–4; Steiner, 2012, 49.

[52] For example, Lee's (2011) interviews with practitioners of civic forums suggest that women are easier to recruit to forums on social issues, youth, and creative visioning, but harder to attract to forums about technology, planning, toxics and waste, and budgeting.

[53] Our discussion of community policing meetings draws especially on Fung 2004, as well as Skogan and Hartnett 1999.

recruited this group to participate and an especially good reason for their perspectives to be included. Contrary to most public meetings, beat meetings attracted residents of low-income neighborhoods at higher rates than residents of more affluent areas. By 1998, around 10 percent of city residents had attended at least one meeting, and even among attendees, some residents participated far more regularly and extensively than others. Still, because the meetings were open, anyone who chose to could attend.

Forums that address relational issues which are open to all citizens (quadrant II) can maximize access for all affected by the issue, but also need to be concerned about whether they achieve proportional or even over representation of those most deeply affected by the issue, because their perspectives are especially valuable to the goals of the deliberation. Many forums that address social problems and relations between communities (ethnic, religious, and the like) fall into this category.

For example, in 2002–2003, a coalition of voluntary associations working to reduce domestic violence in West Virginia held a series of deliberations around the state to increase understanding of the issue and identify the public's preferred strategies for addressing the problem.[54] Based on extensive interviews with citizens, the organizers developed three major approaches to the problem, each with its own policy steps for deliberators to discuss. These issue framings included increasing community support for victims, stiffening punishment for perpetrators, and transforming public attitudes to domestic violence. While the meetings were open to all, the organizers especially recruited victims, perpetrators, abuse prevention professionals, and law enforcement personnel, all of whom are most deeply affected by the issue, and all of whom deliberated together in the same small forums. By over sampling those who were disproportionately influenced by the issue, the forums increased the likelihood of gathering multiple perspectives from each group, rather than if one or a handful of people had represented victims or perpetrators. Because the forums were one phase in a longer process of developing advisory recommendations, over representing some perspective holders was not necessarily a democratic liability. The organizers followed up by holding additional forums to discuss specific responses to domestic abuse in especially disadvantaged communities, including people with disabilities, African Americans, immigrants, and lesbians, gays, and bisexuals. Each community is situationally disadvantaged with regard to the issue, for example, by physical dependence on caregivers or by higher levels of

---

[54] Our discussion of these forums is based on Fagotto and Fung, 2006, 45–51.

mistrust of the police or courts. This illustrates another way of incorporating enclaves into a larger deliberative process, in this case, *after* the forum through successive rounds of consultation.

A different principle of inclusion can be applied to forums that can only preserve deliberation by limiting admission to a selected group of citizens who represent other citizens (quadrants III and IV). Most often, this occurs when forums address issues on a larger social scale, affecting more people than can be accommodated by an open invitation. There are excellent reasons to hold such gatherings in increasingly diverse, complex, and large-scale polities. Yet this requires some form of representative sampling. We can speak meaningfully of a *representative* sample only after defining a population and what characteristics within it ought to be represented. We have argued that forums are most legitimately inclusive when organizers articulate defensible criteria for identifying all affected perspectives on the issue and including them in appropriate proportions.

What proportions are appropriate? Many theorists contend that forums practice inclusive equality best when they aim at random selection because each member of the population has an equal *probability* of participating.[55] Random selection is also touted for creating a more demographically diverse group than would enroll through self-selection, election, or network recruiting alone.[56] However, unless the polity is

---

[55] Barber 1984, 293; Carson and Martin, 1999, Chapters 5–6; Fishkin 2009, 25–31; Gastil 2008, 200–201. We say that civic forums *aim* at random selection as an ideal, because none achieve it fully at present, for the same reasons that public opinion polls do not. First, recruiters do not begin by drawing from a complete list of the population, relying instead on lists of voters (which omits the unregistered) or random-digit dialing (which omits those without telephones, and often those without land lines because mobile phone numbers cannot be linked confidently to one's place of residence). Second, because anyone can refuse to participate, there is always an element of self-selection (Smith 2009, 79–81; Fishkin 2009, 117). This role of self-selection in all civic forums means that they probably over represent better deliberators – people who are most capable of listening to others, reconsidering their own views, and coming to independent-minded agreements through public reasoning. There are stronger and weaker deliberators among people of all perspectives. Therefore, over representing strong deliberators of all perspectives is acceptable for purposes of equality as long as deliberative skills are not concentrated among those who come from one perspective over another.

[56] Hendriks 2011, 48. As Hendriks notes, theorists and organizers of deliberation raise additional arguments for random selection, which we see as claims about increasing the quality of its public reasoning. Compared with other methods, choosing by lot is valued for recruiting citizens who are thought to be more open to reconsidering their preferences than the kinds of people attracted to public hearings, who tend to attend because they have already formed their views and are there to express them, not to deliberate. Random recruitment is also said to reduce pressure on participants to hold themselves accountable to a particular constituency or to those who share a descriptive

very small or the sample is very large, random selection is likely to conflict with representative selection. An equal probability of each citizen being chosen often does not translate into an equal opportunity for all relevant perspectives to be represented. When the population is very large and the deliberating group small, random recruitment alone can yield a sample that is highly unrepresentative of the population in ways that deprive deliberation of necessary perspectives. For example, if a national forum on abortion in the United States selected 24 people at random to deliberate out of a current population of around 315 million, it is quite possible that all of the people chosen would be male or female, Republicans or Democrats, or children or people past child-bearing age. Random sampling is especially likely to fail to include people from minority ethnic, religious, or cultural groups, presenting a problem for many forums about issues that center on inter ethnic, inter religious, or inter cultural relations.

These problems can afflict forums of all sizes. Clearly, random selection alone is insufficient for achieving representativeness in small forums, such as Consensus Conferences and Citizens Juries, which tend to recruit fewer than 25 deliberators to represent polities as large as a nation-state. Yet even in larger forums that recruit hundreds or thousands of deliberators, such as Deliberative Polls or 21st Century Town Meetings, deliberation happens in multiple small groups, so the composition of each group may influence participants' thinking as much or more than the composition of the whole forum. In these situations, stratified sampling can be used to ensure that at least some perspective bearers most relevant to the issue are included. Better yet, a critical mass of people who come from each relevant perspective can be included, by which we mean enough to disperse into many or all small-group discussions without being isolated tokens. Of course, deciding which perspectives are most relevant to the issue is a powerful choice that organizers must make carefully. However, as we argued in Chapter 1, organizers have to make consequential decisions about the boundaries of the public and the composition of those who will represent that public in *every* civic forum. Few issues map cleanly onto the borders of existing political jurisdictions or affect all people similarly.

Nonetheless, there is something valuable about random selection. Even if sponsors and organizers of deliberation will always have a strong hand

---

aspect of their identity (such as race, gender, age, or occupation), freeing participants to think of themselves as representing the citizenry as a whole, to consider arguments more impartially, and to seek solutions that serve a common good.

in defining the population and criteria for representing them, random selection in the final stage keeps organizers' fingerprints off of the particular individuals who are chosen. This prevents organizers from choosing the most or least persuasive people to represent a particular perspective. Random selection also keeps organizers from imposing their view of the kinds of people who can most authentically represent a social group's interests or what the group's interests might be. Thus, the best argument for preserving an element of randomness often is not that it enhances representativeness, but that it acts as a check on manipulation and paternalism. Of course, another legitimate way to choose citizen representatives can be to have other citizens elect them.

If we are right, holistic forums that must rely on some principle of representation (quadrant III) should aim for a stratified sample of all perspective holders affected by the issue. They can be recruited by random selection, or, in some cases, by asking citizens themselves to elect other citizens among them. In general, proportional representation is most desirable, as long as there are sufficient numbers of salient perspective holders to be heard in group deliberation, including those who would be under represented in the absence of active recruitment.

The Participatory Budgeting process pioneered in 1989 in Porto Alegre, Brazil, provided a practical realization of this ideal in a forum empowered to decide for the public.[57] Each year, citizens attended open meetings in one of the city's 16 districts to review the previous year's budget with officials and to elect fellow citizens to represent their neighborhood in upcoming budget deliberations. Neighborhoods accrued more representatives based on how many of their residents attended these initial meetings, giving citizens a strong incentive to participate and neighborhood associations that represented the least privileged a strong reason to help recruit them. The city also committed to a funding formula that directed larger public investments in infrastructure to the poorest neighborhoods, giving the least well-off residents another incentive to participate. As a result, over a thousand people might turn out for each of these initial meetings. These gatherings were too large for all to deliberate together,

---

[57] While Participatory Budgeting has spread globally, making it one of the most widely used civic forum designs in the world, there are significant differences in the way it is practiced in different locales, especially the degree to which citizens can exert direct authority over budget decisions (Wampler and Hartz-Karp 2012). In addition, there have been changes in the Participatory Budgeting process in Porto Alegre (Baiocchi 2005; Baiocchi, Heller, and Silva 2011; Wampler 2012). Our analysis applies to the specific process developed in Porto Alegre in its initial decade.

but they held officials accountable for their performance at implementing the previous year's spending on local projects and gave all attendees a chance to elect citizen delegates to represent them in budget talks. The real deliberation began among these 40 to 60 delegates, who convened over several months to discuss the district's priorities. Eventually, these district councils voted on their spending requests and elected a smaller group of citizens from among them to a citywide budget council, which harmonized budget priorities from each district.

In effect, the Participatory Budget stratified the district council by neighborhood, and the municipal council by districts. This stratification was justified because the Participatory Budget funded public goods that were most deeply felt at the neighborhood and district level, and therefore best prioritized at that level. The choice of whether to extend a sewer line or paved road first to a *favela* was one that its residents could make most legitimately because it allowed them to exercise their autonomy within the constraints of the city's resources. City officials took part in meetings at each stage and regularly adopted citizens' priorities in the city's final budget. In each phase, election of citizen representatives provided proportional geographic representation and achieved a critical mass of perspectives that were historically under represented in city government, including low-income residents, the less educated, women, and blacks.[58] Planning at the neighborhood and district levels provided opportunities for enclave deliberation among delegates from the city's poorest areas before electing representatives to participate in the city-wide municipal budget council. None of these achievements required complex social scientific sampling. The promise of a more powerful political voice, an opportunity to vote for delegates, and redistribution of city resources to its poorest neighborhoods did the job of engaging low-income constituencies in the annual budget.[59]

Similar principles can be applied to inclusion in relational forums that rely on representation (quadrant IV), except that proportional representation or over-representation of the most affected becomes more important. Over sampling to ensure a critical mass of the least powerful is especially

[58] Each group participated at rates proportional to their share of the general population in the initial district meetings, although representation of less educated and female citizens dropped off somewhat among the elected delegates to the district councils and citywide council. Even so, each group was represented significantly in the municipal council, at rates from around 5 percent for blacks to over 30 percent apiece for women and low-educated residents. These figures are from 1998, about a decade after the establishment of the process in Porto Alegre (Baiocchi 2003, 54.)

[59] Wampler 2012.

clear in forums that address claims made by groups that they should be
treated as a distinct people within the state, as in many issues regarding
indigenous groups, or by one demos in relation to another, as in many
multinational and transnational issues. Failing to include representatives
of such groups or states sufficiently to participate in each small-group
discussion, and in the forum as a whole, seems to reject their claims to
distinct treatment before the forum even begins. It is difficult not to see
them as groups most affected by this kind of decision.

Comparing two Deliberative Polls, both of which addressed the conditions of politically disadvantaged minority ethnic groups, illustrates
the need to over represent the least powerful at times. A 2007 Deliberative Poll on treatment of the minority Roma ethnic group in Bulgaria
fulfilled this standard using stratified random sampling alone. Because
Roma made up about 10 percent of the overall population of seven million, and were included in similar proportion in the overall sample of
255, there were enough members of the minority group to disperse into
the small-group discussions.[60]

However, another national Deliberative Poll on reconciliation with
the indigenous conducted in Australia in 2001 legitimately oversampled
the indigenous, who made up around 2.5 percent of the population
and therefore might have been chosen in very small numbers despite
the fact that their relationship to the wider polity was the topic of the
forum. In addition, prior to the forum, organizers conducted a series
of regional discussions among indigenous citizens alone, forming these
enclaves to identify policy strategies for reconciliation, to craft questions
for the experts who would testify at the national Deliberative Poll, and
to select some of the participants to take part in the national event.
At the national Deliberative Poll, organizers randomly assigned multiple
indigenous participants to around half of the small groups that deliberated about the issue. While all groups became more supportive of reconciliation policies, groups that included indigenous people became more
supportive than groups with no indigenous participants. The organizers
attribute this difference to the airing of "first-hand personal stories of
disadvantage from the indigenous Australians, as well as first hand views
of what indigenous Australians want to see done about the disadvantage,
both symbolically and practically."[61] In the organizers' view, oversampling indigenous participants, which recruited enough to disperse into
half of the small-group discussions, allowed their voices to be heard.

---

[60] Fishkin 2009, 163–4.   [61] Issues Deliberation Australia et al., 2001, 49.

James Fishkin, the inventor of Deliberative Polls, expresses some reservation about how this forum compromised the principle of proportional representation by over sampling the indigenous. Fishkin notes that because groups that did not include indigenous participants also grew more supportive of reconciliation, although not as much, it may have been enough to include indigenous perspectives prominently in the briefing materials and in the balance of experts who presented to the forum.[62] But we strongly suspect that even participants in groups without indigenous deliberators were influenced by the presence of a critical mass of indigenous citizens in the forum as a whole. The indigenous participated in framing questions posed to expert speakers during full plenary sessions, and their presence likely served as a constant reminder that their perspectives were worthy of consideration. The conference report addressed the disparity legitimately by reporting the final views of the randomly selected participants and indigenous deliberators separately, allowing readers to compare the differences and draw their own conclusions about how much weight to give to each set of opinions. By providing both relevant samples of opinion, the forum met the goal of presenting a picture of well-informed public opinion on the relationship between a severely marginalized sector of society and the society as a whole. This ability to present multiple representations of opinion is one advantage of an advisory forum over an empowered one, which must arrive at a single enforceable decision.

To summarize, civic forums can legitimately employ a plurality of principles of representation, depending on the forum's place in the deliberative system. Forums can incorporate and speak to the demos as a whole when they open their doors and supplement self-selection with affirmative recruiting of those who would likely be under represented otherwise. When these holistic forums must limit participation, they can recruit a stratified random sample and a critical mass of under represented perspective holders, so that their views can be raised and heard sufficiently. Forums that focus on improving relations between social sectors or demoi can provide equal access for all affected, when possible, or a stratified random sample of all affected, when necessary. In either case, recruitment that aims for proportional representation of the least advantaged is optimal. However, when the forum's topic is the relationship between a disadvantaged group and the rest of society, it can be most legitimate to over sample the least powerful because their presence in small-group

---

[62] Fishkin 2009, 39.

discussions makes a vital contribution to the consideration of their perspectives.

Enclave deliberation can be incorporated in all of these approaches to representation without excluding the perspectives of the larger public. The forum itself may be an enclave of low-income neighborhood residents that co-governs with officials who are held accountable to serve the broader public, as in the Chicago beat meetings, or with officials and other citizens that represent a larger polity, in the way that the Participatory Budget district councils flow into the city-wide municipal budget council. Enclave deliberation may precede and inform the forum, as in the regional discussions of the indigenous that fed into the national Australian Deliberative Poll. As the West Virginia meetings on domestic violence show, enclave deliberation may also follow a microcosmic forum, deepening or broadening policy development by considering it from the perspectives of different communities that are uniquely affected by social problems.

Building motivation of the disempowered

Politically disempowered people, who have lived on the wrong side of durable inequalities for decades or centuries, have good reasons to be suspicious of political engagement of all kinds. This rational cynicism based on repeated experiences of disappointment and disrespect may lead the politically weak to reject invitations to engage in deliberation with more privileged citizens and with officials. And politicians are rarely interested in hearing the views of those who feel that officials have been unresponsive.

Yet we should not assume, as some critics of deliberation do, that disempowered people do not want to deliberate about politics. Many of them demonstrate interest in civic forums, if given the resources to participate, an opportunity to talk about issues that matter to them, and a real chance of affecting political decisions. For example, Michael Neblo and his coauthors recently studied Americans' attitudes toward a hypothetical opportunity to deliberate online with their congressional representative about immigration policy, finding high levels of interest among all citizens, but especially among those who are least engaged by partisan and interest group politics. Youth, people of color, and lower-income people were more interested than other citizens in deliberating, and the less educated were as interested as more educated citizens.[63]

---

[63] Neblo et al. 2010. Some of these findings may be attributed to the issue of immigration, in which low-income people and people of color have a strong stake, or the prospect of

Disadvantaged citizens' interest in deliberation is not only hypothetical. Many civic forums, including the examples we have just discussed, succeed at recruiting members of marginalized groups by offering them a more substantial opportunity to be heard than in other forms of public consultation. In particular, successful recruitment by co-governance forums, such as Brazilian Participatory Budgeting and Chicago beat meetings, suggests that the least powerful are most likely to attend when they can confer with others who are psychologically and physically proximate about how to address their most pressing needs, and have a direct channel to decision makers.[64] When the disempowered are geographically clustered, as in poor urban neighborhoods, forming enclaves can often be accomplished by holding meetings in these neighborhoods, rather than at a central site that is less convenient or more intimidating (City Hall, a university, and so on). At the same time, even the most representative forums often find it difficult to include proportional numbers of less privileged citizens – especially by education, income, race, and political interest.[65] Moreover, the voices of the least advantaged who attend forums may be muted by being dispersed across many small discussion groups.

Urban redevelopment in New Orleans offers a good example of how the interplay of enclaves and wider, microcosmic discussion can inspire broad and effective participation. After Hurricane Katrina ravaged New Orleans in 2005, the city's initial redevelopment plan slated the Broadmoor neighborhood for destruction and replacement by a park. Given just five months to propose its own rebuilding plan and convince the city not to bulldoze its damaged homes, the neighborhood organized itself into three planning committees, one for a largely poor and African-American area, one for a more affluent and white area, and one for a mixed area. In response to a history of racial mistrust, one organizer explained, "we didn't want the white folks . . . telling the black folks . . . what their part

deliberating online, which may be more attractive to youth. Yet it is a pleasant surprise to see that the prospect of Internet deliberation did not dampen the interest of the less affluent and educated, given concerns about the digital divide.

64 Fung and Wright 2003; Newton 2012b; Barrett, Wyman, and Coelho 2012. In addition, Walsh's (2006) study of community meetings on race relations in the United States, although more focused on dialogue than deliberation, finds that their emergence was "driven by the needs of a community's marginalized racial groups just as much if not more than by the desires of affluent community members to engage in talk about other racial cultures. Such a result challenges complaints that civic dialogue programs are 'all talk and no action' or that members of marginalized communities see little utility in deliberative democracy" (31).

65 Jacobs, Cook, and Delli Carpini 2009, Chapter 6; Lee 2011; Ryfe and Stalsburg 2012; Esterling, Fung, and Lee 2010.

of the neighborhood was going to be... We [had] to create a situation where people had a voice over their own part of the neighborhood... because that's what we hated about the [city's proposed redevelopment plan] – that outsiders were telling us what was going to happen with our neighborhood."[66] Meetings in all three areas were well attended. Residents of the entire neighborhood also met together periodically to seek agreement on a common, coherent proposal to the city. The mix of enclave discussion, whole neighborhood meetings, and technical support from universities and other partners succeeded in producing a widely accepted vision for rebuilding the area, which saved it from destruction.

The ability to confer in their own enclaves at some point in a deliberative political process may boost the motivation of the least advantaged to participate in civic forums, especially if the alternative is the prospect of being a token of one's social group. It can be a great burden to be the only member of a disadvantaged group in deliberation. To be a token is often to feel hyper-visible and constantly scrutinized, uncomfortably different from others, the subject of others' generalizations about one's group, and the need to contend with others' expectations that one speaks for or represents one's group. Tokens often feel they must devote much attention to managing impressions of themselves, adjusting their speech and behavior to guard against criticism from their in-group for betraying their "own kind" and to preclude attacks from out-group members for confirming negative stereotypes about their group. In reaction to these stresses, tokens may isolate themselves or disassociate from social interactions in which they are physically present.[67] Deliberation is a challenging form of political communication under any circumstances, but especially so when one is laboring under the psychological conditions of tokenism. For example, with regard to gender tokens, research finds that women typically speak less, are less likely to mention issues of distinctive concern to women, are less likely to receive positive feedback from men, and are seen as less authoritative when they are the lone female member of their group, while there are no comparable effects of tokenism on men.[68]

Many of the civic forums that have been most successful at attracting a critical mass of the marginalized have worked with voluntary associations of the least powerful, who help attract these citizens or testify to them in public hearings connected to the forums. It is no coincidence that many

[66] Scott 2008, 13–14.
[67] On the psychology of tokenism, see Fiske and Taylor 1991; Kanter 1977; Niemann 2003; Saenz 1994.
[68] Craig and Sherif 1986; Johnson and Schulman 1989; Karpowitz and Mendelberg 2014.

forum organizers turn to associations to help recruit the disempowered because associations often provide the main, or even the only, trusted connections that disadvantaged people have to public life. A robust line of research on democratic associations and social movements has shown how they can create incentives for the least powerful to engage in politics by providing what Sara Evans and Harry Boyte call "free spaces" for political discussion, "in which people are able to learn a new self-respect, a deeper and more assertive group identity, public skills, and values of cooperation and civic virtue."[69] Within these kinds of organizations and networks, people who share a disempowered perspective imagine and define their interests and values, and how members might act to pursue common political preferences. When they participate in forums, as recruiters and sources of testimony, associations of the disadvantaged can provide some counterbalance to the power of government sponsors, offering alternative points of view and holding government and citizens accountable to listen to the views of the least powerful.[70]

While participating in democratic associations and civic forums can have some similar benefits for citizens, we are not suggesting that it is ideal for the disadvantaged to deliberate identically in both settings. Each context can create democratically valuable but different spheres of political activity with their own aims. Internal deliberation within democratic political associations of the marginalized is primarily focused on building relations of solidarity among members, conferring over strategy and tactics, and planning what are sometimes necessary but non-deliberative actions to command attention from the public and the powerful.[71] Civic forums create expectations for engaging in more respectful and mutual justification with a broader cross-section of citizens, in which the disempowered are likely to encounter greater disagreement over political ends, not only over means. These differences suggest potential tensions between convening enclaves for the sake of inclusion and the quality of public reasoning in civic forums, which we will address further below. For now, let us say that the promise of deliberating with people of shared perspectives may help to get the disempowered in the door, where they can also engage with experts, officials, and other citizens as part of a larger forum or political process, increasing the presence of the weak and thereby potentially informing and broadening everyone's views. When

---

[69] Evans and Boyte 1992, 17. See also Hardin 1995; Polletta and Jasper 2001.
[70] Fung and Wright 2003; Hendriks 2011; Talpin 2012.
[71] Fung 2005; Hendriks 2011, Chapter 2; Levine and Nierras, 2007; Warren 2001, 170–76; Young 2001.

inequality relevant to the issue under discussion is profound and inclusion is difficult, enclave deliberation in forums may be worth the risks to the quality of public reasoning.

Participation and influence

If creating enclaves of the disempowered might advance inclusion, what effects might they have on the equality and quality of participation and influence in civic forums? In Chapter 1, we defined these ideals of deliberative equality as applying to how speaking time about each major topic is shared, the capacity to introduce topics and arguments, the ability to command others' attention to one's concerns and reasoning, and the capacity to shape one's own and others' conclusions. We think that enclaves in forums can improve equality in the deliberative system, especially with reference to the forum's relationship to advocacy associations of the disempowered. Within the forum, enclaves can enhance the equal consideration of arguments on their merits by strengthening the political voices of the weak, decreasing differences in status and power among participants, while avoiding some of the well-known dangers that can arise when people talk in exclusive and homogeneous groups in other political contexts.

Advocacy and deliberation in civic forums

Participatory democracy in advocacy organizations and democratic deliberation in civic forums are not necessarily antithetical. Many scholars see the quality of deliberation within democratic associations and movements of the marginalized as an important factor that helps to explain how well the disempowered can define their interests, develop new arguments, present them successfully in the public sphere, and model the kind of democratic politics that these movements want to see in the broader political system.[72] Democratically organized and politically focused

---

[72] della Porta 2013; Dryzek 2010, Chapter 2; Eliasoph 1998; Mansbridge 1996; Polletta 2002; Rucht 2012; Wood 2012. Scholars have diverse views of what *kinds* of deliberation strengthen or undermine associations' public power. Scholars who see internal deliberation as a potential asset focus on its ability to generate novel ideas and practices, diffuse them across movements, help organizations respond to changes in the world, sharpen collective goals and strategies, increase members' stake in the organization, build stronger social ties among members, and embody the democratization that some movements seek in the wider political system. In contrast, some argue that associations that are more internally deliberative may also have weaker public voices because it is harder for them to issue clear, consistent, and forceful political messages. See, e.g., Levine and Nierras, 2007; Warren 2001, Chapter 5.

associations of the weak can act as schools of democracy, developing many of the same civic capacities in members that civic forums aim to enhance, such as building political knowledge, skills, efficacy, trust, and reciprocity.[73] Yet we have noted that, in other important ways, the goals and talk typical of associations and civic forums differ.

If the two institutions have separate purposes, why not pursue equality by developing the voices of the disadvantaged in associational enclaves, while sticking with cross-cutting talk among a microcosm of the citizenry in civic forums? After all, associations and movements of the weak can influence forums in many ways that do not require enclave deliberation within the forum. These advocacy organizations can change the conversation in the larger public sphere that shapes the range of views aired in the forum. Representatives of advocacy organizations are sometimes asked to sit on multi-stakeholder advisory boards that review briefing materials for forums and are invited to testify in public hearings held for participants.

Carolyn Hendriks finds that advocates of weaker interests are often more willing to engage with forums than representatives of stronger interests (especially business and trade associations). Some associations of the marginalized see forums as opportunities to put their issues in the spotlight, inform the public, promote their expertise, and advocate for their positions on more favorable terms than are often presented by lobbying, legal advocacy, elections, and demonstrations. Hendriks suggests that it is most realistic to expect that advocates who participate in forums will remain firmly motivated by the pursuit of their own interests. Thus, their most appropriate contribution is not to deliberate within forums, but to serve as presenters, process advisors, and part of the attentive audiences for participants' conclusions. In these ways, advocates can remain at the edge of the forum, yet add to the diversity of views that informs the unorganized citizens within it. She finds that this role of "strategic deliberator" can have beneficial effects on advocates' openness to deliberate as well. In response to expectations of impartiality created within the forum, some advocates' engagement may induce them to make their arguments in more public-minded terms, and even to reconsider aspects of their own positions.[74] They may present themselves more legitimately as *experts* about a disadvantaged community, rather than making specious identity claims to *represent* or *speak for* that community.[75]

---

[73] Cohen and Rogers 1995; Elstub 2008; Hirst 1994; Warren 2001.
[74] Hendriks 2011, Chapter 10.   [75] Carson 2001.

However, if the communicative power of advocates for the weak is to circulate on equal terms with the claims of more powerful actors, there need to be effective transmitters from outside the forum and working receivers inside it. In some situations, the transmitters shut down, as advocates choose not to cooperate with forums. Hendriks finds that advocates especially refuse to take part in forums that do not seem likely to affect political change in the near term, or that raise issues which are governed by stable and inflexible policy paradigms or are controlled by a closed network of political actors (of which resistant advocates may be a part), or that address a debate that is highly polarized. As she observes, it is often in these situations that deliberation is most needed in a healthy democracy.[76] When advocates for the disempowered avoid the forum, enclaves of the disempowered within it may help these citizens to fill in the missing arguments by discussing their shared perspectives.

Sometimes, the transmitters are weak or non-existent. Advocates for the least powerful may have little knowledge of an emerging issue, like the ones raised in some forums that convene "anticipatory publics" to help steer the development of new technologies.[77] These long-term scientific and technical developments are rarely on the radar of advocacy organizations for racial and ethnic groups. In their absence, others may need to convene enclave forums or disadvantaged communities' voices will be muted. For example, after the US National Institutes of Health conducted a public consultation on genome technology and reproduction that attracted few African-Americans and Latinos, a partnership of academics, churches, and local health care organizations convened enclave forums with more members of these ethnic groups. These forums yielded distinctive policy priorities and recommendations for how genomics research could be designed to benefit rather than discriminate against both ethnic groups, who tend to be less well-served by and trusting of health care institutions.[78]

Sometimes, the transmitters are defective. Not all associations and movements for equality are internally democratic or effective at moving beyond expressing grievances to define goals and strategies to address inequality. While these organizations can still contribute something valuable to democracy, they are not the only option for the disadvantaged, and sometimes may not be the best. If the alternative is joining an organization that is autocratic, dogmatic, hierarchical, distant, or ineffective,

[76] Hendriks 2011, 204–5.   [77] Mackenzie and Warren 2012.
[78] Bonham et al. 2009, 325–59.

it may be more empowering for the marginalized to confer in enclaves within civic forums. This might also provide a better training ground for future collective action. In civic forums with enclaves, people can be drawn into political engagement by learning to deliberate over multiple policy options with others who share a common social position, to choose a common set of priorities with them, and then to test those priorities in discussion with more privileged citizens and officials. Some of these forums have inspired participants to join associations or form new ones.[79] This kind of experience might develop a taste for more empowering forms of activism than obeying charismatic leaders, giving time or money to distant organizations that do not consult their memberships, or settling for spectacular protests against injustice without taking additional focused actions to redress it.[80]

We are not arguing that civic forums should *replace* activism by the disadvantaged, but rather that the two can be mutually beneficial, and that the experience of deliberating over policy solutions in a forum may strengthen participants to demand more deliberative decision making within some organizations of the disempowered. In a larger deliberative system, the example of civic forums with enclaves could compensate for the lack of internal deliberation in some advocacy groups and hold their leaders more accountable to consult their membership. While there is always a possible tension within organizations between deliberation within and united action aimed without, it is possible for advocacy groups to ask their members to talk first and then pursue the strategies and goals that emerge from discussion with strong and effective commitment.[81]

Equalizing capacities for participation
Sometimes the transmitters in associations of the disadvantaged are working but the receivers within the forum are not. As a result, the arguments of organizations of the disempowered may fail to get a fair hearing. Because these organizations usually have limited access to the public sphere and

---

[79] Fagotto and Fung 2006; Kinney 2012; Leighninger 2012.

[80] On social stratification within associations and movements, and limitations to their internal democracy, see Schlozman, Verba, and Brady 2012, chapters 12, 13; Skocpol 2003, Chapters 4 and 5; Warren 2001, Chapter 6. On the benefits of deliberation in more internally democratic movements, see the sources cited in note 73.

[81] Fung (2005) outlines an ethic of "deliberative activism," which focuses mainly on the conditions in which advocacy organizations are more and less obligated to deliberate with opponents. We see the need for a similarly well-developed ethic of internal deliberation, which would specify when leaders of advocacy organizations have a stronger or weaker duty to foster deliberation among their constituents.

political system, their views are likely to be less familiar to citizens who attend forums. Authority, status, numbers, money, and muscle typically weigh more heavily against the ideas promoted by advocates of disempowered groups. Publicly marginalized views may not be included in the range of policy options and arguments provided in briefing materials, hearings, and agendas. This risk is highest in forum designs that predefine a fixed range of choices, such as some Citizens Juries. Even in more open designs, such as Consensus Conferences, participants enter having been exposed to dominant ideas more than marginalized ones in public discourse. Many forums that do not practice random selection of participants try to weed out citizens who appear to be "activists" on the issue and to attract people who are assumed to be more willing to deliberate with open minds.[82] To preserve broad inclusion and the possibility of open deliberation in microcosmic forums, it is legitimate to protect the participant pool from being flooded with members of advocacy groups on one side of an issue. Yet raising the bar against anyone who does not appear to be a "blank slate" poses a serious risk of banishing the perspectives of those who are most affected and in the weakest political or situational position in regard to the issue at hand, based on presumptions about how they will define their interests and their ability to reconsider their views.

In addition, organizers may unnecessarily omit policy options and arguments, intentionally or not. It is *extremely* difficult for even the most experienced and even-handed organizers to anticipate all of the views and policy choices that will be aired in a forum, including ones that will be raised by large numbers of participants. This is the case even for expert practitioners and especially for novices. While it is much easier to critique a forum than to organize a good one, it is critical to consider how limitations on participants and ideas can undercut the forum's ability to receive and deliberate over policy proposals made outside the forum on behalf of the disadvantaged.

Incorporating citizen enclaves at some point in the deliberations can be a valuable way to check and compensate for omissions that can curb full participation in the forum. These omissions can degrade participants' abilities to introduce important topics, attract full attention to them, and influence the group's conclusions. Recall that some participants in the "Our Budget, Our Economy" meetings, discussed in the introduction, challenged organizers at the forum to include national health insurance

---

[82] Hendriks 2011, 50; Irwin 2006: Lee 2011.

as an option for lowering the budget deficit without cutting services. Adopting a single-payer insurance policy was mentioned in passing in the briefing materials, but not included in the list of policy options citizens were asked to consider. The groundswell among some participants to include a national insurance plan as a deficit-cutting strategy was probably influenced from outside by liberal activists, who organized demonstrations at some meeting sites on the day of the forum and mobilized some of their members to participate in the discussions.[83] The organizers quickly expanded the menu of policy options to accommodate these demands. To dismiss this development as tainted by improper intervention of organized interests in the forum would be to miss the contribution to deliberation that came from a less powerful viewpoint being added to discussion by citizens aligned with advocacy groups. This allowed citizens within the forum to correct an important omission.

This check might have been exercised less controversially had the process involved organizing enclave discussions beforehand, or brief enclave discussions during the forum among those who were in the most vulnerable position in relation to the major issues on the agenda, and fed their views into the larger conversation. With regard to health care spending, an enclave of the uninsured, or of recipients of Medicare and Medicaid (the two existing public health insurance programs for senior citizens), might have alerted the forum's organizers that cutting the deficit by adopting national health insurance should have been added to the list of policy options for all to consider. The forum was not only about the deficit, but also about everything that organizers suggested might be cut or taxed in order to reduce the deficit.

We saw the value of enclave deliberation in a different way through our own experience in organizing and evaluating a forum on municipal broadband, discussed more fully in the next chapter. This was an enclave forum that convened only citizens from social groups with least access to high speed Internet service. Participants were asked to deliberate over whether a proposed municipal broadband system in Silicon Valley was a desirable option for addressing the digital divide, and, if so, how the project should be designed to meet the needs of the underserved. The project aimed to inform officials, who were in an early stage of planning such a system, and who were interested in considering how it could extend service to the unconnected. In drawing up the agenda and briefing materials, one of us who co-organized the forum failed to anticipate

---

[83] Hickey 2010; Hoexter 2010.

and address an issue that ended up being among the most important to participants: protecting their privacy and security online. The issue was introduced by a blind participant with dial-up Internet access who told the story of having his identity stolen online. Others chimed in with similar concerns, extending the conversation to fears of lost privacy on the Internet. Because the forum used a Consensus Conference format, citizens could raise this issue without having to resist the organizers' agenda, request additional information about privacy and security, and craft relevant questions for the experts who testified at the public hearing.

Most importantly, because all participants in the forum shared the perspective of groups on the wrong side of the digital divide, these enclave deliberators were able to identify and explore this concern in depth without prompting from the briefing materials or the initial presentation by the organizers. We think it is unlikely that the issue would have risen to the top of the forum's agenda had the participants been dispersed in many small groups with more privileged deliberators who did not share the experience of people without Internet access, anti-virus software, and knowledge of the major security threats to avoid online. In an enclave, participants' conclusions on this issue ended up forming a major, and unexpected, part of the group's recommendations. The personal experiences of all members of the group help them to link issues that the organizers – including a university professor who regularly taught about the digital divide, online privacy, and security – failed to connect beforehand.

Enclaves may also compensate for inequalities of voice among citizens. When politically or deliberatively disempowered people come to a forum, they often enter at a disadvantage. The more the participants reflect the composition of society, the more likely it is that members of some disempowered groups will bring less developed political capacities than other citizens. These differences are based on experience, not inherent differences in ability. It is likely that they stem in part from inequities in civic education. A growing body of research indicates that active and collaborative teaching methods are most successful at developing students' civic knowledge, skills, attitudes, and intent to participate in civic life.[84] These methods include projects involving service learning and civic problem solving, student governance, and participating in simulations, such as mock trial or Model United Nations. Most relevant to

---

[84] Gibson and Levine 2003; Feldman, Pasek, Romer and Jamieson, 2007; Gould 2011; Keeter, Zukin, Andolina, and Jenkins, 2002.

deliberation, these methods also include discussions of current events, as well as an open classroom climate in which students can voice differing perspectives on public controversies. American schools offer fewer of these kinds of opportunities to students who are low-income, African-American, Latino, low-performing academically, or least engaged in civic life.[85]

Inequalities in educational attainment and income appear to be the most powerful influences on how much experience adult Americans have with many kinds of political discussion. Diana Mutz's survey research finds that low-SES adults talk about politics less in their daily lives.[86] Lawrence Jacobs, Fax Lomax Cook, and Michael Delli Carpini's representative survey of Americans finds that less educated people are less likely to engage in many kinds of "discursive participation," including discussions about politics in face-to-face public meetings, informal conversation, Internet discussions, and talk aimed at influencing others' political opinions or votes.[87] Low-income people, women, African-Americans, Latinos, and the young also take part in some of these kinds of political talk less frequently. In particular, each of these groups except youth is less likely to try to persuade others about a political issue, which is the stuff of civic forums. However, many of these inequalities are mitigated by differences in social capital (such as belonging to an organization, religious attendance, and length of residence) and political capital (efficacy, trust, knowledge, partisan and ideological strength, and tolerance). The fact that some forums recruit a portion of their participants through organizations, and that these participants tend to be among the politically and deliberatively disadvantaged, may help decrease inequalities of political voice within the forum. But not all forums turn to organizations to help attract participants, and those that do tend to recruit fairly small percentages of citizens in this way.

John Dryzek is right to remind us that "we should also be wary of the implicit condescension involved in claiming that materially disadvantaged people are necessarily the poorest communicators."[88] On the contrary, members of marginalized groups and communities often express

---

[85] CIRCLE 2010; Kahne and Middaugh 2008; Kahne and Sporte 2008; Torney-Purta and Wilkenfeld 2009.

[86] Mutz 2006, Chapter 5

[87] Jacobs, Cook, and Delli Carpini 2009, 24–6, 35–6. While the authors present this work as a study of deliberation, it includes many forms of public talk that may or may not be deliberative. Therefore, we treat it as a picture of Americans' experience of political discourse, broadly defined.

[88] Dryzek 2000, 172.

extraordinary resilience, creativity, and understanding of their situation. Sometimes, they succeed in piercing stereotypes voiced by other partici- pants in forums.[89] But within forums, there can be a great burden on one or two people in a discussion group to gain a hearing for non-mainstream ideas, which depends in part on their individual status and deliberative skills. Face-to-face communication closely associates an argument with a particular speaker. In her observational study of New England town meetings, Mansbridge notes that "points of information reach the floor of town meeting dressed in the personality of particular human beings."[90] She finds that speaking up in a public meeting can be especially anxiety- producing for low-status individuals or those who are less practiced in political persuasion, because of fears of being mocked by officials or higher-status citizens. Many lower-status individuals who attend Town Meetings refrain from speaking, unless they are deeply moved, often by anger, which can confirm stereotypes of the less powerful as wild and emotional. Therefore, groups of lower-status citizens often caucus the night before a meeting to rehearse the major points of their argument, gather their courage, and appoint one of the group to speak on their behalf.

More extensive opportunities for enclaves in forums could help such people to explore non-mainstream ideas in discussion and prepare indi- viduals to present them more confidently and skillfully to a larger and more diverse group of citizens. None of this guarantees that the marginal- ized will persuade others in deliberation, nor should it, but it helps level the field of deliberation for those who are politically or deliberatively disadvantaged.

Measuring equality and equity in deliberation
Experimental and observational research on small group discussion often raises concerns about equal participation and influence in deliberation among heterogeneous groups. However, many civic forums have taken steps to try to remedy the problems uncovered in the lab. It is important to

[89] For example, newspaper columnist David Boldt (1999, 101), who observed one of the first Deliberative Polls, wrote that "almost everyone had a story about a diatribe against welfare mothers suddenly modulating when a [participant] would disclose that she was a welfare mother." Anecdotes such as this are encouraging. But they do not substitute for a more systematic understanding of the effects of the presence of the disadvantaged. For example, we do not know whether participants changed their policy positions on welfare as a result of these interactions or simply practiced more civil discourse about it in the forum.

[90] Mansbridge 1983, 63.

consider what experimental studies can tell us about deliberative inequalities in the absence of the kinds of interventions used in civic forums. We focus on experimental work on gender differences in deliberation because it offers some of the most rigorous research and because it touches on a kind of deliberative disempowerment that may affect half of humanity. Clearly, we also need to look at the nascent research on equal talk within forums. This evidence suggests that some cross-cutting forums can create conditions for disempowered citizens to speak on more equal terms than they do outside the forum, some forums can improve in this regard, and research can measure equality of participation and influence better than it sometimes has in the past. The picture that emerges from this early stage of research indicates that forums without enclaves do not inevitably condemn the disempowered to be silenced or ignored, but leaves enough unsettling questions that we cannot declare the problem of inequality solved.

An extensive body of research on gender and groups – summarized by Christopher Karpowitz and Tali Mendelberg – finds evidence of a gap between the participation and influence of men compared to that of women, a gap that tends to grow when the gender composition of the group favors men.[91] The literature suggests three factors may contribute to these disparities. First, when women are a numerical minority they have lower status in the group, which discourages their authority. Second, status differences between the genders are especially large in discussions of politics, which is still seen as more of a masculine than a feminine arena. Third, when males outnumber females, the group is more likely to adopt a stereotypically masculine style of communication, emphasizing assertiveness and competitiveness, which can stifle women's participation. In contrast, when women deliberate in all-female groups, they are more likely than women in mixed groups to initiate discussion and to be addressed by others.

Mindful of these gendered group dynamics, Karpowitz, Mendelberg, and their colleagues have recently conducted some of the first systematic studies of gender in experimental groups that deliberate over politics. Unlike prior work, this research examines the interaction of gender composition within groups and the rule they use to arrive at decisions. In their study, 94 groups of five members apiece deliberated over a question of distributional justice – how money that group members were about to earn during the experiment should be allocated among themselves and

---

[91] Karpowitz and Mendelberg 2014; see also Karpowitz, Mendelberg, and Shaker 2012.

in society. Before deliberating, participants were informed about several principles of distribution, including no redistribution (each keeps what he or she earns), protecting each person against falling below a poverty level, and equal redistribution (each member gets the same amount, independent of their work performance). Group discussions, which lasted 25 minutes on average, touched on issues such as "the nature of equality, the needs of the poor, the importance of incentivizing work, the possibility of economic mobility, the fairness of various systems of taxation, and the value of charity."[92] This research design lends the study greater external validity to how people discuss distribution in politics than some other experimental studies, which sometimes have only minimal group discussion or group discussion that is only tangentially related to larger social and political issues.[93]

The researchers assigned each individual at random to discussion groups characterized by one of six gender compositions (ranging from 0 to 5 women) and that used one of two decision rules (unanimity or majority rule). After the group discussion, participants were asked privately who they thought was the most influential member of their group during deliberation. Participants then performed work tasks, such as correcting as many spelling errors as possible within a limited time. They earned money based on their performance, which was allocated according to the distribution principle the group chose during its deliberation. The research controlled for several other factors that might explain differences in participation and influence, including prior attitudes toward egalitarianism, race and ethnicity, and individuals' level of agreement with the group decision.

The study found that in groups deciding by majority rule, the average woman participated much less than the average man in mixed-gender groups with few women. This gender gap in speaking time was strongly correlated with perceived influence: those who spoke more were also seen as more influential by the other members of the group. The decision rule also mattered: in groups deciding by unanimity, the gender gap in participation and influence was much smaller (though men still tended to talk somewhat more than women). These group-level factors thus mediated the relationship between gender and influence. The authors demonstrate similar effects of gender composition and decision rule on

---

[92] Karpowitz, Mendelberg, and Shaker 2012, 537.

[93] For an overview of experimental studies of deliberation, see Karpowitz and Mendelberg 2011.

the issue agenda and the policies the group endorses as well as on the internal dynamics of the group, such as the ways in which men and women interrupt each other.[94] Women were more likely to advocate for a more generous safety net for the least well off, and to speak up about the issues of distinctive concern to them – the issues women are more likely than men to mention in public opinion surveys, including a commitment to the welfare of children, families, and the poor; and they were better able to influence the group by raising those issues when they were empowered by the combination of decision rule and gender composition. Similarly, men's issue agenda also showed signs of shifting toward women's as the number of women in the group increased. Men's interrupting behavior also changed, with men more likely to express positive support for women's statements, when women were empowered.

Karpowitz and Mendelberg thus show that attending carefully to who is in the room and the rules by which the group is asked to make decisions can have a significant effect on the group's dynamics and its decisions. Especially relevant to our concern for enclaves, these researchers also show that women benefit in several ways when they deliberate amongst themselves, in groups comprised entirely of women. In such groups, regardless of decision rule, group talk times increased, women raised issues of distinctive concern to them often, they were less sensitive to critical or negative comments from others, they generated a group norm that was especially warm and inviting, they articulated a preference for more generous support to the poor, and the group made decisions that were in line with those more generous preferences.[95] Put differently, women were able to more fully articulate their perspectives and to generate outcomes that better matched their preferences when they gathered in enclave groups.

These findings hold several implications for civic forums, in which deliberation is typically designed to occur in mixed-gender groups. One is that if forums take no steps to correct for the deliberative disempowerment of women in mixed groups, women are likely to continue to be less frequent and influential contributors. Another is that groups that do not use unanimity or that lack female majorities are likely to arrive at

---

[94] Mendelberg, Karpowitz, and Goedert 2014; Mendelberg, Karpowitz, and Oliphant 2014.

[95] Karpowitz and Mendelberg 2014. Karpowitz and Mendelberg also find confirmation of the results on length of group discussions in a sample of school boards from around the country. Boards composed entirely of women tend to have longer meetings than mixed-gender boards or those composed entirely of men.

conclusions that are less favorable to equalizing distribution outside the forum. Yet forums can mitigate this inequality by changing group composition and decision rules.

As the authors suggest, there are multiple principles that could promote gender equality in forums, which can be tailored to the forum's contribution to the larger political context:

> When women are outnumbered by men, use unanimous rule; when women are a large majority, decide by majority rule. To avoid the maximum inequality, avoid groups with few women and majority rule. To minimize male advantage, assemble groups with a supermajority of women and use majority rule. To maximize women's individual participation, gender homogeneous groups are best.[96]

In some forums it is not practical to decide by unanimity because people cannot agree on all recommendations or decisions, or because the forum aims to offer a representation of public opinion rather than a decision. In these cases, creating female supermajorities or enclaves of women within groups are two ways to equalize women's and men's voices and consideration of their policy preferences. Enclaves may be most appropriate when we should especially want to know what women think about politics, either because they are most affected by an issue, or have been consulted least about it outside the forum, or because we want them to generate new solutions to problems that might be especially attractive to women. These enclaves might help women to inform larger mixed-gender forums more forcefully and influentially than if women's presence is diluted across many small groups.

How comparable are the findings of gender inequality in the groups research to the conclusions drawn in studies of civic forums themselves? Some potentially important conditions can be different in forums, especially the presence of moderators who are trained to foster equal and inclusive discussion.[97] Studies of equal participation and influence in forums that convene heterogeneous groups of citizens offer some encouraging evidence, but the number of studies is small and some of the results are mixed. Moreover, many of them do not attend to the group-level factors that Karpowitz and Mendelberg argue are key. Some of these

---

[96] Karpowitz, Mendelberg, and Shaker 2012, 545.
[97] Experimental researchers have good reasons to exclude moderators because differences in their facilitation styles and ascriptive characteristics (such as gender) would introduce extraneous variables that might influence the results.

studies indicate that forums can succeed at diminishing these patterns of inequality, even without enclaves of the disadvantaged.

Some studies employ indirect measures of equal participation and influence. One method is to ask participants whether they thought the facilitator or the forum created opportunities for each person or viewpoint to be heard on even terms. Laura Black's review of the literature on this point finds that most facilitators and forums score well on these measures, while some forums are criticized for exerting too much control over the framing of issues, and some facilitators are faulted for excluding some participants' views or dominating the conversation.[98] Another indirect measure asks participants to rate their own contributions to the forum. Using this method, Maija Setälä and her colleagues found that men and the more highly educated rated themselves as more active contributors to discussions in a mini-public about the future of nuclear power in Finland.[99]

A handful of studies provide direct evidence of participation. For example, David Dutwin's research on civic forums held to identify policy priorities for the next mayor during the 1999 Philadelphia mayoral race found no significant differences by race or gender in three measures of equality of participation in deliberation – the amount one spoke, the number of topics one raised, and the number of arguments one introduced.[100] Nor did higher levels of political sophistication (combining political knowledge, education, and interest) predict participation in deliberation. However, while the study controlled for the number of participants in the deliberating group, it did not control for other group-level factors, including the number of men or women, the number of political sophisticates, or other measures that might have affected patterns of participation within the group.

Other evidence presents a more complex picture. In a study of five Deliberative Polls conducted by Alice Siu, higher-income speakers participated more (as measured by number of words spoken), participation by race and education were mixed, and there were no differences among males and females (though Siu did not specifically control for the gender balance or other group-level factors within each small group, and these might have an important effect on patterns of participation within the group).[101] Siu did, however, measure shifts within groups toward or away from the initial issue positions held by more privileged participants,

[98] Black 2012.   [99] Setälä, Grönlund, and Herne 2010.
[100] Dutwin 2003.   [101] Siu 2008.

which is an especially useful indicator of influence. It is encouraging that in each case she found no significant pattern of movement toward the initial preferences of whites, males, the wealthier, or the more educated. Groups shifted toward the preferences of each of these advantaged citizens about half the time. James Fishkin finds similar results in his study of a Deliberative Poll on infrastructure development priorities in the Chinese city of Zeguo, in which deliberators moved away from the initial positions of the more educated on half of the issues discussed and away from the economically advantaged on four-fifths of the issues.[102]

These studies are encouraging but limited in scope. Most of this research comes from a single forum design, the Deliberative Poll, which does not ask participants to come to a group decision, which may make it more imperative for citizens to persuade others or to reach agreement within the time allotted by the forum. Most of the analysis examines individual-level participation or opinion change but does not account for the demographic characteristics of groups. This work also suggests that researchers can assess equality of participation and influence better by using multiple measures, direct and indirect, which would strengthen the case that opinion shifts are based on mutual reasoning rather than status, and that people take part and affect each other's views equally *because* of good conditions in the forum rather than *despite* bad issue framing or facilitation. Data on participants' impressions of participation and decision making would be more convincing if it were disaggregated to show whether less privileged participants feel similarly to more advantaged citizens. Finally, while data on the movement toward or away from the initial views of the advantaged are perhaps the most powerful evidence of equal influence, these data alone cannot tell us whether the initial framing of the issues allowed less powerful participants to express authentic views or accommodationist ones, in which the weak adjust their aspirations to the limits of their power, or whether the weak are aware of a broad range of policy options they might pursue. The studies also do not distinguish participation and influence by those who are situationally disempowered by the issues under consideration. For example, infrastructure projects typically create disproportionate disruptions and benefits to residents of different neighborhoods. Pointing out these limitations is much easier than addressing them carefully in research, but worth pursuing given their importance.

---

[102] Fishkin 2009, 108. Because the study did not ask about income levels directly, participants identified as "entrepreneurs" were considered the economically advantaged.

Avoiding groupthink and group polarization

So far, we have shown that experimental research has uncovered persistent inequalities with respect to characteristics like gender, but that such inequalities can be offset, at least to some extent, with careful attention to features of the group and conditions of deliberation. In the case of gender inequality, enclaves appear to have some signal advantages for women. But what are the dangers of enclaves? Some research on group communication and psychology suggests that there are reasons to be cautious: enclaves can limit both the equality of deliberators' voices and the diversity of views that are seriously considered within the group. At its worst, enclave deliberation may breed groupthink, in which maintaining the unity of the group comes to outweigh all other aims. Such groups tend to make poor decisions because members rely on incomplete or biased information and fail to weigh alternatives fully. The classic signs of groupthink include overestimating the group's power and moral justness, sharing an illusion of unanimous opinion among members (often based on self-censorship and quashing dissent), and ignoring evidence that contradicts the group's views.[103]

However, a large body of research on groups suggests that enclave deliberation is not doomed to result in groupthink, but that deliberative outcomes can be shaped by multiple contextual factors. Reviews of the literature surprisingly find little or no clear support for the claim that preexisting group cohesion breeds groupthink.[104] In part, this may be because the original statements of groupthink theory did not offer a clear definition of cohesion and so the concept has been measured in multiple ways. For example, at least one study has found that groupthink is not cultivated by a shared focus on a single task, but by shared socioemotional ties;[105] not by ties of friendship, but by group identification and social attraction (and, even here, there are some exceptions);[106] and is not affected by the strength of the group's shared goals before deliberation.[107] Acknowledging the intuitive appeal of groupthink theory, and the weight of the empirical evidence against it, Robert Baron has pronounced it a theory that is "so right, it's wrong."[108]

Consider a recent study that illustrates the potential diversity of enclaves that share common perspectives and values, and their ability to

---

[103] Janis 1972; Janis 1982.
[104] See Baron 2005; Rose 2011; and the essays collected in Turner and Pratkanis 1998.
[105] Bernthal and Insko 1993.   [106] Hogg and Hains 1998.
[107] Tetlock et al. 1992.   [108] Baron 2005, 219.

deliberate over politics among themselves. Many scholars of deliberation see churches as especially poor contexts for developing deliberative skills because it is assumed that church members are homogeneous in their views and share a strong sense of common identity as co-religionists, which is reinforced by the authority of the clergy.[109] However, a particularly rigorous study employing surveys and participant-observation of adult education meetings in almost 100 Catholic and Protestant churches in the United States finds fairly strong conditions for deliberation, including in some evangelical churches.[110] In these meetings, the topics of discussion were framed as political issues rather than exclusively theological matters. Most clergy tended to act as discussion moderators rather than as opinion leaders. The researchers and most participants reported encountering diverse viewpoints on politics, as well as exercising freedom to disagree with other church members and with clergy. These findings contrast strongly with research on informal conversation in the context of social networks, which finds that political discussion partners met through churches are significantly less likely to have different views than partners found through most other voluntary associations.[111] But informal dyadic conversation is a very different context than a structured group discussion in which deliberative norms are set, as appears to be the case in many church-based adult education classes. If informal social networks of American co-religionists do not appear to be promising sites for discussion of a plurality of views, group education meetings in many churches seem to foster deliberation among participants who share a common religion yet can discuss diverse political preferences.

Experimental research in social psychology sometimes finds that homogeneous groups are also more vulnerable to group polarization, in which "members of a deliberating group predictably move toward a more extreme point in the direction indicated by the members' predeliberation tendencies."[112] For example, the theory would predict that in a group in which the majority favors restricting women's ability to obtain late-term abortions before deliberating, more members will end up supporting this majority view after deliberation, and those who supported it initially will be more convinced of their initial preferences. In addition, when group members think of themselves as sharing a common identity, they

---

[109] Sunstein 2002; Scheufele, Nisbet, and Brossard 2003.
[110] Neiheisel, Djupe, and Sokhey 2009.   [111] Mutz 2006, 37.
[112] Sunstein 2000, 74; Brown 1986, 200–48.

may be more likely to overestimate the homogeneity of opinion within their in-group and the differences between their opinions and those of out-groups.[113]

Two group dynamics especially foster polarization. A group can fail to change or moderate its initial views because of social comparison, as members fear loss of reputation by being in the minority,[114] or because the majority can supply more arguments for their position and thereby strengthen their confidence in their views, win over the undecided, and silence opponents.[115] In either case, group members do not decide based on the strongest arguments, a criterion that is at the heart of deliberative democracy. Some democratic theorists, most notably Cass Sunstein, therefore warn that greater homogeneity, including among groups of the disempowered, could intensify members' alienation from government and citizens outside the group.[116] Such groups may feel that they have little power to influence politics or may pursue extremist positions.

However, as Sunstein notes, even if group polarization occurs, this is not an inherently undesirable outcome. At any given place or time, a laudable position that is perceived as "extreme" by the majority – such as calling for the abolition of slavery in the United States in the early 1800s – may be more just than a "moderate" stance on the issue. Thus, to reject all instances of polarization within disempowered groups would be to adopt a conservative bias against innovative views or a centrist bias against "extreme" positions. In at least some instances, polarization among disempowered groups may be a sign of deliberative breakthrough, not deliberative dysfunction.

Similarly, legitimate deliberation in civic forums does not have to end in *any* movement away from participants' pre-discussion attitudes. The quality of deliberation depends not on how many people change their opinions or in what direction, but on why they hold their positions after deliberation and whether those positions are reasonable. If participants seriously consider a broad range of reasons and conclusions, if they are well-informed by evidence, and if participants deliberate as equals, then it can be as legitimate for their discussion to reinforce or strengthen their preexisting positions as to change those positions. From the standpoint of deliberative theory, the question is not whether groups move further in a direction to which they were previously inclined, but whether they

---

[113] Hogg, Turner, and Davidson 1990; Haslam et al. 1999.
[114] Moscovici and Zavalloni 1969.   [115] Burnstein, Vinokur, and Trope 1973.
[116] Sunstein 2000.

do so for bad reasons, including fear of the social judgments of their members or a failure to consider opposing views, or whether they shift for good reasons, such as achieving a well-informed and duly considered "moral clarity."[117] Therefore, we should only be concerned about *coercive* polarization, which arises from social pressure and limited argument pools.

While findings of polarization are more robust across the literature on groups than findings of groupthink, polarization is a tendency in enclaves, not an iron law. Groups seem to be most likely to polarize if they meet all three of the following conditions: they see themselves as sharing an identity that is made salient to them during deliberation (such as party affiliation, race, gender, or profession), they meet regularly over time, and they insulate themselves from competing views.[118] However, the critical factor is that members of the group share predeliberation preferences about a decision.[119] These conditions are so different from what happens in cross-cutting civic forums that it is not surprising to discover that several studies find that group polarization is not a threat.[120]

These conditions also differ from the kind of enclave deliberation we are proposing. We have argued that well-structured enclave deliberation of the disempowered should put people in groups based on their *perspectives* – their common structural locations in society – not their pre-deliberation *preferences* on the issue at hand. We have suggested that these enclave discussions should be one step in a larger public discussion that includes cross-cutting talk among participants from different social groups, experts, or elected officials. In a deliberative system, that kind of talk can happen within the same civic forum (in which participants meet in enclaves and in more diverse groups), between multiple civic forums (some held among enclaves and others among broader groups), or between enclave forums and political representatives whose role is to represent the interests of the larger public. Thus, while it is possible that enclaves of perspectives will prime participants to embrace a common identity, we are not suggesting that forums that incorporate enclaves should demand that participants feel a shared identity, or hold similar

---

[117] Goodin 2009.
[118] Abrams et al. 1990; Mercier and Landemore 2012; Spears, Lea, and Lee 1990; Turner et al., 1987.
[119] Baron 2005; Mercier and Landemore 2012.
[120] Farrar et al. 2009; Fishkin 2009, 131–3; Luskin, Fishkin, and Jowell 2002; Siu 2008. Admittedly, these are all studies of Deliberative Polls, in which groups do not have to come to a collective decision, which create more social pressure to arrive at agreement.

policy views, or that they should meet alone for long stretches of time in isolation from other citizens and officials.

Like all discussions in civic forums, enclave discussions should encourage participants to explore both their commonalities and their differences. Exposure to balanced arguments and information about an issue can dampen polarization for the wrong reasons as individuals moderate their views in response to diverse viewpoints.[121] Unreflective polarization – stemming from social pressure and inadequate exposure to diverse arguments – may be avoided by encouraging enclave participants to consider how their interests, values, beliefs, and preferences are both similar to and different from other members of the group. Much can depend on how issues are framed. For example, a deliberative enclave of immigrants – some of whom are legalized citizens and some who are not – might be asked to define immigration criteria on which it may be easier for them to agree (e.g., reuniting members of immediate families) and harder to agree (e.g., appropriate levels of immigration from different countries and the optimal size of the US population). As in microcosmic forums, thoughtful, attentive facilitators – while not a panacea for every inequality – can referee the conversation when necessary to help ensure that a few voices, views, or ways of speaking do not dominate. If people are unwilling to contend with opposing arguments, moderators can take the same steps they take in other forums, for example, by asking participants to list the strongest arguments that are raised by people who think differently. Polarization may be less likely if the group is confronted with an issue that is just emerging into public discourse and therefore is not easily incorporated into group members' existing political schemas (such as whether to invest in new technologies for tracking immigration applications).[122]

A study conducted by Kimmo Grönlund and his colleagues tests directly whether enclaves within a typical mini-public forum can overcome group polarization.[123] This study of a deliberation on the controversial topic of immigration policy in Finland divided participants into multiple enclaves of pro-immigration, anti-immigration, and mixed groups. Note that this study formed enclaves of preexisting political

---

[121] Myers and Bach 1974; Vinokur and Burnstein 1978.

[122] Research in cognitive and political psychology indicates that direct experience and oft-repeated mass media messages are the main influences on shaping individuals' political schemas (Graber 1989). People typically have a lack of both kinds of information on complex emerging policy issues.

[123] Grönlund, Herne, and Setälä 2013.

preferences, a much more likely condition for breeding group polarization than the more loosely connected enclaves of shared *perspectives* based on common structural locations that we have suggested. The event involved the typical elements of a mini-public, including exposure to information and competing arguments in a plenary session, facilitated small group breakout discussions, and a final survey of individual views on the issue. On average, all participants moved toward greater support for immigration during the forum, including the mixed groups, and both sets of enclave groups. While the pro-immigration group polarized very slightly by becoming more friendly to immigration, the anti-immigration enclave dramatically depolarized by shifting toward greater acceptance of immigration. These changes were confirmed by a follow-up survey a month after the forum, by which time 40 percent of all participants had switched from their initial positions against immigration to support a more permissive immigration policy and none had switched to the anti-immigration stance. Almost identical numbers of people who had deliberated in the anti-immigration groups (16 out of 42) and mixed groups (18 out of 44) switched their positions. In comparison, in a control group whose members did not participate in the forum, both anti-immigration and pro-immigration citizens shifted toward the middle on the issue.

These results suggest that the forum had a dramatic effect on attitudes toward immigration among participants as a whole and that the effects of participating in the forum overcame the threat of polarization within the anti-immigration enclaves. The slightly polarized shift in the pro-immigrant enclaves might raise greater concerns that the change was a product of social coercion or inadequate scope of arguments if participants as a whole had not also moved in the same direction. This evidence that enclaves based on preferences can change their minds in deliberation suggests that it is certainly as likely, and probably more so, that enclaves of perspectives can deliberate without polarizing for bad reasons.

More generally, the literature on groups shows that careful attention to broader features of the forum, such as its decision rule, can reduce the probability of unhealthy polarization. As Tali Mendelberg writes in her review of the empirical literature on small-group deliberation, evidence shows that in groups of friends, women, or social equals, requiring unanimity rather than majority rule can spark "deliberation that makes people more open-minded and willing to listen to minority views, resolving conflict properly and leaving deliberators feeling that everyone received a fair hearing."[124] Such participation can significantly alter the content of the deliberation, as new ideas, perspectives, and values are introduced into the discussion. Though such outcomes are not always to be found, they may be especially likely in groups that develop a strong sense of community with shared interests and norms.[125] This evidence contradicts the polarization research, which tends to find that groups that see themselves as having a shared identity, opinion, or interest are more likely to limit the argument pool and exert social pressure on members to conform to group preferences.

Public reasoning

We have argued that incorporating deliberation of the disempowered within broader civic forums or policy-making processes can help to ensure that the breadth of voices and views in the wider public sphere can be heard in the forum. In turn, forums with enclaves can contribute to broadening the range of views in the public sphere and government. This is a contribution to public reasoning. As Sunstein observes of enclaves in association and movements,

> A certain measure of isolation will, in some cases, be crucial to the development of ideas and approaches that would not otherwise emerge and that deserve a social hearing. Members of low-status groups are often quiet within heterogeneous bodies, and deliberation in such bodies tends to be dominated by high-status members. Any shift... that increases the number of deliberating enclaves will likewise increase the diversity of society's aggregate 'argument pool.'[126]

Enclave deliberation in civil society can thus serve the larger cause of a fully inclusive public discourse by giving marginalized groups an opportunity to develop their own unique arguments and preferences. Mansbridge writes that citizens need a variety of deliberative arenas in civil society, which allow the weak to develop their political views and voices as they "oscillate between protected enclaves, in which they can explore their

---

[124] Mendelberg 2002, 179. See also Karpowitz and Mendelberg 2007; Karpowitz and Mendelberg 2014. Similarly, Setälä, Grönlund, and Herne (2010) find little or no evidence of polarization in multiple groups that deliberated over energy policy and issued consensus policy statements in a Finnish mini-public.

[125] Karpowitz and Mendelberg 2008.   [126] Sunstein 2000, 105.

ideas in an environment of mutual encouragement, and more hostile but also broader surroundings in which they can test those ideas against the reigning reality."[127]

Public-mindedness

Of course, there is also a danger that creating enclaves within the forum will breed sectarian thinking and selfish bargaining with those outside the group. Even disempowered people ought to take others' basic interests into account, even if it is only for the sake of persuading them expediently. In Chapter 1, we argued that forums should not ask disadvantaged participants to put aside their own interests, which are important contributions to public understanding of the effects of policies on the social whole. At the same time, in the ideal, all citizens would justify their interests in terms that link participants' sense of what is best for them to ideas of what is true, fair, or good for others who are affected by the issue. Enclaves can contribute to an enlarged pool of definitions of the common good. When what is best for all, or universally true, or natural and inevitable, has been defined ideologically in ways that serve the powerful, civil society enclaves have often swept away many of the little clods of hegemonic common sense that once defined the common good – that slaves need the protection of their masters, a woman's place is in the home, we should support the troops by supporting the war, and so on. Within the forum, enclaves might help challenge and supplement partial definitions of the common good with new ones.

Not all of these definitions will be good ones, just as many of the definitions of the common good by the powerful are not worth embracing. Thus, enclaves also need to test their views in deliberation with others. Compared with activist enclaves, the process of discovering self and group interest in enclave forums is different. Forums tend to recruit the unorganized more than the organized. In forums, participants are less familiar with one another than they are in organizations, are not initially united by commitment to a particular cause, interact for briefer periods, and are expected to abide by discussion rules established by forum organizers. Most important, the goal of many forums is to represent or make decisions on behalf of a social whole, rather than a part. These differences suggest that we should expect enclaves in forums to be less prone to intensely sectarian thinking.

---

[127] Mansbridge 1996, 57.

In addition, there are several reasons why it may be easier for people to *reconsider* their views in peer groups than in more diverse settings. In mixed civic groups, pressure to build communal ties rather than to exchange and resolve conflicting views – to observe what Nina Eliasoph has called a sometimes debilitating "civic etiquette" – can steer people away from political talk entirely.[128] Alternatively, when more heterogeneous groups are able to talk politics, it may be more salient for minority tokens who feel threatened by the majority, or burdened with representing their social group before others, to defend their interests and opinions against the majority or fall silent than to seek agreement with them. In contrast, discussions of differences among perceived peers may help to counteract the "false consensus effect," which leads individuals to overestimate their peers' agreement on a particular preference.[129] This misperception can lead individuals to swallow their reservations and continue espousing positions mistakenly attributed to their group, creating a cycle of group adherence to these positions. Enclave deliberation among members of the group might correct such misimpressions and subject them to questioning in ways that Dan Kahan and his colleagues summarize well:

> If participants come to see either that a particular belief is less dominant among their cultural peers than they had imagined or that cultural peers who deviate from the dominant belief are not censured as severely as they had anticipated, participants are likely to revise their view about the social cost – or more accurately the social meaning – of changing their mind.[130]

It is often deliberation within enclaves that can be most effective at helping individuals to rethink their positions as they discover that "people like me" can and do think differently about politics. Experimental research on the power of social group cuing finds that even participants who employ systematic reasoning are still more likely to accept arguments presented to them by a source with whom they share a perceived group allegiance. For example, experimental participants have been found to be more favorably disposed to a policy position if they think it is proposed by their own political party than by an opposing party, even when the proposed policy was the same.[131] In well-facilitated enclaves, people should be able to hear multiple arguments from people with whom they share a perspective,

---

[128] Eliasoph 1998, Chapter 9.
[129] On the false consensus effect, see Quattrone and Jones 1980. Our arguments in the remainder of this paragraph are indebted to Kahan et al. 2006, 1102–3.
[130] Kahan et al. 2006, 1102 (citation omitted).   [131] See Cohen 2003, 808–22.

rather than uniform group cues about how "people like us" agree on an issue.

Empirical research on civic forums can study the enlargement of citizens' thinking from group interests to common interests more carefully than has been done thus far. Mansbridge's observations of New England town meetings found some decisions were made on the basis of common interests, understood in three different ways: as overlapping private interests, as empathy, or as attachment to the common good of the town.[132] However, attempts to measure this kind of thinking in deliberative opinion research have been less successful because they measure citizens' motives indirectly and at a great remove. For example, Fishkin argues that opinion shifts in some Deliberative Polls indicate a movement toward motivations to serve the public good rather than private interests when citizens become more supportive of funding infrastructure projects that benefit a wider community, such as renewable energy, or revenue sharing by towns to support regional development.[133]

Fishkin may be right, but his surveys do not measure directly people's motives for their opinion changes; it may be that people supported wind farms because they became more informed about how to protect their own health, and may have supported regional investment because it seemed more likely to benefit their town. Elsewhere, Luskin and Fishkin measure shifts toward communal thinking with the survey question "when voting, people should always put the interests of the public as a whole before those of themselves and their family."[134] Unfortunately, this question does not capture the movement toward connecting self-interest to collective interest well because it pits the two against one another, perhaps unnecessarily. In an experimental study, Neblo finds reduced influence of age, gender, race, and ideology on post-deliberation opinions about three issues, which he interprets as evidence of deliberators' expanded perspectives. He also finds that subjects' post-deliberation opinions are less influenced by their political ideology (liberal or conservative), which he attributes to a "shift from a market frame ('what is it that I, as an individual, *prefer*?') to a forum frame ('what is it that we, as a group, *should do*?')."[135] Here, too, Neblo does not directly assess people's motives for shifting their opinions, and the assumption that a weakening effect of ideology indicates a shift from self-interested to collective thinking is especially questionable. It is not clear that people hold liberal or

---

[132] Mansbridge 1983, 72–3.   [133] Fishkin 2009, 142.
[134] Luskin and Fishkin 2002, 9.   [135] Neblo 2010, 4.

conservative viewpoints on politics for self-interested reasons, rather than out of a conviction that prioritizing values such as egalitarianism or liberty is best for society as a whole.

Mutual justification and respect

Should we worry that putting disadvantaged participants in enclaves will make them less open to learning and weighing new arguments for and against their positions? Interestingly, some research suggests that it may be the deliberatively privileged who are both most familiar with the broadest range of arguments on an issue and least open to changing their minds. Joseph Cappella, Vincent Price, and Lilach Nir developed the concept of argument repertoires, which are the range of arguments people know in support of and against their stance on political matters.[136] The authors found that participants in an online deliberation over health care policy who scored highest in argument repertoire were also highly committed to party and ideology. These deliberators were also more likely to be highly educated, older, White, interested in politics, to talk about politics in larger social networks, and to perceive their networks to hold more diverse views. These people were also more interested in joining in deliberative forums and highly participative in them. In other words, they are among the kinds of people that civic forums are most likely to attract if they recruit passively. Now, it may be that partisan people have arrived at their views after engaging in mutual justification by examining arguments from both sides with a diverse crowd, which is good for deliberation. Or it may be that they memorize opposing arguments in order to refute them, which is not so good for deliberation. This is an open question.

Meanwhile, we should not assume that enclave deliberators will be less open to opposing views. In a comparative study of two Consensus Conferences on nanotechnology policy based on interviews with participants, Daniel Lee Kleinman and his colleagues found that one of the conferences recruited citizen deliberators who entered the forum as techno-skeptics (most of whom were suspicious of new technologies and of government's willingness to regulate them in the public interest), while the other conference was peopled by techno-enthusiasts (who were optimistic about new technologies and excited to learn more about nanotechnology). Neither group had specific policy preferences about what was a new and mysterious technology, but each had strong and distinct views. We would call them enclaves of shared values and beliefs, which are more specific ties

---

[136] Cappella, Price, and Nir 2002.

than shared perspectives, which we have suggested as the basis for forming enclaves. Despite their different orientations, the two groups arrived
at similar policy recommendations. The authors conclude that "a well-
facilitated process in which participants have prior perspectives (although
not clear instrumental interests) on the issues at stake might still produce
a fair and reasonable outcome."[137]

Jürg Steiner and Didier Caluwaerts' research in Belgium on divided
communities of Flemish (Dutch-speaking) and Walloons (French-
speaking) asked participants to make policy recommendations on how
the country could accommodate each language group. The participants
met in multiple groups separated by language, and also in several groups
that mixed speakers of each language using translation. The researchers
counted statements in which speakers explicitly recognized the value of
one another's positions. Steiner hypothesized that in the linguistically
homogeneous groups, individuals would feel more social pressure to
express respect for others' positions than in the more divisive mixed-
language group, yet found no differences among the groups in how often
speakers acknowledged the merit of each other's views.[138] These are
hopeful findings in enclaves of shared cultural identity who deliberated
in a linguistically and politically divided society.

Knowledge

We argued in Chapter 1 that citizens' judgments are best informed and
most autonomous when they are supported by knowledge that is in least
dispute among relevant experts *and* among citizens with direct experience
that bears on an issue. In forums, citizens often confront knowledge produced by governments, corporations, advocacy associations, academics,
and others who can have strong commitments to their own interests and
theories. Therefore, deliberators need to inquire into the pedigree of the
knowledge presented to them – its sources, funders, methods, and reception in its field, and how it is viewed among citizen experts who can
compare it with their own experience of the situation.

Citizens need to accrue the benefits of expertise while remaining aware
of the risks posed by interested knowledge that presents itself as neutral
or self-evident. All citizens in forums must rely to some degree on expert
knowledge and are potentially disempowered in relation to it. But the
problem of dependence on expertise is especially acute for the politically
disadvantaged, for several reasons. First, those who are less educated may

[137] Kleinman, Delborne, and Anderson 2011, 235.   [138] Steiner 2012, 150.

be less conversant with complex methods and findings in different fields. More important, they may be less familiar with how to assess ways of producing knowledge, such as whether and when to trust academic peer review, comparative policy analysis, the judgments of charismatic public figures, or the direct experience of citizens. Disempowered citizens should not have to make a false choice between trusting the most impressive expert at the dais or the most eloquent purveyor of homespun wisdom sitting at their elbow. As much as possible, the politically disadvantaged need to be able to sift knowledge for themselves.

In addition, the interests that produce complex knowledge can be least responsive to the economically and politically disempowered because they are considered weak markets for sales, votes, or grant money. As many theorists have noted, the production of knowledge can be class-interested and parochial.[139] In response to those who see truth seeking as at odds with democracy because it subjects expert policy knowledge to popular prejudice and ignorance, Thomas Christiano argues persuasively that, in fact,

> democracy is a necessary condition for the truth sensitivity of the community of experts... it is only when all the different sectors of society have the means of articulating their diverse points of view that social science can generate a process of knowledge production that is sensitive to the conditions of all the different parts of society. Under these conditions social science can generate a competitive struggle of ideas that... is responsive to a lot of different sources of evidence.[140]

These comments on the social sciences apply to the natural sciences and to policy analysis as well. In this view, democratic deliberation can help the weak to demand attention to unexplored issues, evidence, and ways of knowing, helping to check the individual and institutional biases and blind spots of policy analysis and the sciences.

Enclave forums of the disempowered may be among the best possible places for this kind of inquiry to begin. Those who share a weaker position can identify common concerns and questions that they want to answer more effectively than in mixed forums. These citizens can subject political and scientific experts to public questioning from people whom specialists often have little professional incentive to consult, given the institutional

---

[139] Christiano 2012; Fischer 1995; Mackenzie and Warren 2012; Mansbridge et al. 2012; Parkinson 2012a.

[140] Christiano 2012, 49.

conditions in which most experts work. Civic forums can promote less adversarial encounters than in many public hearings, allowing experts to engage more respectfully with citizens, rather than in defensive and technocratic "toxic talk," which understandably elicits angry responses from citizens. Forum organizers have valuable experience in working with specialists to help them translate complex knowledge for lay citizens without distorting what citizens need to know to make better informed decisions. Forums also create valuable arenas for adult learning, in which the disempowered are treated respectfully and given a strong incentive to sift knowledge because this process is immediately applicable to their political choices.

Of course, disempowered people have valuable knowledge of their own to contribute, which may circulate best when the least advantaged speak in their own forums. Our discussion in Chapter 1 illustrated how a regulatory process based on chemical risk assessment put much more trust in risk assessors' abstract calculations, which employed controversial assumptions that often minimized risk estimates, rather than in the situated knowledge of farm workers and community residents exposed to toxic chemicals, which indicated significant harms. This situated knowledge was hard won, gathered over many years through individual stories and then by more systematic "popular epidemiology" studies conducted by community-based organizations, sometimes with help from sympathetic academics.[141]

We think this kind of local or situated knowledge is more likely to resonate within forums of people who experience issues from the same structural or geographic perspective in society than in mixed forums. In enclaves, this kind of knowledge is also likely to elicit more relevant local knowledge on the topic from participants. This is not to try to create conditions within the forum that ensure every claim to local or popular knowledge is accepted on faith. Enclave deliberators should receive and interrogate input from many sources, including each other. We simply think this can be done more extensively in a forum, or in groups within forums, in which people are similarly situated in society. Among government conveners of forums, it may be social service agencies that most frequently commission enclave forums. Their main purpose and value are more managerial, about improving effectiveness within current policy and budget constraints, than democratic, about what policies are

---

[141] Cole and Foster 2001; Corburn 2003; Gibbs 1994.

most just.[142] These forums may be useful, but we are suggesting bringing enclaves together as groups of *citizens* to discuss policy, not only as *clients* to discuss the delivery of services. The experience of being a client can certainly inform policy prescriptions, but only if people are asked to think as citizens too.

What can studies of cross-cutting civic forums tell us about how they develop knowledge? To date, the research in this area has been very narrowly focused. Academic and evaluation studies of forums have tended to ask what citizens learn rather than what they teach officials and experts. There are good reasons to assess citizens' learning because it can help show whether their conclusions are better informed than if they had not participated in the forum. Yet it would also be useful to know more clearly what kinds of knowledge advantaged and disadvantaged citizens introduce and how it is perceived and used by officials, associations, and others in the forum. Most of the existing research tests citizens on whether they gain factual information imparted in briefings about the issue. It is also important to know whether citizens learn more about how knowledge presented in the forum was produced and how to evaluate it. Most of these studies show that participants as a whole accumulate new facts in microcosmic forums.[143] However, very few studies disaggregate the learning gains clearly enough to say whether people who enter the forum with less issue knowledge learn as much additional information as others, or whether politically or deliberatively disempowered people learn as much new information as more privileged participants. Even fewer tell us what we should most want to know about equality: do the disempowered achieve *equitable levels of knowledge* with more powerful deliberators? In other words, do the least informed close the gap with the most informed?[144] That would be the strongest evidence that cross-cutting forums can help the least educated and politically aware participants to form equally well-informed opinions, and, therefore, to make equally autonomous choices.

---

[142] Hendriks 2011, 52; Parkinson 2006a.

[143] For summaries of the literature on knowledge gains, see Collingwood and Reedy 2012; Fishkin 2009; Gastil 2008; Pincock 2012; Steiner 2012.

[144] For example, Jacobs, Cook, and Delli Carpini (2009, 131) report that, compared to a non-deliberating control group, participants in a forum on Social Security all increased their knowledge of the issue, with no significant differences among people of different ages, incomes, or education levels. However, this does not tell us whether each demographic group ended up *equally knowledgeable about the issue* before forming their final opinions on it.

Should we be concerned that citizens in enclaves will learn less than they would in microcosmic forums, where participants' views might be enriched by more diverse citizen perspectives? The Finnish immigration study mentioned earlier provides the only direct test of this claim of which we are aware. Recall that the researchers sorted participants into some groups based on their pre-forum policy preferences, while we are suggesting looser-knit enclaves of shared perspectives. The researchers found no significant differences in information gains about immigration or general political knowledge between enclave groups (for or against immigration) and mixed groups.[145] While that is encouraging, we think the most important questions for research to answer are about whether enclaves of disempowered deliberators can assess situated knowledge that would not be considered as fully in mixed forums, evaluate expert knowledge and its pedigree more extensively from disempowered perspectives, and contribute their own considered local knowledge more fully in enclave settings, thereby enriching a larger deliberative political process.

Agreements for self-rule

Enclaves of the politically, situationally, and deliberatively disempowered might also enhance these citizens' ability to structure conflicts, form more coherent views, and exercise greater autonomy over their decisions and the deliberative procedures in forums. While it may be more difficult to imagine the wider society authorizing recommendations made by enclave forums rather than open or microcosmic ones, some existing examples indicate that it is possible.

We have argued that it can be valuable for deliberation to focus the range of reasons and conclusions that are acceptable to a group, whether the group reaches consensus or concludes deliberation with a rational vote on the remaining alternatives. Within a larger forum or political process, enclaves would help the disempowered to identify which values, beliefs, interests, and policy preferences are most important to them. This is often fodder for deliberation within civil society associations that operate democratically. In forums, this process is less one of arming the disadvantaged for battle with other citizens by adopting a common line of reasoning and demands. Enclave members would still be expected to deliberate with officials and experts within the forum and with other citizens in the larger forum or political process.

---

[145] Grönlund, Herne, and Setälä 2013.

In doing so, the disadvantaged would have a clearer and more authentic sense of their own priorities, including the *range* of arguments and outcomes that these citizens can and cannot accept. When confronting polarizing moral issues, the weakest can benefit from discovering consensus values among themselves that are also shared by others and that could guide policy. When faced with conflicting and interested knowledge, enclaves can identify their shared beliefs, defending all citizens against manipulation by experts. Especially in matters focused on the distribution of power and resources, the disadvantaged could discover whether they have shared interests that need to be prioritized in public deliberation. Enclaves can help widen the scope of available preferences if they are limited by organizers or prevailing political discourse in ways that ignore or diminish the preferences of the disempowered.[146] Thus, enclaves might also help the marginalized to monitor the fairness of deliberative procedures within forums. We have argued that enclaves can allow the disadvantaged to spot and challenge biased issue framings and develop alternatives. We have shown initial evidence from the Silicon Valley case study, to which we will return in Chapter 3, which indicates that enclaves can add important issues to the agenda that organizers have not anticipated and widen the scope of information provided to citizens in briefing materials.

This process should also help individual participants *align* their values, beliefs, perceived interests, and political preferences into more coherent and durable views, which they can express more clearly and effectively to those outside the enclave in subsequent deliberation. Of course, this does not guarantee that their views will be correct or even that they will respect democracy. Hence, disempowered enclaves would still need to subject their views to deliberation under good conditions in a larger forum with the public or their representatives. Research on several mini-publics, especially Deliberative Polls, finds that these cross-cutting deliberations can develop participants' consistency of opinions.[147] Some experimental research in randomly assigned discussion groups suggests that deliberation helps participants withstand elite manipulation of opinions,[148] as do studies of several mini-publics.[149] However, like the research on knowledge gains, these studies do not tell us whether the politically or

---

[146] Our discussion in this paragraph adapts John Dryzek and Simon Niemeyer's (2010, 115) arguments for these benefits of deliberation among all citizens to deliberation in enclaves of the disempowered.

[147] Fishkin and Luskin 2005; Niemeyer, Ayirtman, and Hartz-Karp 2008; List et al. 2013.

[148] Druckman and Nelson 2003.   [149] Niemeyer 2004; Dryzek et al. 2009.

situationally disadvantaged aligned their views as well as other deliberators or resisted elite framings as strongly.

One of the most important reasons that organizers gravitate toward
microcosmic forums is that they can offer a symbolic representation of
an existing territorially defined polity. In contrast, enclave deliberation
can appear partial in both senses of the word – partisan and incomplete.
It is difficult enough for most microcosmic forums to gain authorization of their conclusions in the political process. How could enclaves
possibly achieve this legitimacy? As we observed at the outset of this
chapter, enclaves operate within many existing democratic institutions,
officially or unofficially. In regard to civic forums, the clearest examples of
authorized enclaves are co-governance institutions, such as the Brazilian
Participatory Budget, in which people deliberate in their neighborhoods
before sending representatives to district- and city-level discussions. Gianpaolo Baiocchi, Patrick Heller, and Marcelo Silva conclude that because
the Participatory Budget that is drawn up each year in Porto Alegre is
not legally binding upon city leaders, its authority depends upon "an
instituted – that is, rule-bound – process that is effective only to the
extent it produces a set of demands that enjoy a high degree of public legitimacy." Thus, priorities defined in the relative enclaves of each
neighborhood must survive a "procedurally rational and substantively
deliberative mode of legitimacy-producing reason," both at the district-
and city-wide levels.[150]

While disentangling the policy effects of civic forums from other factors
in the political process is always difficult, under the right conditions co-
governance experiments seem to have gained wide legitimacy and have
contributed to impressive results. At their best, these innovations have
integrated deliberation among local enclaves into a larger political process that yields substantive improvements in public services and good
governance. In particular, Participatory Budgeting in Porto Alegre and
other Brazilian cities has been credited with increasing the transparency of
public spending, reducing corruption and clientilistic dependence on government patronage, redistributing public investment to the most neglected
neighborhoods, and increasing civic engagement, solidarity, and the perceived legitimacy of local government.[151]

Comparative research on the rapid spread of co-governance experiments, and their uneven results, also suggests the conditions that

---

[150] Baiocchi, Heller, and Silva 2011, 165.
[151] Baiocchi 2003; Baiocchi 2005; Baiocchi, Heller, and Silva 2011, 54–5.

appear to enable more homogeneous local deliberations among the most disempowered to contribute to improving governance. In order to engage the least politically active and least privileged residents, governments that initiate the practice must be committed to sharing power with citizens and civil society organizations that participate in the process. Citizens must enjoy a high degree of empowerment over consequential decisions, rather than a merely consultative role. Governments may also need to make an up-front commitment to redistributing resources to the least privileged in order to show that their participation will be worthwhile. A vibrant and autonomous network of voluntary associations is often needed to mobilize popular participation in co-governance and maintain its independence from the state. And transparent evaluation of the effects of civic input on policy making, and of policy making on the lives of citizens, must be possible, so that citizens can see the fruits of their labors.[152]

These conditions are rare. Many of the initial co-governance experiments depended in part on the election of left-leaning governments that needed to mobilize new constituencies to stay in office. Yet the success of some co-governance reforms has generated pressure on subsequent administrations and on others elsewhere to perpetuate and spread these institutions. Hundreds of thousands of citizens in scores of cities around the globe now participate regularly in Participatory Budgeting, which has become one of the most widely used civic forums in the world.[153]

Conclusion

The stigma sometimes attached to enclave deliberation is unnecessary and unwise. It is possible to reap the benefits of enclaves of the disempowered and protect against their dangers if we incorporate them carefully in the wider deliberative system. As Cass Sunstein, the theorist who is often most associated with sounding the alarm against enclaves, writes, "For a designer or leader of any institution, it makes sense to promote ample social space both for enclave deliberation and for discussions involving a broad array of views, including views of those who have been within diverse enclaves."[154] In any civic forum, there are likely to be people who are politically, situationally, or deliberatively disadvantaged. Choosing institutional designs of popular assemblies and co-governance

---

[152] Talpin 2012, 201; Fung and Wright 2003, 24; Baiocchi, Heller, and Silva 2011, 142–65; Sintomer, Herzberg, and Röcke 2008, 175–6.
[153] Wampler and Hartz-Karp 2012, 2.   [154] Sunstein 2000, 113–14.

institutions, and sampling strategies used in mini-publics, that allow these people to confer in enclaves based on their common perspectives could advance equality of inclusion, participation, and influence in deliberation.

Enclaves of the disadvantaged in forums need not undermine the quality of public reasoning. On the contrary, these enclaves can contribute to broadening the range of views in the public sphere and policy process. If facilitated well, enclaves can make it easier for the least powerful to consider their common and divergent interests, helping these deliberators to reconsider their views in a safer setting than if they were tokens in mixed groups. There is good evidence that enclave deliberators can remain open to opposing views. Compared with heterogeneous groups, it is reasonable to think that enclaves of the weak will be in a better position to consider situated knowledge relevant to their place in society, to interrogate expert knowledge, and to impart their own local knowledge. This should improve the quality of deliberation in the larger forum or political system in which enclaves meet.

We think there is good cause to believe that enclaves can help marginalized participants align their own views, structure the dimensions of disagreement and agreement rationally, and win authorization of their conclusions in the larger political system under the right institutional conditions. We are not arguing that these enclaves will have privileged access to truth or justice, or that enclaves should determine the outcomes of deliberation, even by exercising a veto over decisions. We do not presume that forums with enclaves of the disempowered will always choose to redistribute power and resources downward, only that they will make better and more legitimate political decisions in keeping with deliberative theory than forums would otherwise and sometimes do now. In Chapter 3, we offer additional evidence of the benefits of enclave deliberation in a unique case study.

3

Enclave deliberation about the digital divide
with Allen S. Hammond IV

In Chapter 2 we noted that people's opinions are often shaped in part by enclave discussions within a broad range of democratic institutions, from legislative caucuses to voluntary associations to social networks that influence polling responses. We also showed that many civic forums incorporate stages of enclave deliberation before, during, or after cross-cutting discussion among more heterogeneous groups of citizens. We argued that enclaves of the least powerful can advance equality in deliberation and should be less worrisome than they are sometimes seen to be. Many of our examples came from popular assemblies and co-governance forums, in which citizen deliberation has become an authorized and routine input into political decision making. Some of these forums are open to all who want to participate.

In contrast, many mini-publics are advisory and have a less established relationship to political power. These kinds of forums are usually selective about who can participate in order to attract a quasi-representative microcosm of some public, and therefore may seem to depend more heavily on cross-cutting deliberation for their legitimacy. Thus, it is not surprising that there are few examples and systematic studies of enclaves within mini-publics. In this chapter, we begin to fill this gap by presenting a case study of a mini-public that recruited an enclave of people who shared a disempowered perspective on the digital divide. We examine how well the forum met our criteria for equal participation and influence among participants, for public reasoning, and for arriving at democratic agreements that are rationally structured, autonomous, and authorized by the surrounding political system.

The policy context

In response to the slow and uneven extension of commercial high-speed
Internet service in the United States, in the years 2004–2006 hundreds
of municipal governments began considering whether to build their own
broadband networks, triggering a robust policy debate over whether
cities should invest public funds in these networks at all, and, if so,
whether to subsidize access for those least likely to have it.[1] Propo-
nents of municipal broadband systems argued that they would confer
multiple benefits, including enhancing local economic competitiveness,
educational opportunities, government services, and civic engagement.
Supporters also contended that municipal networks would inject competition from new providers into local broadband markets, bringing
down subscription costs. Because municipal networks would offer free
or affordable service and would have a stronger public service mission
than the cable and telephone companies that were the main sources
of high-speed service, the new networks would help close the digital
divide by making broadband more widely available. In contrast, most
commercial broadband providers strongly opposed municipal networks,
arguing that they would be inefficient and pose unfair competition
to existing private providers. At the telecommunications companies'
behest, at least 15 states had passed laws by 2006 prohibiting their
municipalities from building, owning, or operating broadband networks.
However, most municipal projects involved public-private partnerships
in which cities and counties contracted with private companies to build
and operate these networks with government oversight.

In Silicon Valley, where the conference was held, an alliance of over
40 cities had begun to plan one of the largest regional wireless broadband
networks in the country. Some municipal broadband projects, in cities
such as Philadelphia and San Francisco, put a high priority on the goal of
offering affordable broadband to all residents to close the divide between
those with high-speed service and those without it. However, in its initial
stages the Silicon Valley broadband network was driven primarily by
the goals of improving economic competitiveness and the internal communications of government agencies.[2] The project was spearheaded by

---

[1] Hammond IV and Raphael 2006.
[2] Wireless Silicon Valley, the project's organizer, presented the benefits of the network to
the community as consisting of: "support for emergency response teams; save mobile
workers, including police, fire, public works, sales people, and construction workers,
from having to return to the office to file reports or get work orders; attract conventions

Wireless Silicon Valley, a task force led by city and county information technology managers, which also included local electrical utilities, county sheriff departments, and public transportation authorities.

In a context of low public attention to the project, two academic centers based at Santa Clara University – the Broadband Institute of California and the Center for Science, Technology and Society – organized a Consensus Conference in October 2006 on municipal broadband and digital inclusion.[3] They aimed to inform the government task force about whether underserved people would value the network and, if so, about their recommendations for digital inclusion. Like most Consensus Conferences, this one convened a public hearing at which experts testified in response to the citizen panelists' questions, in addition to deliberation among the panelists themselves. The academic organizers convinced the Wireless Silicon Valley task force to lend a willing ear to the project.[4] The task force's director agreed to sit on the conference's advisory board, testified at the public hearing, and participated in follow-up meetings with the organizers to discuss the recommendations. At the outset, the organizers posed several broad questions for the conference participants to address, especially with reference to the planned Silicon Valley network:

1. Should governments become involved in creating municipal broadband networks?
2. If so, how should municipal broadband networks be paid for and operated to maximize public benefits, especially to underserved communities?
3. If so, will digital inclusion require governments to provide additional resources to help underserved communities use broadband to meet their economic, civic, and cultural needs?[5]

by making it easy for visitors to connect; offer an alternative broadband service provider to businesses and residents; create opportunities for local wireless companies to develop new products and services; reinforce Silicon Valley's reputation as a center of innovation" (Joint Venture: Silicon Valley Network 2005).

[3] The Broadband Institute of California seeks "to identify, document, address and publicize the broadband and advanced network technology needs of California and the impact of state and federal policies on California's needs" (Broadband Institute of California 2006). At the time of the conference, the Center for Science, Technology, and Society's mission was to promote "the common good of society by providing an independent forum for public dialogue and interdisciplinary inquiry into the social and cultural dimensions of technological change" (Center for Science, Technology, and Society 2006).

[4] Two of this chapter's authors (Hammond and Raphael) organized the conference, while the third author (Karpowitz) served as the external evaluator.

[5] The term "digital inclusion" emerged in the early 2000s to refer to the closing of the "digital divide," or unequal access to Internet service among different groups. Digital

As these framing questions suggest, the main tensions involved whether the telecommunications industry would continue to oppose municipal broadband projects, or acquiesce to them, and even cooperate by bidding to manage the networks. A second question was about how much governments would commit to the goal of reducing the digital divide, given their other goals for municipal broadband, such as fostering economic development and more efficient emergency and police services.

The conference offered the first substantive effort at public consultation about the Silicon Valley project, in an environment of sparse media coverage of the proposed network and no organized attempts to influence its direction by civil society organizations of the disadvantaged. Although some of the contours of the network had been defined already – including private ownership and management – much was still to be determined, including subscription costs and digital inclusion efforts. Therefore, the community panel had a unique opportunity to influence the project's decision makers, although it was clear that the panel's recommendations were advisory.

Forum design

The project adapted an established format for cross-cutting deliberation – the Consensus Conference – to foster deliberation among a disempowered enclave about their interests. Consensus Conferences aim to promote informed public deliberation among small groups of community members to arrive at policy recommendations by unanimous decision. Developed by the Danish Board of Technology and adopted by government and civil society groups around the world, Consensus Conferences have mainly focused on science and technology policy. In a typical conference, the project's organizers appoint an advisory panel of stakeholders on the topic at hand to oversee the fairness and inclusiveness of the conference. The advisory panel reviews the process of selecting and educating a panel of 12 to 25 community members. Conference organizers provide the community panel with background briefing papers about the issue, some of which may be written from a neutral perspective on the issues,

inclusion refers not only to the extension of Internet service, but also to the computer hardware and software required to access the Internet, training in computer and Internet literacy, provision of relevant content (e.g., in users' own languages), and resources for users to contribute their own content on the Internet. See National Telecommunications and Information Administration 2000.

while others may reflect the views of different stakeholders. The organizers and advisory panel select a group of experts representing a wide range of perspectives on the controversy. A facilitator helps the community panel to identify the questions they want to pose directly to the experts at a public hearing. After the hearing, the facilitator leads the community panel in structured deliberation to produce a consensus statement of policy recommendations. Significantly, the community panel is not restricted to choosing between options provided to them by others on a predetermined agenda of issues, but is free to add their own issues and solutions throughout the process. Their findings are presented publicly to government, the news media, and the public to amplify the panel's voice, attract attention to the issue, and stimulate ongoing deliberation.

However, the traditional Consensus Conference is vulnerable to the same concerns about political, situational, or deliberative inequality that we have reviewed in Chapter 2. The organizers and advisory panel may subtly marginalize some views in their selection of briefing materials, community panelists, and experts. Norms of rationality and consensus may discriminate against community panelists who have less education, deliberative experience, and socio-economic status. Consideration of the common good and the goal of consensus may lead to coercion of those with minority viewpoints. To address these concerns, the conference organizers in this case study departed from standard practice by exclusively recruiting members of disempowered groups to form the community panel. Instead of assembling a community panel reflective of Silicon Valley as a whole, the organizers formed an enclave, each of whom was a member of at least one of the groups that had the lowest rates of home access to commercial broadband in the United States at the time: low-income people, African-Americans, Hispanics, seniors, the disabled, and rural residents.[6] All of these groups were represented on the panel, and many participants fell into more than one of these categories (e.g., African-American and disabled). Thus, the panel formed an enclave in the sense that all shared a structural *position* as belonging to a group that was least served by home broadband Internet service.[7]

---

[6] U.S. Government Accountability Office 2006.

[7] In deliberation, panel members often drew conclusions from their personal frustration with barriers to securing and affording broadband service, and they frequently referred to underserved groups as "we" rather than "they." In the panel's final report, it wrote,

> The community panel worries about potential "disconnects" between the underserved and other stakeholders in broadband networks. Those who plan such networks need to reach out actively to underserved communities and strive to see the digital world

Although the conference brought community panelists in contact with the views of government and industry leaders through background readings and the public hearing, the group's deliberation about its policy recommendations focused on the task of articulating the interests of a group with a shared perspective of situational disempowerment relative to the issue of broadband access. Participants were asked to consider the common good, but not necessarily to weigh everyone's interests equally. The initial questions posed on the agenda did not ask how to come up with recommendations to meld the public interest with the interests of telecommunications companies, which feared competition from municipal networks, or to accommodate the interests of other residents who could easily afford broadband access, and who therefore might not have been as willing to invest tax dollars in providing access to those who could not afford it.

Other elements of the project adhered to the typical Consensus Conference format. The organizers recruited an advisory panel of 11 stakeholders from local governments, civil society organizations working on digital inclusion (but not yet on the Silicon Valley network), and the technology and telecommunications industries. The advisory panel approved plans for recruiting community panelists, reviewed a briefing paper to ensure that it was fair and inclusive of major perspectives on the issues, and approved the composition of the experts who testified at the public hearing. As described in more detail below, the citizen panel was recruited through community organizations. The 12 panelists received the briefing paper about one month prior to the conference. During the first weekend of the conference, the organizers gave community panelists a presentation on the issues summarized in the briefing paper to refresh their memories and responded to the panel's questions. A professional facilitator helped the group prioritize and define their questions about the issues for the experts and identify additional readings for each member based on her or his interests. During the second weekend, the community panel posed their questions to 11 experts from industry, government, and community organizations who testified at the public hearing, then began their deliberations as a full group and in small-group breakout sessions focused on specific issues identified by the panelists. During the

from the perspective of those who have the least. Making claims about "broadband for all" without understanding the needs of the underserved could create a false – and ultimately disappointing – level of expectations (Santa Clara University Center for Science, Technology, and Society and Broadband Institute of California 2006, 4).

third weekend, the facilitator helped the full group to come to consensus on policy recommendations. The organizers publicized the community panel's policy recommendations widely to government, industry, community organizations, and the news media.[8] In addition, several months later the organizers convened a follow-up forum by videoconference to discuss the community panel's recommendations with 60 representatives of municipalities, community groups, and municipal broadband service providers in four California cities where similar projects were planned or underway, including Los Angeles, San Diego, Sacramento, and Silicon Valley.

In its recommendations, the panel agreed that local governments should commission and control municipal broadband networks, with private companies building and operating the networks, especially to reach the underserved. The panel also made detailed recommendations on how cities could extend broadband access to underserved groups by subsidizing computer hardware and software, provide training, design networks to be accessible to people with disabilities and non-English speakers, protect users' privacy and security, serve rural areas, and involve the public in network planning and oversight.[9]

Evaluation of the forum

While the forum was designed first and foremost as a political event rather than an academic research project, it also offered an opportunity for close study of enclave deliberation. Therefore, in addition to the community panelists, we enlisted a second group of citizens who were demographically similar but who did not deliberate; they served as a control group with whom we could compare the participants' attitude changes during the forum. The community panel and control group were recruited by distributing applications to approximately 80 social service agencies and

---

[8] For a sample of news coverage see Bowker, Hammond and Raphael 2006; Ostrom 2006. Coverage of the recommendations appeared on over 20 websites about the telecommunication industry or telecommunication policy, as well as public, community, and independent media sites. The press release announcing the panel's recommendations was also distributed to the community organizations that helped recruit Community Panel members and through the professional networks of many Advisory Panelists. In the year after the panel issued its recommendations, they were downloaded almost 900 times in English, Vietnamese, or Spanish from the conference website (http://broadbandforall. org), which drew visitors from 48 countries.

[9] See Santa Clara University Center for Science, Technology, and Society and Broadband Institute of California 2006.

community-based organizations. Almost all of the members of each group were clients of these organizations. Two in the community panel (or 17 percent) and four in the control group (or 27 percent) were staff members (computer instructors to the disabled or elderly), but none occupied leadership positions in their organizations. To encourage open deliberation, applicants who were employed by or belonged to an organization that had previously taken a public position on municipal broadband were excluded from both the community panel and control group.

From the 95 applications received, the organizers selected 12 community panel members and 15 control group members, each of whom belonged to at least one group with the lowest rates of home broadband access: low-income people, African-Americans, Hispanics, seniors, the disabled, and rural residents.[10] However, to ensure that each group had enough experience of home broadband access to discuss whether it was valuable, the organizers required that at least half of the community and control group had home access. Table 3.1 reports the characteristics of each group. Although assignment to the control group was not strictly random (availability on the conference weekends sometimes determined placement in control or community group, for example), the two groups were fairly evenly matched, with two exceptions. The control group had slightly fewer years of education on average (although the difference is mainly between those with some college and a college diploma), and the control group had somewhat greater access to broadband at home.

We evaluated the forum primarily through a series of surveys administered to many different groups involved in the Consensus Conference process, including the community panel, a non-deliberating control group, the advisory panelists, the experts who appeared at the public hearing, and the participants in the follow-up event on municipal broadband in California. The community panelists responded to surveys one month prior to the start of the conference, at the end of each weekend of the conference, and again one month following the conference's completion.[11] The control group completed survey questionnaires prior to the

---

[10] Low-income was defined as having household earnings below 50 percent of the median income in the four counties from which participants were drawn. The fact that just one rural resident was recruited reflected the scarcity of rural dwellers in a largely urbanized area.

[11] Pre- and post-conference surveys were administered over the telephone by a research assistant. During the conference, community panelists completed a self-administered pencil-and-paper questionnaire as the last task on the schedule at each conference weekend. Blind panelists were assisted by graduate student research assistants. Conference organizers left the room during the administration of the surveys.

Table 3.1 *Community panel and control panel characteristics*

	Community panel (n=12)	Control panel (n=15)
Household income		
Below median	92% (11)	100% (15)
Below 50% of area median	50% (6)	60% (9)
Education		
High school graduate or less	8% (1)	7% (1)
Technical school graduate	16% (2)	7% (1)
Some college	16% (2)	47% (7)
College graduate	50% (6)	27% (4)
Postgraduate or professional degree	8% (1)	13% (2)
Race or ethnicity		
African-American	25% (3)	33% (5)
Hispanic	33% (4)	27% (4)
Asian or Pacific Islander	25% (3)	20% (3)
White	25% (3)	20% (3)
Other	12% (1)	0% (0)
Age		
60 years or older	25% (3)	20% (3)
31–59 years	50% (6)	40% (6)
Under 30 years	25% (3)	20% (3)
Gender		
Female	58% (7)	60% (9)
Male	42% (5)	40% (6)
Physical disability	25% (3)	27% (4)
Rural resident	8% (1)	8% (1)
Home broadband access	58% (7)	86% (13)

Notes: Household median income was $87,400 for the four counties of Santa Cruz, Santa Clara, Alameda, and San Mateo, California. Some respondents identified with more than one racial or ethnic category. Some percentages may not total 100 percent because of rounding.

conference and again one month after its completion.[12] Advisory panelists and experts who testified at the public hearing completed online questionnaires one month prior to the conference and one month after its completion. The experts and advisors were about evenly split between the telecommunications industry (n=5); civil society organizations working for digital inclusion (n=7); and representatives, consultants, and service providers to local governments (n=6). Follow-up event

---

[12] These were administered over the telephone by a research assistant.

participants (n=57), who were asked to review the recommendations of
the community panelists, were about evenly split between the government and civil society categories. The response rate for the community
and control panels was 100 percent, for the advisors and experts 39 percent, and for the follow-up event participants 61 percent.[13] (We present
operational measures along with our findings.)

These data present limitations and strengths. Like many case studies,
this one involves a quasi-experimental design involving a small number
of participants in a unique context, all of which requires some prudence
about the external validity and the generalizability of our findings. On
the other hand, our case study approach also offers some signal virtues
for assessing the quality of enclave deliberation. Most of the research
on enclave deliberation involves one-time discussions in a lab setting
among college students. In contrast, we were able to train the analytical
microscope in fine detail on the dynamics of participant attitudes over
an extended period of deliberation about a current issue of real-world
significance. Repeated inquiry about community panelists' impressions
of both the process and the substance of the issues allows us to show how
participant attitudes changed (or remained constant) during the course of
the deliberations.[14] Much research on deliberative forums has been critiqued for failing to distinguish the effect of providing participants with
more information on a topic from the impact of deliberation itself. The
skeptics suggest that if the benefits attributed to deliberation are in fact
merely the result of being more informed about a range of policy positions by briefing materials, or exposure to public officials, then perhaps
deliberation is unnecessary.[15] Our research design surveyed participants
before they received a briefing paper, at the end of all three weekends of
deliberation, and one month after the conclusion of the conference. This
design allows us to discern the effects of the initial provision of information and discussion on a number of outcomes more precisely than
much prior research. In addition, we are able to assess the external legitimacy of the deliberation through surveys of a diverse group of policy
advocates, industry, and government decision makers. In all, this case

---

[13] Approximately 89 percent of the expert and advisory panelists responded to the pre-
conference survey, but only 39 percent completed the post-conference survey instrument,
which included the questions assessing the community panelists' recommendations. This
post-conference survey was administered more than one month after the conference's
conclusion. In addition, our analysis of the attitudes of follow-up event participants is
restricted to those who had actually read the community panel recommendations.

[14] On the importance of studying the dynamics of deliberation over time, see Steiner 2012,
189–91.

[15] Mutz 2006, 59.

Table 3.2 *Community panelists' views of participation*

Question	Weekend 1 mean	Weekend 2 mean	Weekend 3 mean
1. I am finding it difficult to state my ideas as well as I would like.	1.42 (0.26)	1.58 (0.31)	1.75 (0.35)
2. A few members of the community panel are dominating the discussion.	2.33 (0.33)	2.17 (0.32)	2.75 (0.35)
3. The facilitator made sure that everyone's opinions were heard.	6.50 (0.19)	6.17 (0.37)	6.50 (0.29)
Post-conference evaluation	Rarely	Occasionally	Frequently
How often did you speak during the consensus conference?	8.3%	16.7%	75.0%

Note: Responses to questions 1 and 2 are on a 1–5 scale, with 1 meaning "strongly disagree" and 5 meaning "strongly agree." Responses to question 3 are on a 1–7 scale, with 1 meaning "never" and 7 meaning "very often." Standard errors in parentheses.

study provides some of the most systematic, detailed empirical data available of structured enclave deliberation among the less powerful.

Equality

How well did the conference meet the criteria we defined in Chapters 1 and 2 for equal participation and opportunity to influence decisions? We suggested that, in ideal terms, equality of participation means that participants feel that speaking opportunities are distributed fairly, and that no participants dominate the floor or feel dominated by others. This can be measured by triangulating data on participants' speaking patterns, panelists' perceptions of whether they felt that their ability to speak was inhibited, and the perceptions of observers at the forum (such as facilitators, organizers, or evaluators). Table 3.2 shows responses to several survey questions posed to panelists about their impressions.

For the most part, panelists agreed that they were able to state their ideas adequately. On a scale from 1 to 5, where one indicates strong disagreement and five means strong agreement, the average panelist registered somewhere between "strong" and "somewhat" disagreement with the notion that it was difficult to state their ideas as well as they would like. Panelists expressed slightly more agreement with the notion that a few people were dominating the discussion, but on balance, the average panelist was still below the midpoint on the five-point scale with respect to that question. When asked to offer a self-report of how much they spoke up during the panel deliberations, fully three-quarters of panelists said they did so "frequently." These self-reports are seconded by the subjective impressions of the conference organizers. While some spoke more often than others in the full group, no one person appeared to dominate consistently, and in small breakout sessions that were held as panelists developed and refined their recommendations, nearly every participant appeared to participate often.

Surprisingly, panelists' concerns about whether they could state their ideas effectively and whether some were dominating the discussion *increased* slightly over the course of the conference's three weekends. Even with our small number of observations, these differences approach or reach statistical significance.[16] As we will discuss in greater detail below, the third weekend was the time when panelists were asked not just to consider different perspectives but also to come together around a set of consensus recommendations. The evidence in Table 3.2 is consistent with the notion that the conversation during the decision process was more difficult and that panelists struggled slightly more to voice their own perspectives as fully as they might have liked to on the third weekend. Nonetheless, this conclusion comes with the caveat that the change in means is quite small and that most participants still felt that they participated a great deal.

Were members of the group able to exert equal influence over their own and others' reasoning and conclusions? Given the concerns in the literature about enclaves being prone to groupthink (failing to consider diverse views in order to maintain group unity) and group polarization (in which the group moves further toward supporting positions to which it is initially inclined because of social pressure or unwillingness to raise a full range of arguments), we especially want to know whether participants succumbed to these problems. We also want to know whether participants felt they expressed authentic and autonomous preferences rather than being steered toward particular positions by the conference organizers.

We expected that if panelists eluded groupthink and polarization, they would be able to recognize points of common agreement, but also to

---

[16] For the "difficult to state my ideas as well as I would like" question, the difference between the Weekend 1 mean and the Weekend 3 mean falls short of significance at $p=0.22$ (two-tailed difference-of-means test), and the difference between the Weekend 2 and Weekend 3 mean for the "few people dominate" question is significant at $p=0.04$ (two-tailed test).

acknowledge the presence of disagreement when it existed.[17] In contrast, groupthink would be characterized by a heavy focus on consensus without recognition of a diversity of opinions within the panel. Group polarization sparked by social pressure would be indicated by an extreme shift in policy preferences in order to avoid conflict within the group.

Early in the process, most community panelists did not perceive differences of opinion among the group. As Figure 3.1a reveals, after the first weekend most participants rejected the notion that "important disagreements" separated the panelists. In response to an open-ended query about what the panelists "disagreed most" about, many panelists could not name any point of disagreement. However, the first weekend's activities focused on learning about the issues, identifying needs for additional information, and forming questions to pose at the public hearing, rather than on deliberation about the benefits of different policies. It is likely that the group perceived little discord because their group activities that week were focused on seeking information rather than taking positions.

As participants shifted into deliberation over their policy recommendations during the second and third weekends, their impressions of group differences changed, and they reported an increase in disagreement about the issues under discussion and a much greater variety of perspectives being discussed (see Figures 3.1a and 3.1b). By the end of the final weekend, all 12 participants could name at least one important difference of opinion among group members in response to open-ended queries. In their assessments of the conference one month after its conclusion, community panelists judged that allowing "people to air differences of opinion and discuss different points of view" was one of the most important goals of the conference (mean=6.75, SE=0.18 on a 1 to 7 scale, where 1= "not important at all" and 7 = "very important").[18]

Despite their perception of more differences being aired as the conference proceeded, the participants generally found these different perspectives were welcomed, considered, and respected, rather than being a source of discomfort (see Table 3.3). Even on the final conference weekend, when disagreements were confronted directly and the sometimes

---

[17] See, e.g., Mansbridge 1983.

[18] No other potential conference purposes scored as highly on the 1–7 scale: "To teach people about municipal broadband in a neutral, factual way" (mean = 6.50, SE=0.29); "To help people come to agreement about municipal broadband" (mean=5.42, SE=0.63); "To persuade people to support a specific approach to municipal broadband" (mean=4.25, SE=0.68).

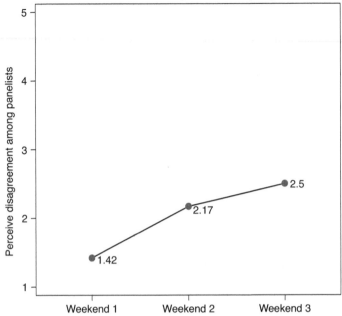

(a)   At the end of this weekend, important disagreements remained
among the community panelists with regard to
the issue of municipal broadband policy

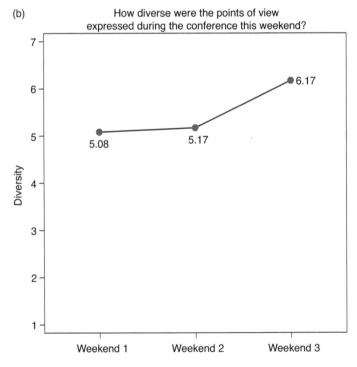

(b)   How diverse were the points of view
expressed during the conference this weekend?

Figure 3.1 (a) Recognition of disagreement. (b) Recognition of diversity of views

Table 3.3 *Community panelists' views of agreement and disagreement*

Question	Weekend 1 mean	Weekend 2 mean	Weekend 3 mean
1. All different perspectives about municipal broadband were welcome during the group discussions	4.5 (0.23)	4.7 (0.19)	4.5 (0.29)
2. This weekend's community panel discussions are helping me see new perspectives I had not considered before.	4.8 (0.13)	4.5 (0.19)	4.6 (0.26)
3. The community panelists carefully considered all sides of the issue.	4.5 (0.19)	4.2 (0.30)	4.5 (0.23)
4. Some important perspectives or ideas about municipal broadband were not adequately considered or discussed.	2.3 (0.40)	2.7 (0.38)	2.1 (0.42)
5. Members of the community panel were too quick to agree with each other.	2.5 (0.26)	2.4 (0.29)	2.3 (0.30)
6. Community panelists respected each other's ideas, even if they disagreed about some important issues.	4.5 (0.23)	4.6 (0.15)	4.6 (0.23)
7. The group discussions this weekend made me uncomfortable because there was so much disagreement.	1.1 (0.08)	1.4 (0.23)	1.6 (0.37)

Note: All responses are on a 1–5 scale, with 1 meaning "strongly disagree" and 5 meaning "strongly agree." Standard errors in parentheses.

arduous work of forging agreement in the face of strong and diverse opinions took place, most panelists still felt relatively comfortable with the deliberative exchange (though levels of discomfort were higher than on the first weekend). Most said the process helped them to consider alternative points of view rather than closing off consideration of diverse opinions. When asked a month later whether the conference process had caused them to rethink their initial positions about municipal broadband, only two panelists said that it had not. In the end, the panelists were able to come to consensus on ten pages of detailed policy recommendations.

These findings run in precisely the opposite direction expected by critics of enclave deliberation. Instead of groupthink, in which consensus is based on limiting the argument pool, silencing dissent, or adopting an illusory sense of unanimous agreement in the interests of group unity, participants increasingly recognized that their consensus emerged from a

climate characterized by real differences of opinion. Rather than undesirable group polarization, in which members tip unreflectively toward
an extreme position in which the group inclines in order to save face
or follow perceived group norms, participants became ever more acutely
aware of conflicts amongst themselves, but still achieved consensus on
many policy preferences.

On the two issues that provoked the longest debates, the panel
hammered out carefully considered agreements that were inclusive
compromises rather than a movement toward an extreme position. One
debate focused on the role of private companies in operating municipal
networks. After much discussion, the panelists agreed that "municipal
governments should be involved in developing and controlling broadband networks and should require private companies to operate the networks in ways that provide public benefits."[19] The panel suggested that
"a broadband oversight committee could be established with equal representation of public, private and municipal interests. Ongoing public
input should inform decisions about these networks. However, private
companies should build and operate the networks."[20] This recommendation expressed a nuanced compromise between panelists who prioritized
private firms' expertise at building networks and participants who prioritized government oversight to protect the public interest.

Similarly, although the panelists agreed that broadband was a necessity, they recognized that they could not come to consensus on whether
a free tier of service should be offered to low-income residents. Some
participants felt a free service would be accompanied by a significant
drawback – that some low-income people like themselves would fail to
value and use the service if they did not have to pay something for it. They
also worried that a free tier would mean something less than full equality
of access, given the likelihood that free service would include fewer online
tools and benefits than paying households would get. However, a deeply
committed minority was unwilling to cede their view that free service was
integral to digital inclusion. Thus, after a long and sometimes contentious
discussion about the meaning of equality for disadvantaged groups and
the tension between the price and quality of service, the panel agreed
to recommend a "free or discounted tier" for low-income residents, but

[19] Santa Clara University Center for Science, Technology, and Society and Broadband
Institute of California 2006, 3.
[20] Santa Clara University Center for Science, Technology, and Society and Broadband
Institute of California 2006, 3.

insisted that the lowest-price tiers, whether or free or not, should offer the same speed, privacy, and security as a full-price tier of service offered to paying households.[21]

These results contradict the groupthink and polarization theories of enclave deliberation. The panelists appeared to have achieved a high-quality consensus based not on the absence of disagreement, but rather a willingness to engage differences productively and to press forward together to achieve outcomes acceptable to all, even if some important disagreements remained (as they inevitably will in any real-world political process). The experience of the community panel thus seems to support claims that consensus-oriented deliberative processes must also incorporate elements of adversarialism to sustain consideration of diverse views, encouraging participants to explore their differences and allowing room for negotiating them.[22]

To what extent were the consensus recommendations authentic, rather than imposed on dissenters by other participants, or forced on the panelists as a whole by the facilitator or the organizers? The battery of questions we asked participants, reported in Table 3.4, indicates that panelists felt their individual and group choices were their own. They strongly disagreed with the notion that the facilitator dominated the conversation or was too quick to overlook concerns or objections, even on the conference's final weekend, and they strongly agreed that the facilitator worked to make sure all different perspectives were aired. After the conference had concluded and panelists had a chance to reflect on their experience on their own, apart from the conference organizers, they expressed nearly unanimous strong agreement with the notion that "the community panelists' recommendations came from the panelists themselves, not from the conference organizers," and they strongly disagreed with the idea that the conference organizers "dominated the discussion" or "influenced the panel's recommendations too much." The self-reports thus suggest that the panelists were fairly autonomous.

In addition, if the panelists perceived their choices as having been manipulated, it is plausible that they would have left the forum with a diminished sense of personal political efficacy. Yet we find just the opposite: participants' sense that they were well-qualified to participate

---

[21] Santa Clara University Center for Science, Technology, and Society and Broadband Institute of California 2006, 3.
[22] Karpowitz and Mansbridge 2005.

Table 3.4 *Community panelists' views of autonomy*

Question	Weekend 1 mean	Weekend 2 mean	Weekend 3 mean	Post-conference evaluation
1. The facilitator dominated the conversation.	1.42 (0.19)	1.42 (0.23)	1.25 (0.18)	
2. The facilitator made sure that all different perspectives were on the table.	4.83 (0.11)	4.83 (0.11)	4.83 (0.17)	
3. The facilitator was too quick to overlook some concerns or objections.	1.58 (0.23)	1.67 (0.28)	1.25 (0.18)	
4. Conference organizers dominated the discussion.				1.42 (0.19)
5. Conference organizers made sure all different sides of the issue were on the agenda.				4.67 (0.19)
6. The conference organizers were too quick to overlook some concerns or objections.				1.58 (0.26)
7. The conference organizers influenced the panel's recommendations too much.				1.33 (0.19)
8. The community panelists' recommendations came from the panelists themselves, not from the conference organizers.				4.92 (0.08)
9. I fully support all of the community panel's policy recommendations.			4.67 (0.14)	4.67 (0.19)

Note: Responses to all questions are on a 1–5 scale, with 1 meaning "strongly disagree" and 5 meaning "strongly agree." Standard errors in parentheses.

in community politics increased after the forum (see Figure 3.2, where increasing agreement is represented by higher scores). While the control group trended slightly in the opposite direction, community panelists tended to feel more confident about their abilities after participating in the conference, moving approximately one-half point on the

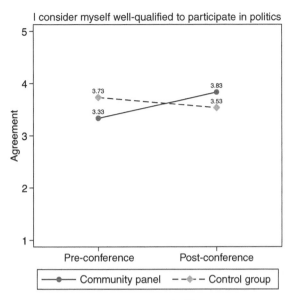

Figure 3.2 Internal efficacy

5-point scale, a change that is significant at the 90 percent confidence level (p=0.06).

Authentic decision making also depends upon whether the range of information provided to panelists, the initial framing of the issues by organizers, and the spectrum of policy choices that citizens considered were inclusive of the range of information, frames, and preferences in the larger political environment on the issue. The best available evidence we can provide here consists of the impressions of the experts who testified in response to panelists' questions at the public hearing and the advisory panelists who vetted the briefing materials, some of whom overlapped. Table 3.5 shows responses from experts and advisors to several questions about the diversity of viewpoints at the conference. On average, these outside observers strongly agreed that the range of viewpoints on the issue presented at the hearing was diverse and these perspectives were treated fairly. It is not surprising that the expert observers tended to feel that some of their own preferred issues and ideas were not represented in the panel's final recommendations. Indeed, we should be more worried about both the diversity of views presented to the panel and about the panel's ability to decide for itself if it had accepted every idea put forth by the advisors or expert witnesses.

Table 3.5 *Expert evaluations of diversity of views*

Experts who testified at the public hearing represented a broad range of views.	4.50 (0.29)
At the public hearing, all different perspectives about municipal broadband were treated fairly.	4.75 (0.25)
Some of my preferred issues and ideas did not make it into the community panel's recommendations.	2.86 (0.46)

Note: All responses scored on a 1–5 scale, with 1="strongly disagree" and 5="strongly agree." Standard errors in parentheses. N of Expert and Advisory Panelists = 7.

Public reasoning

Public-mindedness

One aspect of public reasoning is the effort to present reasons to other citizens in terms they might comprehend and accept. Public-minded thinkers do not disavow their own interests but consider them in relationship to others' interests as well, making arguments about what is true, just, or good for themselves and others who are affected by the issue. In Chapter 2, we suggested that research on civic forums should expand the range of ways in which we study whether citizens link group interests to common interests. In particular, we should study deliberators' motives and arguments more directly, rather than assuming that a particular policy preference better serves the common good and imputing public-minded motives to those who hold that preference. A concern about enclave deliberation is that it may foster exclusive consideration of group interests among those with a narrow shared perspective, rather than a more enlarged concern for the social whole. If enclaves are not exposed to diverse perspectives and encouraged to consider them, participants may turn inward and justify their positions only to themselves, rather than in terms that others could accept.

We can present several kinds of data that shed light on whether the panel linked their interests to larger social interests, although each kind of evidence has its limits. The evidence, reported above, that panelists and expert observers perceived the forum as having aired diverse policy views is relevant, although it does not say whether the panelists weighed these views with an eye toward some idea of the common good as well as their group interests. A month after the conference, participants were asked whether the panel's recommendations "reflect the public interest" and whether they "reflect my interests." Panelists overwhelmingly agreed that both their individual interests and the public interest were reflected in their collective conclusions.[23] We did not ask whether panelists saw a conflict between their interests and the public interest, but in the participants' self-reports, they expressed a belief that their recommendations had done well on both counts.

A less subjective measure is provided by the panelists' responses to survey questions posed before and after the conference that asked participants to list as many reasons as possible in favor of municipal broadband. Because participants ended up endorsing this position, their answers to these open-ended questions can be analyzed for whether panelists based their preferences in more personal or public-minded terms before and after the conference. We coded each panelists' responses in three ways: for the presence of appeals to each panelist's own group interests in relation to broadband access (such as a disabled participant's response that municipal broadband would especially benefit "people with disabilities"), for appeals to the interests of other underserved groups (such as an urban resident's argument that municipal broadband would help connect people "in rural areas" or appeals to the needs of "underserved communities" in general), and for appeals to more generalized public interests or principles (such as "effective emergency response during crises," "economic growth," or "to achieve equal access.").

The pattern of responses was remarkably similar before and after the conference (see Table 3.6). While two additional panelists argued in part from their own group interests after deliberation, almost all panelists grounded their arguments in some claim to a general public interest or principle before and after the forum. Enclave deliberation did not appear to narrow panelists' arguments for their positions to the pursuit of their own group interests or even to limit their concern to underserved groups at the expense of the larger population. Panelists' ability to explain their views in terms that appealed to widely shared interests in economic development, education, civic engagement, and the like was also evident in the final report and recommendations of the conference, which are analyzed in Chapter 5. At this point, we can say that enclave deliberation appears to have allowed panelists to recognize and perhaps even further clarify their

---

[23] On a scale from 1 to 5, where 1="strongly disagree" and 5="strongly agree," mean agreement with the statement that "the community panel's recommendations accurately reflect *my* interests" was 4.67 (SE=0.14), and agreement with the statement "the community panel's recommendations accurately reflect the public interest was identical."

Table 3.6 *Panelists' rationales for municipal broadband*

	Appeal to own group interest	Appeal to other underserved group interest	Appeal to generalized interest or principle
	% of panelists (N)	% of panelists (N)	% of panelists (N)
Pre-conference	33.3 (3)	33.3 (3)	77.7 (7)
Post-conference	55.5 (5)	33.3 (3)	77.7 (7)

Note: N of Panelists = 9. Rows do not add up to 100% because each panelist's reasons may contain appeals to more than one interest. Three panelists who could not offer reasons for municipal broadband during the pre-test were omitted from the analysis.

individual interests without losing their ability to ground their arguments in larger public interests.

Respect

Ideally, participants in civic forums practice reciprocity, empathy, and magnanimity, allowing them to consider others' perspectives and arguments fully, even if participants do not end by agreeing with others. Respect should extend to citizens inside and outside the forum. We gauged respect within the forum by asking each respondent to report whether "community panelists treated each other with respect and courtesy" and whether "community panelists respected each other's ideas, even if they disagreed about some important issues." These measures tap whether the deliberation created an environment of respect for persons and for ideas.

On both measures, panelists expressed overwhelming agreement that the Consensus Conference norm was respectful: average agreement with the respect for persons measure exceeded 4.8 on the 5-point scale every weekend, and respect for ideas averaged 4.5 or better on all three weekends. As we mentioned earlier, when we introduced Table 3.3, we also asked whether the disagreements between the panelists made them feel uncomfortable. In general, the answer to that question was "no"; panelists did not feel disturbed by the group deliberation, with every weekend's average responses remaining under 2 ("somewhat disagree") on the 5-point scale of agreement. We have already shown, however, that panelists perceived increasing levels of disagreement over the course of the conference, and consistent with those changing perceptions, Table 3.3 also shows that some felt less comfortable with that disagreement. By the third weekend, average levels of reported discomfort were about half a point higher than on the first weekend.[24]

The Consensus Conference's ability to build respect between deliberators and others outside the forum can be gauged in part by the forum's impact on participants' attitudes toward other citizens and local governments – the two main audiences for the forum's recommendations. Participants in heterogeneous deliberative groups often develop greater trust in their fellow citizens, more faith in citizens' political competence and ability to consider the common good, and increased trust in government.[25] Of course, whether this trust is desirable depends on whether it is warranted in a given political context. Regardless, these attitudinal changes may depend on interacting with a diverse set of deliberators. Enclave deliberation, especially among the disempowered, could lead to a greater sense of disempowerment, difference, or alienation from government and more empowered citizens outside the group, increasing enclave deliberators' resentment or mistrust.[26] Therefore, we administered a plethora of measures of these attitudes before and after the conference to the community panel and control group.

Our findings were mixed. The forum had no significant effect on participants' trust in local government, assessments of local government decision-making processes, confidence in the competency of average people to deal with a complex political world, or belief in the ability of ordinary people to consider all opinions or to back up their opinions with good reasons. On the other hand, the conference did not lead to any meaningful declines on these measures of civic attitudes, either. Participants did not leave the conference more cynical about government or citizens' ability to handle public policy issues. In addition, forum participants began with fairly high confidence in the capacities of ordinary citizens, so the lack of change on these measures may be attributable to a ceiling effect. With respect to trust in local government or assessments of local decision making, it is not clear that the conference should have provoked much change, as community panelists had little direct exposure to local politicians or decision-making processes, aside from the public testimony from the leader of the consortium of cities that was planning

---

[24] Specifically, the discomfort measure moves from 1.08 (strong disagreement) to 1.58. This difference falls short of statistical significance, however (p=0.19, two-tailed difference-of-means test).

[25] See, e.g., Pincock 2012.   [26] Levine and Nierras 2007; Sunstein 2000.

the Silicon Valley broadband network. Because the consortium had not decided how to pursue digital inclusion before the post-conference survey of panelists, participants did not have enough information to judge this decision.

However, community panelists' levels of interpersonal trust and their sense of ordinary individuals' commitment to the common good increased moderately over the course of the conference. Interpersonal trust was measured with a three-item scale coded to range between 0 and 1, with higher numbers indicating greater trust.[27] Mean levels of trust among the control group did not change at all, while the community group saw an increase of over 11 percentage points on the scale. This change is significant at the 0.10 level, which we interpret as meaningful movement, considering the small sample size.[28] As Figure 3.3a shows, the difference between the control group and the community panel increased over time, with the post-conference difference between the two groups reaching nearly a quarter of the trust scale, a difference that achieves solid levels of statistical significance for our small sample (p=0.06).

Similarly, the community panel showed an increased commitment to the notion that most people can overcome their self-interest and pursue the common good (see Figure 3.3b). The survey question asked respondents how much they agree or disagree with the statement: "Most people are too self-interested to agree on solutions that serve the common good." While the control group showed very little change, the community panel moved sharply away from the notion that self-interest overwhelms an ability to serve the common good. Among the community panelists, the pre-conference mean was 3.5 (1="strongly disagree", 5="strongly agree"), while the post-conference mean decreased to 2.92 – not yet strong levels of disagreement, but definite movement in that direction. This change exceeds standard levels of statistical significance (p=0.03). As a whole, these results contradict concerns that enclave deliberation inevitably diminishes participants' respect for other citizens or for

---

[27] The interpersonal trust measures were a scale composed of three separate questions: "Generally speaking, would you say that most people can be trusted, or that you can't be too careful in dealing with people?"; "Do you think most people would try to take advantage of you if they got a chance, or would they try to be fair?"; and "Would you say that most of the time people try to be helpful, or are they just looking out for themselves?" These are classic measures, used most famously by Robert Putnam (2000) as evidence of social capital.

[28] Levels of significance are based on two-tailed difference-of-means tests.

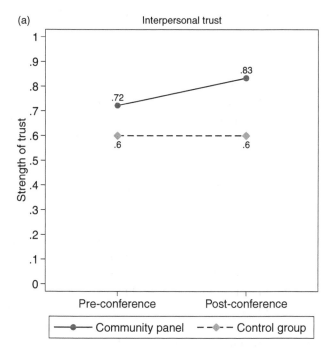

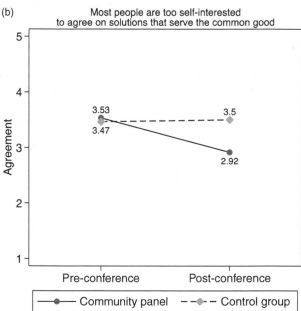

Figure 3.3 (a) Interpersonal trust. (b) Self-interest and common good

government, leaving the disempowered more alienated or cynical about mainstream politics.[29]

Knowledge

The quality of the panel's arguments and conclusions depends also on whether it was well-informed. A potential concern about deliberation in homogeneous disempowered groups is that participants may not gain sufficient knowledge about an issue because they will not be exposed to evidence that supports alternative positions and will not have to deploy facts that support their positions to persuade others. The enclave panelists might have lacked basic information, given their relatively low levels of Internet access and familiarity with municipal broadband prior to the conference.

We begin with some objective measures of panelists' knowledge, which are broad indicators of basic learning that do not attempt to capture the sum of participants' issue knowledge. However, panelists' inability to report this information would raise doubts about whether they were sufficiently well-informed. The evidence shows that participants came to know important facts about broadband technology over the course of their involvement with the conference. Whereas only two-thirds of panelists could describe the difference between broadband and dial-up Internet service without prompting prior to the conference, more than 90 percent correctly answered the question one month after the conference's conclusion (see Figure 3.4a). Knowledge levels of the control group also increased, but by only 7 percentage points, as opposed to the 25 points among the community panelists. In addition, compared to their pre-conference responses, community panelists were able to generate a significantly longer list of activities computer users could engage in with broadband but not with dialup access. As can be seen in Figure 3.4b, community panelists were able to offer, on average, almost one more advantage of broadband after the conference than before it (p=0.017) – an increase of nearly 70 percent, compared with little improvement in the control group.

Community panelists also gained a better sense of how access to broadband within the United States compares to access in other countries.

[29] In Chapter 1, we also argued that deliberation should help citizens to clarify how their values align with their policy preferences. While we did not measure whether individual panelists clarified how their values applied to municipal broadband, in Chapter 5 we evaluate how well the group as a whole did this in its final report, showing that the group grounded its arguments in several norms.

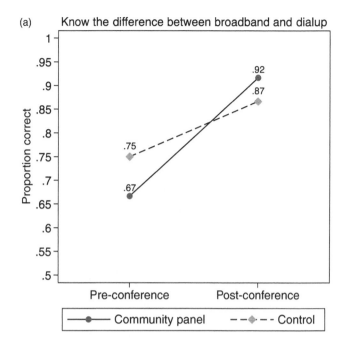

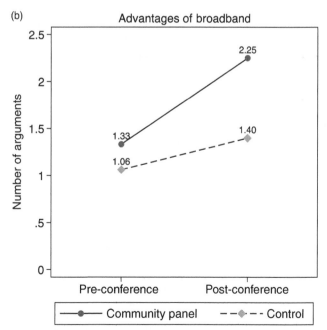

Figure 3.4 (a) Knowledge of broadband. (b) Knowledge of broadband's advantages

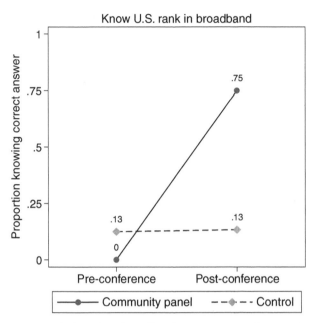

Figure 3.5 Knowledge of US broadband penetration ranking in the world

Whereas prior to the conference no community panelist could correctly rank the United States among OECD countries in broadband subscribers per capita, fully three-quarters of community panelists could do so one month after the deliberations, while the control group exhibited essentially no change (see Figure 3.5).[30]

These objective measures of information are strengthened by the subjective impressions of both conference participants and outside observers. Table 3.7 highlights participants' sense of their own levels of knowledge after each of the three conference weekends as well as at-a-distance summary judgments from advisory panelists and experts who testified to the panel at a public hearing. From the first weekend onward, participants

---

[30] Answers were given in response to the following open-ended question: "Imagine a list that ranked the countries of the world by what percentage of their residents had access to broadband Internet. The country with the highest percentage of residents who had broadband access would be first on the list. What number on this list do you think the United States would appear?" The United States ranked twelfth at the time. In both the pre- and post-tests, correct answers were counted as a ranking of between 10 and 14 or, if participants did not provide an exact number, a more general answer that expressed familiarity with the idea that the United States ranks low relative to other similar countries.

Table 3.7 *Impressions of community panelists' knowledge of the issues*

Questions	Community panelists' impressions		
	Weekend 1 mean	Weekend 2 mean	Weekend 3 mean
The conference organizers provided sufficient information to enable the community panelists to make informed policy recommendations.	4.6 (0.23)	4.6 (0.23)	4.8 (0.13)
I learned new information about the issue of broadband access that I did not know before this weekend.	4.8 (0.11)	4.9 (0.08)	4.5 (0.33)
I do not yet understand enough to make a good recommendation about municipal broadband policy.	3.0 (0.32)	2.7 (0.40)	1.3 (0.26)

Questions	Experts' impressions
	Post-conference evaluation
The Consensus Conference provided sufficient information to enable the community panelists to make informed policy recommendations.	4.3 (0.29)
Questions and comments from community panelists [at the public hearing] showed that they understood well the important issues related to municipal broadband.	4.5 (0.29)
The community panel's recommendations show that the panelists understood well the basic issues surrounding municipal broadband.	4.6 (0.20)

Note: All responses are on a 1–5 scale, with 1 meaning "strongly disagree" and 5 meaning "strongly agree." Standard errors in parentheses.

felt that they were receiving high-quality information about municipal broadband, and they expressed strong agreement with the idea that they were learning new information and considering new points of view. Just as importantly, community panelists appeared to grasp that they had much to learn and that such learning would continue over the course of each conference weekend. In other words, participants felt that they gained new information as the deliberation proceeded across each weekend. For them, learning about the issues appeared to include more than simply reading the background briefing paper, and their subjective sense of learning continued through the final full weekend of deliberation. After the first two weekends, participants were, on average, unsure whether they understood enough to make effective recommendations, but by the end of the last weekend, when they completed their policy recommendations, the panelists felt strongly that their conclusions had been backed by sufficient information.

Perhaps the strongest evidence supporting this point is provided by the outside experts who observed or testified at the conference's public hearing and read the group's policy recommendations. As Table 3.7 highlights, these experts tended to share participants' impression that they were provided with sufficient information to produce well-grounded policy recommendations. In addition, the experts who observed the public hearing came away satisfied that the community panelists were conversant in the important issues and found the panel's policy recommendations exhibited a solid understanding of "the basic issues surrounding municipal broadband."

We interpret this combination of evidence as cause for optimism about well-structured enclave deliberation's ability to inform disempowered participants sufficiently. These results suggest that information relevant to a broad range of arguments can be provided through background briefing papers, presentations, hearings, and facilitation that gently challenges participants to support their arguments with factual claims as well as other forms of evidence. These findings also suggest that the effects of the initial provision of information in the briefing paper, exposure to experts at the public hearing, and deliberation among the group cannot be as neatly disentangled as skeptics of deliberation suggest. Participants did not simply stop learning after reading the briefing paper. Instead, they strongly agreed that they learned new information and discovered new perspectives on all three weekends of the conference (see Table 3.7), including the third weekend devoted entirely to their deliberations among themselves. The assumption that non-experts could absorb all the information they need from reading a paper, or from interaction with experts, is not borne out by our data. Rather, the community panelists repeatedly indicated that they learned in part through discussion with their peers. Given the striking consistency of their responses, it seems unlikely that these benefits can be attributed entirely to upfront provision of information or exposure to experts, and not at all to deliberation.

Agreements for self-rule

Structuring of views

Ideally, deliberation results in a meta-consensus among the group, which focuses the range of reasons and conclusions that are acceptable to all participants. In some cases, this meta-agreement focuses choices enough for members to engage in a rational vote on the remaining alternatives. In other cases, this winnowing can result in a genuine group consensus on reasons and preferences. In this case study, the group arrived at consensus on 32 recommendations about several dimensions of the issue, including whether cities should commission their own broadband networks, how they should be financed and operated, public oversight of the networks, and how cities might make high-speed Internet service fully accessible to a variety of underserved groups, while protecting users' privacy and security. As we noted above, although the group agreed on the common goal of extending service to as many low-income residents as possible, it could not resolve disagreements over whether the best means would be to offer a free tier or a reduced-price tier, so it included both options in its recommendations. We have also shown that panelists felt they arrived at their own recommendations, rather than having preferences imposed on them by dominant group members, the facilitator, or the conference organizers. On the whole, this evidence suggests that the enclave panel achieved extensive and authentic agreement.

Citizen deliberation should also help each participant to arrive at a more coherent set of values, beliefs, perceived interests, and political preferences. Prior to the conference and after every weekend of meetings, we asked the participants to tell us "how strong" their "opinions about municipal broadband" were. Over the course of the conference, average strength of opinion increased by nearly a point on a four-point scale ranging from "not strong at all" to "very strong" (see Figure 3.6). This increase is statistically significant at $p < 0.01$ (two-tailed difference-of-means test). We asked the same question again a month after the conference had concluded, and strength of opinion had declined somewhat but was still significantly stronger ($p = 0.01$) than pre-conference averages. Among the control group, we see no such pattern of change; if anything, they become less certain of their opinions.

One opinion that was especially strengthened among the group was on the question of whether broadband access was a necessity or a luxury. Panelists moved quite sharply in the direction of believing that high-speed

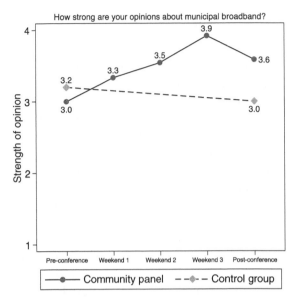

Figure 3.6 Opinion strength

Internet access was a "necessity" and not a "nice luxury," which aligns well with their recommendations that cities should commission networks and take affirmative steps to ensure that they were accessible to underserved citizens. Prior to the conference, the panelists were, on average, non-committal about this statement, neither agreeing or disagreeing with it. By the end of the conference, however, the panelists expressed strong endorsement of the idea that high-speed Internet access was a necessity of contemporary life, and this strong attitude persisted one month after the conference's conclusion.[31] Not only did average opinion change, but individual opinions also clustered more tightly around this new mean.[32] In other words, most panelists rallied around this newfound sense of priorities. In contrast with this dramatic change, control group attitudes remained essentially flat, and the few small changes come nowhere close to statistical significance.

---

[31] Among conference participants, the difference between opinions prior to the conference and opinions one month after the conference's conclusion is significant at p=0.059 (two-tailed difference-of-means test).

[32] The standard deviation of the post-conference mean is half as large as the standard deviation of the pre-conference mean.

Autonomy

Citizens are best able to exercise autonomy when they can help shape deliberative procedures, especially the agenda. Skeptics of enclave deliberation might fear that participants will reject elements of the agenda that are on the table in mainstream political debate, thereby marginalizing the forum and rendering it irrelevant to political decision making. Skeptics of deliberation among the disempowered might wonder whether these participants will be emboldened enough to expand the agenda and range of policy preferences beyond the initial framing offered by conference organizers. Neither outcome appears to have happened in this case. In part, this is because the Consensus Conference format gives participants' more freedom than many other kinds of forums to add issues and policy preferences to the agenda.

In the broadband conference, panelists added several issues during deliberation that were not mentioned in the briefing materials or in the initial questions posed by the organizers. These issues included protecting Internet users' privacy and security, as well as ongoing citizen participation in implementing and overseeing municipal broadband networks. While organizers had not provided any initial information about these issues, panelists were able to request additional background readings and gather information relevant to their concerns at the public hearing. The panel ended up defining privacy and security protections as part of the "basic needs" that all municipal networks should meet and recommending that "privacy and security protections should be made available equally across all tiers of service."[33] Panelists also called on local governments to affirm that personal information about users' online behavior should not be tracked or sold to third parties, that network providers should not share users' personal information with government agencies without a court order, that information about potential privacy and security risks should be made easily accessible to all network users, and that privacy and security policies should be stated in terms that users could understand and disseminated in multiple languages. The panel also recommended that cities create a "broadly representative public advisory board which includes members of underserved communities" and several specific steps for involving the board in reviewing requests for proposals to build municipal networks and for monitoring network providers' performance over time. This recommendation seems to us to

---

[33] Santa Clara University Center for Science, Technology, and Society and Broadband Institute of California 2006, 3.

meet our second criterion for deliberative autonomy as well. We have argued that a forum's conclusions are more legitimate if they preserve conditions for all citizens to deliberate about public issues in the future. The proposal for a public advisory board seems to us to be one that would facilitate, rather than curtail, citizens' capacity to exercise their autonomy.

Perhaps the strongest evidence of the panel's autonomy was that its report countered conventional thinking about Internet service and added some original recommendations to the debate over municipal broadband at the time. The dominant model among telecommunications companies and many municipal broadband providers was one in which cheaper service should provide fewer benefits or recoup its costs through increased exposure of users to advertising. In contrast, the panelists asserted that low-cost service should offer the same speed as higher cost tiers of service. The panel's focus on equal protections for privacy and security for all users was especially novel. We compared the panel's final report with comparable reports issued within the same six-month period, one of a national meeting of well-informed activists for broadband access, and another of Wireless Silicon Valley's focus groups conducted with representatives from local public works, public safety, parks and recreation, and convention and visitor departments.[34] The panel's concerns about protecting the public's privacy and security on wireless broadband networks do not appear in either of the other two reports. In contrast, the community panel not only raised these issues but also made specific recommendations about how they should be addressed.

Authorization

Another way of evaluating agreements is the extent to which they are authorized within the larger political system by citizens and officials. We have suggested that the strongest kind of authorization occurs when the substance of a forum's conclusions is validated by further deliberation within other parts of a democratic system. When other political actors do not render a verdict on the content of a forum's policy proposals, but trust the forum enough to consider it a proxy for public judgment, then this is a somewhat weaker version of authorization. In this version, the forum earns its authority because others trust in its inclusiveness, its

---

[34] New America Foundation and Center for International Media Action 2006; Wireless Silicon Valley 2006.

deliberative process, or its expertise. However, policy recommendations that emerge from more homogeneous deliberation by marginal groups may be seen as illegitimate by stakeholders on the issue, especially if they do not agree with the recommendations.

Here we have two relevant sources of data – first, the impressions of the advisory panelists who supervised the conference and the experts who interacted with the panel at the public hearing, and, second, a summary judgment by the group of advocates, industry representatives, and local government officials who read the panelists' recommendations and attended the follow-up event several months later. These stakeholders tended to evaluate the work of the community panelists quite positively. As we have already seen (in Table 3.5), the outside experts and advisory panelists believed the presenters at the public hearing reflected a diverse set of views and that all different perspectives were treated fairly, even though these observers tended to feel that some of their own preferred views were not embraced by the community panel in its final recommendations. In addition, we saw (in Table 3.7) that advisors and experts expressed solid agreement with the idea that community panelists' recommendations were grounded in sufficient factual information.

The experts and advisory panelists also expressed moderate levels of confidence that the panelists' recommendations could actually influence subsequent debate and affect the perspectives of stakeholders (see Table 3.8). At the same time, the experts also recognized that the panelists' recommendations would not be embraced by all sides and would likely be opposed by some interests. In other words, the outside experts judged the panelists as having made a substantial contribution to subsequent deliberation and decision making on municipal broadband, articulating perspectives that would be taken seriously but that were not simply parroting already-existing views and would likely provoke opposition from some quarters. The experts also judged the panel's recommendations as well-grounded and realistic, even if they did not perfectly match the ideas and perspectives of the experts themselves. On average, experts and advisory panelists reported moderate levels of support for the recommendations, although participants in the follow-up event who had read the panelists' report were somewhat more enthusiastic. We conclude that the stakeholders who observed this enclave forum or read its recommendations expressed fairly strong approval of both the deliberative process and the substance of the panel's conclusions, which we consider as both strong and weak authorization.

Table 3.8 *Expert views of the consensus conference*

	Expert and advisory panel	Follow-up event participants
Impact		
The Consensus Conference will have an impact on public policy decisions about municipal broadband.	3.86 (0.26)	
The conference will affect the thinking of stakeholders in the municipal broadband issue.	4.00 (0.44)	
The community panels' recommendations are likely to be opposed by important stakeholders or interests.	3.71 (0.57)	
Panel recommendations		
The community panels' recommendations are not realistic.	1.57 (0.30)	
I fully support all of the community panel's recommendations.	4.00 (0.22)	4.46 (0.18)
N	7	13

All responses scored on a 1–5 scale, with 1="strongly disagree" and 5="strongly agree." Standard errors in parentheses.

While the long-term impact of the panel's recommendations is beyond our scope here, there were several short-term impacts. The recommendations were taken up by others in the policy process, such as the advocacy groups that attended the follow-up event in four California communities. The panel's conclusions informed public debate through the extensive media coverage and almost 900 downloads of the recommendations from the conference website within a year. The forum helped legitimate municipal public involvement in broadband and digital inclusion by providing the first organized expression of citizen interest in the Wireless Silicon Valley project and efforts to include the underserved in its plans. The public hearing exerted the first organized form of citizen oversight on the Silicon Valley project, which had received almost no media coverage and had held no public hearings on its direction before the conference sparked both. The conference organizers were later asked by one of the partners in Wireless Silicon Valley to organize further public consultations in other parts of the state where the organization was bidding on municipal broadband projects, offering some further evidence of increased attentiveness to citizen voices in network planning. At the time of this writing, the

Wireless Silicon Valley project was proceeding slower than planned, having piloted service in just one community, amidst uncertainty about funding commitments from local governments and private partners in the project. The national financial crisis of 2008 was the major brake on the project, starving local government budgets of capital to build the project and refocusing them on struggling to continue providing basic services.

Conclusion

This case study suggests that structured enclave deliberation among the less powerful that involves immersion in a broad range of policy information and arguments could help resolve concerns about whether the marginalized can deliberate on equal terms, while also fulfilling criteria for public reasoning and arriving at autonomous agreements. Participants in the Consensus Conference saw themselves as participating and influencing each other fairly equally. Panelists' reasoning appealed to broader public interests and principles, not simply to their own group interests. Instead of adopting groupthink or dangerous forms of polarization, participants perceived greater diversity of views the longer they deliberated, yet were able to arrive at a long list of policy recommendations. Panelists demonstrated respect for each other's arguments and for the claims of others outside the forum, rather than growing alienated or cynical about civic engagement. These citizens increased their knowledge of municipal broadband and were seen by expert observers as having a good grasp of the issues. The group achieved consensus on multiple recommendations, and members' views became clearer and more coherent during the conference. In their deliberations, the group members contributed their own perspectives to the larger policy debate and did not simply parrot the issue agenda outlined by conference organizers. Panelists saw their conclusions as their own autonomous views and contributed unique recommendations about equal protections for privacy and security to the public debate over digital inclusion. Both the participants and observers in government, industry, and advocacy groups perceived the deliberative process and the group's conclusions as legitimate.

We have argued that enclave discussion is compatible with the theory of democratic deliberation if enclave deliberation is preceded and followed by exposure to the larger public sphere. Convening enclave deliberation among the disempowered can be justified on behalf of equality if it improves upon deliberative forums' ability to attract participation by the marginalized, to develop their political knowledge and skills, to discover common interests and positions without coercion from the privileged or from each other, and to contribute a broader range of arguments to the larger public sphere. What might this mean for deliberation's practitioners and researchers? Comparative research on civic forums that include enclave deliberation and those that do not would be most helpful at identifying whether and how more homogeneity can boost deliberative quality and equality. Because this case study had no comparison group that was more heterogeneous, we cannot offer evidence that structured deliberation in more homogeneous groups was *better* according to our measures than deliberation in more heterogeneous groups, only that the former need not lead to some of the problems foreseen by traditional deliberative theory and its critics. Comparative research on equality in civic forums with and without enclave discussion would be helpful, but it would depend upon convincing forum organizers to include more homogeneous groupings of the marginalized.

Comparing the quality of deliberative forums is complex because forums are shaped by many contextual dynamics.[35] Especially salient factors include who deliberates, on what issues, and using what deliberative mode. First, our case study involved a group that did not share a powerful group bond at the outset, but shared a structural position in relation to the issue of broadband access and during deliberation developed a stronger collective identity as representatives of the underserved. Cases in which participants recognize a more cohesive group identity from the start would provide stronger tests of whether enclave deliberation among the less powerful can avoid some dangers, such as polarizing for the wrong reasons.

Second, our case study group deliberated over an issue that was only beginning to surface in the public sphere. Emerging issues may be ideal for the quality of enclave deliberation because participants' interests, identities, and commitment to policy options are undiscovered territory. Under such conditions, information tends to be scarce, issues are not yet clearly located in prevailing political frames, and interest groups' and policy makers' positions are still relatively fluid. At these times, deliberation among the dispossessed may be most likely to be educative, open, autonomous, and influential on policy making.

Other aspects of the issue may have favored good deliberation as well by helping clarify participants' stakes. There was a strong local angle

---

[35] For a summary, see Fung 2003.

(Silicon Valley's municipal broadband plans), the issue required discussion of both facts (such as whether people take full advantage of free services) and values (such as equal opportunity and privacy), and it allowed deliberators to draw on their personal experience (of using the Internet). Research on enclave deliberation about issues that are more established, less local, more fact-driven or value-driven, and less accessible to personal experience could illuminate whether and how these kinds of issues provide the same opportunities for high-quality enclave deliberation. This could help practitioners decide whether the benefits of forming enclaves outweigh the risks.

Third, research could help inform organizers about whether other kinds of civic forums besides Consensus Conferences offer more or less congenial homes for productive deliberation by the marginalized. Spaces for enclave deliberation could feasibly be incorporated into all such forums, but they differ in design and purpose in numerous ways.[36] Features of the Consensus Conference that may be most relevant to deliberative quality in enclaves include opportunities to interact directly with policy makers and activists, allowing participants to generate their own policy options rather than simply choosing among those presented by organizers, and requiring that recommendations be agreed to by consensus rather than majority rule.

Of course, these findings also suggest the need for additional research into the mechanisms that might have promoted such an apparently successful blending of consensus and adversarial approaches, such as the role of the facilitator in establishing group norms that prize both civil agreement and a willingness to air differences. We note, too, that the nature of the questions that the community participants engaged may have played a role in the Silicon Valley outcome. The community panelists tackled only one closed-ended question (about whether governments should be involved in municipal broadband), a question on which they quickly agreed. On the further, open-ended questions (about how governments should be involved and what is needed to achieve digital inclusion), the panel achieved hard-won consensus amid conflict. But the outcomes may have been different if the panel had disagreed more on the initial closed-ended question or if their further deliberation had centered on other, closed-ended questions. More research is needed to better understand the ways in which the nature of the questions under consideration shape enclave deliberation.

[36] See Gastil and Levine, eds. 2005.

Perhaps the most important factor that may influence the quality of enclave deliberation is how empowered these forums are in relation to government and other institutions. Our case study involved a one-time forum with an advisory relationship to officials and activists. In contrast, in merely educative forums the stakes may be too low for participants to sustain a commitment to the hard work of deliberation. Although we are not aware of civic forums in which disempowered people alone enact policy decisions directly, and the prospects for such forums look dim, were they to come to pass they might present the same barriers to reaching agreement seen in legislatures, as interest groups attempted to "rig the jury" with their surrogates and bring other pressures to bear on behalf of their positions.[37] Ongoing advisory groups of the least powerful might increase in deliberative quality as they build issue knowledge and discussion skills. But prolonged relations with government could also undermine their deliberative capacities by presenting possibilities for co-optation by more powerful policy actors.

Our proposal for enclave deliberation need not involve a naïve belief that deliberative quality and equity can be entirely perfected, only that they can be improved. These case study results suggest the need to know more about the conditions under which enclave deliberation is likely to result in the sorts of encouraging outcomes we found in the Silicon Valley conference. At the same time, research should take seriously the possibility that these factors of group composition, issue, deliberative mode, and level of empowerment may interact and be mutually reinforcing, such that the whole of deliberative success is more than the sum of its parts, not all of which can be neatly and easily separated. For example, we found in this study that information acquisition cannot be easily separated from deliberation itself. Instead, the community panel discovered new information and perspectives throughout the conference, including during the final weekend when they deliberated as a group and finalized their recommendations.

Research that simply demonstrates that deliberation succeeds or fails to reach ideal standards is less useful than studies that illuminate *when, how, and why* deliberation might achieve greater equity and quality. We have suggested more comparative research on forums with and without enclaves of the dispossessed. Another strand of comparative work might assess whether our enthusiasm for civic forums as venues for enclave deliberation would be better invested elsewhere. This research

[37] Steiner et al. 2004.

could examine the extent that deliberation in forums of disempowered people satisfies criteria of equality, public reasoning, and self-governance compared with other political arenas open to them. Do civic forums offer better prospects for discussion among those who hold different views in ways that lead to empowered participation compared with discussion in informal social networks, where talk with political opposites can lead to dispirited withdrawal from politics?[38] Do forums provide better possibilities for the least powerful to discover and express collective interests than in some social movement organizations that have become managed by distant professionals, hierarchical, and focused on single issues?[39] Do forums inform and interact with deliberation within other movements, such as the global justice movement, revitalizing earlier forms of popular discussion in the interests of leadership accountability, political education, and mobilization?[40] Do forums allow the deliberation of the disempowered to exercise more influence than at typical public hearings, which are often designed in ways that make it especially difficult for disempowered groups to contribute meaningfully to the decision-making process?[41] If so, then there is a strong case for forums to provide opportunities for people to talk among others who share their social location, or their situation in regard to the matter at hand, or who face some of the same barriers to equal participation in deliberation itself. In Chapter 7, we provide a list of guiding questions that can help organizers design enclave deliberations and integrate them into broader forums or political processes.

However, strengthening equality by incorporating well-designed enclaves is only half of our prescription for civic forums. In medicine, combined therapies can sometimes enhance success and prevent pathogens from developing resistance to either treatment. In politics, enclaves of the marginalized are much more likely to strengthen the body politic and stave off resistance from the powerful if they are accompanied by a healthy dose of publicity. As we noted in the Introduction, deliberation tends to be most democratic when participants feel accountable to a larger public. In enclaves of the marginalized, as in more heterogeneous groups of citizens, transparency tends to elicit more public-minded arguments,

---

[38] Mutz 2006.   [39] Skocpol 2003.

[40] On deliberation within the global justice movement, see della Porta 2006. On the deliberative strains in the American New Left, civil rights, and feminist movements, see Evans and Boyte 1992; Polletta 2002.

[41] Gastil 2008, 177–212.

which are more likely to be grasped and accepted by others. Just as important, publicity holds sponsors and organizers accountable for designing a fair-minded forum, in which participants must consider a broad range of interests, values, and policy preferences. Without publicity, it is hard to imagine how enclaves of the disempowered will get a hearing from decision makers and other citizens, much less their approval.

Part II

Publicity

4

Deliberative publicity

We now turn to the second major challenge for integrating civic forums within a more deliberative political system: communicating what happens in the forum to the wider public and decision makers. The controversy over the "Our Budget, Our Economy" forum, discussed in the introduction, illustrated several problems that many civic forums face. Critics of the budgeting forum suggested that its sponsor would manipulate participants' opinions, that citizen participants would not be representative of the country as a whole, and that the organizers failed to give a transparent explanation of how participants were selected. Like "Our Budget, Our Economy," many forums are new institutions on the political landscape, their procedures are unfamiliar and murky to many political observers, and these forums' roles are not always clearly authorized within the political system. Compared with traditional ways of consulting public opinion (through polls, public hearings, and the like) and involving the public in decision making (through elections and juries), most civic forums need to work harder to make a case for their own legitimacy simply because they are new and less well understood by powerful actors in the political system (officials, journalists, interest advocates, and the like).

In addition, we have noted that deliberation requires a small group, and therefore often involves excluding most people who are affected by the forum's conclusions from the discussion. Because the whole polity cannot directly participate in even the most ambitious deliberative event, the perceived legitimacy and influence of civic forums depend in large part on how they communicate to others in the political system. It is primarily through forums' external communication that policy makers and the public will be able to assess the legitimacy of citizens' deliberative decisions and weigh whether to agree with them or not.

If civic forums are to thrive, they will need to establish some widely understood and accepted standards for conducting and reporting them. While comparable institutions do not always operate legitimately, they benefit from established criteria for judging how they are supposed to work and how they should be made public. In the United States, we know that elections are supposed to be open to all registered voters, that voters are permitted to cast secret ballots, and that election officials should count each vote equally and report the results in a timely manner. Courts are empowered to resolve disputes over voter eligibility and electoral procedures. Political actors and savvy citizens know that opinion polls should be expected to draw representative samples of the public, report their margin of error, reveal when the poll was conducted, disclose question wording and response options, and so on. Journalists and others critique poorly conducted polls and "push polls," which construct biased questions to sway opinion to one side of an issue. At present, there are no comparably well-established criteria and procedures – formal or informal – for reporting and evaluating civic forums.

In this chapter, we propose a set of public benchmarks for assessing whether forums should be considered more or less legitimate, so that observers can make better judgments about how much to trust to the results of a particular forum. These benchmarks need to include common criteria for evaluating civic forums, which are just beginning to emerge in the field, but also need to encompass how many other kinds of information about the forum are made public. We begin with some initial thoughts about how to distinguish the goals of deliberative publicity from other kinds of strategic political communication, building on recent writing about the role of rhetoric in a deliberative democratic system. In the bulk of the chapter we adapt and distill widely shared criteria for good deliberation within forums to create conceptual and operational measures that can begin to assess external communication in deliberative terms. By drawing on contemporary deliberative theory and practice, we propose a set of metrics, which we call the Legitimate Publicity Indicators (LPI), that clarify how civic forums should report participants' arguments and practice transparency about how the forum was conducted.

Publicity as deliberative rhetoric

Although the principle of publicity is central to many theories of deliberation, how civic forums communicate externally is still largely undiscovered country for theory and research. Given the growth of civic forums, it is surprising how little attention has been paid to how they disclose their deliberative processes and express their arguments. Instead, scholars have been much more interested in how the forum design affects the quality of participants' deliberation, the effects of forums on participants' political attitudes and behaviors, and forums' influence on the political process. Unfortunately, this often involves skipping over what is likely an important step: the reporting of deliberative groups' decision-making process and recommendations to policy makers, citizens, and the news media.

There may be a number of reasons for this gap in much of the thinking about civic forums, some stemming from practice and others from theory. Some open forums, such as New England Town Meetings and Chicago's community policing meetings, follow long-established procedures for transmitting what happens within public meetings convened by government. Legal requirements stipulate that minutes are published and that meetings are open to all citizens and the news media. But most civic forums involve private and public phases, and most of the deliberation occurs in private. In many cases, organizers lack funds to publicize the forum beyond convening a public hearing and delivering a final report of the forum to sponsors and other intended audiences.

There may also be theoretical reasons for scholars' relative lack of attention to this aspect of publicity. As discussed in Chapter 1, some theorists focused initially on defining an ideal deliberative procedure, which assumed that a good process guaranteed a good outcome. This did not lend much urgency to the question of how to convince others outside the forum of its legitimacy. In addition, claims about the epistemic benefits of deliberation directed researchers' attention to examining the quality of citizens' conclusions and reasoning. In response to critics who charge that citizen deliberation is ineffective, research and practice have also focused on the impact of deliberative forums on policy. Yet the perceived legitimacy and influence of any deliberation surely depend in part on publicity, which shapes how deliberators' process and conclusions are communicated to decision makers and the public.

The turn to systemic thinking about deliberation especially raises the question of how civic forums communicate to other elements of the political structure. In the Introduction, we noted that scholars adopted systems thinking in response to the problems that arise from basing a theory of legitimate decision making in a perfect "micro-deliberative" procedure.[1] Instead, many theorists now advocate for an improved macro-deliberative

---

[1] Parkinson 2006a, 6.

system, in which better deliberation is infused in many arenas, from representative government to consultative bodies, voluntary associations, social movements, and journalism. One hope is that shortcomings in the deliberative quality of any one element of the system might be offset by other elements.

Clearly, this approach depends upon the quality of communication between different elements of the system. If such a system is to work, civic forums must be able to convey their views effectively to other citizens and institutional decision makers. Legitimate external communication becomes the glue that binds a forum to a deliberative political structure. Organizers of civic forums may practice many forms of publicity as they recruit citizens and advisory panels, enlist experts to testify, solicit attention from decision makers and journalists, and issue final reports and evaluations of forums. Practiced well, this publicity can make a crucial contribution to developing a more deliberative political system, one in which all state and civil society institutions become more responsive to well-informed public opinion, and can apply checks and balances on each other's democratic deficits. We agree that this is a good vision for democratic theory, but it demands more clarity about how deliberative bodies should communicate with those outside the forum.

Organizers cannot simply attribute or delegate responsibility for publicity to mediating institutions, such as the news media. This does not mean that the news media's role can or should be overlooked. How the organizers of a forum present their work is likely to affect whether and how the news media cover it. However, as several studies suggest, the shortcomings of contemporary journalism mean that many civic forums will be ignored or reported in ways that are oversimplified and sensationalized.[2] Fortunately, in a world in which new information sources are bypassing traditional media gatekeepers, many nonparticipants can have ready access to the websites, reports, and messages sent directly by forum organizers and sponsors. Therefore, if citizens' arguments are to be conveyed in terms that comport with deliberative theory's norms and are to influence policy making, forums must pay

---

[2] Parkinson 2006a; 2006b; 2006c; Page 1996. Both Parkinson and Page discuss how reporting on deliberation can conflict with the news media's economic imperatives, its space constraints, and its priorities for political reporting, which tend to focus on controversy, conflict, and the actions of those who are assumed to hold power over decision making (see also Cooper and Smith, 2012, 25). Moreover, when journalists report on citizens' political activities, the focus is typically not on citizens' political analyses, but on their personal experience or spectacular demonstrations designed to grab public attention (see, e.g., Eliasoph 1998, 176–87).

attention to communicating both to the news media and *around* them to the public and decision makers.

This is not simply because of journalism's faults. Even the kind of ethical publicity that civic forums should practice involves something journalistic reporting does not: the need to persuade onlookers that the forum's process and arguments are trustworthy. Therefore, this unique sort of publicity is best thought of as a form of deliberative rhetoric rather than judged by the ideal standards for impartial journalistic reporting.

While one strand of deliberative theory has been highly suspicious of rhetoric, there is a growing appreciation of the need and value of some kinds of rhetoric in a deliberative system. Simone Chambers traces this debate back to the Greeks.[3] Plato attacked political speechmaking as an exercise in manipulative flattery of the audience aimed only at obtaining power, which he feared was endemic to democracy. In Plato's view, rhetoric is the enemy of deliberative reasoning. While deliberation requires reciprocal communication, rhetoric implies asymmetrical talk in which orators speak and the audience listens. While deliberation demands small groups that are protected from the need to play to the gallery, rhetoric is designed to appeal to the interests and emotions of the crowd. In contrast, Aristotle's approach to rhetoric counsels acceptance of the necessary role for rhetoric in all politics, but also of the need to define the legitimate democratic uses of rhetoric. For Aristotle, persuasion always depends on appeals not only to *pathos* (the psychology and interests of one' audience), and *ethos* (the character of the speaker), but also to *logos* (the merit and coherence of rational argument).

John Dryzek argues that rhetoric serves an indispensable function in a deliberative system by connecting "differently disposed actors, forums, and institutions."[4] He argues that, compared with the existing machinery of democracy, each new civic deliberation must create conditions of its own perceived legitimacy. As a practical matter, it is difficult to see how any forum could communicate to the larger political structure without employing rhetorical persuasion. Empowered forums, such as some popular assemblies and co-governance forums, need to persuade citizens and officials that these forums are accountable to them and have chosen wisely. These forums rely on other levels of government to approve, implement, or at least cooperate with their decisions. Advisory forums

---

[3] Chambers 2004. John Dryzek (2010, 70) sees this line of thinking as extending through the political philosophies of Kant, Rawls, and Habermas, who retain a suspicion toward rhetoric as undermining public reason.

[4] Dryzek 2010, 74.

especially need to persuade the public to support their recommendations and decision makers to implement them.

However, rhetorical persuasion always poses some danger of descending into what Chambers calls "plebiscitary reason." In this kind of rhetoric, "speakers still appeal to what they think are common or public values but with a twist: under the 'glare' of publicity these arguments may become shallow, poorly reasoned, or appeal to the worst that we have in common."[5] Persuasion is motivated by manipulation, pandering, or image maintenance, rather than sincere justification. Chambers' examples suggest that she is most concerned about political candidates and officials engaging in this kind of purely strategic communication. We should be less worried about citizens in civic forums deploying this reasoning, given the good conditions for deliberation within most forums and the fact that participants are not vote-seeking politicians, who have much stronger incentives and resources to pander or polish their individual images.

We should be more attentive to the possibility that authors of publicity about forums, who are often the organizers or sponsors, may be tempted to engage in this kind of rhetoric. Even if this is rare in our experience, politics being what it is, there will always be some who *suspect* that forums are designed to manipulate participants and broader public opinion. We saw this in the budget deficit forum example with which we began this book. In addition, forums need to demonstrate that they are not selectively reporting or interpreting citizen participants' views to match sponsors' policy interests. They need to dispel suspicions that organizers' interest in presenting the deliberative process as having been conducted well has tempted them to burnish the forum's credentials by using manipulative rhetoric. Publicity helps build confidence in the process by inviting non-participants to understand the purposes, rules, dynamics, and outcomes of the forum. Just as a gerrymandered political district might undermine confidence in electoral democracy, forums have a responsibility to show that organizers have not rigged the process or the outcomes in one direction or another. In short, civic forums need to build trust among decision makers and members of the public who did not directly participate.

In the Introduction, we raised potential concerns about the marketization of the field of public consultation. We noted that this can bring the benefits of professionalization, but also pose risks as forum

---

[5] Chambers 2004, 393.

organizing and evaluation become products designed to suit the preferences of officials or other customers, which must compete for business in a
market for consultation services. For example, Carolyn Hendriks rightly
criticizes some forum organizers for making inflated claims that small,
randomly selected panels of citizens are "representative" or "typical" of
all perspectives and characteristics of a larger polity, in order to make a
stronger bid for legitimacy.[6]

There are other well known trade-offs associated with deliberating in
public. A public setting can make it more difficult for people to change
their minds for fear of losing face, and it can present opportunities
for intimidation or bribery.[7] When deliberators are highly polarized, or
the surrounding political context is rife with conflict, secrecy can foster
greater trust, sincerity, and empathy among a group.[8] Empirical studies
suggest that these values of secrecy are realized, especially in citizen groups
discussing difficult racial issues and in legislatures.[9] But the importance
of publicity for democracy increases when participants in deliberation
are empowered representatives who can enact policy directly, because
publicity can make them more accountable, and when there is a danger
that some with legitimate claims may be excluded, because publicity can
increase pressure to make groups more inclusive. Thus, we agree with
Jane Mansbridge that the best solution is "some mixture of protection
and publicity in the early stages of a deliberative process, but maximum
feasible publicity in the final stages."[10]

---

[6] Hendriks 2011, 49; see also Smith and Wales 2000, 56–7. James Fishkin (2009, 21–4)
   dismisses the ability of smaller forums to represent a whole, likening them to "self-
   selected listener opinion polls" (SLOPs). Despite their representative limits, we think
   that small forums can make valuable contributions to public debate because they create
   much better conditions for public reasoning than are found in SLOPs, including exposure
   to information and diverse views, to experts, and to deliberation with other citizens. In
   contrast, Dryzek claims that the thousands of citizens who take part in 21st Century
   Town Meetings "probably produce results little different from the smaller forums"
   (2010, 74). While we value the deliberative capacity of small forums, a forum that
   engages thousands of people should be expected to encompass more diverse perspectives
   than a forum of 12–25 citizens, and therefore has a stronger claim to representativeness
   of the larger population, even if it is not perfectly representative in a statistical sense.
   Most importantly, as we argue below, our commitment to transparency leads us to
   expect deliberative publicity to explain how its sample is similar to and different from
   the polity the forum aims to influence.
[7] Ferejohn 2009, 209.   [8] Warren 2007.
[9] See, respectively, Walsh, 2007; Steiner et al. 2004.
[10] Mansbridge 1999, 221. See also Parkinson 2006a; Warren 2007. Intentionally or not,
   Mansbridge's call for "maximum feasible publicity" echoes the attempts of 1960s social
   welfare policy to allow for "maximum feasible participation" by the poor in designing

Practicing publicity as a form of deliberative rhetoric may be the best hope that civic forums can offer for reducing the tension between culti- vating necessary protections for citizen deliberation and improving delib- eration in other, wilder parts of the democratic system. Chambers warns that if we think of the civic forum as "the only place that deliberation can take place then we risk falling into the Platonic position of turning our back on the broader democratic public sphere as a place to pursue reasonable politics."[11] This misses the fact that because most civic forums are not empowered to effect decisions directly, they are very much aimed at the public sphere and officialdom, and need to persuade them. Their ultimate goal is to communicate with the political system, not to retreat from it. Good publicity works toward their goals, and Chambers' aims, to improve deliberation within other elements of the system.[12]

What would that kind of publicity look like? Our aim will be to adapt deliberative principles for public reasoning within the forum to communi- cation with those outside the forum. Many theorists specify standards of deliberative rhetoric that are similar to the elements of public reasoning we discussed in Chapter 1: public-minded reasoning,[13] respect for others' views,[14] clear appeals to values (such as justice),[15] well-informed,[16] and transparent about the deliberative process. We agree with Dryzek's argu- ment that deliberative rhetoric should also be judged by its consequences for the deliberative system by asking, "does the rhetoric in question help create and constitute an effective deliberative system joining competent and reflective actors?"[17] Dryzek would prioritize the systemic criterion over the categorical criteria of public-mindedness, respect, and so on, but we are less concerned about doing so. His point is that even categorically

---

and delivering social programs, which were also motivated in part by making welfare bureaucracies more accountable to the least well off and more inclusive of their views (Zarefsky 1986, 45–8).

[11] Chambers 2004, 400. See also Chambers 2009.

[12] Chambers (2004) is rightly concerned that thoughtful decisions issuing from protected deliberative spaces can be defeated by plebiscitary rhetoric in the public sphere. She points to what she saw as a good plan for constitutional reform developed in regional conferences in Canada in 1995, which was overwhelmed by manipulative campaign rhetoric when put to a referendum. The Oregon Citizens Initiative Review panels, which examine proposed ballot initiatives and advise the electorate on them, as discussed in the Introduction, suggest an institutional solution to the challenge of enabling protected citizen deliberation to provide a counterweight to typical campaign rhetoric (see Gastil and Richards 2013).

[13] Dryzek 2000, 68–70; Spragens 1990, 249.

[14] Kock 2007, 14; Spragens 1990, 249; Young 2000, 77–9.

[15] Yack 2006, 423.   [16] Chambers 2009, 335.   [17] Dryzek 2010, 81.

ugly rhetoric by political leaders engaging in demagoguery may spark a reaction that leads, in the long run, to a more deliberative system. But the good conditions for deliberation in civic forums generally do not result in their issuing demagogic arguments, and so are not likely to pose such conflicts. In addition, we are less clear about whether to credit ugly rhetoric for a good response to it. We should be wary of falling into a kind of optimistic functionalism, in which all developments make some contribution to the best of all possible deliberative systems.[18]

While we agree that non-deliberative rhetoric, such as demonstrations by disempowered groups, can be necessary and legitimate for compelling unresponsive decision makers' attention to important issues, we need a fuller account of when coercive, adversarial, or plebiscitary rhetoric harms the deliberative system, as well as when it helps.[19] For example, in the US context, we see the conservative Tea Party movement's angry rhetoric about deficits and health care reform as having severely undermined the ability of politicians even to bargain, much less deliberate, with each other and with citizens over fiscal and health care policy.[20] The Tea Party and other conservative critics have demonized their opponents so completely that officials and activists fear cooperation would brand them as hypocritical, weak, or foolish. The result of such rhetoric has not been a movement toward principled compromise, but rather a calcification of the debate into opposing positions that cannot be bridged without great political costs to each side.[21] This gridlock has imposed

---

[18] In Voltaire's *Candide*, Dr. Pangloss typifies this type of functionalism when he argues, "'Tis demonstrated ... that things cannot be otherwise; for, since everything is made for an end, everything is necessarily for the best end." As Candide wonders, "If this is the best of all possible worlds, what are the others?" (Voltaire 1949 [1759], 230, 241).

[19] On the value of social protest in a deliberative system, see Mansbridge et al. 2010. Fung (2005) articulates a sensible ethical framework for how citizen groups can use the coercive rhetoric of protest to compel attention from more powerful actors when they refuse to address the arguments of the less powerful. Drawing on rationales for civil disobedience, Fung emphasizes that "deliberative activism" should follow an attempt to engage the powerful in deliberation and demand opportunities for future deliberation with them. Deliberative activism should employ rhetoric that does not destroy the possibility for future deliberation.

[20] For a review of Tea Party ideology more generally, including the tension between extreme rhetoric and the ability to compromise, see Williamson, Skocpol, and Coggin 2011; Skocpol and Williamson 2011.

[21] Sarah Palin's accusation that the Affordable Care Act would put elderly citizens' health care decisions in the hands of government "death panels" is one of the more famous examples of overheated rhetoric. For another example, at one of the more infamous 2009 Town Hall meetings between congressional representatives and their constituents, Representative Barney Frank was confronted by an activist who opposed the Democrats'

significant costs on the country, including brinksmanship regarding the nation's debt ceiling, difficulty passing regular budgets, and an unpopular and economically damaging government shutdown.[22]

In other words, not all adversarial rhetoric contributes to a more deliberative system. By the same token, not all civic forums contribute to a better functioning system either. For example, Karpowitz and Mansbridge highlight the case of a local forum on town planning that did not give sufficient space for different perspectives and conflicting interests to be expressed, resulting in frustration and less confidence in the forum among some participants as well as non-participating members of the community.[23] Those who were dissatisfied with the process at the forum resisted the claims of forum organizers and were more likely to take their concerns to other, more adversarial forums, such as meetings of the local town council. More attention to the principles of effective deliberative publicity, especially to the relationship between the civic forum and other institutions for local decision making, would have helped the forum play a more effective role in the community.

What systemic consequences should we want from deliberative publicity? Drawing on the ideal criteria for deliberation articulated in Chapter 1, we can say that publicity should contribute to self-rule by those outside the forum. Concern for *ethos*, which in civic forums includes the character of both the citizen participants and the custodians of the deliberative process, should motivate them to practice accountable argumentation and transparency about how the forum was organized. This kind of rhetoric ought to allow others to make well-informed decisions about whether to accept the forum's process and argumentation. This may reflect acceptance of the forum as a proxy for public judgment,

---

health care reforms, demanding to know why he supported what she repeatedly called a "Nazi policy." Frank, who is Jewish, responded,

> When you ask me that question, I am going to revert to my ethnic heritage, and answer your question with a question. On what planet do you spend most of your time? ... You want me to answer the question? As you stand there with a picture of the President defaced to look like Hitler, and compare the effort to increase health care to the Nazis, my answer to you is as I said before, it is a tribute to the First Amendment that this kind of vile, contemptible nonsense is so freely propagated. Ma'am, trying to have a conversation with you would be like trying to argue with a dining room table. I have no interest in doing it.

[22] Yen 2013. Of course, we are not arguing that Tea Party rhetoric is the *only* cause of ineffective governance, but that it has been a significant obstacle to deliberation and negotiation.

[23] See Karpowitz and Mansbridge 2005; Karpowitz 2006.

because of trust in the *ethos* of the citizens who participated, for example, if they are seen as representative of the polity or well-informed about the issue. Trust may be warranted as well by the *ethos* of those who conducted the forum if they are seen as having conducted it fairly and competently. Agreement may also be achieved on more substantive grounds, such as acceptance of the participants' arguments, or *logos*. Even if a forum does not arrive at recommendations, publicity can argue for meta-agreements about what are the central issues, values, and knowledge claims at stake in the debate. Deliberative publicity should also serve public reason as forum members anticipate their audience's response. Giving an account of their positions should motivate group members, or groups as a whole, to clarify, prioritize, and strengthen their arguments (*logos*). The prospect of communicating with the larger public or decision makers may also help translate narrow interests into more public-minded reasoning, demonstrating respect for those outside the forum by addressing their views and values (*pathos*), even if they are not physically present in the forum. As Chambers observes, the need to appeal to an audience does not have to inspire plebiscitary rhetoric, but also "brings the asymmetry of rhetoric in line with the reciprocity of deliberation" through anticipatory consideration for and sympathy with others.[24] At its best, this kind of publicity might prompt non-participants to be more interested in taking part in civic forums or other aspects of decision-making processes in the future.

The Legitimate Publicity Indicators

How can we assess the quality of deliberative publicity practiced by civic forums? In the rest of this chapter, we construct a set of Legitimate Publicity Indicators (LPI), which we will use to evaluate publicity in final reports of civic forums in later chapters. Our hope is to identify a set of metrics that will allow outsiders to tell when they ought to pay attention to the results of a particular forum. Our strategy is to derive many of our conceptual and operational definitions of the LPI by adapting and distilling criteria that are used to assess the internal deliberative process of groups, supplemented by the expectations for deliberative rhetoric outlined above. Our main challenge is that deliberative democrats do not share a single vision of these evaluative criteria, as we saw in Chapter 1. In response to this diversity of perspectives, we aim to define

[24] Chambers 2004, 403.

criteria that reflect what we see as the most broadly shared views in the current literature. We translate them into operational definitions, which can be used to assess civic publicity using quantitative content analysis.

We also contrast the criteria with the most intricate coding scheme for assessing the quality of public deliberative talk – the Discourse Quality Index (DQI) developed by Jürg Steiner and his colleagues.[25] The DQI offers an especially useful point of comparison for several reasons. It was inspired by Jürgen Habermas' theory of communicative ethics, which has stimulated many of the theoretical debates over deliberation during the past three decades. In addition, because the DQI was created to evaluate parliamentary discourse, contrasting it with our approach allows us to highlight how evaluative criteria must be tailored differently to civic deliberation. The DQI also raises important methodological questions, especially whether it is valid to construct an overall index of the quality of deliberation and of publicity about it. The DQI has been widely applied and adapted in empirical research. Its authors have also reflected on it extensively and made some alterations to it, which reveal changes in thinking about deliberation over the past decade.[26] Our aim is build on the strengths of the DQI, while improving upon a few of its weaknesses, as we adapt it to evaluate publicity about citizen deliberation.

Several clarifications are in order at the outset. First, we aim to measure the quality of communication *about* deliberation, not of deliberation within the forum. Excellent deliberations may be communicated poorly to the public, for example, by reporting that reveals nothing of the group's reasoning and process. Poor deliberations can be dressed up after the fact such that they appear to be communicated well, for example by publicity that supplements the group's actual discussion with reasons it did not consider or that presents a misleadingly rosy view of its process. Thus, we are not attempting to offer an indirect measure of the legitimacy of a group's deliberation by assessing the publicity about it. Our focus, instead, is on the messages that are communicated to an audience beyond the forum.

Second, we are concerned here with the *formal* aspects of publicity that are widely supported within deliberative theory. Therefore, our measures do not assess the *substantive* legitimacy of publicity. For example, while the LPI can capture whether a report appeals to norms, such as conceptions of rights or justice, our measures do not attempt to distinguish good norms from bad ones. As we saw in Chapter 1, deliberative decisions

---

[25] Steiner et al. 2004, Chapter 3.   [26] Bächtiger et al. 2010; Steiner 2012.

should be grounded in norms and judged normatively, but there is less agreement among theorists about all of the specific rights or principles that decisions must respect. Thus, we want to explore whether broadly stated norms – such as appeals to any version of rights, justice, the common good, and so on – are communicated at all. At the same time, if formal quality is necessary but insufficient to identify good arguments, our measures can identify weak arguments that fail to appeal to norms, evidence, and so on.[27]

Third, we aim to propose realistic standards for any deliberative publicity by a group that seeks to affect public opinion or policy making, rather than an ideal standard, such as Habermas' Ideal Speech Situation. We think that publicity can incorporate each of the elements of argumentation and transparency, at least briefly, regardless of the issue, context, or audience for the deliberation, unless doing so would expose the participants to external pressure that undermines the very possibility of deliberation. For example, in regard to argumentation, even highly moral issues (such as abortion) involve disputes over evidence (such as when human life begins or the experiences of women who have had abortions). Even the most technical issues (such as the safety of genetically modified crops) implicate norms (such as the rights of consumers to full information about the ingredients in their foods). None of the kinds of transparency we define require that all deliberation be held in public or even that the deliberators' identities be revealed. In the following chapters, we demonstrate that each element of publicity is fulfilled by at least one of the final reports of deliberative forums that we analyze. In Chapter 7, we suggest ways in which all forum organizers could incorporate both argumentation and transparency more effectively.

Fourth, while we think that practicing high-quality publicity is likely to be necessary for most forums to influence public opinion or policy decisions, we make no claims that deliberative publicity is sufficient to determine policy. It would be naïve to ignore the role of political expediency, including the timing of conclusions to fit windows of opportunity, costs of proposals, fit with interests of powerful constituencies, and so on. But it would also be naïve to assume that communicative legitimacy has *no* bearing on the adoption of conclusions. Moral authority is always a resource in politics.[28] In addition, many elements of good publicity as we define it overlap with aspects of effective policy analysis and writing.

[27] For a similar point about the DQI, see Bächtiger et al. 2010, 41.
[28] Kratochwil 1989.

Scholarship on the rhetorical aspects of policy analysis and public policy textbooks emphasize the persuasive value of offering thorough rationales for proposals, credible evidence, and clear evaluative criteria (normative reasoning), as well as addressing multiple alternative courses of action and trade-offs (i.e., exploring counter-arguments).[29]

There are trade-offs to our approach. If it involves some transcendence of debates over the many conceptual distinctions that have marked deliberative theory, it also involves relinquishing some of the specificity that is valuable and interesting in those debates. Thus, the LPI may appear somewhat generic. Yet its value is that it allows future research to build theory by preserving a core set of measures that can be employed consistently across studies of how civic deliberation is made public. It also allows researchers to supplement these basic measures with additional criteria to examine more specific concepts unique to particular deliberative theories. Qualitative analysis should also be used to offer a deeper analysis of the extent to which publicity is legitimately deliberative. As we show below, many of our core measures reflect broadly shared values among deliberative theorists about what makes for legitimate deliberation, such as arriving at conclusions; supporting them with reasons, evidence, and normative claims; giving respectful consideration to opposing views (or reciprocity); and practicing transparency about multiple aspects of the deliberative process. Other measures are more tailored to the challenges of reporting civic forums, such as how faithfully authors reflect the group's views. We organize these measures into two broad categories: argumentation (reporting the *content* of deliberation) and transparency (disclosing the deliberative *process*).

Argumentation

When a civic forum reports its conclusions to external audiences, the participants' deliberation is transformed into an argument, which can be assessed using many of the categories that are basic both to the theory of democratic deliberation and to the study of argumentation. These categories include the group's conclusions, reasons, evidence, norms, and consideration of and respect for opposing views (see Table 4.1). While we derive these categories below from the literature on deliberation, they also overlap with most of the elements of Stephen Toulmin's classic model

---

[29] On policy rhetoric, see Fischer 1995; Majone 1989. For a policy textbook that emphasizes these elements of argumentation, see Bardach 2009.

Table 4.1 *Argumentation indicators*

Conclusions	Reasons	Evidence	Norms	Opposing views
Recommendations	Events	Statistics	Rights	Contrary conclusions
Decisions	Conditions	Research	Duties	Contrary reasons
	Ideas	Stories or anecdotes	Justice	Contrary evidence
	Needs	Testimony	Fairness	
	Values	Analogies or contrasts	Morality	
	Affects			

of argumentation, in which rhetors base claims (conclusions) on data (reasons and evidence) and address rebuttals (opposing views).[30] We suggest that the most legitimate kind of deliberative argumentation will include each of these elements and connect them to each other coherently.

Conclusions

We have defined democratic deliberation as a search for agreement among political equals engaged in public reasoning. When group agreements are publicly reported, they become recommendations (from advisory forums) or decisions (made by some popular assemblies or co-governance institutions). Yet, as shown in Chapter 1, theorists do not agree on what kinds of agreements (on shared procedures for discussion, on values, or on specific policies) should count; whether collective agreements must be binding upon all members of the group; or whether agreements must be made by group consensus, or can be made by individual voting or polling after deliberation. For the purpose of inclusiveness, we define any agreements reached by a group as its *conclusions*, which we construe broadly as including all decisions or recommendations that are publicly presented as having been endorsed by at least a majority of the deliberators. Our operational definition of a conclusion includes any sentence containing a statement about what should or must be done, as well as descriptions of what the deliberative group or its allies want or aim to do, or are trying to get others to approve or pass. This approach needs some unpacking.

[30] Toulmin 1958.

Specificity of agreements
In our view, conclusions vary in their specificity because deliberative
theory is not of one mind about what kinds of agreements matter. Deliberation may end with all of the elements of meta-consensus discussed in
Chapter 1, including expressions of agreement on common definitions
or understandings of a situation, on procedural goals or strategies for
addressing it, or on more detailed policy prescriptions. Thus, we define
conclusions broadly as including any of these kinds of agreements, as
long as they are expressed as what at least a majority of the group thinks
should or must be done, or as their wants or aims.

For example, consider the report of the *Broadband for All?* Consensus Conference we discussed in Chapter 3.[31] Embedded in the recommendations are agreements on many mutual understandings of complex
terms. A call for subsidizing "equal access to service" specifies a shared
understanding that equality must include comparable Internet speed and
protections for privacy and security for all. The group agreed that local
governments should pursue several goals, such as full accessibility of
broadband for the disabled; a host of related strategies, such as ensuring
that broadband networks are compatible with screen reader programs
for the blind; and specific implementation steps, such as requiring city-
sponsored computer training programs to consult with adaptive technology specialists in the academic and nonprofit sectors. The report also
called for procedural measures to ensure ongoing citizen participation
in oversight of broadband, such as creating a municipal public advisory board. Our definition of conclusions would capture all of these
agreements on goals, strategies, implementation, and future procedural steps, and the common understandings that are embedded in these
conclusions.[32]

Force of agreements
In our view, conclusions also may vary in their binding force upon the
group and others. Conclusions include *decisions* that are enacted into
policy by forums that are empowered to do so and *recommendations*

---

[31] Santa Clara University Center for Science, Technology, and Society and the Broadband
Institute of California 2006.

[32] Because we are coding deliberative rhetoric, how a statement is phrased matters greatly.
Our definition of conclusions omits shared understandings that are not phrased as a
statement about what should or must be done, as an aim, or as something that the
participants want to get others to approve or pass. Examples would include straight
definitions of terms, such as "Equal access is . . . " or "Equal access means . . . " Instead,
we would code these as *reasons* for the group's conclusions.

by less empowered forums. For example, Deliberative Polling presents participants' views after deliberation as having a "recommending force" to policy makers and as offering "the rest of the population some conclusions that they ought to take seriously."[33] Similarly, organizers of Citizens Juries, which conclude with individual voting, contend that they should "have an impact on public policy and empower a microcosm of the public to do its best job of producing sound policy recommendations in the public interest."[34] The results of deliberations in National Issues Forums are regularly presented to officials and the public at congressional briefings, at press events at presidential libraries, and on public television.[35] Organizers of each kind of forum often involve officials in the process and disseminate the results to politicians and the news media; in rare cases, Deliberative Polls have been used to settle electoral or policy questions more directly.[36] Whether participants in these advisory minipublics consider their views to be any less binding upon themselves and others because they use voting or polling as a decision rule is an empirical question. However, it is reasonable to assume that participants expect that their participation in these forums can have some kind of collective influence on policy, even if their own views are expressed within a composite representation of considered public opinion, rather than as a group verdict that affects policy more directly. Each participant in a mini-public is still asked to answer the question "What should we, as a society, do?" and to discuss potential answers with others.

What about educational forums, which may seek common ground on basic understandings of a situation but not specific agreements on policy preferences? Do they lack conclusions entirely? As we will see in coming chapters, it is very difficult to summarize a group's discussion without expressing any points of agreement. All of the reports we examine, including reports of the most educational or dialogic forums, present some agreement as shared by all or a majority of the group, even if it is expressed as an affirmation of shared understanding (such as a problem definition), values (such as tolerating difference of opinions), future procedural steps (such as continuing to engage in discussion), or goals (such

---

[33] Fishkin 2009, 27.   [34] Crosby and Nethercut 2005, 114.

[35] Melville, Willingham, and Dedrick 2005, 44–56. For more evidence of the policy impacts of National Issues Forums, see also Fagotto and Fung 2006.

[36] Deliberative Polls have directly affected energy policy in Texas, infrastructure in China, and a party primary in Greece. In the Texas case, participants' policy choices were subsequently ratified by energy companies and regulators; in the Chinese case, these choices were ratified by local party officials. In the Greek case, participants directly elected their party's candidate for mayor. Fishkin 2009, 150–8.

as seeking common ground), rather than specific policies or strategies. For us, all of these kinds of agreement, if they are presented in publicity as endorsed by at least a majority of the group, count as conclusions.

Extent of agreements

How extensively must citizens agree if we are to say that the forum has endorsed a conclusion? The decision rules used in civic forums vary widely, sometimes not including a formal *collective* choice at all. In some deliberative designs, such as Consensus Conferences, participants arrive at agreement by consensus and their conclusions are presented publicly as having been endorsed by all deliberators in the forum. In formats that conclude with voting or polling, or with majority and minority statements, participants' views are often presented as a series of consensus, majority, plurality, or minority opinions on discrete policy questions. We have noted that organizers intend these expressions of public opinion to be seen as recommendations that should inform policy. However, as we analyze reports of such forums in Chapters 5 and 6, we will find that these reports are not always clear about when a majority, plurality, or even minority view should be considered as a group recommendation. How do we handle this wide variety of approaches? For our purposes, we consider a conclusion by the group to be any majority view after deliberation that is not omitted or disclaimed in public communication by the forum's organizers.[37] To do otherwise would seem to violate the intent of these forums' goals and their claims about the public opinion that emerges from these events.

Some deliberative democrats may wonder why we have not restricted the definition of conclusions to consensual statements, or at least prioritized them as more normatively attractive than majority views. As noted in Chapter 1, few deliberative democrats still see consensus as the only desirable outcome of deliberation, or even as the best one. Faced with this lack of agreement, we employ a broad conception of conclusions that counts everything crossing the minimal threshold of endorsement by a majority of deliberators. This move seems especially appropriate to the analysis of *deliberative* publicity, in which one goal may be to express

---

[37] While the reports we analyze contain no examples of recommendations that are disclaimed in publicity, this is a theoretical possibility. For example, authors of publicity may reject or discount some conclusions if they see participants as misinformed, manipulated, or uncertain. A more likely possibility is that some conclusions are not reported publicly because authors are not fully aware of them as they were not adequately recorded in the forum, or because these conclusions are objectionable to sponsors.

not just agreements but also the extent of agreement among the group. And, as we will see in our discussion of opposing views below, this definition still allows us to recognize the diversity of opinions that may be present in any forum.

Reasons

Legitimate public communication of deliberation does not simply list conclusions but supports them with reasons. For many theorists, democratic deliberation's "first and most important characteristic . . . is its *reason-giving* requirement."[38] Reason giving has been presented as more legitimate than other ways of resolving differences, such as bargaining and voting, because of its many anticipated effects on participants and decisions. As we noted in Chapter 1, under good conditions, public reasoning is said to enlarge participants' perspectives; to foster mutual respect, tolerance, and trust; to encourage critical reflection on taken-for-granted values and preferences; to inform political leaders about the public's knowledgeable and considered views; and to hold deliberators more accountable to the public. As a result, reason giving is seen as yielding more legitimate decisions than procedures that do not involve rational discussion. Publicity should be guided by similar ideals, as citizens within the forum present their reasoning to those outside the forum to promote understanding of the forum's conclusions and further deliberation about them.

Conceptually, we define a reason broadly as any statement that "answers the 'why' question" about the basis for one's position.[39] Our operational definition of a reason is any statement that explains why a conclusion is desirable, but which is not immediately backed by evidence in the same sentence (in order to distinguish evidence from other kinds of reasons). We include not only rational argumentation but also affective reasoning (or justifications based on emotion), which is increasingly recognized as making a valid contribution to deliberation.[40] Reasons include presentations or summary descriptions of events, conditions, ideas, needs, values, and affects that justify conclusions. For example, reasons found in the sample report mentioned above include claims that Internet access must be expanded because those who lack it "miss out on basic social, economic, and political opportunities" (an event); privacy must be better protected because "users are often unsure how the information they

---

[38] Gutmann and Thompson 2004, 3. See also Benhabib 1996, 69; Cohen 1989; Habermas 1996, 107.

[39] Mansbridge 2007, 261.

[40] Mansbridge 2003; Ryfe 2005; Gastil 2008, 36–7; Black 2003.

provide to the broadband provider will be used" (a condition); Internet training should be subsidized because "training programs can themselves generate economic opportunities and growth" (values) and "residents need to know and use basic safe practices" (a need); and access should be subsidized because "[t]he panel worries about potential 'disconnects' between the underserved and other stakeholders in broadband networks" (an affective reason).[41]

Privileged reasons

Have we defined reasons too broadly? Are there some kinds of reasons that should be ruled out or prioritized as more and less legitimate? We do not see sufficient agreement among deliberative theorists to warrant excluding or ranking different kinds of reasons. We have defined public reasoning within the forum as involving mutual justification, characterized by an exchange of reasons employing persuasion rather than coercive threats or inducements. Similarly, publicity should aim to offer reasons that could be accepted by others who would be affected by the forum's conclusions. However, it is not clear how one can identify reasons that would be accepted by others in public communication, such as a final report of a forum. Gutmann and Thompson acknowledge that whether there are indeed claims that can be accepted by all "can often be discovered only in the process of deliberation itself."[42] This question of whether a forum's reasoning is acceptable to others is best answered not in the heads of researchers, but by studying the reactions of others outside the group, in subsequent deliberation or through formal evaluation of the forum by citizens, officials, and expert observers.

The problems that can arise from distinguishing reasons that are thought to be acceptable to others from those that are not is illustrated in Cappella, Price, and Nir's study of online deliberation. The authors were confronted with the problem of weeding out "off-topic" postings to unmoderated message boards on the Internet, where the likelihood of such comments can be high. While this is defensible in the interest of identifying a coherent object of study, the authors define relevant reasons as claims

> that are acknowledged in public discourse as plausible reasons (e.g., for [one's] support of the Republican party). Plausible reasons might

---

[41] Santa Clara University Center for Science, Technology, and Society and the Broadband Institute of California 2006, 3, 4, 6, 9.
[42] Gutmann and Thompson 1996, 56.

include the Republicans' policies regarding smaller federal government and lowered taxes. Irrelevant reasons could include a person's statement that he or she liked Republicans or knew some Republicans.[43]

How should we distinguish reasons accepted in "public discourse" from those that are not without reference to further deliberation or public evaluation? Whose public discourse counts? *The New York Times*? *The National Enquirer*? Furthermore, why exactly is knowing and liking Republicans (or Democrats) not a valid reason for liking the party? The authors rely on a particular version of rationality based on abstract policy calculations, excluding experience and social affiliation as illegitimate sources of reasoning. This seems to reflect a belief that good citizens engage in independent cognition about politics, while inadequate citizens decide in part based on their social ties.[44] As we have noted, this may privilege a brand of deliberation that favors those who have greater experience with this kind of reasoning or who engage in it more often in response to social expectations, including people with more education, status, and income, not to mention testosterone.

Indeed, early deliberative theory often saw abstract reasoning as more worthy than other types of reasoning. Elster distinguishes reason as "impartial, both disinterested and dispassionate."[45] In his early work, Dryzek writes that decisions should be "based on good cognitive reasons."[46] Reflecting this traditional view of reason, the Discourse Quality Index (DQI) considers a claim to be better if it incorporates an appeal to abstract principles, such as "social justice, quality of life, peace."[47] In contrast, Chambers sees a clear shift among many theorists away from the "highly rationalistic view of reason-giving that stresses a model of impartiality rising above all difference" toward "a flexible and pluralistic idea of reason-giving" that sees rationality as more context-bound and culturally specific, and as inextricably (and rightfully) affective as well as cognitive.[48] Therefore, our approach does not privilege abstraction only for abstraction's sake. However, as discussed below, we think that normative discourse makes an important contribution to deliberation, and so we would credit an appeal to social justice as revealing the values that motivate a group's arguments.

---

[43] Cappella, Price, and Nir 2002, 77.
[44] On these different visions of the good citizen, see Schudson 1998.   [45] Elster 1998, 6.
[46] Dryzek 1990, 218.   [47] Steiner et al. 2004, 20; Steiner 2012, 271.
[48] Chambers 2003, 321. Chambers sees this shift in Bohman 1995, 253–79; Dryzek 2000; Mansbridge 1999.

Should we privilege reasons oriented toward "the formation of a public conception of the common good,"[49] eliminating or discounting appeals from self-interest or group interest? In Chapter 1, we sided with theorists who argue that public-minded reasoning can incorporate self-interest or group interest, as long as it links them to some larger argument about truth, justice, or fairness for society as a whole. Moreover, even those who would preserve some notion of the common good, and would put appeals to it closer to the heart of deliberation, share no common definition of the common good. For example, the initial version of the DQI uses the following hierarchy to rank how well statements invoke the public good: at the top are appeals that refer to helping the least advantaged in society (all of which are assumed to be justified in terms of Rawls' difference principle); second best are utilitarian appeals to the greatest good for the greatest number; next come statements that do not appeal to the common good; the lowest rung is reserved for appeals "concerning group interests."[50] This is certainly a departure from Habermas' deliberative theory, which was the main inspiration for the DQI.[51] Steiner appears to have abandoned it in his revised version.[52]

---

[49] Cohen 1989, 19; see also Habermas 1989, 82–3, 195.   [50] Steiner et al. 2004, 58.

[51] As Jane Mansbridge (2007) notes, the DQI's validation of utilitarian appeals does not square with Habermas' communicative ethics. If, for the early Habermas, consensus is the ultimate and inherent aim of communication, it is not a consensus reached through utilitarian cost–benefit analysis, which assumes that pleasure is people's ultimate goal and aims to aggregate individuals' amount (and perhaps intensity) of happiness to arrive at just decisions, rather than submitting them to deliberation. In addition, Habermas justifies more equal distribution of resources differently than Rawls. Rawls' argument depends on a counterfactual agreement that individuals make behind the veil of ignorance, in which they do not know who they will be in the world and therefore aim to protect themselves from being on the wrong end of inequality by agreeing to minimize inequality itself. Rawls' (1971, Chapter 3) rationale stems from a liberal social contract: individuals, who are assumed to have pre-political rights, identities, and interests, meet behind the veil and strike a deal to protect their individual interests and freedoms. However, in Habermas' (1996, 122–3) attempt to meld liberalism with republicanism, the right to basic living conditions is justified because it is necessary for both exercising rights of individual liberty and being fully included in exercising popular sovereignty. In addition, the examples of legislative discourse given by Steiner et al. (2004) do not contain the kind of specific rationales for the common good that are found in Rawls' difference principle or utilitarian philosophy. Not every rationale for ameliorating poverty is Rawlsian, and not every majoritarian argument stems from the principle of utility. For example, one can argue that reducing poverty increases economic demand, fueling economic growth, or that we need to honor the majority's wishes because they are more powerful than we are and will defeat us in the next election if we do not bend to their will.

[52] Steiner 2012, 268–71.

Other theorists raise additional views of the common good. Deliberative democrats influenced by the republican and communitarian traditions tend to favor thick or comprehensive definitions of the common good focused on shared traditions and values, while other deliberative theorists who are more influenced by liberalism seek only a common good of shared principles and procedures.[53] Chambers differentiates more legitimate appeals to the public good from "plebiscitary reason," which addresses commonality, but with "shallow, poorly reasoned pandering to the worst we have in common."[54] Mansbridge calls for a plural understanding of the common good that includes many "noncongruent, contested meanings" of the term, including

> The good of a functional or organic whole, the correct result of reasoning on a problem, an aggregative entity that includes every individual but for different individual reasons, an aggregative entity that need include only more than a majority (or a supermajority), the good of each in his or her role as member of the public, or other meanings.[55]

The many visions of the common good that Mansbridge finds in the literature suggest the extent of disagreement over its meaning. Although researchers who are especially interested in comparing these different visions of the common good in public discourse might operationalize multiple definitions, that is not the best task for an instrument that aims to assess aspects of deliberative publicity about which most theorists agree.

Reasons without conclusions?
But perhaps the problem is that we construe reasons not too broadly, but too narrowly? Recall that we operationalize reasons as any statements that explain why a conclusion is fair or effective. We do so because there is a logical problem with defining reasons separately from conclusions: a reason must be a reason *for* something. As Cohen writes, reasons are "considerations [that] count in favor of proposals."[56] Even an explicit call to inaction is a call for a particular response to a situation. Otherwise, it is something else – a consideration, observation, impression, or the like, but not a reason. However, this means that publicity about a deliberation that does not identify any conclusions also cannot present any reasons. This might be expected to occur especially in accounts of

---

[53] Gutmann and Thompson 2004, 26–9.   [54] Chambers 2005, 260.
[55] Mansbridge 2007, 262.   [56] Cohen 1997, 413.

educative forums that do not aim to reach agreements on specific policy recommendations. As noted earlier, we have not found a report of a forum that failed to endorse a basic understanding of a situation or future procedural step for addressing ongoing disagreements, both of which we would count as conclusions. Of course, this does not mean that participants in a deliberation who do not agree on a position have not exchanged reasons about it. However, our aim is not to analyze deliberation itself, but how it is made public. In the context of publicity meant to inform or persuade a larger audience, reasons are communicated in support of conclusions. A report of a deliberation without conclusions endorsed by at least a majority of the group may present what were given as reasons in deliberation as background considerations, but on our accounting, they are not collective reasons for a group position.

Evidence

Good deliberation is also based on broad access to information.[57] In published conclusions, information is presented as *evidence*. Evidence is a particular form of reasoning that consists of the "empirical or quasi-empirical claims on which moral reasoning often depends to achieve its practical purposes."[58] Publicizing evidence especially enhances the epistemic functions of deliberation for those inside and outside the forum, so it is worth measuring separately from other kinds of reasoning. In real-world policy documents, evidence can be difficult to distinguish from other kinds of reasons, so we define evidence operationally as any claim that supports a conclusion and that is accompanied with immediate backing in the same sentence or in a footnote to it. As we note below, backing may include statistics, stories, and so on. These kinds of backing distinguish evidential statements (e.g., "75 percent of Americans believe X will solve this problem") from other kinds of reasoning (e.g., a non-evidentiary reason, such as "X would solve this problem quickly and cheaply").

Not all kinds of evidence may be considered equal by different branches of deliberative theory. For example, affective reasoning, storytelling, and personal testimony are now increasingly recognized as valid additions to early deliberative theory's narrow focus on cognitive argumentation.[59] Steiner's revised version of the DQI now includes storytelling as a form of reasoning.[60] However, not all deliberative democrats may agree that

---

[57] Fishkin 2009, 34; Gastil 2008, 9.   [58] Gutmann and Thompson 1996, 56.
[59] Ryfe 2005, 58–60; Thompson 2008, 505; Young 2000, Chapter 2.
[60] Steiner 2012, 57–62, 271.

stories and testimony are as legitimate forms of evidence as references to more abstract or generalizable knowledge, such as social science research.

Rather than attempting to resolve such debates, we code each piece of evidence under the following subcategories so that different conceptions of evidence may be explored. A *statistic* refers to any numerical statement: for example, "fifty percent of Americans," "600 people," "a majority of women," "an increasing number of robberies," as well as probabilistic claims about what is more or less likely to occur, such as "a one in five chance of winning." *Research findings* include any claim attributed to a specific study or to "research" in general, whether a source is cited or not. *Stories or anecdotes* about others include specific, real-world examples of people, organizations, and events, such as "A man who lost his Internet service ended up losing his job."[61] While stories and anecdotes are about people outside the deliberative group, *testimony* refers to personal or collective experiences or projects in which a member of the group has participated directly. *Analogies or contrasts* involve explicit comparisons with or distinctions from other issues or examples. In addition, we argued in Chapter 1 that citizens' judgments are better when they are informed by knowledge that is least disputed among relevant experts *and* among citizens who have direct experience that is relevant to the issue. Though it is not explicitly coded in the LPI, qualitative and quantitative analysis of the larger information environment can help to assess these grounds for evidence deployed in publicity, and we will consider possibilities for such analysis in the concluding chapter.

Normativity

We have argued that deliberation should clarify the values at stake in policy making because deliberative legitimacy is enhanced by making the moral bases of one's position public. The theory of democratic deliberation is itself a normative theory about how politics ought to be conducted, one which aims to incorporate discussion of moral reasoning into politics. This is a vision of what ought to be, not only about what would be most effective or strategic. Therefore, deliberative publicity should communicate the values that motivate forum participants' conclusions. The DQI does not distinguish normative and non-normative claims, which

---

[61] Stories do not include hypotheticals, such as "If a person loses his Internet service, he might lose his job," or claims about general conditions, such as "People who lose their Internet service also lose their jobs."

is surprising given that Habermas demands that law and democracy be justified by citizens and officials in moral terms.[62] Although there is no perfect ratio of normative to non-normative reasoning in a policy document, we think that more legitimate expressions of policy conclusions and their underlying rationales will involve clearer explication of their normative bases.

We code all conclusions and reasons as *normative* (i.e., which explicitly state why a conclusion or reason is morally right, just, or fair) or *non-normative* (which state reasons or conclusions solely in terms of their effectiveness or efficiency). Normative statements explicitly refer to individual and group rights, duties, or obligations, or to justice, fairness, or morality, and to their opposites, such as exploitation, discrimination, or immorality. For example, the report on Internet access mentioned above bases its demand for privacy protections on users' "right to keep their personal information personal." Non-normative statements may be stated in strategic terms ("If [users] do not feel their information is secure, they will be less likely to use the network") or presented without reference to justice or effectiveness ("Providers and governments should take steps to protect users").[63]

Opposing views

Deliberative theory's call to pursue agreement through reciprocal reason-giving means that the theory also prizes consideration of *opposing views*. For many theorists, participants' openness to revising their own views in response to counter-arguments helps distinguish deliberation from other forms of communication, such as strategic bargaining, which may be motivated by a combination of promises and threats rather than genuine exchange of reasons.[64] Willingness to engage with opposing views also manifests mutual respect, a central element of public reasoning as we have defined it. We have also noted that a variety of cognitive biases can make it difficult for people to hear, accept, and weigh arguments that challenge their existing views. However, well-structured deliberation can overcome these biases by exposing citizens to a diversity of viewpoints.

---

[62] Habermas 1996, Chapter 1, 104–18.

[63] Santa Clara University Center for Science, Technology, and Society and the Broadband Institute of California 2006, 6.

[64] Cohen 1989, 22–3; Dryzek 2000, 2; Elster 1998, 6; Gutmann and Thompson 1996, 57–8. At the same time, many theorists of deliberation see interest group bargaining as a necessary feature of the political landscape, but stipulate that bargaining procedures be agreed upon through deliberation. Gutmann and Thompson 2004, 114; Habermas 2005, 384–92; Mansbridge 2007.

Like deliberation, deliberative publicity is more legitimate to the extent that it addresses a greater variety of arguments for and against the majority's position.

For us, an opposing view includes any statement that is explicitly presented as contradicting a conclusion endorsed by the majority of the group, or the reasons or evidence that support the majority's conclusions. Here is an example found in our Internet report:

> While some argue that governments are too inefficient to provide service, or that government involvement in broadband represents unfair competition with private companies, the panel believes these concerns are outweighed by the benefits of government involvement.[65]

In this example, the group's conclusion that city governments should take steps to expand broadband access is accompanied by two opposing views: government is inefficient and government should not compete with private firms. Because we have defined conclusions broadly – as understandings, perspectives, agreements, or decisions endorsed by a majority of the group – conclusions of the minority within the deliberating group and their supporting reasons and evidence are counted as opposing views. For example, some of the reports we will analyze in the next chapter include results of surveys of deliberators about their policy views. Policy options that garnered support from a minority of deliberators during or after deliberation are counted as opposing views.

One of the DQI's strengths is its attention to measuring the level of respect with which counter-arguments are treated in discourse, and we follow its lead. Opposing views may be presented *neutrally*, without explicit comment on whether they are worthy of consideration, even if they are ultimately rejected, as in the example given above. Counter-arguments can also be presented as *illegitimate* when they are introduced as unworthy of consideration through attacks on the arguer's motives (e.g., "Companies, *who care only about their profits*, object to government involvement in broadband"), use of negative adjectives or adverbs ("Some people *mistakenly* argue that government has no role to play in broadband"), caricature ("Some people seem to think that government involvement would *lead straight to communism!*"), or other pejorative language, such as negative language that opponents would not use themselves in public to characterize their position ("The telecommunications

---

[65] Santa Clara University Center for Science, Technology, and Society and the Broadband Institute of California 2006, 2.

industry thinks its *monopoly is good for consumers*"). Alternative perspectives can also be presented as *legitimate*, even if they are not embraced ("We agree with some people's concerns about government inefficiency, but still think that cities should initiate broadband projects").[66]

Coding the level of respect accorded to opposing views helps to address the problem of sincerity in reports of deliberation. While the developers of the DQI and others value sincerity in deliberation, they acknowledge that it is an internal state that is very difficult to measure in discourse.[67] Earlier, we noted that we often cannot know whether participants indeed address counter-arguments with the kind of open and fair-minded consideration that many deliberative democrats value. Deliberators may simply consider opposing views strategically, for example as a way of strengthening one's ability to refute one's foes in debate or to appear reasonable when this is socially desirable.[68] Dennis Thompson resolves the problem by arguing that "the appeal beyond self interest does not have to be sincere if it is plausible on the merits; actual arguments are what matter, not motives (except insofar as the motives are predictors of future arguments)."[69] Evaluating the respect with which opposing views are presented publicly offers one useful way to judge whether reports of deliberation consider opposing views in ways that are plausible on the merits.

Coherence

High-quality reporting of deliberation does not merely include the elements discussed above, but makes clear the connections between participants' conclusions and related reasons, evidence, opposing views, and norms. In our view, deliberation is better when a group arrives at a meta-consensus that focuses the range of reasons and conclusions that are acceptable to the group, sometimes to the point of consensus, and sometimes just enough for members to engage in a vote on the remaining alternatives. More legitimate deliberation also helps to align each participant's values, beliefs, perceived interests, and preferences. Therefore, publicity should try to put coherent arguments to the public and decision makers, so that they can assess whether the forum allowed participants to arrive at a group position or individual arguments that are internally consistent.

---

[66] We should note that the examples in this paragraph are hypothetical, not taken from the report of the civic forum on broadband.

[67] On the challenges of observing sincerity empirically, see Bächtiger et al. 2010; Steiner 2012, Chapter 7.

[68] Frey 1986, 59.   [69] Thompson 2008, 504; see also Warren 2007.

We should not expect the same degree of coherence in publicity issued by civic forums that we would expect from academic political theory, which struggles to make consistent arguments under much more favorable conditions of production.[70] As a threshold measure of coherence in the final reports of civic forums, we code for whether each conclusion in the document is supported by at least one reason, piece of evidence, and so on elsewhere in the report. Similarly, the DQI codes whether each conclusion in a legislative speech or parley is accompanied by some justification, although our measures are a bit more precise in that they can tell us whether each accompanying justification is a reason, a piece of evidence, a norm, or a contrast with opposing views.[71] However, because supporting each conclusion with some justification is a fairly low standard for deliberative publicity, we also offer a summary judgment about the explicitness of the connections between conclusions and the other categories in the entire document. This measure focuses on whether the supporting elements of argumentation are consistently connected to conclusions *proximally* (in the same section of the document) and *logically* (related specifically and directly instead of vaguely or ambiguously). In this way, we aim to draw on the strengths of content analysis, which offers more precise measurement of individual statements, and discourse or narrative analysis, which are better suited to characterizing the interconnections between statements.

Transparency

In addition to practicing comprehensive argumentation, civic forums also honor publicity by practicing transparency about their process. We argued above that civic forums must build trust in their *ethos*, which includes both the character of the citizen participants and the custodians of the deliberative process. Publicity should allow the public and their political representatives to make autonomous decisions about whether to trust the forum as an authentic representation of public opinion, a proxy for public judgment, or a legitimate decision-making entity. We have also argued, in Chapter 1, that transparency can foster equality of inclusion, participation, and influence among citizens.

---

[70] While this may be a rare instance in which academics would prefer *not* to cite themselves, we would certainly admit that we find it challenging to make coherent arguments about complex political theory and empirical evidence.

[71] Steiner et al. 2004, 57.

Table 4.2 *Transparency indicators*

Control	Design	Intended influence	Evaluation	Fidelity
Convener's mission	Participant selection	Purpose	Of deliberation	Authorization
Funding	Representativeness	Audiences	Of participants	Accountability
Partnerships	Agenda			
	Structure and facilitation			
	Deliberative format			
	Decision rule			
	Decision dynamics			

We define transparency as disclosing information about the control, design, intended influence, and evaluation of the deliberation, as well as the fidelity of the publicity to the deliberation it represents.[72] Transparency is not measured directly in the DQI because it was designed to evaluate publicly available transcripts of legislative committee discussions and parliamentary debates. In this context, the control, design, and intended influence of deliberation are governed by established legislative procedures; there is no tradition of formal evaluation; and the authors of publicity are stenographers to the deliberators. In contrast, most civic forums do not have long-established parliamentary procedures, formal evaluation is increasingly conducted to demonstrate deliberative legitimacy to outsiders, and participants' comments are summarized in final reports that are often written by others. Given these differences, the DQI cannot be applied easily to assess the transparency of most civic forums. We code for five types of transparency (see Table 4.2).

Control

First, we measure any disclosures about the control of the deliberative process, including the mission, activities, and staffs of organizations that convened the deliberation; their partner organizations; and their funders or sponsors. As Alison Kadlec and Will Friedman note, in deliberative events, "proper control is a prerequisite for proper design, because control by a partisan entity with a stake in a specific outcome can put

---

[72] The first three categories are adapted and expanded from the discussion in Kadlec and Friedman 2007.

problematic constraints on the deliberative process," such as who is included, what questions are open to discussion, and what solutions are considered within the realm of possibility.[73] Even in forums organized by and for partisans, such as social movements, there is likely to be a diversity of views about goals and strategies. Thus, control can shape whether or not each of these kinds of deliberations are open to public and equal discussion about shared ends and means, or are dominated by the views of better-resourced or more eloquent speakers.

In many practitioners' views, government-organized, partisan, and non-partisan forums are likely to be more legitimate if no one party controls the process; "instead, non- and multi-partisan entities should operate to ensure that the deliberative context is inclusive and egalitarian."[74] Some government forums and many non-partisan forums are organized by independent entities and overseen by advisory boards with representation from multiple stakeholders, who review the agenda, the briefing materials, and the composition of deliberators and experts who will testify, to ensure that the process is open to a range of viewpoints and participants. Similarly, partisan forums can be overseen by diverse members of a larger coalition or movement to minimize inequalities of power among groups. Whether deliberation's organizers are partisan or not, deliberative publicity is best served when the entities controlling and organizing the event are identified clearly, facilitating outsiders' judgment of their openness to diverse perspectives.

Design

We also record revelations of the design of the forum, which encompasses the inclusion of participants and the process by which they deliberate. If a sample of citizens is to deliberate on behalf of the larger polity and aims to influence it, the group's legitimacy depends upon the criteria and process used to select it, and its representativeness of the larger demos. Not everyone shows up to open forums, such as some popular assemblies and co-governance forums, and mini-publics restrict admission by design. To what extent did the forum include those who are most affected by the issue? How broadly did the forum include voices that should be heard on the issue but are least likely to participate in politics? As discussed in Chapter 1, these are difficult questions to answer, and the answers are highly dependent on the issue and political context. We argued that transparency requires that organizers justify how and why

---

[73] Kadlec and Friedman 2007, 7.   [74] Kadlec and Friedman 2007, 8.

they assembled a particular group of participants. This explanation can also reveal whether safeguards were placed against some of the dangers of traditional forms of public consultation, including under representation or exclusion of disempowered groups and domination by those who hold opinions most intensely or who represent organized interests without disclosing so.[75] Therefore, we code for whether publicity mentions the criteria used for recruiting and selecting participants, as well as the group's representativeness of the larger population.

In addition, publicity should mention the major design factors that can influence deliberative quality. The agenda given to participants (initial questions, tasks, briefing materials, statements, issues, or points of view posed) establishes the grounds for discussion, positioning deliberators and framing the issues for them, sometimes in subtle but powerful ways. Public opinion research teaches us that people's policy framings and preferences can shift depending on which of their many values or interests (economic, moral, political, etc.) and perspectives (citizen, consumer, taxpayer, parent, woman, African-American, etc.) are made most salient in a particular context.

How issues are named, framed, and ordered can also influence participants' reasoning and preferences.[76] Research on message priming and framing indicates that the public's thinking can be shaped by how news stories and polling questions foreground particular criteria for evaluating issues.[77] For example, a deliberation that asks employed participants to discuss how much public funding should be spent on supporting the unemployed may proceed differently if it begins with the question "How generous should our country's safety net for the unemployed be now?" (which may evoke "welfare" programs that benefit a narrow segment of the population) than if it starts with the question "How much should we spend to stimulate the economy now?" (which can orient participants' thinking toward managing economic demand for the common good). However, research on framing effects suggests that they can be moderated by several factors, including the strength of a frame and of the predispositions of individuals exposed to it; and, perhaps most relevant to deliberation, the presence of competing frames may neutralize the effects of any one frame.[78] Thus, revealing the range of frames offered by

---

[75] Fishkin 2009, 21–3; Gastil 2008, 188–92.
[76] Bishop 2005, 48–49; Kinder and Sanders 1996, Chapter 7; Bartels 2003, 48–82.
[77] Iyengar and Kinder 1987; Zaller and Feldman 1992.
[78] Recent reviews of the literature on framing indicate that people may respond to competing frames in a number of ways, including reaffirming one's prior values as multiple

organizers at the start of a forum helps us to understand how susceptible deliberators may have been to framing effects.

The structure and facilitation of deliberation – including its length, its location, and the role of the facilitator – can also influence outcomes, so we code for any mention of these factors as well. Because deliberation demands much of people, the length of time available for discussion likely influences how fully they can absorb new information and perspectives, relate them to values, discuss trade-offs between different positions, and arrive at thoughtful conclusions. Location can matter, including whether the meeting site is seen by deliberators as neutral ground or controlled by a particular party. Even the "physical setting used for deliberation, such as the official markers of authority (quality of furniture, seating arrangement of citizens) . . . may serve as indicators of preferred values or ways of interacting."[79] As discussed in Chapter 1, facilitation can shape all aspects of the deliberative quality of the conversation.

Other influential aspects of design that are important to reveal include the deliberative format, decision rule, and dynamics of deliberation. Deliberative formats, such as Consensus Conferences or Citizens Juries, each involve different processes, strengths, and weaknesses.[80] Perhaps the most important aspect of any format is the decision rule by which deliberators come to conclusions, such as consensus, various systems of voting or polling, or leaving it to the organizers to resolve or prioritize the group's views. In Chapter 1, we saw that the means of decision making can influence the deliberative process and outcomes in dramatic ways, although no decision rule is guaranteed to do so. In our discussion of conclusions, we also saw that deliberative theorists see different kinds of decision rules as more and less legitimate. Some theorists viewed consensus as the highest goal, while others were more comfortable with majority rule, and still others were satisfied with individual polling. In addition, there are several other dynamics of deliberation that are important to report, including the strength, speed, or ease with which the group came to agreement on major conclusions. These dynamics can help distinguish which agreements are more and less robust, but also may reveal areas in which the group failed to grapple with alternative views fully enough. Insufficient consideration or high levels of disagreement may send a signal

---

frames cancel each other out, being driven in conflicting directions, or becoming more motivated to evaluate alternatives. See Chong and Druckman 2007; Borah 2011.

[79] Gastil, Knobloch, and Kelly 2012, 216.

[80] For comparisons, see Button and Ryfe 2005; Fung 2003; Fishkin 2009, 21–31, 54–60; Smith 2009, especially Chapter 1.

that more deliberation among the public or officials is needed outside the forum.[81]

Intended influence

Transparency requires disclosing the intended influence of the forum. Publicity should plainly reveal the forum's purpose, including the reasons or goals for convening the deliberation; the intended impact of the conclusions, such as to spark wider discussion among the public or to be adopted directly by decision makers; and the intended audiences, such as particular government entities, or specific publics, such as a community or nation. Many organizers of deliberative forums believe it is best practice to tailor forum designs to each particular issue, context, and goal.[82] As Martín Carcasson observes, sponsors often have multiple, sometimes conflicting, aims for forums. Organizers must often resolve the tension between these goals, especially between building a community's capacity for long-term deliberation and addressing a short-term issue, by designing forums that begin with both ends in mind.[83] To assess the forum, onlookers need to understand the justification for the organizers' choices in light of the sponsor's aims. Given the sometimes controversial nature of civic involvement, the purpose of and audience for deliberation require some explanation if political actors outside the forum are to give their consent to it.

Evaluation

A fourth area of transparency entails reporting evaluation data. In the Introduction, we noted that the professionalization of the field of public consultation might increase expectations that mini-publics will be independently evaluated. Many co-governance forums hold citizens and officials accountable for their performance through reviews by higher levels of government, such as the municipal budget councils that review regional councils' proposals for annual spending priorities in Brazilian Participatory Budgeting.[84] We have also observed that market logic may dissuade organizers from publicizing negative findings to protect their reputations,

---

[81] Mackenzie and Warren 2012.

[82] Cooper and Smith 2012, 12; Lee 2011, 19. As Lee points out, customized forums tend to cost more than standardized designs, which often limits the former to communities and organizations that can afford to pay more.

[83] Carcasson 2009, 3.   [84] Fung and Wright 2003.

and government sponsors of forums can have an incentive to cherry-pick evaluation data to make the forum appear most legitimate in the public's eyes.

The presumption should be that all evaluation data will be made public after the forum. In most contexts, the prospect of post-forum publicity about how well the participants deliberated and how well they thought the organizers conducted the forum is more likely to encourage both groups to hold themselves accountable to the larger polity than it is to chill useful speech within the forum. When government agencies convene forums, it is especially important to practice evaluative transparency about them, for the same reasons that many governments have passed "sunshine" laws requiring disclosure of the time, place, and minutes of all public meetings. In a democracy, citizens have a right to know about how government is spending public money to conduct its business on the public's behalf, including how government consults the citizenry.

Of course, exceptions are possible. If the surrounding political environment is highly divisive and prone to violence or other retribution, it may be necessary to limit publicity if it would make deliberation impossible. When government sponsors or organizes a forum, prior authorization by the public to protect some aspects of citizen deliberation from the spotlight would make it more legitimate. However, even advisory forums that only aim to offer a picture of well-informed public opinion enhance their legitimacy and fulfill their mission better when they release all evaluation data because this fosters better informed deliberation about the forum's process and conclusions in the wider public sphere, and gives officials a clearer understanding of the nature of this unique form of public opinion.

Summaries of the many evaluation studies conducted by practitioners and scholars reveal that they have used numerous overlapping or incompatible measures.[85] Combined, these literature reviews identify over 40 distinct indicators of the quality of the deliberative process and its impacts on participants or the policy community. Some evaluation criteria are narrowly administrative in nature, such as cost-effectiveness, perceptions of the forum by government agency staff, and contribution to faster development of regulations by agency staff. Some measures do not seem to be clearly motivated by deliberative theory, such as participants'

---

[85] Abelson and Gauvin, 2006; Gastil, Knobloch, and Kelly 2012; Haug and Teune 2008; Lyu 2008; Rowe and Frewer 2004.

comfort and convenience. Other indicators, such as "process flexibility," are too vaguely defined to be generalized from one forum design or political context to another. Fortunately, the common themes in these evaluations bear some strong similarities to the argumentation and transparency criteria we have outlined above, especially coming to agreement (conclusions), exchanging reasons, respecting opposing views, and many elements of transparency (including participants' representativeness, and fair and constructive facilitation.)

Looking across the evaluation literature, we see two core areas for transparency about evaluation that should be reported. One consists of formal, systematic assessment of the fairness and effectiveness of the deliberative process – especially the briefing materials, facilitation, and discussion – by participants and observers of the process. Another area encompasses evaluation of the participants, especially the development of their knowledge, attitudes, or dispositions during the deliberation. These measures are motivated by common concerns among theorists and practitioners that deliberators should be able to engage in public reasoning free of manipulation, should be equal in status during deliberation, and ought to be well-informed about the issues they discuss. These indicators also help to evaluate some of the common claims about the benefits of deliberation for fostering civic autonomy and collective knowledge. Therefore, we also code publicity for the presence of any data that emerge from formal assessment of the forum's deliberative process and of the participants. We omit evaluation of the impact of forums on policy because much publicity occurs prior to any reasonably expected effects of the forum and, most importantly, because the quality of publicity is itself a likely influence on those outcomes.

Fidelity

Finally, transparency also involves disclosure of the fidelity of publicity to the deliberative forum. This includes explicit reporting on the group's authorization of the publicity – the criteria used to decide how the major elements of argumentation (conclusions, reasons, evidence, and consideration of opposing views) were included in publicity and whether these criteria were agreed to by the group as a whole. Fidelity also involves a measure of authorial accountability to the deliberators – a disclosure of whether group members thought the authorizing criteria were applied accurately in the final form of the publicity.

Unlike our other categories, fidelity is not widely mentioned in the literature. However, it is crucial for ensuring that publicity's authors are accountable to the deliberators themselves. The potential for authorial infidelity means that as citizens' views are issued into the political system funny things can happen to them on the way from the forum. The kinds of distortion that some theorists fear can happen *within* deliberation can also be committed against the group *after the fact* by the authors of reports. Reports may align participants' views with sponsors' or organizers' own preconceived issue framings and positions, rather than listening to the emergence of new ways of understanding and resolving disagreement.[86] Authors may be drawn to present an illusory consensus, to suppress conclusions and reasoning that conflict with sponsors' views, to airbrush opposing views and conflict within the forum, and the like.

A focus on fidelity also helps us to distinguish the legitimacy of the deliberation itself from the quality of the publicity about it. For example, if a deliberation did not succeed at getting participants to discuss opposing views, then the deliberation is to blame, not the publicity (although the publicity could be expected to acknowledge this failure). As we will see in Chapters 5 and 6, crafting publicity involves more than a simple process of "writing up the forum." The outputs of civic forums – such as individual or consensus statements, the results of majority or plurality voting, or shifts in opinion polls – rarely speak for themselves. Instead, authors must actively interpret, synthesize, and resolve the diverse arguments and conclusions expressed in deliberation, sometimes apart from deliberators and long after the forums have ended.

Fidelity is especially challenging to measure without going beyond reading reports of deliberation. Our definition puts the burden of proof on authors to present evidence of their criteria for summarizing the group's reasoning and conclusions, that the group agreed to those criteria, and that the group felt they were used appropriately by authors in the final product. Of course, authors may present misleading evidence of all three elements of fidelity. If our definition can be applied feasibly and reliably to code reports, it involves a trade-off that may sacrifice some validity. When possible, it would be ideal to supplement content analysis of reports with case studies or evaluation research by independent parties that involves surveying or interviewing participants in deliberation directly about publicity's faithfulness.

[86] Moore 2011.

Expectations for legitimate publicity

How can these measures be used to distinguish more and less legitimate examples of deliberative publicity? A basic threshold for judging
legitimate publicity is that it should include each element of argumentation (conclusions, reasons, evidence, norms, and opposing views) at
least once. Higher quality publicity would involve more *comprehensive*
argumentation, which employs each element more often. For example, a
report that includes more evidence than another would be more legitimate on that dimension of publicity. However, this measure still fails to
address the quality of the connections between each element, or their relevance to one another. Therefore, more legitimate argumentation would
also be more *coherent*, meaning that more conclusions would be directly
supported by at least one reason or piece of evidence, norm, and discussion of an opposing view somewhere in the document; and the example
of publicity as a whole would be structured and worded in a way that
clearly links conclusions and supporting elements. Conclusions would
be linked both proximally (in the same sections of the document) and
logically (a non-specialist in the issue would be able to see how reasons
and evidence support conclusions, for example). Comprehensiveness and
coherence do not always go together. As we show in the following chapters, some reports are much stronger on one set of measures than the
other. Finally, more legitimate publicity would also be fully *transparent*
by disclosing each aspect of the deliberation's control, design, intended
influence, evaluation, and fidelity.

Unlike the DQI, our measures aim to capture and compare a set of
individual indicators, not to create a single index of legitimate publicity of civic deliberation. While it is possible to aggregate our measures
into an index in order to compare reports, we are wary of doing so.
It may be misleading to assign a consistent weight to each element of
publicity in all contexts. Dennis Thompson argues that aggregating to a
single indicator of deliberative quality may obscure the distinct strengths
and weaknesses of different kinds of deliberation, and the same is true
for publicity.[87] For example, it may be that a report that boils down a

[87] Thompson (2008, 509) writes, "Composite standards (which combine several different
measures of the quality of deliberation) may be appropriate for some purposes, but using
separate standards is more useful for identifying conflicts and trade-offs" among the ideals for good deliberation. Other ways of integrating measures of deliberative quality
without reducing them to a single index are suggested in Gastil, Knobloch, and Kelly
2012, 227–8. At the same time, it is important to note that Steiner et al. (2004) had a

welter of competing policy proposals to a handful of conclusions, that is mindful of some major opposing views, and that is highly transparent about its process, is superior to a report that lists many more conclusions and counter-arguments but reveals nothing about how the group chose between them. Furthermore, it may be misleading to deploy an index of legitimate publicity as an independent variable to predict the effects of a deliberative group's report on policy outcomes. For example, it is not reasonable to expect that a report that offered a single conclusion, or conclusions that strongly conflicted with elite opinion that violated widely shared norms, but scored high on all other measures of good publicity would have a greater influence on policy than a report that offered multiple and mainstream conclusions but had low scores on all other measures.[88]

Our goal, then, is to offer criteria for assessing each of various elements of deliberative publicity and to see how those elements are distributed both within and across the final reports of deliberative groups. Understanding the different strengths and weaknesses of any report or set of reports means attending to the distribution of scores across multiple categories. Ideally, this also requires additional qualitative and case

---

stronger rationale for using the DQI as an index to measure the quality of legislative deliberation than we do for publicity about civic forums. Steiner's research team wanted to explore the effects of political institutions on official deliberation. Their comparative study of deliberation in four countries – Germany, Switzerland, the United Kingdom, and the United States – yielded interesting and plausible results. For example, the authors found that deliberative discourse among politicians was enhanced in political systems with multiple parties and proportional representation in elections, and in legislatures that afforded minority vetoes and a strong tradition of second-chamber debates. These findings tested and confirmed some claims in the literature in a more deductive manner than the effects of publicity by civic forums can be tested at present. We suspect that there are more factors than institutional design that may mediate the effects of a forum's publicity on its perceived legitimacy by different audiences and on policy uptake.

[88] Diana Mutz (2008, 532) offers a similar critique of attempts to build a single index of deliberative quality:

> Most human behavior is sufficiently complex that mere additive models are unlikely to account for it. Instead, it is likely that many of the factors [theorists' identify with good deliberation] interact with other factors in influencing these outcomes. Thus, it would not be logical to ask how well a given deliberative encounter stacked up on all of the factors, create a combined score of deliberative goodness, and expect more beneficial outcomes associated with higher scores. This approach would be parsimonious, but it is unlikely to work because (*a*) not all necessary conditions are critical for producing each consequence, and (*b*) many of the factors are likely to interact with one another.

study analysis of how fully the publicity engaged with the range of contemporary arguments on the issues in the wider public sphere and how
well it practiced transparency about the forum, based on a thorough
understanding of what happened in the forum.

Conclusion

We have argued that deliberative democratic theory needs to pay greater
attention to how civic forums communicate their process and conclusions
to those outside the group. Such communication is necessary because civic
forums are relatively new, compared to more established institutions of
public discourse and decision making, and they must work harder to
establish their legitimacy in the eyes of the public. Although theorists of
deliberation value publicity, empirical research has yet to systematically
assess the public communication of civic forums. Thinking about civic
forums' publicity as a unique kind of deliberative rhetoric helps to identify ideal standards for how forums can communicate with other citizens
and with officials. Drawing on contemporary theory, we have derived a
set of measures of the quality of publicity about deliberative processes
and decisions – the Legitimate Publicity Indicators (LPI). These indicators include the comprehensiveness and coherency of major elements of
argumentation (conclusions, reasons, evidence, norms, and consideration
of opposing views). The LPI also evaluates transparency, including disclosure of the control, design, intended influence, evaluation, and fidelity
of publicity.

We are indebted to the Discourse Quality Index (DQI), which was
developed to measure the quality of deliberation in legislative discourse.
Its strengths and weaknesses help illuminate how we can best measure
publicity. The DQI needs to be adapted in several ways to the study of
publicity of civic forums. In some ways, the DQI relies too heavily on
Habermas's early thinking about reasoning, consensus, and the common
good, some of which Habermas himself has since questioned. At the same
time, the way in which the original version of the DQI prioritized Rawlsian and utilitarian appeals to the common good runs counter to the
theory of democratic deliberation as it is understood by most theorists
today. The DQI omits some important categories implied by deliberative
theory, including evidence and normative appeals. Because it is designed
to measure parliamentary discourse, it does not grapple with the challenges of demonstrating transparency, which is a critical concern for
reporting on civic forums. And the DQI aggregates deliberative qualities

into a single index that does not appear to be a logically or universally valid measure of legitimate deliberative publicity for civic forums. In the following chapters, we put our new set of measures to work, comparing the quality of publicity practiced by a sample of reports of civic deliberation.

5

Argumentation

How can our criteria for legitimate publicity be applied to real-world reports of deliberation? What can this tell us about how different groups contribute discursively to the larger deliberative system? In this chapter, we closely examine the quality of argumentation in ten reports of a broad range of deliberative forums.[1] Our sample of reports is neither representative nor random, but illustrative and diagnostic. Because our research is an initial exploration of different patterns of publicity, our sampling strategy was not to take a random sample of all possible reports of deliberation, but rather to ensure that we covered a wide variety of forum designs on a range of issues. We pursued this strategy in part because drawing a fully representative sample is infeasible. Hundreds or thousands of civic forums have been held, and there is no directory that includes them all.[2] A recent survey of practitioners of civic forums finds that around two-thirds of organizations release public information about their forums, but some do so only through press releases, official testimony, or newsletter articles. Almost one in five organizations confine

---

[1] University of New Hampshire Office of Sustainability Programs and Cooperative Extension 2002; Danish Board of Technology 2005; Doble Research Associates 2006; New America Foundation and Center for International Media Action 2006; Santa Clara University Center for Science, Technology, and Society and the Broadband Institute of California 2006; San Francisco Department of Telecommunications and Information Services 2007; America*Speaks*, Everyday Democracy, Demos, and Ash Institute for Democratic Governance and Innovation 2009; Danish Board of Technology 2009; South Dakota Issues Forums 2009; MacNeil/Lehrer Productions and Center for Deliberative Democracy 2010.

[2] Leighninger 2012. The recent creation of an online archive for civic forums, at www. participedia.net, may help fill this gap in the future.

their findings to internal reports and 13 percent make no effort to publicize the results of their forums.[3] Because we cannot draw a representative sample of reports, we do not aim to make universal claims about the form taken by all deliberative publicity or the causes of its dynamics. Nor do we engage in hypothesis testing. Rather, we strive to develop some initial typologies of how deliberative groups publicize their conclusions and reasoning, and suggest what may explain the similarities and differences found in our sample. Where possible, we compare our findings with those in the broader literature on deliberation and democracy, drawing the implications for claims about civic contributions to the public sphere.

However, we think that several conclusions are supported by our limited sample. First, publicity is not a simple reflection of the underlying deliberation, but is shaped by many authorial choices about what to report and how to do so. Authors choose whether to emphasize a group's decisions, how much of the group's supporting reasons and evidence to convey, whether and how to present alternative views, and whether to present the group's views in more or less normative terms. Second, given the gaps we find between some reports' stated aims and their representation of the group's arguments, authors of deliberative publicity can become more conscious of their own choices and these choices can be guided more clearly by deliberative theory.

The reports

We used several criteria to select examples of publicity. First, we limited our focus to final reports issued by the organization that convened the deliberative forum. Some organizers include other material on their web sites, such as briefing materials, excerpts from the deliberation, presentations to the group, and so on. We trained our lens on final reports on the assumption that they best integrate and represent the elements of publicity in which we are interested: conclusions and reasoning (and, as discussed in Chapter 6, transparency). In addition, it is likely that policy makers and members of the public pay more attention to final reports than to background materials. While supporting materials may be made available on the Internet, final reports reflect organizers' views about what

---

[3] Jacobs, Lomax Cook, and Delli Carpini 2009, 148. In addition, there are over 80,000 legislative and policy advisory bodies at the local, state, and federal levels of government in the United States alone, and some of their deliberations are not easily accessible or made public (Theodoulou and Kofinis 2004, 46).

information they deem most important to share most prominently. These reports are comparable to the front page of a newspaper and the lead story on a newscast – an expression of editorial judgment that reveals the publishers' priorities for publicity. While omitting background materials from our analysis means leaving out some expressions of publicity, our focus on forums that issued final reports means that we also left out forums that practice very little publicity or none at all.[4] Another reason to focus on final reports is that these materials are direct expressions by the organizers themselves and therefore are more clearly under their control than news media coverage or public commentary about forums.

We used several additional criteria to select reports. Of course, we sought reports of forums that included both deliberation and publicity. This means that participants exchanged views in order to arrive at individual positions or group decisions, justified their conclusions to others outside the group, and revealed something of the process by which the group reached its conclusions. We restricted the sample to reports published between 2000 and 2010 in order to analyze contemporary practices. Because scholars have identified many factors that can influence the quality of internal deliberation in public forums,[5] these factors may also affect the quality of these forums' publicity, so we sought reports on deliberation that embodied as many of these variables as possible. These are outlined in Table 5.1, which presents the sample as a whole.

We sought reports on several issues that have been the topics of many recent deliberative forums. Some forums focused on questions of environment and health, including the regulation of genetically modified crops and policy responses to climate change. Other forums examined media policy issues surrounding attempts to extend broadband Internet access to underserved groups. One forum asked state residents to tackle economic issues, including their priorities for government services and economic development, and what sorts of taxes the public was willing to pay to support economic renewal. Several projects addressed the issue of renewing democracy itself, asking citizens to imagine what could be done to foster civic character, community institutions, and political reforms. These forums were organized by the kinds of institutions that have been

---

[4] A recent survey of practitioners of civic forums finds that around two-thirds of organizations release public information about their forums, but some do so only through press releases, official testimony, or newsletter articles. Almost one in five organizations restrict their findings to internal reports and 13 percent make no effort to publicize the results of their forums (Jacobs, Lomax Cook, and Delli Carpini 2009, 148).

[5] For an overview, see Fung 2003.

Table 5.1 *Sample of reports*

Report	Year	Issues	Organizers	Design	Decision rule	Deliberators	Sampling strategy	Length of deliberation	Level	Influence
New Hampshire Just Food Citizen Panel	2002	Environment and health (genetically modified crops)	Academic (University of New Hampshire Office of Sustainability Programs and Cooperative Extension)	Consensus Conference	Consensus	Unspecified number of local citizens	Convenience	5 months	National	Advisory to national government
New GM Plants – New Debate	2005	Environment and health (genetically modified crops)	Government (Danish Board of Technology)	Modified Citizens Jury	Cumulative voting (each participant allocates points to one or more options)	16 Danish citizens	Quota (age, region, occupation, gender)	4 days	National	Advisory to national government
Democracy's Challenge: Reclaiming the Public's Role	2005–2006	Democracy (government reform, civic engagement)	Foundation and NGO (Kettering Foundation and National Issues Forum)	National Issues Forum	Some polling	Over 900 Americans in small groups at multiple sites	Convenience	Up to 3 hours	National, local	Advisory
Wireless Broadband and Public Needs	2006	Media (broadband access)	Foundation and NGO (New America Foundation and Center for International Media Action)	Activist strategy meeting	Aggregative	12 American media activists and service providers	Purposive (expertise and leadership)	2 days plus extra time in small groups	National, state, local	Advisory to foundation, participants, their allies

(cont.)

Table 5.1 (cont.)

Report	Year	Issues	Organizers	Design	Decision rule	Deliberators	Sampling strategy	Length of deliberation	Level	Influence
Broadband for All?	2006	Media (broadband access)	Academic (Santa Clara University Center for Science, Technology, and Society and the Broadband Institute of California)	Consensus Conference	Consensus	12 residents of Silicon Valley, CA	Purposive (race/ethnicity, income, physical ability, age, rural/urban)	3 weekends	Local	Advisory to local governments
San Francisco Digital Inclusion Strategy	2007	Media (broadband access)	Government (San Francisco Department of Telecommunications and Information Services)	Stakeholder task force	Organizer decides	Unspecified number of local leaders in business, nonprofit sector, and philanthropy	Purposive (expertise and leadership)	8 months	Local	Advisory to local government
The Role of Citizens in the Legislative Process	2008–2009	Democracy (civic engagement)	NGO, business, academia (South Dakota Issues Forums and 10 local NGO, business, and academic partners)	National Issues Forum	Some polling	321 South Dakota citizens in small groups in 9 towns	Convenience	Unspecified	State	Educational/advisory to state legislators and the public

By the People: Hard Times, Hard Choices	2009	Economy (development, taxes, government services)	News media and academia (McNeil/Lehrer Productions and Center for Deliberative Democracy)	Deliberative Polling	314 Michigan citizens	Random, representative	3 days	State	Advisory to legislature
World Wide Views on Global Warming	2009	Environment (climate change)	Government, NGOs, and academia (Danish Board of Technology and over 50 local government, NGO, and academic partners worldwide)	Modified Citizens Jury	4000 citizens in 38 countries on 6 continents	Convenience	Up to 1 day	Global	Advisory to global climate policy makers
Working Together to Strengthen Our Nation's Democracy	2009	Democracy (civic engagement, electoral reform, open government)	Academia and NGOs (Ash Institute/ Harvard, America*Speaks*, Everyday Democracy, Demos)	NGO Advisory Panel	82 American academics and activists; 7 members of the Obama administration	Purposive (expertise and leadership)	3 days plus extra work in small groups	National	Advisory to national government

most active at convening public deliberation, including academia, governments, and non-governmental organizations.

Over the past four decades, deliberative practitioners have developed an array of forum designs, each of which is distinguished by some fairly consistent features. We summarized these typical forum designs in the Introduction. Because the organizers of the forums we analyzed sometimes adapted and even commingled these traditional designs, we note these modifications in Table 5.1. The sample encompasses a diversity of forum designs, including Deliberative Polls, Citizens Juries, Consensus Conferences, National Issues Forums, stakeholder task forces, and the like. Each kind of forum involved its own rules for how individuals or the group came to decisions about their policy recommendations, which ranged from group consensus to individual polling and voting, to deferring to the organizers to reconcile and prioritize conflicting views. In the Introduction, we noted that there is a continuum between forums that recruit everyday citizens and forums that convene more expert and activist citizens. Most of the forums in our sample convened lay citizens who were not recruited for their expertise or activism on the issues under discussion. Yet, in the interest of assessing publicity about diverse forum designs, we also include a few reports of forums that brought together citizens in their capacity as stakeholders (community leaders with a direct economic or political interest in an issue) or political activists. Some forums were large-scale efforts that engaged hundreds and even thousands of deliberators in small groups, while others brought together a single group of 12 to 16 participants. Recruitment strategies included representative random sampling of the public, but mostly non-random sampling of deliberators. In some forums, deliberation occurred over months, while in others people met for as little as two hours. The forums asked participants to address issues at many different levels: local, state, national, and global.

The sample also includes variation in the forums' prospects for directly influencing public policy. Some were low-stakes affairs in which participants had little ability to affect policy directly, while others included significant engagement from local, state, or national officials, including representatives of the Obama administration or delegates to a worldwide conference on climate change. The audiences for these reports also differ – some were meant for decision makers in government, some for activists and stakeholders, and some for the general public. In all, the sample offers us ample opportunity to explore how a variety of different deliberative forums sponsored by a diversity of institutions communicate their aims, processes, and results to different audiences.

Each report was analyzed independently by two coders in two stages using the definitions of our categories introduced in Chapter 4. In the first stage, each sentence in each report was coded into our categories for argumentation and transparency. Subject headings and subheadings were excluded because their meanings were too fragmentary or ambiguous to code reliably, while images were coded along with their explanatory captions as a single unit of content, equivalent to a sentence. While we defined our categories to be mutually exclusive (e.g., a conclusion was defined differently from a reason), a sentence could be coded as falling into more than one category (e.g., as containing both a conclusion and a reason).[6]

In the second stage, a new pair of coders assessed each document's coherence by coding whether each conclusion was linked to a relevant reason, evidence statement, norm, and opposing view somewhere in the document, and also by making a summary judgment about the document's coherency as a whole (whether it consistently linked conclusions and other elements of argumentation both proximally and logically).[7] Coders also noted the presence or absence of each element of transparency. Over three-quarters of all coding was done by six different research assistants, while the rest was completed by the authors. Both stages of the content analysis yielded high levels of intercoder reliability.[8]

---

[6] There were two exceptions to this rule. A sentence could not be coded both as a reason and as evidence (because we defined a reason as lacking immediate backing in the same sentence and evidence as accompanied by backing in the same sentence). Nor could a sentence be coded as "other material" and in any additional category.

[7] For some of the longer documents, we employed a random sample of approximately 75 percent of the conclusions in the document in the second stage of coding.

[8] In all, the documents in our sample included 3073 sentences. In the first round of coding, in which sentences were assigned to categories, we established intercoder reliability using a sample of 585 sentences, or approximately 19 percent of the sample. Two coders independently assessed the sentences, and levels of intercoder reliability far exceeded standard thresholds for reliability. Averaging across all documents, Krippendorff's alpha for each of the categories is as follows (percentage in agreement in parentheses): conclusions, 0.96 (98.4%); reasons, 0.93 (98.3%); evidence, 0.92 (99.6%); opposing views, 0.96 (99.7%); transparency, 0.95 (97.7%); and other material not falling into any of the categories, 0.78 (95.7%). Because sentences with explicit normative claims were identified using computerized keyword searches, not human coders, we do not have reliability numbers for that category. To establish intercoder reliability for the second round of coding, we examined a sample of 217 conclusions (approximately 23 percent of all conclusions in the dataset). Average Krippendorff's alpha for coder's assessments of whether conclusions were supported by each of the categories is as follows (percentage of agreement in parentheses): reasons, 0.91 (97.0%); evidence, 0.89 (95.2%); norms, 0.89 (94.5%); and opposing views, 0.94 (97.8%). These results also exceed standard thresholds for

Elements of argumentation

Consistent with our aim to include a wide variety of reports, we find considerable variation in the extent to which the reports in our sample emphasized each element of argumentation. Figure 5.1 shows the extent to which each report emphasized conclusions, reasons, evidence, opposing views, and normative claims, giving the raw number of sentences in each category. The figure highlights the diversity of approaches to deliberative publicity found in our sample. While some reports focused heavily on conclusions, others devoted greater space to reasons or evidence. Across all reports, attention to opposing views and norms was comparatively rare, and some reports devoted no space to those elements of argumentation at all. In the rest of this chapter, we unpack and interpret these basic findings.

Conclusions, reasons, and evidence

Deliberation is oriented toward arriving at conclusions, which we have defined as decisions, goals, strategies, solutions, policies, or recommendations that are endorsed by at least a majority of the deliberators. In our sample, the average report devoted about one-third of its sentences to conclusions. Deliberative theory also values supporting conclusions with reasons and evidence. As we detailed in Chapter 4, reasons encompass any answers to the "why" question for the basis of group preferences, including evidence (statistics, research, stories and anecdotes, testimony, and analogies). In the reports we analyzed, the correlation between the percentage of sentences that mentioned conclusions in each report and the percentage devoted to either reasons or evidence (which we will call "reasoning") was negative and low (−0.14). In other words, the reports that were more likely to emphasize conclusions were not necessarily the reports that devoted more space to reasoning. Some reports had few conclusions and considerable reasoning; others included many conclusions and little reasoning; still others had a rough balance between the two. Thus, there is no inherent trade-off in publicity between stating policy conclusions and the reasoning that supports them. Authors can, and sometimes do, choose to report both extensively.

The balance of conclusions and reasoning can be seen more clearly in Figure 5.2, which shows the pattern that results from computing the log

reliability. For the document-level assessments, two coders achieved perfect agreement in all categories on a sample of three reports (30 percent of the reports in the sample).

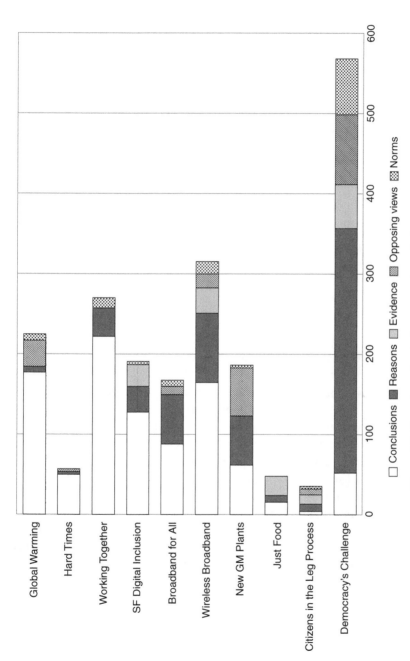

Figure 5.1 Overview of coded sentences in each document

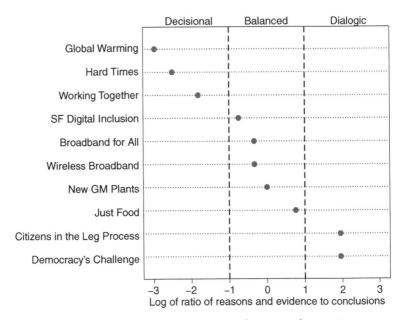

Figure 5.2 Relationship between conclusions and reasoning

of the ratio between the percentage of sentences devoted to conclusions and the percentage of sentences devoted to reasons and evidence.[9] This figure shows the relative weight of conclusions to underlying reasoning in each document. An equal balance between conclusions and reasoning would be at 0 on the scale, with reports containing more conclusions than reasons and evidence appearing to the left of 0 and reports with more reasoning than conclusions to the right of 0.

Figure 5.2 suggests a typology of reports based on the relative weight of conclusions to reasons and evidence in each.[10] Though the conclusions–reasoning spectrum is continuous, the reports tended to cluster into three basic types. *Decisional* reports were focused primarily on communicating conclusions, with much less attention to reasons and evidence. This does not necessarily mean that the deliberators failed to engage in a

---

[9] Other methods of assessing this relationship, such as computing the difference between the percentage of conclusions and the percentage of reasons and evidence, produce the same pattern.

[10] Although our typology overlaps with Button and Mattson's (1999) "deliberative styles" in some ways, it is also distinct, as ours is focused on the way that groups communicate a deliberative event to other audiences, not on the internal dynamics of the event.

thoughtful discussion before deciding, only that the reports highlighted the group's decisions rather than the reasoning behind them. *Dialogic* reports showed precisely the opposite pattern, devoting much greater attention to the reasons and evidence discussed by the group. While conclusions were mentioned, they were not discussed as extensively as the rationales that underpin deliberators' choices. *Balanced* reports gave approximately equal weight to conclusions and reasoning.

Why are some reports decisional and others dialogic, while some strike a fairly even balance? In our sample, one factor that seems especially important is the deliberation's relationship to the policy process. Some of the deliberative forums from which these reports emerged were timed to important political decisions, while other reports had a less direct connection to immediate policy making. Decisional reports tended to be more strategic about influencing policy in their timing and intended influence. They aimed to take advantage of the prospect of governmental action by offering specific prescriptions or issue positions. For example, *World Wide Views of Global Warming* sought to influence negotiators at the COP15 summit, a global intergovernmental meeting about climate change policy. *Hard Times Hard Choices* sought to provide detailed citizen perspectives to Michigan lawmakers deciding how to balance revenues and expenditures during a deep recession. *Working Together* aimed to promote opportunities for civic engagement offered by President Obama's incoming administration, which had specifically committed to such action, including by sending representatives to the deliberative forum.

Similarly, balanced reports also tended to be pegged to upcoming windows of policy action. The *San Francisco Digital Inclusion Strategy* was developed by a municipal agency charged with designing this element of the city's broadband project. The *Broadband for All?* report was timed to affect the design of a regional broadband initiative in Silicon Valley. *Wireless Broadband and Public Needs* appeared amidst national ferment over several communication policy issues in the US courts and before the Federal Communications Commission. The *Danish GM Plants* report was commissioned by the federal government to inform parliamentary debates on revising regulations of genetically modified crops. While *Just Food*, issued by an academic center at the University of New Hampshire, addressed the same issue as *Danish GM Plants*, the New Hampshire report was not as closely tied to any immediate policy action (and it was also closer to the dialogic end of the spectrum than any of the other balanced reports).

The dialogic reports in our sample tended to communicate initial efforts at structured deliberation about long-term and diffuse issues, rather than strategic efforts to influence pending legislation, regulation, or ongoing projects. Both *Democracy's Challenge* and the South Dakota report on *Citizens in the Legislative Process* represented early efforts at the national and state levels to promote civic engagement. In contrast to the *Working Together* conference, which was also convened to address the challenge of civic engagement, the window for policy action (and direct participation) provided by the Obama administration was absent in these earlier projects. Thus, the context of the deliberative event, especially its relationship to more official forms of decision making, appeared to influence how much attention the reports paid to expressing policy preferences or to reasoning about them.

A second factor that appeared to influence the balance of reason giving and conclusions was the design of the deliberative forum. For example, the purpose of Citizens Juries is for the group to make a choice among a range of preselected policy options, and the chief aim of Deliberative Polls is to provide a picture of well-informed public opinion; therefore, organizers of both kinds of forums generally do not preserve deliberators' rationales for their positions.[11] With this focus on outcomes, it is not surprising that these formats produced more decisional reports. A partial exception to this finding is the *Danish GM Plants* document, which was a Citizens Jury, but modified to focus more on reasons and argumentation. In addition to seeking agreement on policy outcomes, the organizers asked citizens to develop and prioritize *arguments* for and against genetically modified crops, and chose to report them in the final document. The result of this important decision was a more balanced report than one might expect from many Citizens Juries, which tend to focus on the citizens' policy "verdicts."

Similarly, the *Wireless Broadband and Public Needs* forum was a strategy-setting brainstorm among social movement activists, rather than an event that asked participants to choose between predefined options. The topic of deliberation was tactics, not necessarily outcomes (on which the activists presumably already agreed). In creative brainstorms of this sort, participants and organizers may see reasons and evidence as critical elements to be communicated in the final report. For example, the report includes strategic discussions of how to frame issues in ways that would most effectively counter telecommunication companies' frames. As

---

[11] Parkinson 2006b.

with the *Danish GM Plants* report, this document shows that the tasks organizers ask participants to complete can have a strong influence on the nature of communication about the event – but only if the authors choose to include this material in the final report. Our argument is not that the design of the deliberative forum *determines* the report; rather, the aims, purposes, and elements of the forum can shape the way authors conceive of their task, including how much attention they will pay to reporting conclusions and reasoning.

The deliberative format can also influence the "raw material" available for inclusion in final reports. For example, several of the dialogic reports in our sample employed the National Issues Forum (NIF) format. NIF forums are structured to focus deliberators on weighing the pros and cons of several broad approaches to framing a problem. The aim of these events is to "provide a way for people of diverse views and experiences to seek a shared understanding of the problem and to search for common ground for action," rather than to achieve consensus or majority approval of specific policy solutions.[12] In the *Democracy's Challenge* events, for example, participants discussed three frames developed by the organizers, which attributed democratic malaise to individual citizens' failings (self-indulgence and self-absorption), community failings (the loss of cooperative skills and spaces), or government failings (a political system captured by special interests). Each approach was "presented with explanations for supporting and opposing it, along with some tradeoffs and drawbacks. People considered that each approach or course of action involves risks, uncertainties, sacrifices and consequences, and therefore that their preferences were associated with costs."[13] One of the longest sections of the report was devoted to discussing unresolved "tensions in the deliberations," either within individual participants or between them.[14] Thus, the organizers and facilitators of the event focused discussion on weighing reasons for and against some broad ways of framing the problem, rather than on more specific decisions about what should be done about it. It is not surprising, then, that publicity associated with the event devoted relatively less attention to the collective agreements of the deliberators.

The report of the South Dakota forums, *Citizens in the Legislative Process*, also followed the basic pattern of NIF events, and its organizers similarly devoted almost no space to conclusions in their report. Organizers provided three frames for discussing the relationship between citizens

---

[12] Doble Research Associates 2006, 43.   [13] Doble Research Associates 2006, 3.
[14] Doble Research Associates 2006, 12–20.

and the legislative process, including "citizen as learner," "legislators and officials as collaborators," and "citizen as participant."[15] The report described each approach at length and gave many examples of the participants' comments during deliberation. Unlike *Democracy's Challenge*, however, the South Dakota report gave scant attention to reason giving, spending most of its pages on describing the deliberative process instead. This difference between the two documents emerged partly because the approaches discussed in *Democracy's Challenge* were more clearly associated with policy solutions, such as the need for increased character education or the teaching of civic skills in schools. Much of the document could thus be read as offering reasons for or against the policies associated with these approaches. However, the approaches found in the South Dakota document did not include many policy solutions, and with few conclusions came very few reasons.

If the design of the deliberative forum and its relationship to policy decisions were important factors in the balance between conclusions and reasoning, other aspects of deliberation seemed to have little or no effect on publicity. For example, while one of the key choices in the design of deliberative forums is about who participates, we find only a weak relationship between the identities of the deliberators and the nature of publicity. Two of the three decisional reports were stakeholder deliberations – *Wireless Broadband and Public Needs* and *Working Together*. Surprisingly, *Working Together*, which reported recommendations for increasing civic engagement made by leading advocates of civic participation and deliberation, showed relatively less concern for communicating reasons to those outside the group. By contrast, balanced and dialogic reports tended to include participation from citizen deliberators, though we also find the activists who wrote *Wireless Broadband and Public Needs* in the balanced category.

In addition, the size of the deliberative group had relatively little to do with a decision to privilege conclusions over reasons. Presumably, it can be easier to record participants' reasons and evidence in a smaller group than in multiple groups, a view that finds support in the fact that the most heavily decisional report was *World Wide Views of Global Warming*, a deliberative event with more than 4,000 deliberators spread across 38 countries and 6 continents. In addition, each of the balanced reports emerged from single, relatively small deliberative forums rather than from larger efforts like the international global warming event. But size was by no means determinative. The most reason-heavy report, *Democracy's Challenge*, emerged from a multigroup national deliberation of almost a thousand Americans spread across a variety of different sites. Small groups may make recording reasons easier, but it is possible to capture and report reasons even in large and diverse forums held at multiple locations. *Democracy's Challenge* did this through a mixture of post-forum surveys, interviews with moderators about the main concerns aired in small groups, and direct observation or analysis of video recordings of some groups by researchers.[16]

Evidence

Legitimate publicity also includes sufficient information for outsiders to understand the quality of the knowledge that underpins the group's reasoning. Many reports referred to background briefing materials or other evidence playing a role in the deliberative process, but little of that supporting evidence made its way into most post-deliberation reports (see Figure 5.3). Four reports included no evidence whatsoever, and a fifth (*World Wide Views of Global Warming*) contained only one sentence coded as evidence. Three of the remaining reports devoted less than 10 percent of the sentences in the document to evidence. The *San Francisco Digital Inclusion Strategy* – written by full-time city employees with some expertise in policy analysis – contained a slightly higher percentage of evidence sentences (approximately 13 percent), and the University of New Hampshire Consensus Conference report on genetically modified crops contained the most evidence by far, with over 42 percent of sentences coded in the category. The New Hampshire report was relatively brief (only 57 sentences in all) and unlike most of the other reports in our sample, was written in a style more typical of academia than of other forms of public communication. Two of the document's four pages consisted solely of footnotes, which contained multiple references to scholarly studies or other evidentiary details.

When we look closer at the nature of the evidence included in the reports, we also find that different reports emphasized different kinds of support for their claims. These differences are summarized in Figure 5.3, which shows the percentage of evidence sentences falling into different categories. In our sample, statistical evidence and research studies tended to offer data that are systematic and abstract. Other kinds of evidence were more narrative and experiential in nature. These experiential forms

---

[16] Doble Research Associates 2006, 38–9.

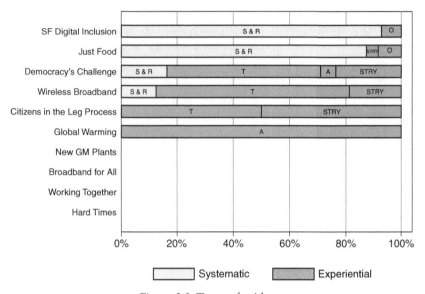

Figure 5.3 Types of evidence

Note: S & R=Statistics and Research, T=Testimony, A=Analogies,
STRY=Stories, O=Other

include personal testimony (references to the personal experiences of deliberators or projects in which a member of the deliberating group had participated directly), stories or anecdotes (narratives about real-world people, organizations, or events), analogies or contrasts (explicit comparisons with other places, issues, or examples), and other evidence (forms of evidence that did not fall into any other category). Deliberative theory increasingly values both of these two broad forms of evidence, which we will refer to as systematic and experiential data. In Figure 5.3, systematic forms of evidence are shown in light gray. More experiential or narrative forms of evidence are shown in dark gray.

The two documents with the most evidence – *New Hampshire Just Food* and the *San Francisco Digital Inclusion Strategy* – relied almost exclusively on statistics and research findings. By contrast, the three reports in which evidence made up between 1 and 10 percent of the document – *Citizens in the Legislative Process, Wireless Broadband and Public Needs,* and *Democracy's Challenge* – tended to rely on very different sources of support, such as stories or personal testimony. None of these three documents employed statistical evidence frequently, with the percentage of evidence sentences in these documents coded as statistics or research never rising above 16 percent. Of the evidence sentences in *Democracy's Challenge*, for example, more than three-quarters were counted as containing stories or personal testimony. The activists responsible for the report on *Wireless Broadband and Public Needs* relied even more heavily on these forms of evidence, and all of the evidence sentences in the South Dakota report on the *Role of Citizens in the Legislative Process* came from the experiences of the participants or from the stories they told about others.

Once again, the nature and purposes of the deliberative forum appeared to have an important effect on forms of publicity. Of the three reports that included more than one sentence with evidence and that leaned more heavily toward experiential or narrative forms of support, two emerged from National Issues Forum gatherings and one from a brainstorming session for activists. All three deliberative events were designed to encourage participants to share their experiences with each other. These purposes were reflected in the way the reports were written.

We might be tempted to assume that the amount of systematic evidence was solely a function of deliberators' or authors' policy expertise. In our sample, the *San Francisco Digital Inclusion Strategy* and the New Hampshire *Just Foods* documents were unusual, not only in the amount of attention paid to evidence but also in the nature of the evidence they provided. The two reports both concerned somewhat technical issues, with the New Hampshire event designed to elicit the informed views of ordinary citizens on genetically modified foods and the San Francisco task force designed to coalesce policy stakeholders' visions for extending broadband access to underserved groups. The reports themselves were authored by academics (in the case of the New Hampshire report) and city officials trained to communicate about technical policy issues (in the case of the San Francisco document).

But the presence of academics or technical communicators as either authors or deliberative participants did not necessarily mean an increased role for systematic evidence across our sample. *Working Together*, a gathering of high-profile policy advocates, academics, and government officials, includes no forms of evidence. *Broadband for All?*, a report that we had a direct hand in producing, also failed to report evidence considered by the group. When we look across our sample, the overriding impression is one of relative lack of attention to evidence, with systematic forms of evidence being especially sparse, regardless of who deliberated and who authored the final reports.

Nor can the lack of evidence in many of these reports be traced consistently to the information inputs the group received or a lack of competence in assessing that evidence. For example, participants in the Danish Board of Technology's global Citizens Jury were provided with background briefing papers on several highly technical issues, such as debates over the optimal target for reducing greenhouse gas emissions and proposed international institutions that would transfer technology and financial support to developing countries likely to bear the brunt of climate change.[17] In the *Broadband for All?* Consensus Conference, deliberators received a briefing paper, presentation, and expert testimony at a public hearing on debates over whether cities should invest in broadband, appropriate pricing and speeds of service, a range of possible technologies for delivering broadband, and a host of social issues, such as reaching non-English speakers and extending broadband to rural areas.[18] Reports from each of these forums offer pages of detailed policy recommendations, indicating that the deliberators were quite capable of choosing amongst a range of technical policy options. But the specific pieces of evidence on which deliberators might have based their recommendations are absent.

Given our interest in questions of equality, we also asked whether certain kinds of evidence were deployed more often in reports of deliberation by relatively disempowered participants. As we discussed in Chapter 1, some theorists caution that deliberative appeals to the common good can frustrate the efforts of the least powerful to enter into public discourse. If deliberation is, as Lynn Sanders puts it, "a request for a certain kind of talk: rational, contained, and oriented to a shared problem," then it may privilege the discourse and the norms of the well-educated or the powerful.[19] Sanders advocates testimony instead of deliberation as a model of public discourse. "What is fundamental about giving testimony," she argues, "is telling one's own story, not seeking communal dialogue."[20] Sanders' argument thus hinges on the idea that testimony – in which citizens tell "their own stories, in their own ways, to each other" – is in tension with deliberation, rather than potentially a part of it.[21] She also suggests that testimony by the disempowered is oriented more toward their individual or group interests, rather than to the good of the community or the larger collectivity. This might lead us to expect that reports that rely more on narrative forms of evidence will advance the particular interests of the disempowered, while systematic evidence would primarily

---

[17] Danish Board of Technology 2009, 7.
[18] See www.broadbandforall.org for the background briefing papers and Chapter 3 for a fuller description of the Consensus Conference process.
[19] Sanders 1997, 370. See also Young 2000, 40–4.
[20] Sanders 1997, 372.   [21] Sanders 1997, 372.

support more holistic recommendations aimed at advancing the common good.

Yet a close reading of our sample cautions against assuming that narrative evidence always leads to particularistic conclusions or systematic evidence always supports communal ones. In our sample, reports of forums that included activists on behalf of the disempowered (such as those who participated in *Wireless Broadband and Public Needs*) and disempowered citizens (such as the young voters at the South Dakota forums on civic engagement or the many Americans who felt they had lost control of their communities and governments in *Democracy's Challenge*) tended to feature more testimony and storytelling, as Sanders would expect. But these forms of evidence also supported conclusions that connected particular interests to the general interest. Testimony and storytelling were deployed by the authors of *Citizens in the Legislative Process* to promote the common good in the form of greater civic engagement and better relationships between South Dakota's legislators and youth for the benefit of the state and its citizens. For example, a section on the importance of citizen involvement in the legislative process included the following testimony: "a college student in Aberdeen told her fellow participants that her family members in previous generations were not allowed to vote, which makes her not take opportunities for granted."[22] The report connected this individual student's reason for voting with the importance of "education as an example of an issue that can affect everyone and that cuts across all levels of government."[23]

In addition, systematic evidence was employed on behalf of arguments for serving the needs of the less powerful. For example, the *San Francisco Digital Inclusion Strategy* report provided ample research and statistics on demographic groups who had the least access to broadband service to support its conclusion that "investing in [underserved] residents will promote innovation, economic growth and social justice within the City"– in other words, the interests of less well-off residents and the city as a whole.[24] Thus, it was not the case that deliberative publicity always employed testimony, stories, and analogies to appeal to the particular interests of the disempowered or that research and statistics bolstered appeals to broader considerations alone.

The lack of evidence in many of these reports and the types of evidence employed appear primarily to reflect authorial strategy rather than the

[22] South Dakota Issues Forums 2009, 3.   [23] South Dakota Issues Forums 2009, 4.
[24] San Francisco Department of Telecommunications and Information Services 2007, 6.

nature of the deliberators or the information to which they had access. Often, even when evidence was presented or discussed in forums, the authors simply chose not to communicate it. Most reports not only omitted the more systematic information found in many briefing documents, but also the experiential evidence that participants exchanged in deliberation. For example, the *Broadband for All?* report failed to include influential testimony that participants gave about their own experiences. As discussed in Chapter 3, the group decided to make recommendations on how to protect Internet users' privacy and security after one participant told how he had become a victim of identity theft online, even though this was not an issue that the conference organizers put on the initial agenda for the group to discuss. However, because we looked to reports of Danish Consensus Conferences as our models for how to report our own, we followed their lead by focusing on reasons and policy conclusions, rather than reporting the evidence that most swayed the participants.

The influence of forum design and authorial strategy on the presentation of evidence can be understood as a "genre effect." Genres are "widely used schemes for classifying texts that shape how their makers create them and their audiences interpret them."[25] For example, the "romantic comedy" genre sets a common set of expectations for filmmakers and audiences alike: two potential mates will meet, exchange witty banter as they grapple with conflicts and misunderstandings between them, and engage in some personal growth that allows them to come together by the end of the film. As Daniel Chandler notes, if "particular features which are characteristic of a genre are not normally unique to it . . . it is their relative prominence, combination and functions which are distinctive."[26] Characters fall in love in many genres, but things rarely turn out well when they fall in love in a Greek tragedy. Deliberative reports also appear to be shaped by genre expectations for how to report particular kinds of civic forums, which seem to influence authors and perhaps audiences. Because civic forums are diverse and relatively new developments, the expectations for reporting them are not as fixed as Hollywood film genres, but there are patterns to be found.

While many genres likely shape the use of evidence in deliberative publicity, four genres emerged in our sample. The two NIF forums on civic engagement adopted a *populist* genre that valued the authenticity of citizens' experiential evidence as expressed in their own voices. As the

---

[25] Raphael 2005, 174.   [26] Chandler 2000, ¶ 12.

authors of the South Dakota report wrote, "This report reflects what was heard in the forums – the forums belonged to the participants – this is their voice."[27] Both the South Dakota and *Democracy's Challenge* reports tended to introduce broad themes in the discussion and illustrate each with multiple examples of citizen testimony and storytelling. Evidence was used to present a nuanced picture of public opinion more than to make a forceful case for particular policies.

In contrast, reports such as the *San Francisco Digital Inclusion Strategy* were written to meet the expectations of *policy analysis*, in which both the nature of the forum (stakeholders familiar with technical arguments) and the primary audience (stakeholders and decision makers in local government) favored more systematic forms of evidence. This evidence was presented to demonstrate lack of access to services (as in a "needs assessment" conducted by a social service agency) and to make an argument for the citywide benefits of a set of policies to expand broadband access. Both forms of policy analysis prize systematic, often quantitative, evidence.[28]

The *Just Foods* report, produced by a university-based center, had an *academic* bent. Half of the report consisted of footnotes studded with citations to research on the risks of genetically modified crops. Conventions of academic argumentation explain the emphasis on drawing conclusions from systematic evidence found in published research, as in a literature review. The *Wireless Broadband and Public Needs* report, which summarized a deliberation among policy advocates, took an *activist* approach, foregrounding the testimony of advocates for the disempowered about their own campaigns and pilot projects to provide broadband access. This report also emphasized brief stories about how communities and individuals struggled without Internet access, or were ignored or exploited by telecommunication companies. While the same kinds of stories may be found in the policy analysis genre, in activist discourse this experiential evidence contributes to larger accounts of abuse and inequality – "injustice frames"– that aim to motivate others to join movements for change, rather than make the case for ameliorative social services alone.[29] This

---

[27] South Dakota Issues Forums 2009, 3.   [28] Bardach 2009.

[29] On injustice frames, see Snow et al. 1986. The report was intended to summarize local organizers' advice to a national think tank on broadband policy work and to build an advocacy coalition among them and other activists beyond the group. As part of this goal, the organizers asked participants to "provide stories, data, and examples of actual community experiences that can be used to support and bolster public interest positions in spectrum/wireless policy advocacy." New America Foundation 2006, 1.

evidence supported an array of common goals and strategies for winning the public argument about how to expand Internet access. More than other kinds of reports, the activist genre wielded evidence *against* an identifiable foe – the telecommunications companies.

Our findings highlight potential dangers for authors who use the populist genre alone to represent citizen voices, especially the voices of the disempowered. We pay special attention to this genre because it was adopted in most of the reports we sampled. In response to critics such as Sanders, we would argue that exclusively adopting populist discourse may be a well-intentioned effort to include the experiences of less powerful citizens as legitimate evidence in deliberation, but it can also become a rhetorical straitjacket on participants. Within mainstream journalism, social documentary, and political discourse, there is a long tradition of ambivalence about extending power to lay citizens, and especially the marginalized, to analyze the causes of their own situations and propose policy remedies. Often, this involves restricting the disempowered to the role of "victims who testify about personal experience to illustrate or dramatize a larger point made by experts or journalists."[30] The "victim tradition," in the words of Brian Winston, "substitutes empathy for analysis, it privileges effect over cause," and therefore does not afford disempowered speakers a chance to set their experience within a larger analysis of social life.[31] In judicial and media discourse, testimony is a double-edged sword that gives the marginalized a right to speak about their conditions in a public setting, but within tightly constrained rules of evidence that do not allow citizens to argue with the design or application of law or policy. The role of testifiers is subordinate to the role of experts – journalists, judges, and attorneys – who are empowered to analyze, synthesize, and resolve social conflicts.

Authors of reports of deliberation who relegate citizens, and especially the disempowered, *solely* to presenting stories, anecdotes, and testimony about their own experience may unconsciously further this discourse of victimization. Limiting participants to communicating these kinds of evidence can prevent citizens from demonstrating their ability to generalize from their own experience, analyze and resolve systemic or structural problems, and stand on equal ground with experts (including the authors of publicity themselves). As a result, citizen voices may come across to expert audiences as less authoritative than those voices could be. This discourse also restricts citizens from communicating *public* reasoning that

[30] Raphael 2005, 52.   [31] Winston 1988, 274.

links their interests to the common good, which is likely to be more persuasive to other citizens and to officials than a discourse of personal testimony, and which would be more in keeping with deliberative theory. In addition, organizers who overemphasize the value of citizens' experiential and anecdotal evidence may structure the forum in ways that discourage participants from considering more systematic evidence. As we argued in Chapter 1, deliberation is most valuable when it empowers participants to compare the best available knowledge generated by experts and citizens, and to resolve differences between them. Often, this requires a deep understanding of how expert and citizen knowledge are created and assessed by interested parties who aim to influence public policy.

While all kinds of evidence can be valuable, we think that organizers and authors of publicity should see their role as enabling citizens inside and outside the forum to make autonomous decisions based on a strong grasp of a wide variety of evidence. While organizers of civic forums are not in a teacher–student relationship with participants, the skills of critically evaluating different kinds of evidence are no less important in forums than in classrooms. As educators, we do not see our role as protecting people from discussions of research and statistics. Rather, our job is to help people understand how these kinds of evidence are assembled in order to question them, and then to decide whether to accept and deploy them in arguments. For example, it is important for citizens who are discussing issues of distributive justice, or reading a report of other citizens' deliberation on these issues, to know how statistics that shape the allocation of public resources, such as the unemployment rate and poverty rate, are constructed by experts, in part so that citizens can decide whether those statistics understate or overstate the problems of joblessness and poverty. The populist genre does not easily enlist citizens in that kind of conversation. If early deliberative theory has been rightly critiqued for its bias toward cognitive and abstract argumentation, a bias toward experiential and particularistic civic discourse may be just as disempowering to citizens inside and outside the forum.

Of course, genres can be changed or creatively merged. Some of the most interesting films, novels, and deliberative reports draw on multiple genres or consciously alter our expectations for a given genre. This suggests that the authors of deliberative reports can be more conscious of the various sets of expectations that influence their choices, including the expectations of deliberative theory more broadly. The more that authors are mindful of established genres of deliberative publicity – populist,

policy analytic, academic, activist, and others we have yet to identify –
the more likely it is that publicity will reflect thoughtful and critical
choices about how to report evidence rather than unthinking adoption
of genre expectations. In our sample, reports would have met the criteria
for good deliberative publicity more fully by presenting more evidence,
by including both the systematic and experiential evidence that helped to
shape the deliberation, and by questioning whether existing genres are
faithful to core values of deliberative theory, especially the importance of
helping citizens to relate their views to the views of others and to argue
on equal ground with experts.

Opposing views

Evidence is not the only element of publicity that could be strengthened in our sample of reports. Theories of democratic deliberation prize
careful consideration of differing perspectives on contested issues, but as
Figure 5.4 shows, three documents included no statements that opposed
the conclusions, reasons, or evidence endorsed by a majority of the deliberators. In another five documents, less than 10 percent of coded sentences
included references to alternative perspectives. This is surprising because
many of the reports described their deliberative process as involving the
exchange of multiple views.

Three examples show that it is possible for reports to include substantive discussion of alternative perspectives, whether the deliberation was
oriented mainly toward dialogue or arriving at decisions. In *Democracy's
Challenge*, a section entitled "Tensions in the Deliberations" devoted
eight pages to conflicts that emerged among deliberators. As the introduction to this section of the report put it,

> Sometimes... people do not reach... common ground. Their unre-
> solved tensions may be within individuals, as participants find them-
> selves drawn to more than one of their own deeply held values. Or
> their tensions may be external, as participants disagree with each other
> about different approaches or policy particulars.[32]

By devoting an entire section of the report to these tensions, the authors
of *Democracy's Challenge* made clear their commitment to publicizing
not only areas of agreement but also differences among the deliberators.

We might expect that more extensive consideration of alternative views
is easier when the purpose of the deliberation is closer to exploratory

---

[32] Doble Research Associates 2006, 12.

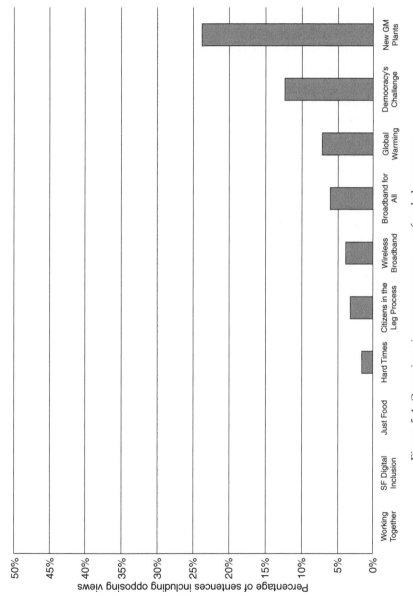

Figure 5.4 Opposing views as a percentage of coded sentences

dialogue, as in *Democracy's Challenge*. Yet the report of the Danish Citizens Jury, which issued multiple policy recommendations to national leaders on the controversy over genetically modified plants, also made differing perspectives within the deliberation clear. The report accomplished this by detailing citizens' arguments for and against every policy the group considered and including in the report a comprehensive catalogue of voting results at every stage of the process. The deliberators formulated arguments about each question they were asked, and they then expressed their support for the arguments and counter-arguments – and ultimately for policy recommendations – in a series of seven votes held over the course of the event. In each voting period, participants were given multiple votes that could be distributed to support multiple arguments. Participants could allocate up to half of their votes for a single recommendation or argument. By disclosing the results of the weighted-preference voting process, the final document allowed readers to review every vote taken and to gauge, with actual vote tallies, the support for every substantive argument debated by the citizen participants. This approach offered readers a precise sense of which reasons were most persuasive for deliberators and which alternatives they rejected.

World Wide Views of Global Warming, which also presented many policy conclusions, exemplifies a closely related approach to incorporating opposing views. Because the report included participants' voting tallies on an array of policy recommendations for addressing climate change, the responses that garnered minority support presented alternatives to the majority's recommendations on many issues. Whereas the *New GM Plants* report presented opposing reasons, the *Global Warming* report provided opposing conclusions.

These three reports suggest that the design of the deliberative forum may have some influence on the attention paid to opposing views in the resulting publicity, but again, forum design does not appear to be the sole determining factor. One report of a dialogic NIF forum scored high on reporting opposing views (*Democracy's Challenge*), but the other (*Citizens in the Legislative Process*) was in the middle range among our reports. One report of a Consensus Conference was in the middle range (*Broadband for All?*), while one reported no opposing views (*Just Foods*). Forums that involved voting or polling about conclusions, rather than agreeing by consensus or "agreeing to disagree" in dialogue, sometimes presented more opposing views than average (*New GM Plants*, *World Wide Views of Global Warming*), but sometimes presented almost no alternative views (*Hard Times Hard Choices*). Once again, we find that publicity is independent of the deliberative event; similar kinds of forums may be publicized quite differently, based on authors' decisions.

Although we cannot assume that the reports offer simple reflections of the underlying deliberations, we can see that the reports of deliberation among stakeholders tended to pay less attention than reports of citizen deliberation to opposing views. While reports of citizen forums appeared at the top, middle, and bottom of the range of attention to multiple perspectives, the forums that convened the most expert deliberators almost all scored low. Here, we also need to remember the impact of political context and intended audiences. Two of the three documents that omitted any opposing views reported on task forces of experts who had been invited by policy makers to make recommendations on live issues: the *San Francisco Digital Inclusion Strategy*, in which municipal officials asked stakeholders to help craft the city's broadband access policy, and *Working Together*, in which advocates of citizen engagement and deliberation responded to the Obama administration's invitation to offer advice on its civic engagement strategies.[33] In each case, the fact that the groups enjoyed some official sanction, and perhaps felt the need to present a unified series of policy proposals, seemed to outweigh deliberative concerns about addressing multiple, conflicting views. Nonetheless, it is important to note that several reports of citizen deliberation pegged to policy windows, such as *World Wide Views of Global Warming*, did address some alternative viewpoints. Therefore, it seems reasonable to think that these expert reports might have done so as well, even if only to explain why they rejected other policy choices and rationales, or to address conflicting evidence.

Consider the contrast between the *San Francisco Digital Inclusion Strategy* and *Broadband for All?*, both of which focused on broadband access in the San Francisco Bay Area, and were published within three months of each other. The latter report, of citizen deliberation, paid significantly greater attention to opposing views than the government-organized San Francisco report. This is surprising. The San Francisco task force gathered input from a diverse range of interested parties in the

---

[33] The third report that presented no opposing views was *Just Foods*, an anomalous report of a citizen Consensus Conference. As we explain in the next chapter, the organizers and all of the expert witnesses opposed genetically modified foods, and it is not clear what relationship the citizen deliberation had to the final report. *Wireless Broadband and Public Needs*, the third report of deliberation among relative experts in policy matters, indeed reported alternative views, but it presented them as illegitimate foils for the activist group's views, as we discuss below.

corporate, non-profit, and philanthropic sectors. Policy analysts, such as the author of this report, are trained to demonstrate discursively that they have considered trade-offs, unintended consequences, and potential objections to policy options.[34] But the goal of the city telecommunication agency that organized the San Francisco task force was to gather advice from this group about how a planned municipal broadband network could best reach underserved residents, not to consider contentious issues such as *whether* the city should build the network, who should operate it, or how its tiers of service should be priced. Our follow-up interview with the forum organizer revealed that the opposing views expressed within the committee on these contentious issues were not reported because the city staff member who authored the report was empowered to frame this debate as outside the group's purview. In other words, opposing views were mentioned frequently in the deliberation, but simply were not reported.

Respect

Deliberative theory also highlights the need for *respectful* treatment of opposing views. As we explained in Chapter 4, alternative perspectives may be presented as legitimate (worthy of consideration), neutrally (with no comment either positive or negative), or as illegitimate (unworthy of consideration because of attacks on the arguer's motives, negative adverbs, caricature, or other pejorative language). The extent to which each document included these differing forms of opposing views can be seen in Figure 5.5. The documents that presented opposing views treated most of the alternative perspectives as legitimate or neutrally. For example, because the counter-arguments in the Danish Citizens' Jury on genetically modified plants emerged from the deliberators themselves, 100 percent were presented as legitimate. All or nearly all of the counter-arguments in *Democracy's Challenge, World Wide Views on Global Warming*, and the South Dakota report on the role of citizens in the legislative process were presented neutrally.

Only the *Wireless Broadband and Public Needs* document presented a significant percentage of opposing views as illegitimate, depicting them in pejorative language not likely to be used publicly by the group's opponents. Organizers asked the group to identify opposing views raised by private telecommunications companies in order to hone arguments that could be used against the companies. For example, the activists contrasted

---

[34] Bardach 2009.

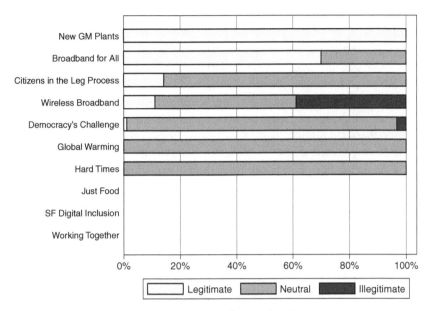

Figure 5.5 Varieties of opposing views

their efforts on behalf of "freedom to innovate" with telecommunications' companies' "opposing agenda" designed to "Control/limit threatening innovation and competition."[35] The purpose of the activists' deliberation was to discuss among themselves how to forge a common approach to the larger political conflicts in which they were engaged. Thus, their deliberation occurred within an enclave that was attempting to form a coalition, rather than to find common ground with their opponents.

While we certainly do not suggest that activists are always obligated to show respect for opponents' views, reports such as this one, even if aimed at an audience of other activists, may achieve greater deliberative legitimacy by addressing disagreements *within the group* more explicitly (and, presumably, they would do so respectfully). As we saw in Chapter 2, this can help spark useful internal conversation within social movements about the common goals and strategies its members might embrace. Our interview with the forum's facilitator indicates that there were disagreements within this activist group about what steps were most likely to be effective at creating change, which steps should be prioritized, and how to share control over the coalition's agenda between the national think tank that organized the event (the New America Foundation, or NAF) and the

[35] New America Foundation 2006, 2.

local organizations represented in the deliberation. These tensions are also evident in some of the published conclusions, such as recommendations that future meetings of the group "need to include open space, i.e. not just NAF agenda" and that the group needed "to get clear on what NAF wants/needs from group + what influence Committee has."[36] However, the report presented potentially conflicting priorities and organizational roles as a long list of bullet-pointed recommendations for the coalition, rather than attempting to rank or resolve these differences. This meant that disagreements that were present among the deliberators were muted or difficult to decipher in the final report, and they were almost never coded as "opposing views."

The respect shown to opposing views in most reports is a sign of good deliberative publicity, but the small space given to alternative perspectives in most reports suggests that authors could think more carefully about how to represent disagreement among participants and between the group and others. The fact that, at least in our sample, reports of deliberation among more expert participants who were closer to decision makers were least likely to grapple publicly with contradictory goals, strategies, reasons, and evidence may be especially surprising, and worrisome from the standpoint of democratic deliberation.

Norms

Because theories of deliberation are especially concerned with how to resolve moral disagreement, the presence or absence of normative claims – which state why a conclusion or reason is morally right, just, or fair – is an important element of deliberative publicity. For the sake of reliability, our strategy for coding appeals to norms was to focus on the manifest content of the document, using keyword searching to find any explicit assertion of individual or group *rights*, *duties*, or *obligations*; reference to principles of *justice*, *fairness*, *equality*, *religion*, or *morality*, or to their opposites (e.g., *injustice*, *unfairness*, *exploitation*, *discrimination*, and *immorality*).[37] The limitation of this method is that it can overlook latent references to norms. For example, the phrase, "All members of the community should be consulted" may imply that the authors value egalitarian principles, but we would not have coded it as a normative appeal because it does not explicitly mention equality. Thus, it is possible that we understate the

---

[36] New America Foundation 2006, 17.

[37] All variants of each keyword were searched (e.g., *right*, *rights*, and *rightfully*). A full list of words coded is available from the authors.

normative content of the reports, yet we believe it would be unusual for appeals to equality, morality, or justice to avoid such words entirely.

Even with these methodological limits in mind, the relative absence of normative claims in our searches is perhaps the most striking result of our analysis. Deliberative theory asks citizens to foreground their moral arguments, and deliberation is often said to help citizens perceive how their deeply held values can better inform their policy preferences. As shown in Figure 5.6, two documents contained no normative appeals at all, and an additional five reports included norms in between 1 and 3 percent of coded sentences. In no document did such claims comprise more than 10 percent of coded sentences. The San Francisco broadband report, for example, contained only two sentences with norms, and these referred only briefly to the rights of all city residents to "digital inclusion and digital empowerment."[38] *Broadband for All?* also contained a small number of normative statements (only seven sentences out of 167), but it rooted its claims in a richer set of appeals to equal access, equal economic opportunity, and equal privacy protections for all Internet users. The activists who participated in *Wireless Broadband and Public Needs* raised a broad range of norms that might underwrite increased Internet access, including broadcasters' public interest obligations, public rights to the spectrum, treaty obligations to Native Americans, the public good, and a healthy democracy.

The document with the most references to moral argumentation, *Democracy's Challenge*, contained multiple references to citizens' views about the role of religion in public life, the obligations of citizens, and the need for citizens to embrace moral values that would support the common good. This report appears to have included more normative appeals because the NIF organizers framed each of the three approaches to civic life that provided the forums' agenda in explicitly moral terms and the report's authors seem to have chosen quotes from participants that reflected these moral concerns. In *Democracy's Challenge*, the three approaches to the problem of civic engagement focused on individual character issues ("Democratic Values: Rebuilding Democracy's Moral Foundation"), strengthening community ties ("Web of Connections: Reinventing Citizenship"), and political reforms ("By the People: Bringing the Public Back into Politics.")[39] Copious quotes from citizen participants appealed to notions of individual duties and rights,

---

[38] San Francisco Department of Telecommunications and Information Services 2007, 6.
[39] Doble Research Associates 2006, 40–1.

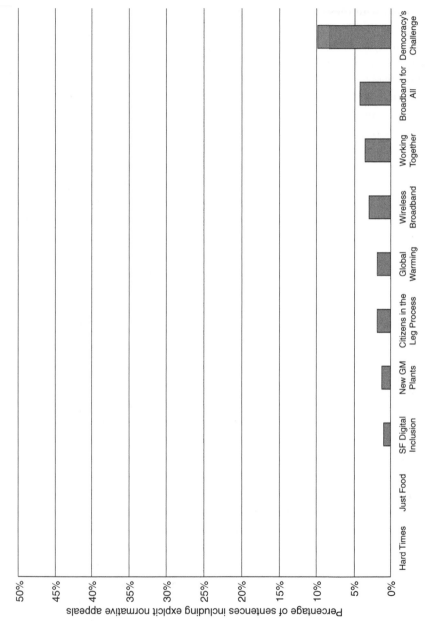

Figure 5.6 Normative appeals as a percentage of coded sentences

community obligations, and desires for a more just political system. In contrast, the *Working Together* report, also on civic engagement, reflected the professional discourse of advocates for engaging the citizenry, more than the moral and ethical reasons for doing so. The authors of *Working Together* phrased policy recommendations in technical terms, such as "Improve Federal Public Participation and Collaboration," "Explore Lessons from the Open Government Dialogue," and "Create on Ongoing Mechanism for Sustaining Leadership."[40]

Given the extremely small numbers of sentences falling into the normative category, it is difficult to draw any firm conclusions about the reasons why moral claims are present. Our key finding is, simply, that explicitly normative statements are surprisingly rare. We do not claim that there is a "correct" percentage of normative appeals in a report because a small number of them can still place important standards of moral reasoning on the agenda for readers. Nonetheless, when a report makes few or no clear moral claims that ground its conclusions in some notion of rights, equality, justice, or fairness, then it is difficult to say that deliberative theory's requirement of deep engagement with moral reasoning has been met.

There may be several reasons why reports steered away from moral argumentation, and these are worthy of future research. One possibility is that citizens avoided making explicit normative claims in the forums. In her summary of research on civic deliberation, Laura Black finds that citizens often introduce moral considerations indirectly, by asking questions or telling stories that imply their values but do not name them. For example, she notes that in an evaluation of the Oregon Citizens Initiative Review panels, which issue recommendations to other citizens about how to vote on ballot initiatives, researchers rated participants' ability to consider their underlying values as the least effective aspect of the panels' deliberations.[41] Similarly, Nina Eliasoph finds that even in the grassroots voluntary organizations she observed citizens self-censor normative discussion among themselves and in public because they sense that overtly moral talk will spark conflict or mark speakers as political ideologues.[42] Another possibility is that authors refrained from identifying and reporting statements about the underlying values that motivated

---

[40] America*Speaks*, Everyday Democracy, Demos, and Ash Institute for Democratic Governance and Innovation 2009, 1.

[41] Black 2012, 67–9. See Knobloch et al. (2013) for the evaluation of the Oregon Citizens Initiative Review.

[42] Eliasoph 1998, 255.

deliberators' policy choices, perhaps for the same reasons that citizens can be reluctant to speak in normative terms. Finally, if deliberators and authors refer to moral claims indirectly, they are not easily discovered by content analysis, which is better at measuring explicit meaning than subtext.

Coherence

In our approach, publicity's legitimacy depends not only on including the elements of deliberative argumentation but also on how well they cohere into a clear overall argument. To this point, our analyses have focused on the extent to which reports emphasize different elements of argumentation. However, high-quality deliberative argumentation depends upon not only the sheer percentage of conclusions reached but also the extent to which each is grounded in reasons, evidence, norms, and comparison with opposing views. For this reason, in our second round of coding, a new set of coders assessed each conclusion to identify whether it was supported by a reason, evidence statement, or norm, and whether it was challenged by an opposing view. This represents a threshold standard of coherence, as the relevant support for (or opposition to) the conclusion could occur anywhere else in the document.

Table 5.2 presents the percentage of conclusions in each document supported by each of the other elements of argumentation. The table shows a strong relationship between the decisional, balanced, or dialogic nature of the report and the percentage of conclusions associated with either reasons or evidence. On average, only 56.5 percent of conclusions in the decisional documents were supported by reasons or evidence, while 83.4 percent of conclusions in the balanced reports were supported, and nearly all the conclusions in the dialogic reports were supported (97.1 percent).[43] This strong relationship can also be seen in Figure 5.7, which plots the log of the ratio of conclusions to reasoning against the percentage of conclusions supported by some form of reasoning. These two measures are nearly perfectly correlated ($r=0.96$). The line in the figure is the fitted regression curve. The results thus comprise a helpful check on the validity of our initial conclusions. For example, this second round of coding highlights the fact that sentence-level coherence comes from making reasoning a clear priority in the report: the more reasons and evidence found in a document relative to each conclusion, the more likely that every conclusion is supported by at least one reason or piece of evidence.

---

[43] The differences between these average percentages is significant at $p<0.01$ for each pairwise comparison.

Table 5.2 *Percentage of conclusions associated with other categories*

		Reasons	Evidence	Reasons or evidence	Norms	Opposing views
Decisional	Global Warming	45.9	0.7	46.7	50.4	74.8
	Hard Times	55.1	0.0	55.1	0.0	24.5
	Working Together	67.8	0.0	67.9	36.2	0.0
Balanced	SF Digital Inclusion	69.3	48.0	79.5	41.7	0.0
	Broadband for All	79.3	0.0	79.3	42.5	40.2
	Wireless Broadband	81.0	45.7	82.6	52.6	49.1
	New GM Plants	88.5	0.0	88.5	1.6	80.3
	Just Food	26.7	80.0	86.7	0.0	0.0
Dialogic	Citizens in the Legislative Process	100.0	100.0	100.0	66.7	66.7
	Democracy's Challenge	90.2	60.8	94.1	64.7	82.4

In the case of dialogic reports, achieving a high level of support for conclusions is not a difficult task because the number of conclusions tends to be very low. The strength of a report like *Democracy's Challenge*, for example, is that nearly half the document is devoted to reasoning. With only 7 percent of the sentences coded as conclusions, nearly every conclusion is supported by a reason. South Dakota's *Citizens in the Legislative Process*, on the other hand, achieves high sentence-level coherence despite the fact that less than 10 percent of the document is devoted to reason-giving. This is because the report contains only three relatively vague conclusions. As we have indicated, then, the challenge for documents like the South Dakota report is to articulate clearer, more specific policy recommendations that emerged from the deliberation. We will return to this issue below.

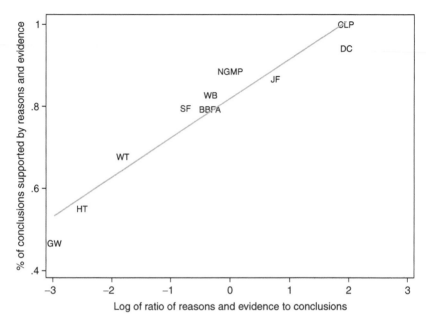

Figure 5.7 Ratio of conclusions to reasoning

The reports that fit our balanced category are in many ways more impressive, as they also tended to show a very high level of sentence-level coherence, even though they generally included a higher proportion of conclusions to reasons than the dialogic reports. On average, nearly 40 percent of the sentences in the balanced reports included a conclusion, and in *Broadband for All* and *San Francisco Digital Inclusion Strategy*, the number rose to more than half. Even so, both reports supported 80 percent of their conclusions with reasoning of some sort. The other balanced reports showed even higher levels of reasoned support for each conclusion. In the decisional category, on the other hand, a significantly lower percentage of conclusions were supported by reasons. In reports of this type, nearly half of the conclusions were not buttressed by any reasons or evidence.

However, Table 5.2 also shows that a commitment to supporting conclusions with reasoning does not necessarily result in an increased connection between conclusions and other important aspects of deliberative publicity, such as opposing views or norms. While the correlation between the percentage of conclusions supported by some form of reasoning and the log of the ratio of conclusions to reasoning was extremely high

($r=0.96$), correlations between that same log ratio and the percentage of conclusions supported by opposing views or by norms were considerably lower ($r=0.28$ and 0.31, respectively). In other words, an increased commitment to reasons and evidence did not necessarily result in increased attention to reporting other elements of deliberation that are important to deliberative theory.

Thus, while our decisional-balanced-dialogic typology of argumentation captures well the patterns of coherence with respect to reasoning, it does not fully explain the choices made by report authors about other elements of legitimate publicity. While the dialogic reports again scored relatively high on both measures – on average, two-thirds of conclusions were supported by a normative claim, and nearly three-quarters of conclusions were complemented by opposing views – this can again be explained by the fact that these reports contained relatively few conclusions, so nearly any normative claim or opposing view was more likely to be related to the conclusions that were present. The decisional and balanced categories, by contrast, showed considerable variation in the extent to which their conclusions were buttressed by normative claims or tested by attention to competing perspectives. Even in the reports that made more connections between conclusions and norms, or between conclusions and opposing views, significant percentages of conclusions were not grounded in normative claims or accompanied by competing views.

These basic patterns can be seen in Figure 5.8, which presents summary measures of the level of support for each conclusion in the document. In the figure, reports are arranged along the x-axis from decisional (on the left) to dialogic (on the right). The figure shows the extent to which conclusions in each document were either fully supported or completely unsupported. Fully supported conclusions were defined as being linked to at least one form of reasoning (either evidence or other kinds of reasons) *and* one norm *and* one opposing view. Unsupported conclusions were not linked to any reasons, evidence, norms, or opposing views. Overall, in no document were more than two-thirds of the conclusions fully supported.

Figure 5.8 shows that dialogic reports tended to fully support a relatively high percentage of their conclusions – nearly 63 percent, on average, for the two dialogic documents. Conversely, only a very small percentage of conclusions received no support. But in both dialogic documents, this increased coherence came at the cost of arriving at a smaller number of conclusions, and in the case of the South Dakota report, the gains in reason giving were offset by vague and unclear policy conclusions.

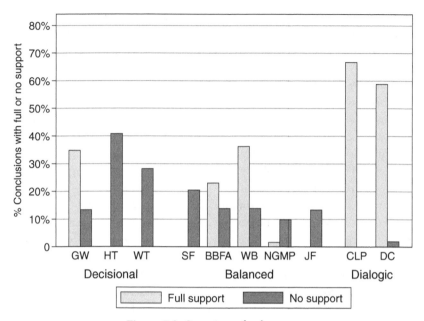

Figure 5.8 Overview of coherence

The balanced and decisional reports show considerable variation. While no document in either category rose to the level of full support found in the dialogic reports and the average level of full support never exceeded 15 percent for either category, some presented more coherent forms of argumentation than others. For example, *Broadband for All*, *Wireless Broadband and Public Needs*, and *Global Warming* all gave full support to a relatively high percentage of conclusions and left a fairly small number of conclusions completely unsupported. But others, including *Just Food*, *San Francisco Digital Inclusion Strategy*, *Hard Times Hard Choices*, and *Working Together*, did not fully support any of their conclusions.

Together, Table 5.2 and Figure 5.8 thus lead to a few basic conclusions about patterns of legitimate publicity in our sample. First, the more space a document devoted to participants' reasoning, the more likely that document was to score high in our measures of coherence. That is, the greater the attention to reasons and evidence, the more likely each conclusion was supported in ways that meet the basic expectation of deliberative theory that people should engage in reasoned discourse. But an increased attention to reason giving did not automatically translate into greater attention to the other aspects of deliberative publicity, including the need for moral reasoning or the importance of testing reasons against competing views. In many ways, the choice to give space to norms or opposing views appears to be orthogonal to the balance between conclusions and reasons. These findings imply that authors in our sample can practice deliberative publicity better by showing how citizens supported their conclusions with moral norms, not just with reasons and evidence, and by revealing more about the opposing views against which citizens tested their conclusions.

As a final review, we asked our coders to step back from the sentence-level analysis to consider the relationship between conclusions and the elements of argumentation in the document as a whole. In this step, coders rendered summary judgments about the extent to which the connections between conclusions and the other elements of argumentation were both logical and proximate (close to one another in the document). If we think of argumentation as a web with conclusions at the center and other elements (reasons, norms, and so on) arranged around the conclusions, the sentence-level coding tells us whether threads connect each conclusion to the rest of the web. However, a stronger web would be built of threads that are shorter (proximal) and thicker (logical). This is what the document-level coding tells us: how strong and clear was the connection between conclusions and each of the other aspects of argumentation. These judgments are presented in Table 5.3. In documents marked as "high," the connections between conclusions and reasons, evidence, norms, or opposing views were clear and easy to discern. Those marked as "medium" were somewhat less clear, and in those marked as "low," coders had a difficult time making the connection between conclusions and the other elements of argumentation. This could be, for example, because the conclusions were not located near the supporting reasons or because the logical connections between the conclusions and supporting reasons were muddy. In cases where the document contained no evidence, opposing views, or norms, coders marked "none."

The document-level measures overlap with our sentence-level indicators in many ways, though the relationship is not perfect. The correlation between the percentage of conclusions that are fully supported and the percentage of document-level indicators coded as "high" is only moderate: 0.42. The bivariate relationship between these two measures can be seen in Figure 5.9. For the most part, documents in which a higher percentage of conclusions were fully supported also scored higher on the summary measures of coherence, but there are some important differences. For example, *Hard Times*, *Working Together*, and *San Francisco*

Table 5.3 *Document-level coherence coding results*

Judgments of how clearly conclusions are linked to...	Decisional				Balanced				Dialogic	
	GW	HT	WT	SF	BBFA	WB	NGMP	JF	CLP	DC
Reasons	Medium	High	High	High	High	Medium	Medium	Low	High	High
Evidence	Low	None	None	High	None	Low	None	Medium	High	High
Norms	High	None	High	Medium	High	Medium	Low	None	Low	High
Opposing views	High	High	None	None	High	Medium	Medium	None	Medium	High
% Coded high	50.0	50.0	50.0	50.0	75.0	0.0	0.0	0.0	50.0	100.0

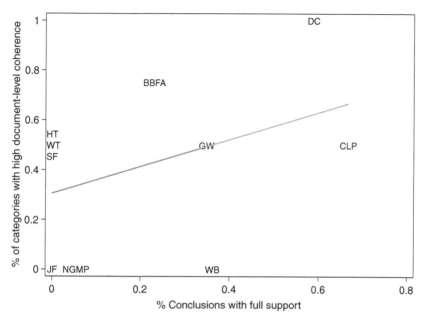

Figure 5.9 Relationship between document-level and conclusion-level coherence

Note: Overlapping labels are jittered for ease of interpretation.

Digital Inclusion had no fully supported conclusions, as each of those documents neglected at least one of our argumentation categories. Nonetheless, all three scored as at least moderately coherent in the document-level summary, meaning that the connections between conclusions and the categories that were present were relatively clear and easy to discern.

Conversely, *Wireless Broadband* included a relatively high percentage of fully supported conclusions (36.2), but scored quite poorly in the document-level measures. In part, this is because of the report's structure, which began with a section on "Why Telecommunication Matters" filled with reasons and evidence, then presented a "Public Policy Agenda" and "Strategies for Action," which were almost all conclusions about articulating demands, how to frame issues, identifying allies and opponents, and identifying resources. In addition, each section tended to present long lists of bullet-pointed text written in fairly dense language that presumed background knowledge of debates over spectrum policy. As a result, coders found it difficult to link conclusions in the latter part of the document with the fragmentary rationales provided in the opening section.

In contrast, reports that scored higher in the document-level assessments tended to be organized by topic (e.g., how broadband could be made more accessible to the disabled, to non-English speakers, and so on), and each section integrated conclusions with supporting reasoning, alternative views, and norms. These reports were written in a more accessible style that presumed little prior knowledge of the topic. If we think of the reports as jigsaw puzzles, reading *Wireless Broadband* was like putting together a partially disassembled puzzle in which most of the elements could be pieced together with effort (at least by those with some prior knowledge of the topic). Reading reports that scored higher on the document-level measures of coherence (such as *Broadband for All?*) was like encountering fully assembled puzzles, even if some of the pieces (such as evidence and opposing views) were missing. In other words, the choices authors make about how to organize the different facets of argumentation have a meaningful effect on the extent to which readers can make the connections deliberative theory encourages. This suggests that creating legitimate deliberative publicity involves attention to not only including all the different facets of deliberative argumentation, but also making the connections between those facets easy for readers to see.

Representing public voices

Our study of these reports reminds us that the products of civic forums are not simply a set of decisions or a collection of reasons exchanged, but *texts* in which authors actively select and communicate the group's arguments and conclusions. As we conclude this chapter, we want to step back from our findings and address what seems to be a fundamental dilemma of deliberative publicity. How can publicity faithfully represent citizens' voices yet also convey a clear message to the political system about what they want to see happen? In other words, how can forums reconcile the duty to report what citizens want to say with how decision makers need to hear it in order to act? In our sample, we see three basic authorial processes – resolution, synthesis, and interpretation – that convert the inevitable messiness of what is said in a deliberative forum into a coherent report of the participants' views.

Resolution
Publicity about deliberative forums that use consensus or voting to arrive at conclusions often involves resolving opinions into a totality, a majority, or a plurality in support of specific policy preferences. Resolution

aims to provide conclusions on which decision makers can act. While some resolution is found in all the reports we analyzed, it was especially prevalent in the decisional reports, which emphasize participants' conclusions at the expense of communicating their reasoning. Whether authors reported on forums that employ consensus, voting, or polling, they faced important challenges.

If the decisional reports amplified citizens' policy recommendations, these reports tended to mute participants' ability to reason with others outside the forum. As a result, these reports could not tell readers directly whether the deliberators considered self-interest, group interests, or common interests when coming to conclusions; the validity of the evidence upon which the participants relied; or whether their reasons were ones that could be recognized as legitimate (even if not embraced) by others. These are all important deliberative criteria. They are especially important for efforts to influence live policy issues, when deliberators are likely to be exposed to intensive efforts to manage public opinion, which can spread contradictory and misleading evidence and a welter of reasons for different positions. It is likely that what deliberators saw as true, good, and fair strongly conditioned the legitimacy of their conclusions. Yet the reports that were most likely to try to influence pressing policy decisions with specific conclusions were least likely to include reasoning.

To address this problem, one basic step that decisional forums can take is to devote greater attention to systematically recording the reasons, evidence, and norms that were most convincing to citizens in the forum. The *Global Warming* report made some effort to accompany its many polling results about what citizens wanted to happen with a few quotes from participants explaining why they supported each policy options. For example, the report illustrated majority support for requiring the most industrialized countries to slash greenhouse gas emissions most with quotes from unnamed participants in Mali ("Industrialized countries must honour their commitments"), Germany ("We demand binding reduction targets which are in accordance with both the capabilities and the responsibility of all countries"), and Uruguay ("Solidarity between countries with different economies").[44] These quotes reveal that some participants reasoned from the importance of keeping international agreements, accepting responsibility for historic emissions, and embracing common interests or fates. But it is not clear that these quotes are representative of participants in each country or globally. *New GM Plants*,

---

[44] Danish Board of Technology 2005, 17–18.

which reported all participants' votes in support of each argument about genetically modified agriculture, as well as in support of each conclusion, provides a better model. This fully transparent approach does not rely on the report's author to select some participants' views as representative of all others, thereby resolving disparate reasons into a coherent whole that may or may not have existed in the forums, even among participants who ended up supporting the same policy options.

Synthesis

Publicity that portrays the "sense of the group" in qualitative terms, crystallizing major agreements and disagreements without attempting to resolve them into group conclusions, involves synthesizing opinions. Synthesis aims to produce a more complex or coherent understanding of public opinion without endowing that opinion with recommending force for external decision makers. While decisional reports must especially grapple with the challenges of resolving opinion, dialogic reports focus more on synthesizing views. Some reports mix both. Synthesis also presents some challenges, including the problems of representing common understandings and actions that citizens suggest could be taken.

When understandings are in conflict, they can be very hard to synthesize and an author may be tempted to declare convergence among them without strong evidence. For example, South Dakota's *Citizens in the Legislative Process*, a highly dialogic report, recounted an initial tension in the forums between some young people's views that government is irrelevant to people's lives and the views of their elders that government affects their everyday existence in myriad ways. Indeed, this is a widespread generational difference in understanding. Research on youth civic engagement finds that young Americans are less likely than older generations to view traditional politics oriented toward influencing government as meaningful, important, or effective.[45] The report introduces the tension this way:

> Several young people in the forums said government and issues do not impact them. Each time, these young people were gently and kindly told otherwise by statements such as this by a participant in Brookings, 'Laws affect everyday life,' and this by a woman in Chamberlain, 'They will affect you some day. You need to look into the future. You will be paying taxes and out on your own some day.' Dr. Pam Carriveau of

[45] Bennett 2008.

Black Hills State University, an opening presenter in Rapid City, gave education as an example of an issue that can affect everyone and that cuts across all levels of government – federal, state, and county.[46]

Later, the report notes, "Many young people in some of the forums said they had not realized that adults in their community welcome and value youth participation. 'I think we learned that we should get involved,' said a high school student."[47] The report goes on to summarize youth participants' experience by noting that "not only did young people leave the forums feeling included and empowered, but adults felt they became more aware of how the younger generation thinks."[48]

It is possible that this synthesis of understandings occurred. Surveys conducted before and after the forum found that agreement "to participate in civic activities that involve public policy issues, voting, and lobbying" increased from 63 percent before the forums to 76 percent afterward.[49] But it is not clear whether young participants moved in this direction, as this is not reported, or whether the young people who attended the forum would agree with the authors' depiction of their views and how they changed. Claims of synthesis should be accompanied by some evidence other than the author's authority.

In addition, it was often unclear in dialogic reports how citizens might build upon their common understandings of problems to develop an authentically unified voice that could inform policy clearly. At the end of *Democracy's Challenge* and the South Dakota report, we are left with a handful of fairly modest policy recommendations for increasing civic engagement and unspecified calls for more dialogue. What remains unclear is citizens' theory of change that would lead us from dialogue to deliberation that generates policy reform commensurate with the problems laid out in each report, which include citizen apathy and cynicism, loss of traditional civic connections, media biases, capture of government by moneyed interests, gerrymandering, and more.[50]

---

[46] South Dakota Issues Forums 2009, 4.   [47] South Dakota Issues Forums 2009, 9.
[48] South Dakota Issues Forums 2009, 10.   [49] South Dakota Issues Forums 2009, 10.
[50] For example, *Democracy's Challenge* summarized participants' common concerns about the current state of government as feeling "misrepresented and disenfranchised from the political system," which they saw as dominated by "the wishes of special, moneyed interests." In response, participants "were also clear about a 'cure,' expressing an overwhelming desire for a greater public voice, more effective or widespread representation, and more accountability with respect to the representation of that voice by elected officials. But when it came to the particulars, they remained far from clear, and certainly less than fully persuaded, about what should be done." The authors say that "these

How might synthesis address these challenges of balancing authenticity of voice and clarity of message? Using consensus as a decision rule is one way, but the presence of synthesis rather than resolution suggests that consensus on understandings or conclusions is not yet possible. Reports of dialogic forums might be more likely to lead to deliberation about policy initiatives if organizers asked citizens to prioritize some concrete follow-up activities that might deepen mutual understanding and identify jointly-held policy priorities. This would involve internalizing recommendations about post-forum steps in the deliberation itself, reducing the distance between deliberation and authoring of reports.

Interpretation

All publicity inevitably involves some interpretation of citizens' opinions to make their meaning comprehensible to intended audiences in a partic-ular policy context. Voting tallies and collections of quotes from deliber-ators do not speak for themselves, or at least, do not tell the whole story of participants' arguments and conclusions. The raw data always need to be framed and contextualized for an audience. For example, our reports often aimed to draw attention to what authors found surprising about the group's outcomes, how they differed from participants' opinions before deliberation or from public opinion as expressed in polls, or how pol-icy makers or the public might respond to the deliberators' conclusions. While interpretation is a necessity, it poses several challenges to reporting citizens' voices authentically, which include explaining the strength of their conclusions, explaining the meaning of these conclusions without imputing reasons to participants, and treating citizens' views equally in publicity.

The first of these challenges, interpreting the strength of conclusions, is especially difficult when deliberators do not make a collective decision.[51] James Fishkin has said that opinions expressed by participants after dis-cussion in his Deliberative Polls should provide policy makers with a

results suggest that a national dialogue focused on public involvement about this deeply troubling issue might be the key to reducing the alienation, mistrust, and cynicism that are so widespread" (Doble Research Associates 2006, 2, 17). But if the participants in these forums were not able to agree on many policy solutions, how would more dialogue of this kind lead them to do so? How would such a dialogue need to be different in order to contribute to political change, not simply spread attitudinal changes?

[51] Recall that in our own coding scheme, we had to make such an interpretation when we decided to count any view that was supported by at least a majority of the group as a collective conclusion.

"recommending force," even if there is no shift in opinion, because deliberation converts "top of the head" opinions to considered opinions.[52] *Hard Times* echoed this when it claimed that the "resulting changes of opinion in the final survey offer some dramatic recommendations for both policymakers and the public."[53] Yet it is not always clear what the recommending force of certain opinion changes should be. For example, how are readers to interpret policy options that were supported by a majority before and after deliberation, when support *declined* after discussion? To take one specific case, *Hard Times* noted that "support for 'increasing the minimum wage' actually dropped significantly from 58 to 52 percent, presumably because of arguments about effects on employment." What is the recommending force of this decline in support for a policy that nonetheless remains the majority opinion? There are also options that attracted minority support before and after deliberation, but which gained substantial backing after discussion. For example, support for increasing tax incentives for small businesses moved from 32 percent to 43 percent. Which options were recommended – ones that attracted greater support after deliberation, or ones that were supported by a clear majority after deliberation? Perhaps most importantly, how would the deliberators themselves view the results? Do they think the movement or the marginal result is the most authentic expression of their views?

Questions of this sort lead to a second potential problem: explaining the underlying reasons for citizens' policy preferences. This is an especially significant issue for decisional reports, which foreground citizens' conclusions at the expense of their rationales, often because citizens' reasoning was never measured or preserved. For example, in *Hard Times*, participants were asked whether they agreed or disagreed that the state of Michigan should prioritize several industries for improving its economy in the future. Proposals to develop five different industries garnered majority support before deliberation and even stronger support afterward. The report interpreted the vote as follows: "After deliberation, all the options had strong support but none predominated. It was as if the participants found a number of ideas compelling but none reached the level of an agreed solution."[54] This interpretation that the forum failed to reach agreement only makes sense if one assumes that citizens ought to have chosen one industry on which to stake Michigan's future.

[52] Fishkin 2009, 34.
[53] MacNeil/Lehrer Productions and Center for Deliberative Democracy 2010, 3.
[54] MacNeil/Lehrer Productions and Center for Deliberative Democracy 2010, 10.

Alternatively, the results might have been interpreted as a very strong agreement among residents of a state that has been heavily dependent on the fortunes of the automotive industry to diversify their economy. These questions did not ask participants to rank each industry, but to express approval or disapproval of promoting each one. Similarly, the authors assume that support for increasing the minimum wage dropped over the course of the deliberation "presumably because of the effects on employment."[55] Deliberative publicity should not have to make such an assumption. To minimize unnecessary interpretation, Deliberative Polls and similar forums that do not end with a collective decision could ask people to rank their major reasons for their positions, as the *New GM Plants* forum did.

Authorial interpretation can also lead to unequal treatment of participants' conclusions and reasons. In some of the reports in our sample, incorrect or misleading evidence raised by participants went unquestioned, while other participants' comments were presented with editorial commentary that may have affected their credibility. For example, to illustrate its concern with the crisis of American politics, *Democracy's Challenge* recounted one participant's (false) claim that voting rates in presidential elections compared unfavorably with participation in elections held by entertainment television programs for viewers' favorite contestants: "Another man pointed out that, 'we had more *American Idol* voters than [in] any presidential [election] in the history of the country." No matter how troubled American democracy may be, things were not quite so dire at the time of the forum as either the participant's claim or the authors' uncritical acceptance of it might have made them seem.[56]

The same report also singled out some speakers and their comments for differential treatment. Opponents of public campaign financing were exemplified by "a San Diego woman with strong moral views," whose highly edited quote reads, "Shouldn't you have the right to donate and do whatever you want? ... [Public financing is] taking away one of our freedoms [by forcing me to contribute to candidates I am morally opposed to]." In contrast, a quote from a Dayton, Ohio, man complaining that

---

[55] MacNeil/Lehrer Productions and Center for Deliberative Democracy 2010, 9.

[56] While an extended treatment of this issue may begin to sound like a late-night comedy program, suffice it to say that vote totals on programs like *American Idol* are inflated by the fact that many viewers can and do vote repeatedly, while it is illegal and difficult for a citizen to cast more than one vote in a presidential election. Even so, the number of votes (not just voters) in the 2004 presidential election exceeded the number of votes in any *American Idol* polls at the time of the forum (Andries 2008).

the excessive focus on teaching to proficiency tests in the public schools had crowded out civic education was immediately followed by backing from an expert voice, who may or may not have attended the forum:

> Commenting on the issue, educator John Hale, Associate Director of the nonprofit, nonpartisan Center for Civic Education, which fosters the development of informed, responsible citizen participation, said, 'There is no subject for which a community connection could be more powerful than civics, yet few states have a civics requirement prior to 12th grade.'

In this report, some citizens' views are supported with expert authority, while others are presented as driven by "strong moral views." One need not assume that the male expert would be more convincing to all readers than the woman motivated by her values to see that their positions on the issues are being personified and presented in very different terms, which resonate with traditional assumptions about male rationality and female emotionality in deliberation.

Forums can begin to reconcile the need to interpret and to respect citizens' views in several ways. Forums can either establish clear standards for group decision making, or, in the absence of a collective choice, give a more transparent argument for how they interpret citizens' voices. Perhaps respecting the authenticity of citizens' reasoning, even if it is incorrect, outweighs the risk of spreading false information when there is not much at stake, as in claims about voting rates for presidents and pop singers. But how should authors treat more consequential flaws in citizens' reasoning, when their preferences are based on beliefs that are strongly contradicted by the best available evidence? When organizers' best efforts to inform all participants through briefing materials and deliberation do not succeed, what kinds of claims ought to be revealed as poorly informed, or even corrected, in publicity? Communication involves obligations to audiences too. Repeating deliberators' false or misleading beliefs without comment may come at the price of serving as an effective and trusted information proxy for the forum's audience.

Once again, one step that would help address many of these challenges would be for more forums to measure and report participants' reasoning for their positions. Authors would be less tempted to speculate about citizens' rationales and attribute them to participants after the forum. Citizens whose preferences are motivated by especially dubious empirical beliefs could be identified, and their views might even be reported separately, so that observers can judge how much credence to give these opinions. In doing so, publicity might report participants' views authentically without abandoning responsibility to the forum's audience.

Conclusion

In this chapter, we have shown that our approach to evaluating deliberative publicity can discover important differences in the ways that it is practiced. This close analysis of a sample of ten reports that emerged from a wide variety of deliberative processes revealed the extent to which each report met the basic requirements of deliberative theory. Our approach allows us to evaluate publicity from a variety of different perspectives – exploring the connections between conclusions and other elements of argumentation, and thinking about the extent to which the elements cohere in a clear and easily discerned argument.

While our sample size does not permit us to generalize about all deliberative publicity, we can begin to identify some of its different forms. Decisional reports emphasize conclusions over reasoning, while dialogic publicity focuses on reasoning at the expense of conclusions, and other documents offer a rough balance between the two. This relationship between conclusions and reasoning can be influenced by factors such as the design of the civic forum and its relationship to formal policy-making processes, but is not wholly reducible to such factors. Especially in its treatment of evidence, deliberative publicity can be influenced by several dominant genres of political discourse – populist, policy analytic, academic, and activist – which can exhibit cognitive or experiential biases about civic argumentation.

Moreover, we found that across all types of reports and forums in our sample, authors often neglected other important elements of deliberative theory. Few reports discussed opposing views, which would have revealed the range of perspectives deliberators considered and how they resolved trade-offs between them. Moral argumentation, which would have shown how deliberators' policy preferences were motivated by their values and how participants reconciled conflicting norms, was also rare.

Among our most important findings is that authors' expectations of their audience and their understandings of the appropriate genre for communicating deliberation appear to play a key role in influencing reports. Deliberative publicity is not a mere function of other aspects of the forum or event, but an independent variable in its own right. In calling attention to the ways in which important elements of publicity are often missing from these reports, we want to underscore the point that authors can attend more carefully to the ways in which their communication is *deliberative*. This is a separate question from whether a forum itself met the hallmarks of high-quality deliberation. No matter how well or poorly deliberation occurred within a forum, the authors of publicity need to consider how they resolve, synthesize, and interpret participants' views for those outside the forum.

To this point, we have primarily examined the content of deliberative argumentation. Just as important, however, is transparency about the deliberative process – and in fact, we have already shown that more transparency about the process can make it easier to perceive arguments and counter-arguments. In the next chapter, we will explore more fully the ways in which such transparency is – or is not – practiced.

6

Transparency

In the previous chapter, we explored how well the reports in our sample disseminated the substance of citizens' argumentation in the forum. But legitimate publicity also depends upon transparency – that is, making clear to audiences the deliberative process that shapes what citizens say about issues and what they think ought to be done about them. Who controlled the sponsorship and organization of the forum? How was it designed to recruit a sample of a larger polity, focus their discussion on a common agenda, and arrive at opinions or decisions? Who were the results meant to influence? Did citizen participants and others who observed the forum think that it was conducted fairly and knowledgably? How do we know that publicity faithfully represented what happened at the forum? We developed these five dimensions of transparency – control, design, intended influence, evaluation, and fidelity – in Chapter 4.

In this chapter, we analyze how well our sample of reports practiced these elements of transparency. This is an important question not only for authors of publicity, but also for all actors within a civic forum and all those who the forum aims to influence. As we argued in Chapter 4, the prospect of disclosing how the forum was conducted tends to hold sponsors and organizers accountable to the larger public and to other political actors, encouraging inclusion and equal treatment of participants and policy arguments, and discouraging manipulation. Transparency can also improve deliberation within most forums by motivating participants to enlarge their personal regard into public reasoning that addresses the views of other citizens outside the forum, engaging in a kind of reciprocity with the public as a whole. Outside the forum, transparency allows audiences to make well-informed decisions about whether to trust and authorize the views of citizen deliberators.

If all civic forums that aim to influence public opinion or decision making need to attend to transparency, different kinds of forums need to pay attention to disclosure for somewhat different reasons. Forums that act in an advisory capacity, such as most mini-publics, especially need to convince officials, the news media, and the public to ratify the forum's conclusions, a decision that often depends in part on accepting that the forum was conducted legitimately. However, even forums in which citizens are empowered to make binding decisions or to co-govern with officials are new and delicate institutions that need to persuade others of their ongoing legitimacy in order to win consent to the institution's decisions and continued existence.

Our sample also includes a few examples of stakeholder and activist forums, which need to be concerned about transparency for additional reasons as well. Stakeholder forums' claims to legitimacy rest in part on how well they deliver on their promise to incorporate the views of community leaders who represent important constituencies, the extent to which more and less powerful interests can speak on equal terms, and whether stakeholders arrive at agreements that serve the public good or cut "back-room" deals that sacrifice the interests of non-participants.[1] Therefore, it is especially important that these forums divulge who was invited to the table, the people for whom stakeholders aim to speak, and whether weaker interests felt their voices were ignored, co-opted, or equally influential.

Activist forums raise other questions that need to be addressed in publicity. Some see civil society as fertile ground for authentic and equal deliberation because it is relatively autonomous from state and market pressures.[2] However, others raise suspicions that movements and interest groups are unlikely to hold themselves accountable to society as a whole because these groups are too narrowly and passionately committed to their own economic or ideological pursuits.[3] Therefore, activist forums need to be especially clear about whose interests were represented as well as the constituencies or audiences to which the participants are most accountable. Because advocates contribute to democracy by advancing particular perspectives and ideas, they do not necessarily have to represent all citizens or views equally, but they do have an obligation to be clear about whom they aim to speak for and why they should be seen as

---

[1] Hendriks 2006; Levine and Nierras 2007. These are longstanding criticisms of interest-group pluralism (see Lowi 1969).

[2] Dryzek 2000; Habermas 1996; Cohen 1989.   [3] See, e.g., Sunstein 2005.

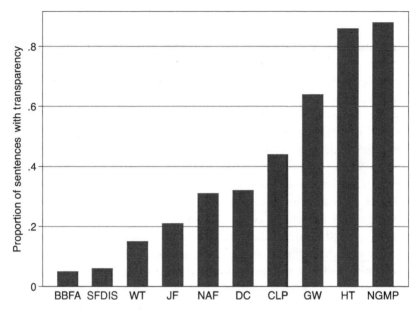

Figure 6.1 Proportion of sentences including transparency

representing their constituencies' interests or views. For example, some advocacy groups created and controlled by narrow business interests are understandably criticized for cloaking their true constituencies behind claims that they speak for everyday consumers or citizens – for being more "astroturf" than "grassroots" organizations.

As in our assessment of argumentation in Chapter 5, we want to understand the extent to which our small but diverse sample of reports fulfills basic expectations of deliberative transparency. Our goal is to identify and explain some major strengths and weaknesses in the practice of transparency, generate additional theoretical insights about its role in legitimate publicity, and lay the groundwork for subsequent discussion of how it might be better served in the future.

Overview

We begin with a summary of the results and their implications for publicity, before delving deeper into each of the major dimensions of transparency. Figure 6.1 shows that many of the reports devoted a significant number of sentences to revealing some element of transparency.[4] In the median report, a little less than one-third of the sentences (32 percent) included some transparency-related information.[5] But, as the figure reveals, there is considerable variation among the reports. In two reports, *Broadband for All?* and the *San Francisco Digital Inclusion Strategy*, only about 5 percent of sentences disclosed some aspect of transparency, while in two other reports, *New GM Plants* and Michigan's *Hard Times Hard Choices*, more than 80 percent of the sentences revealed some information about how the forum was conducted. As we discuss in more detail below, *New GM Plants* and *Hard Times* devoted extraordinary attention to discussing the design of the forums, the demographic composition of the participants, and the dynamics of the deliberation (especially how strongly the participants as a whole agreed with the group's conclusions). *Hard Times* was also notable for its attention to how the deliberators evaluated the quality of their discussions and the moderators.

However, what matters more than the sheer number of sentences devoted to disclosure is whether a report addressed *each element of transparency*. Reports may attend to these elements with a large number of sentences, but they might also meet expectations for deliberative publicity more efficiently in comparatively fewer sentences. Therefore, we made an additional pass through each document, coding the presence or absence of each kind of transparency in the document as a whole.[6] This approach set a relatively low bar – for example, one mention of a given element of control or design in any sentence was enough for us to code the category as present in the document as a whole. Nonetheless, it allows us to identify many aspects of transparency that were not disclosed. In addition, in our discussion below we also look more qualitatively at how extensively the reports divulged each element. Table 6.1 shows all the dimensions of

---

[4] We asked coders to indicate any sentence in which any element of transparency was present. Levels of intercoder reliability for the transparency codes were quite high. In our first round of coding, in which sentences were assigned to categories, we established intercoder reliability using a sample of 585 sentences, or approximately 19 percent of the sample (3073 sentences), which were coded independently by two coders. Krippendorff's alpha for the transparency category was 0.95 (97.7% agreement between the coders).

[5] The average was even higher: 39 percent.

[6] Two coders completed this coding activity independently, and as with all our other content analysis, we checked levels of intercoder reliability by asking both coders to review an overlapping portion of the sample. Intercoder agreement was perfect (100%, Krippendorff's alpha=1.00).

Table 6.1 Transparency coding results

	BBFA	WB	SF	NGMP	DC	GW	HT	JF	CLP	WT	Total (% of reports)
Control											
Org. mission	No	Yes	Yes	No	Yes	Yes	Yes	No	No	Yes	60
Funding	Yes	Yes	No	No	Yes	Yes	Yes	Yes	Yes	Yes	80
Partnerships	Yes	Yes	Yes	Yes	Yes	Yes	Yes	No	Yes	Yes	90
Total (% of categories)	66	100	66	33	100	100	100	33	66	100	77
Design											
Participant selection	Yes	Yes	No	Yes	No	Yes	Yes	No	No	Yes	60
Representativeness	Yes	Yes	Yes	Yes	Yes	Yes	Yes	Yes	Yes	Yes	100
Agenda	No	Yes	No	Yes	Yes	Yes	Yes	No	Yes	Yes	70
Structure and facilitation	Yes	Yes	No	Yes	Yes	Yes	Yes	Yes	Yes	Yes	90
Format	Yes	No	No	Yes	Yes	Yes	Yes	Yes	Yes	No	70
Decision rule	Yes	No	No	Yes	Yes	Yes	Yes	No	No	No	50
Decision dynamics	No	Yes	No	Yes	Yes	Yes	Yes	No	Yes	No	60
Total (% of categories)	71	71	14	100	86	100	100	43	71	57	70
Intended influence											
Purpose	Yes	Yes	No	Yes	Yes	Yes	Yes	Yes	Yes	Yes	90
Audiences	Yes	Yes	No	Yes	No	Yes	Yes	No	No	Yes	60
Total (% of categories)	100	100	0	100	50	100	100	50	50	100	75

	BBFA	WB	SF	DC	GW	HT	NGMP	JF	CLP	WT	Total
Evaluation											
Deliberation	No	No	No	No	No	No	Yes	No	Yes	No	20
Participants	No	No	No	No	Yes	No	Yes	No	Yes	No	30
Total (% of categories)	0	0	0	0	50	0	100	0	100	0	25
Fidelity											
Authorization	Yes	Yes	No	Yes	No	No	No	No	No	No	30
Accountability	Yes	No	No	Yes	No	No	No	No	No	No	20
Total (% of categories)	100	50	0	100	0	0	0	0	0	0	25
Transparency totals											
% of all categories	69%	69%	19%	75%	69%	75%	88%	31%	63%	56%	58%
% of sentences	5%	31%	6%	88%	32%	64%	86%	21%	44%	15%	39%

Note: BBFA = *Broadband for All?*; WB = *Wireless Broadband*; SF = *San Francisco Digital Inclusion*; DC = *Democracy's Challenge*; GW = *World Wide Views on Global Warming*; HT = *Hard Times, Hard Choices*; NGMP = *New GM Plants*; JF = *Just Foods*; CLP = *Citizens in the Legislative Process*; WT = *Working Together*

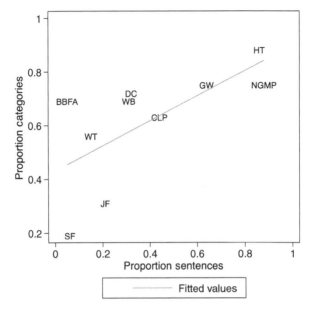

Figure 6.2 Relationship between sentences and categories

Note: Overlapping labels are jittered for ease of interpretation

transparency and their subcategories, providing the full data set we will analyze in this chapter.

Looking at this overview of the data, we can see that several factors that might plausibly account for how transparency was practiced in our reports *do not* end up explaining much. For example, did reports that allocated more space to transparency, or that were simply longer, address more elements of transparency as well? Figure 6.2 shows that there was a strong and positive relationship between devoting more sentences to transparency in the document as a whole and addressing it in greater breadth: the two measures are significantly correlated at $r=0.68$ (p=0.03). However, the relationship between depth and breadth is not perfectly linear, and some reports are well off the trend line. Most dramatically, *Broadband for All?* devoted only 5 percent of its sentences to transparency yet still addressed 69 percent of the categories. While *Broadband for All?*, *Wireless Broadband*, *Democracy's Challenge*, *Global Warming*, and *New GM Plants* varied dramatically in the number of transparency sentences, all covered around 70 to 75 percent of the categories. In addition, we find no relationship between the overall length of the reports and revelation of all aspects of transparency. In fact, the report that covered

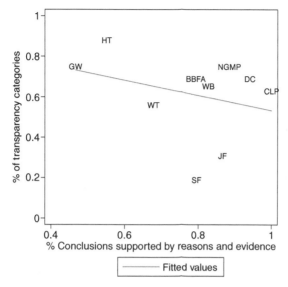

Figure 6.3 Relationship between transparency and argumentation
Note: Overlapping labels are jittered for ease of interpretation

the most categories – *Hard Times* – did so in less than 200 sentences, which is about half the average number of sentences in the reports we analyzed. Even in our small sample, these results indicate that covering a broad range of transparency categories can be done in either many or few words.

The reports' style of argumentation also did not seem to affect how they treated transparency. In Chapter 5, we divided our sample into three types – decisional (which emphasized participants' conclusions), dialogic (which focused more on citizens' reasoning), and balanced (which reported conclusions and reasoning about equally). Yet, as can be seen in Figure 6.3, there was no meaningful relationship between our reports' coverage of transparency categories and the proportion of conclusions supported by reasons and evidence ($r = -0.30$, $p = 0.40$).

Coupled with our findings about how differently civic forums disseminated participants' argumentation, these initial findings about transparency suggest that there were few commonly practiced standards of publicity in our sample. Longer reports were not necessarily more transparent. Disclosure seemed independent of reporting on argumentation. As we will see, the decision to divulge information about the control, design, intended influence, evaluation, or fidelity of the deliberative forum appears to be very much within the author's control, but authors

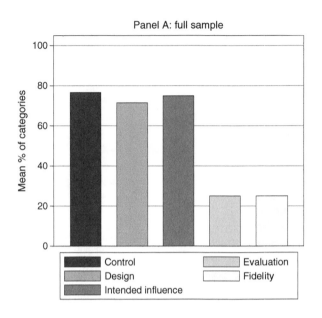

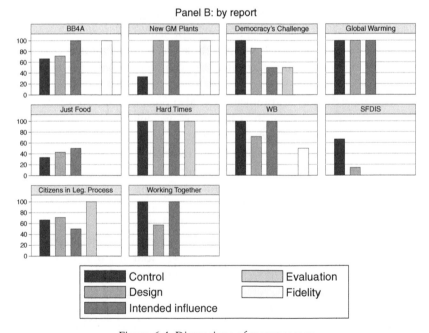

Figure 6.4 Dimensions of transparency

frequently choose not to attend to one or more of these elements of transparency. Just as important, even when they disclose information, authors make important choices about how much detail to provide or omit.

Figure 6.4 reveals how successfully the reports in our sample disclosed at least minimal information about each of the five dimensions of transparency we outlined in Chapter 4. Panel A shows that authors were far more likely to report information about control, design, and intended influence than to touch on evaluation or fidelity. On average, reports included information about 70–75 percent of each of the subcategories in the control, design, and intended influence dimensions. In contrast, only about a quarter of the subcategories for evaluation and fidelity, on average, were found in the documents. This unevenness can be found at the level of the individual report as well. As Panel B makes clear, no report fully covered all the dimensions or categories we have identified as important. Even the reports that were especially attentive to transparency, such as *New GM Plants* and *Hard Times*, were missing a tooth or two. *New GM Plants* did not report some aspects of control and omitted evaluation information entirely. *Hard Times* had nothing to say about fidelity. At the opposite end of the spectrum, the *San Francisco Digital Inclusion* report highlighted some aspects of control, but neglected almost everything else. This underscores that there were few widely shared standards of transparency among our reports. In what follows, we review each of the five dimensions of transparency in greater detail, explaining the importance of the subcategories in our coding scheme and exploring the implications of our findings.

Control

As Peter Levine, Archon Fung, and John Gastil have written, high-quality deliberation "is not self-generating... Someone must organize a discursive process, choose a topic, recruit the participants, prepare background materials or invite speakers, provide facilitators, and raise the funds that are necessary to do these things."[7] Revealing control is about making clear who those people are, which allows outsiders to begin to judge for themselves the legitimacy of the event. Control thus involves disclosing the organizational power behind the civic forum. At a minimum, this element of transparency means revealing the mission of the convening

---

[7] Levine, Fung, and Gastil 2005, 274–5.

organization(s), who funded the forum, and any partner organizations that helped design it.

Recall from the Introduction the controversy over sponsorship of the America*Speaks* "Our Budget, Our Economy" forums. One of the most potentially damning charges made by the forum's critics was that funding from a conservative foundation would skew the forums' briefing materials and agenda, subtly encouraging participants to prize deficit reduction over social and economic spending. While the critics' fears did not ultimately materialize, this controversy nonetheless underscores the importance of divulging control and explaining how the autonomy of the process is preserved when partisan or other interests are involved. This is not to say that "interestedness" is always a weakness or that organized interests ought to be excluded from deliberative events. But full transparency can address real and imagined limits to a forum's fairness and help observers come to well-founded conclusions about whether the forum is trustworthy.

In our sample, control was revealed frequently, though often briefly. The convening organization's mission was revealed in 60 percent of reports, mainly through short descriptions of the broad purposes motivating the sponsor's activities. For example, the *Hard Times* report describes its convening organization, By the People, as a "civic engagement initiative" that "seeks to bring the view of informed, 'ordinary' residents into the discussion of the important issues of the day."[8] *Wireless Broadband and Public Needs* portrayed its sponsor, the New America Foundation, as "an independent think-tank" committed to advancing "work on public interest spectrum policy."[9] *Global Warming* noted that its forums emerged from an alliance between the Danish Board of Technology and many civil society organizations committed to global policymaking and "citizens' sense of ownership in decision making."[10] The report named each of these organizations but did not describe the separate missions of each of these partners in detail. Yet it explained that the Danish Board of Technology is an organization with "a long tradition of involving ordinary citizens in political decision-making processes nationally and on a European scale."[11] In general, the mission statements in our sample are complete enough to give the informed reader a basic sense of the organizers' aspirations, though not always sufficiently detailed to allow people who are unfamiliar with the organization to understand its ideological or partisan commitments.

---

[8] MacNeil/Lehrer Productions and Center for Deliberative Democracy 2010, 2.
[9] New America Foundation and Center for International Media Action 2006, 1.
[10] Danish Board of Technology 2009, 3.   [11] Danish Board of Technology 2009, 5.

The key question for disclosure of organizational mission may be how well-known the organizers are to their audience. For example, *New GM Plants* omits any reference to its organizers' mission. But perhaps the Danish Board of Technology, a government agency that routinely conducts citizen consultations, was familiar enough to its primary audience (the Danish Parliament) and secondary audiences (Danish journalists and other interested stakeholders) that a statement of its mission and purposes was unnecessary. If the report aimed to influence debate outside of Denmark, however, a failure to describe the organizers' aims would be more problematic. Similarly, *Broadband for All?* was designed in part to influence local Silicon Valley decision makers, many of whom participated in the forum as advisory panelists or witnesses at the associated public hearing. But the forum was simultaneously aimed at a broader audience of localities considering the issue of municipal broadband, so more transparency about the goals of the Broadband Institute of California and Santa Clara University's Center for Science, Technology, and Society would have helped those audiences better evaluate the report. In this sense, the most worrisome omissions of organizers' missions may be in the *Just Food* and *Citizens in the Legislative Process* reports. Both divulged the identity of their convening organizations – the University of New Hampshire Office of Sustainability Programs and the South Dakota Issues Forums, respectively – but in both cases, it is unclear whether the reports' intended audiences should have been expected to know much about those organizers (nor is it clear who, exactly, the intended audiences were).

With respect to the second and third aspects of control, disclosure of sponsorship and identification of organizations who partnered with the conveners to organize the deliberation, most of the reports in our sample scored quite well. Eighty percent included some information about the organizations or individuals who paid for the deliberative group to convene, and 90 percent identified partners who helped to arrange the forum. This level of disclosure signaled a commitment to some important pillars of transparency, though in many cases additional information would have helped readers to understand sponsors and partners more fully. For example, civic forums that utilized advisory boards typically listed the names and titles of the advisory board members but rarely provided biographies or other detailed information about the perspectives and roles of the individuals.[12]

---

[12] The only report that did not divulge its advisory panel or partners was *Just Foods*, whose organizers were advised by the Loka Institute (see Dryzek et al. 2009, 272).

A few reports, such as *Global Warming*, referred interested readers to their websites for further information about partners, co-sponsors, and organizers. The reports themselves, however, tended to offer little rationale for recruiting particular advisors and co-organizers – an important omission because these partners can play substantial roles in the deliberative process, including recruiting participants and preparing briefing materials. It is especially worth noting that few reports identified their authors. *Democracy's Challenge* was an exception. The report noted that it was prepared by Doble Research Associates, included biographies of the report's authors, and gave a full page of information on Doble Research, including its mission and a list of its clients and partner organizations.

The reports in our sample could have revealed more about control by addressing further questions. Why did the organizers choose particular partners?[13] What were their views on the issues under deliberation? Were partners chosen because they are "neutral experts," contending stakeholders, or decision makers who are the intended audience for the report, or for other reasons? Were advisors and partners expected to act as delegates from their organizations, or to express their individual views more autonomously? If they were academics, to what major positions, theories, or findings on relevant issues were they committed? To what extent did partners shape the agenda or contribute to briefing materials? How did the distribution of views on the issues among the advisory panel or among co-organizers compare with participants' views before and after deliberation? All of this information, especially the answers that allow readers to judge whether advisory panelists represented multiple perspectives and whether deliberation led citizens to endorse the organizers, sponsors, or partners' issue positions, could be helpful for establishing the extent to which deliberators were autonomous.

Similarly, disclosures about funding sources were often brief and not accompanied by additional information about funders' backgrounds, purposes, mission statements, and, most importantly, whether the sponsors had taken positions on the issues under discussion. Without such information, mere reference to the names of funding sources makes it difficult for observers to understand the relationship between funders and the forum's

[13] For example, *Democracy's Challenge* discloses that it partnered with the New Scholars Program, which is described as helping to bring together "honors students at historically black colleges and universities," and explains that students in the New Scholars Program underwent moderator training and subsequently held forums at various colleges. This background information helps to orient the reader to some aspects of the partner program, but the report offers no rationale for why this program was chosen over others.

aims and purposes. For example, *Just Food* divulged that the citizen panel was funded with a grant from the Nathan Cummings Foundation but offered no further information that might help the reader understand the foundation's mission or perspective on the issue of genetically modified foods. A few reports, though, did disclose helpful further information. For example, *Hard Times* explained that its Deliberative Poll was funded with a grant from the W. K. Kellogg Foundation, which was portrayed as an organization that had invested $50 million in the state of Michigan to facilitate "improving lives for vulnerable children" the year the forum was held, in the belief that "there is no separation between the future of children, the future of our state, and of our nation."[14] This alerted readers to the possibility that the sponsor favored investment in government programs to assist children, which was germane to the forum's topic of how to address the state's budget crisis through tax increases or spending cuts to education, health care, and other programs that affect youth.

Notably, reports sponsored by an official government agency, the *San Francisco Digital Inclusion Strategy* and *New GM Plants*, were the only ones that did not reveal their sources of funding. Perhaps in these cases funding can be assumed. But when government agencies cooperate closely with private sources, as is increasingly common in civic forums, the need for additional transparency about the identities and aims of the funders and partners grows. In a world in which the relationships between new civic forums and more traditional forms of public decision making are still being forged, public information about who is footing the bill and why remains at a premium.[15] The two reports of events that involved the closest public-private partnerships both scored well on revealing basic aspects of control. We have noted above how the *Global Warming* report discussed its partners and funding. In addition, *Working Together* disseminated the results of a conference in which civil society leaders conferred with members of the Obama administration in hopes of influencing the incoming administration's strategies for electoral reform and public engagement in government. The report included a full list of individual participants and their institutional affiliations, including from the administration, and disclosed the event's organizers and funders. It also gave a brief history of the different issues on which participants had been working, and their viewpoints, before the conference.

---

[14] MacNeil/Lehrer Productions and Center for Deliberative Democracy 2010, 2.

[15] For more on the relationship between private and public decision-making forums, see Karpowitz 2006. See also Gastil 2008.

To summarize, most reports disclose at least minimal information about most aspects of control. However, additional detail would often help readers better understand the impetus for civic forums and potential biases in the organizers' perspectives. This is most urgent with respect to the organizational missions of the forum's conveners, but it also extends to funders, and advisory boards or partners, especially when partners are unlikely to be familiar to the outside audience whom the deliberative forum is meant to influence. Greater transparency about control takes on special importance when the relationship of funders and organizers is least obvious (i.e., not a government-commissioned forum), when there is no clear prior relationship between organizers and their intended audiences, and in proportion to funders', co-organizers', and advisors' influence over the conditions of deliberation.

Design

Transparency also encompasses disclosing information about the design of the forum, including 1) the selection of participants (the criteria and process used to choose deliberators); 2) the participants' representativeness of others (the relationship of the sample of deliberators to some larger population); 3) the initial questions, task statements, or points of view posed to participants (including the group's agenda and how the objectives, issues, or questions were framed for the group); 4) the structure and facilitation of deliberation (such as where and when the group met and the presence or absence of moderators); 5) the deliberative format (a Consensus Conference, Citizens' Jury, or the like); 6) the decision rule (whether the group was asked to settle on conclusions by consensus, majority rule, or other means); and 7) other dynamics of the deliberation (such as the strength of agreement or disagreement, the speed with which the group came to agreement, or other qualities of the group's discussion).

Participant selection and representativeness
In our discussion of enclave deliberation among the disempowered in Chapter 2, we argued that not every sample must be random and representative, especially if background conditions of inequality and the goals of the deliberation warrant oversampling marginalized groups or convening entire forums of the disempowered. However, we also contended that any forum's legitimacy turns on how well it justifies the criteria used to select participants. Therefore, organizers of all deliberative forums should practice transparency about the participants' relationship to a larger

populace, allowing outsiders to better understand who was in the room and why they were chosen. Forums that recruit lay citizens especially need to attend to whether people that are least likely to participate in politics are part of the conversation. Stakeholder and activist forums need to account for how they represent a pattern of interests or constituencies.

All of our reports mentioned the representativeness of the sample in at least some minimal fashion, and 60 percent discussed the process of participant selection. Reports addressed these issues in several ways, including disclosing statistics on the demographic diversity of deliberators, biographies of the participants, and group pictures of the participants that revealed some of their characteristics. *Broadband for All?*, for example, provided a large photograph of the consensus conference participants, who were described as "a diverse community panel of Silicon Valley residents from underserved groups," defined as those "least likely to have Internet access now." The picture made clear that the panel differed along lines of gender, ethnicity, age, and even physical ability (one participant was seated in a wheelchair, and two blind participants wore dark glasses). However, the report would have been more illuminating if it had specified which groups had the lowest levels of broadband access, how the organizers selected the 12 deliberators, and how closely the panel's composition mirrored the size of each underserved group in Silicon Valley (not to mention where the borders of Silicon Valley were drawn).[16]

Two reports discussed participant selection and representativeness most extensively. *Hard Times* explained that the organizers convened "a random, representative sample of over 300 Michigan residents" and took the additional step of comparing participants' prior issue knowledge and attitudes to a similarly representative control group that did not deliberate.[17] This close attention to measuring and reporting the representativeness of the forum's sample of deliberators is a unique strength of Deliberative Polls. Among the smaller forums, *New GM Plants* stands out for offering an especially precise discussion of its selection process and its aims in choosing a panel of "laymen with diverse backgrounds":

> The citizens were found by sending an invitation to 2000 randomly selected Danish citizens between the ages of 20 and 65, found through the interior ministry's registry of civil registration numbers. In this

---

[16] While we report much of this information in Chapter 3, none of it was included in the final report.

[17] MacNeil/Lehrer Productions and Center for Deliberative Democracy 2010, 2.

invitation, the citizens were encouraged to write an application for participation in the citizens' jury. On the basis of the 150 applications that the Danish Board of Technology received, 16 participants were selected. The aim was to select a citizens' jury that was representative of the population with regard to gender, place of residence, age, education and occupation. Furthermore, it was a precondition that the citizens did not have particular professional expert knowledge of the subject.[18]

In addition, the report goes on to name each deliberator and list how each contributed to the forum's desired demographic diversity.

Interestingly, the activist meeting in our sample modeled a way in which these kinds of forums can practice transparency about participants as well. The meeting reported in *Wireless Broadband* aimed to represent a movement rather than citizens generally. But it served transparency about its participants with four full pages of biographical information about them and their constituencies. For example, the biography for a representative of the National Hispanic Media Coalition included both information about the NHMC's mission ("to open the door for Latinos in all areas of the media and protect the Latino image as portrayed by the media") and the interest group's constituency ("the Latino community and in general people of color that have historically not had equity in access to affordable broadband").[19] Through biographical information, *Wireless Broadband* helped readers to understand the interests and perspectives that deliberators brought to their interactions, and therefore participants' claims to represent others.

While not all legitimate samples have to be randomly chosen and broadly representative, transparency requires that authors justify their principles of inclusion, clarifying their sample's ability to represent a larger population in social scientific terms, or what standards for recruitment were used as an alternative. Several of the reports we analyzed were not at all clear about their sampling strategies, which posed several legitimacy problems. First, even reports that revealed something about selection criteria often succumbed to the temptation to overstate the group's representativeness of a larger population. It is usually not possible for smaller forums to achieve a statistically accurate representation of a larger public. *Just Food*, for example, described its Consensus Conference

---

[18] Danish Board of Technology 2005, 4.
[19] New America Foundation and Center for International Media Action 2006, 19.

panel as a group of "volunteers of all ages and from all walks of life."[20] No further details were provided, including any sense of the number of people who comprised the panel, let alone a description of the selection criteria or process. Without any additional information, it is impossible for even the most friendly reader to judge the writers' assertions about the diversity of the sample. For non-representative samples, it is especially important to discuss selection criteria to avoid charges of stacking a group with people who will arrive at organizers' foregone conclusions.[21]

Even reports that admit the difficulties of assembling a representative sample can fall prey to this difficulty. *Global Warming*, an ambitious attempt at worldwide deliberation that included many thousands of participants across multiple countries, acknowledged the challenge of achieving representativeness but still made the bold and unproven assertion that the views of the deliberators were broadly generalizable: "Although the sample size of 100 per country or region somewhat limits the national statistical validity of the results, it is nonetheless large and diverse enough to give a sense of general trends in national and international opinions."[22] The report went on to indicate that partners of the Danish Board of Technology helped to assemble panels of deliberators in each country (thus satisfying the minimal requirements of our coding scheme), but offered no details of exactly how these partners selected their participants.

Understanding the nature of this worldwide sample is not easy because the sampling frames differed dramatically across locations, and the partners around the world likely used somewhat different sampling strategies. Some partner organizations only recruited participants from one geographical area, others from whole countries. The report stated that partners were instructed to recruit groups that "reflect the demographic distribution in their country or region with regards to age, gender, occupation, education, and geographical zone of residency (i.e., city and countryside) ... [and] where appropriate, national partners added other demographic criteria, which were relevant to their national context; for example race or ethnic groups."[23] Yet the authors do not report the demographic breakdown of those who ended up participating. Despite a

---

[20] University of New Hampshire Office of Sustainability Programs and Cooperative Extension 2002, 1.

[21] For further discussion of the shortcomings of *Just Food* with respect to these issues, see Dryzek et al. 2009; Dryzek, 2010, Chapter 8. Dryzek et al. found that the process of the New Hampshire conference was "not a neutral forum," which helps explain why it arrived at recommendations that "were more hostile to GM foods than any of the other reports surveyed" by the authors (2009, 272–3).

[22] Danish Board of Technology 2009, 6.   [23] Danish Board of Technology 2008, 8.

Herculean effort at simultaneous global deliberation, it seems unlikely
that the forums could have reliably approximated statistical opinion
"trends" in participating nations, both because the samples were not
large enough and because they were not randomly selected. The sample
cannot represent trends in *international* opinion because entire regions
did not participate. There were very few meetings in Eastern Europe and
Africa, and none at all in the Middle East, the world's main oil-producing
region, which is no small matter in a discussion of climate change.

In addition, the authors of *Global Warming* make the ambitious claim
that because participants were provided with balanced information and a
chance to deliberate before expressing their views, "the WWViews results
can be interpreted as a leading indicator for what conventional opinion
polls will likely find in the future, as populations gradually learn more
about climate change."[24] But the lack of data on whether the sample
reflected the distribution of prior attitudes toward global warming makes
it difficult to evaluate the extent to which self-selection skewed the groups'
discussions in ways that were more friendly to government action on
climate change. The huge majorities (above 90 percent in many cases)
for taking dramatic steps to limit greenhouse gas emissions suggest that
the project probably attracted people who were more concerned about
climate change than the norm.[25]

Do forums that aim more to initiate dialogue than to arrive at decisions bear responsibility for reporting their criteria for including participants? Two reports that did not specify these criteria – *Democracy's Challenge* and *Citizens in the Legislative Process* – were National
Issues Forums (NIFs), which use convenience sampling and are more
dialogic than decisional. Yet some NIFs also want to provide officials
or civil society associations with a snapshot of considered public opinion that could inform policy making or political action.[26] For example,
Democracy's Challenge concluded that the forums suggested the need
for "a national dialogue focused on public involvement."[27] *Citizens in
the Legislative Process* claimed that "voters want ballot initiatives in
simpler language."[28] Reports of NIF and similar forums that claim to

---

[24] Danish Board of Technology 2009, 6.

[25] In a recent journal article, two of the organizers of this forum lamented that "too many
like-minded 'greens' may have been present at WWViews," recounting how "one local
partner distributed T-shirts emblazoned with a 'Save the Earth' slogan that were worn
by all participants at the event" (Rask and Worthington 2012, 561).

[26] Melville, Willingham, and Dedrick 2005.   [27] Doble Research Associates 2006, 2.

[28] South Dakota Issues Forums 2009, 5.

represent public opinion should reveal how they assembled a sample of the public.

Even purely dialogic NIF forums can honor transparency by explaining why they chose the forum sites they did, disclosing more information about the demographic characteristics of the deliberators, and assessing the opinions of participants prior to the dialogue. *Democracy's Challenge* indicated where forums were held (from community colleges to prisons) and offered some demographic data (gender, ethnicity, age) on who ended up participating. The authors described special outreach efforts among disadvantaged populations, including African-Americans and inmates in Pennsylvania prisons, and highlighted ways in which African-American participants' opinions differed from other deliberators' views. These details gave readers some resources to grasp the effects of the selection process and especially to understand the characteristics and opinions of deliberators. Yet the report offered no rationale for this selection process or its aims – the authors never offer even a brief defense for why organizers chose to over-represent African-Americans and prison inmates in discussions of civic engagement.[29] *Citizens in the Legislative Process* revealed less information. The report noted that the series of South Dakota forums attracted "over 300 people ranging from middle school students to retired individuals."[30] Organizers said little about their reasons for especially recruiting young people. Each of the NIF reports could have made more persuasive claims to represent public opinion about the issue of civic engagement if it had reported whether the forums attracted individuals who were already the most likely to take part in politics or brought in citizens who might otherwise have shunned political participation.

Of the reports that did not disclose the participant selection process, the *San Francisco Digital Inclusion Strategy* may raise the greatest alarm because it was a government-organized stakeholder forum with special power to help forge the city's policy on broadband. We have already indicated that the San Francisco report scored very low on many dimensions of transparency. Stakeholder panels are frequently criticized for omitting important interests that are less well-resourced or well-organized, and for including advocates who may not have significant followings and therefore cannot speak for larger communities.[31] It is particularly important

---

[29] Our critique is not that the choice to focus on these groups is wrong-headed, but rather that authors have an obligation to explain *why* these choices were made.

[30] South Dakota Issues Forums 2009, 3.

[31] See, for example, the discussion and further citations in Hendriks 2011, 53.

for these kinds of forums to reveal the composition of the group so that people can assess for themselves whether all important interests were included and how fully each member represents the groups for whom they were chosen to speak.

We recognize that it may be difficult for a report to characterize fully the wide variety of participants' attributes and attitudes that may be relevant to any given deliberative event. Still, our results show that a norm of complete transparency about participant selection does not seem to have developed among the reports we analyzed. Most reports managed to provide at least minimal information about the representativeness of their participants, but in our view, much more detail was often needed to evaluate the characteristics of those participating. In the reports we assessed, disclosure of the representativeness of the deliberators was most feasible when a conventionally defined geographic community or polity was sampled. The Deliberative Poll in Michigan offered the strongest methods for reporting representativeness, including of pre-deliberation opinions. Unconventional communities, such as those that cross traditional borders, posed a greater challenge for reporting representativeness, with *Global Warming* offering the main example. But making assertions about participants' representativeness without providing sufficient information to judge those claims is a serious weakness in publicity. Many of the reports we analyzed overstated these claims. This is not just weak social science. It is also a threat to democratic legitimacy. Full disclosure of sampling criteria is possible under all conditions; every forum can practice this kind of transparency, even those that make use of convenience samples.

To summarize, the fullest reporting of sampling criteria and representativeness is especially important under several conditions. First, when deliberation is most likely to influence policy, decision makers and the public need to know who is speaking to them and who is not. Second, we see increased needs for transparency about representativeness when deliberation is held among members of stakeholder groups. Here, there is a double-sampling decision made by organizers: which segments of the public should be represented and what leaders are most appropriate to speak for each segment. Both decisions need to be explained. Third, the transparency requirement increases when deliberation is held in enclaves, as in *Broadband for All?* We have argued that enclaves can play a valuable role in the wider deliberative system, but this does not excuse organizers of such forums from explaining their goals, being completely forthcoming about the attributes of the participants, and making the case for why the wider public (or some other relevant audience) should attend carefully to what emerges from the enclave group.

Agenda

Political scientists have long held that agenda setting is a consequential form of power, and that is no less true of civic forums than of other political settings.[32] The initial questions, briefing materials, or other tasks for participants in civic forums comprise an agenda, which, in turn, frames the debate, establishes the terms of discussion, and likely influences both the dynamics and the outcomes of the civic forum.[33] Therefore, we examined whether each report included a statement of the group's agenda, including a set of objectives, issues, or questions put to the group.

In our sample, only three reports failed to state the initial agenda. Two of the three – *Just Food* and *San Francisco Digital Inclusion Strategy* – neglected many areas of transparency, and two of the three were reports of Consensus Conferences – *Just Food* and *Broadband for All?* In the consensus conference format, initial agendas are somewhat fluid because participants can add their own concerns. Still, even these kinds of forums typically begin with some structured questions posed by organizers about a focused set of topics; because these can shape discussion, they should be reported. For example, the *Broadband For All?* conference posed three initial questions, which were the starting point for discussions, and therefore should have been included in the report.[34]

The reports that managed to disclose the forum agenda did so in a variety of ways. Some reports explained the organizers' goals especially clearly. For example, *Wireless Broadband* described the forum as an effort to guide the New America Foundation's (NAF's) "policy initiatives to reflect the interests/perspectives of a diverse range of constituencies," to inform advocates "about current and future issues in wireless policy and

---

[32] Bachrach and Baratz 1962; Cox and McCubbins 2005.

[33] For an overview of how framing can affect attitudes, see Bartels 2003, and for a discussion of how frames and counter-frames matter in deliberating groups, see Druckman 2004.

[34] The questions were:

1. Should governments become involved in creating municipal broadband networks?
2. If so, how should municipal broadband networks be paid for and operated to maximize public benefits, especially to underserved communities?
3. If so, will digital inclusion require governments to provide additional resources to help underserved communities use broadband to meet their economic, civic, and cultural needs?

the implications for specific communities," to "provide stories, data and examples of actual community experiences," to "generate opportunities and advice to maximize the usefulness" of NAF research and publications, and to "develop mid- to long-term visions of what NAF and stakeholder allies are working towards." This clear statement of goals for the event helped to place the rest of the report in context.

Other reports revealed the agenda in part by explicating the initial framing of the issue under discussion. *Working Together* explained that "[e]arly in the conference, Prof. Archon Fung presented a graphic overview of how various strands of the democracy movement can help our nation make progress on a wide range of public issues, using health care policy as a timely example."[35] Fung's presentation slides were reprinted in the report, serving as valuable agenda-setting artifacts that detailed the roles and relationships of different civic engagement organizations, some of them working on electoral reform, others on community organizing, public deliberation, government transparency, and the like. This initial framing helped to explain and justify the conference's outcomes, especially to "develop stronger relationships across the democracy reform field" and to create a "new collaborative platform that can serve as a liaison between democracy reform advocates and the [Obama] Administration."[36]

Reports of National Issues Forums in our sample provided another useful model for disclosing the agenda by stating *competing* issue frames that participants were asked to discuss. In the NIF approach, deliberation is typically organized around several broad approaches or perspectives to an issue or problem. Organizers develop these frames before the meeting as a way of helping participants to make sense of the issue and to focus the conversation. For example, the South Dakota *Citizens in the Legislative Process* report outlined three distinct views of the relationship between citizens and lawmaking: a fairly passive vision of citizenship focused on becoming well-informed about politics (citizens as learners), a more active vision in which citizens give frequent input to legislators on policy decisions (citizens as collaborators), and a robust view of citizenship as direct participation in policy making (citizens as participants). *Democracy's Challenge* provided an even fuller "issue map" that included the exact information presented to participants before deliberation. The issue map highlighted three broad approaches to democratic renewal, one focused on strengthening individuals' civic and moral values, another on

---

[35] America*Speaks* et al. 2009, 4.   [36] America*Speaks* et al. 2009, 5.

revitalizing voluntary associations, and a third on reform of the political system. Each of these frames was accompanied by a few specific policy steps, as well as objections (counter-frames) to the approach.

While this pre-framing work by organizers can constrain participants' thinking, it allows for fairly transparent reporting about how participants are asked to approach issues. In Chapter 4, we noted that research suggests that exposure to competing frames can weaken the effects of any one frame on citizens' thinking, ideally by encouraging them to consider multiple alternatives, or, less optimally, because citizens become confused or uncertain. It serves deliberative publicity well when organizers divulge the particular frames that were privileged in discussion and how they conflicted. This should give readers more confidence that organizers did not unduly influence participants to adopt a single frame, while also allowing observers to make better judgments about whether the range of viewpoints given to citizens was sufficiently inclusive.

There were two broad kinds of frames in these reports, which Alison Kadlec and Will Friedman have called *partisan framing-to-persuade* and *nonpartisan framing-for-deliberation*:

> The first involves defining an issue to one's advantage in the hopes of getting an audience to do what you want it to do. The latter involves clarifying the range of positions surrounding an issue so that citizens can better decide what they want to do. Framing-for-deliberation helps citizens engage a range of advocacy frames that are competing for their allegiance without being overwhelmed by their sheer number and volume.[37]

Most of the forums, such as the NIF examples, reported initial framing-for-deliberation among citizens. In contrast, the activist forum, *Wireless Broadband*, also divulged participants' efforts to develop persuasive frames for use in public debates over broadband and spectrum policy, such as appeals to "better opportunities for children," and to citizens desire "to feel like active participants, in society, to have a sense of ownership," even to "help make history."[38]

Both framing-for-deliberation and framing-to-persuade delimit the initial range of options for discussion, albeit to different degrees. Reports that disclosed their initial agendas and how they framed issues helped observers judge whether a forum was designed in ways that might have

---

[37] Kadlec and Friedman 2007, 11.

[38] New America Foundation and Center for International Media Action 2006, 11.

privileged a specific outcome (framing-to-persuade) or whether counter-frames and a range of options were presented to the participants (including the possibility of encouraging participants to critically evaluate the frames given and to come up with their own alternative options). In some deliberative forum designs, such as Consensus Conferences and the advocacy forum we examined, facilitators actively encourage participants to generate their own frames. In other designs, such as some Citizens Juries, participants are asked to make a choice between supporting or opposing a set of policy preferences that are presented by the organizers at the outset. In NIFs, citizens are guided to discuss competing frames and can adopt elements from more than one approach. In each of these kinds of forums, disclosure of agendas, frames, and counter-frames serves deliberative publicity well.

Structure, facilitation, and format

The category of structure and facilitation was defined as including comments about time spent deliberating (in days or hours), where the group met, how their conversations were moderated or guided by facilitation, or background on the process, strengths or weaknesses of the deliberative format (e.g., how Consensus Conferences work). Disclosing the deliberative format involves mentioning the specific type of civic forum or deliberative design chosen by the organizers, such as a Deliberative Poll or Citizens Jury.

All of our reports except *San Francisco Digital Inclusion* included information about structure and facilitation, and 70 percent disclosed the deliberative format they followed. Those that did not report a format – *San Francisco Digital Inclusion*, *Wireless Broadband*, and *Working Together* – were stakeholder and advocacy forums that did not follow a formalized or well-known deliberative format.[39] These groups discussed issues and made decisions, but they did not label their process or approach to deliberation in any formal way – perhaps because their process was not an established one or had no formal label – in contrast, say, to the trademarked Deliberative Poll.

---

[39] Given that *Working Together* was a gathering of educators and activists who are unusually committed to deliberation and civic participation, and who were undoubtedly closely familiar with a variety of well-developed deliberative formats, it is interesting that this meeting did not report whether organizers chose a particular format for their own deliberation.

Organizers who had significant experience with a deliberative format often provided the most helpful information. Reports of events sponsored by the Danish Board of Technology, for example, offered detailed discussion of events and processes that occurred during the forums. *Global Warming* described its worldwide deliberation as follows: "All meetings followed the same schedule: The 100 citizens, divided into tables of 5–8 people, were led by a head facilitator and group moderators through a programme divided into four thematic sessions and a recommendation session."[40] The specific sessions were then described in detail, accompanied by pictures from around the world. Similarly, *Hard Times* offered a description of the goals of Deliberative Polling, provided examples of previous uses of the approach, included pictures of Michiganders deliberating, and even offered a diagram of the basic steps in any Deliberative Poll (see Figure 6.5).[41]

The discussion of format in *Hard Times* also offers a strong argument for Deliberative Polling as a method and its potential uses around the world. This should not be dismissed as mere self-promotion or cheerleading. Even when organizers advocate for their particular approach to deliberation, the discussion can help draw attention to the important differences among deliberative formats. Deliberative transparency would be promoted if more reports included justifications for their chosen process.

However, transparency would be strengthened even further if reports also included an acknowledgment of the potential weaknesses of their deliberative format. Such critical reflection about process is rare to nonexistent in our sample of reports. As we noted in the Introduction, every kind of forum involves trade-offs between desired processes and goals. In James Fishkin's terms, the trade-offs are between how many people can deliberate, how well they represent others, and the quality of deliberation they foster.[42] Others have identified additional trade-offs, for example between the commitment to deliberate and quality of deliberation in partisan and non-partisan forums or high-stakes and low-stakes forums.[43] There is no one-size-fits-all civic forum: the appropriate choice depends on

---

[40] Danish Board of Technology 2009, 9.
[41] We thank James Fishkin for reminding us that Deliberative Polls often include control groups, an element of the process not shown in this figure.
[42] Fishkin 2009.
[43] See Hendriks, Dryzek and Hunold 2007 on partisan and non-partisan forums and Fung 2003 on high versus low-stakes forums.

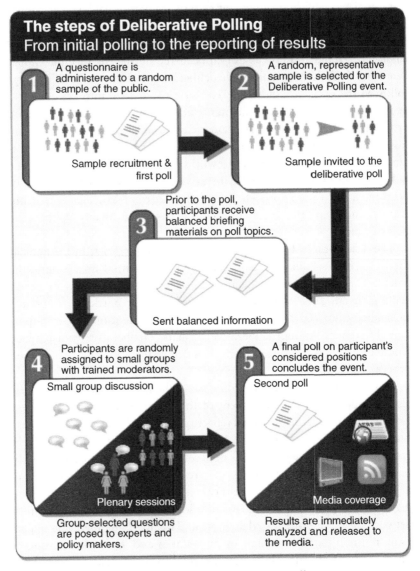

Figure 6.5 Overview of deliberative polling

Source: By the People. 2010. "Hard Times Hard Choices. Michigan Residents Deliberate," p. 4.

the policy and procedural goals of the organizers.[44] Clearer explanations of a deliberative format's particular strengths *and* inevitable weaknesses

[44] See Mackenzie and Warren 2012 for a discussion of the variety of purposes minipublics such as civic forums might serve, and Karpowitz and Mendelberg 2014 on how the

can help those who are unfamiliar with the range of possible formats to understand why organizers chose a forum of a particular kind and how that forum might ultimately inform the wider deliberative system.

Our reports also had little to say about the role of moderators in the forum. Many of the reports mentioned the presence of moderators, but they had almost nothing to say about the specifics of the training, goals, or instructions given to discussion facilitators. As we wrote in Chapter 4, moderators can potentially influence nearly every aspect of the deliberative experience, from the tone and level of civility of the conversation, to the extent to which reasons and evidence are encouraged, to the patterns of participation among group members, to the final decisions made by the group. Studies of the behavior and attitudes of moderators are still in their infancy, and more remains to be done to understand their training and influence in deliberation.[45] In the meantime, we can say that deliberative transparency is fostered when reports indicate not just whether discussion was moderated but *how*.

The contours of this particular challenge come into clearer relief in the *Global Warming* report, which discloses more than most about the role of moderators. In its description of the WWViews process, the report explains that the participants engaged in "moderated discussion at their tables" and that moderators "were trained in advance to provide unbiased facilitation at the tables." The fact that moderators were present and that they had been trained in some way is helpful context that is not always provided by many other reports, but more is needed. What, if anything, did moderators do to encourage all participants to speak, maintain mutual respect among deliberators, and encourage the group to explore a diversity of views, rather than bowing to pressures to conform to the group or avoid conflict? To what extent were moderators expected to actively insert themselves into the conversation, and for what reasons? The number of variables that moderators or facilitators might be asked to attend to during the group discussion is vast, and knowing more about what forum organizers prioritized in the behavior and interventions of moderators could shed light on many aspects of the forum. Complicating the situation further, the behavior of moderators may be quite different across groups as well, both because of the training or personality of the

particular rules of public forums and meetings can affect the dynamics and the outcomes of deliberation.

[45] Initial studies of moderators' influence in face-to-face forums include Mansbridge et al. 2006; Ryfe 2006; Dillard 2013. Davies and Chandler (2012) summarize the research on facilitators in online forums.

facilitator and because of the needs of the group. More transparency about this potentially meaningful, but not yet well understood, feature of group deliberation would allow observers to better understand exactly what happened in the civic forum.

In sum, our analysis leaves us both heartened by the extent to which basic information about structure, facilitation, and format seems to be a common element of the reports in our sample and struck by the extent to which such information is often cursory, with key details about process, facilitation, and the necessary trade-offs involved among deliberative formats often missing. Transparency will be better served as the writers of deliberative publicity seek greater critical distance from which to reflect on both the contributions and the limitations of their specific civic forum.

Decision rule and dynamics

The final two transparency categories associated with deliberative design involve reporting the forum's decision rule and information about the dynamics of discussion. Decision rules are disclosed through statements about how participants are asked to arrive at conclusions, such as discussion that aims to achieve consensus, post-discussion majority vote, and so on. For purposes of transparency, disclosure of the decision-making process does not depend on whether the group succeeded at coming to a decision. What matters is whether reports state what process the group used to *try* to arrive at a choice. For example, one of the NIF Forums, *Democracy's Challenge*, stated that "at the end of the forums, moderators and recorders asked the groups to consider what they had agreed on and what common ground for action, if any, they had identified."[46] While the report notes that many groups did not find common ground, it reveals the process by which participants were asked to seek agreement.

In our definition of decision rules we also include disclosure of individual decision-making processes in deliberative formats, such as the Deliberative Poll, which concludes by surveying participants on their policy preferences. To do otherwise would be to reject the goal of Deliberative Polls to ask participants to arrive at individual opinions after deliberation and to present these citizens' views in the aggregate to policy makers as an expression of well-informed public opinion. Whether one agrees that the outcome represents a composite picture of public opinion or not, our question here is a different one: did the forum practice transparency

---

[46] Doble Research Associates 2006, 4.

about how participants were asked to make up their minds, collectively or individually?

Even using this expansive definition of decision rules, only half of the ten reports we examined disclosed how participants chose their conclusions – the lowest level of transparency of any of the subcategories included in the design dimension. Three of the five reports that did not mention how participants were asked to make choices came from the activist or stakeholder forums (*Wireless Broadband, San Francisco Digital Inclusion,* and *Working Together*). This may be because decision making among these kinds of forums varies more, and has been less carefully considered, than in established mini-public formats. It may also be that activist and stakeholder forums prioritize speaking in a single voice on behalf of policy recommendations. As we saw in Chapter 5, all of these reports paid greater or equal attention to communicating participants' conclusions, compared with their reasoning, and all aimed to exert immediate influence on impending political decisions by government or advocacy campaigns. These forums' intended audiences and focus on influencing their short-term political choices may explain why the reports paid greater attention to advancing policy outcomes than to justifying their decision-making processes.

The other reports that declined to reveal their decision rules offer more evidence that forums adopting the same deliberative format can be reported very differently, depending on authorial choices. Of the two NIF forums, *Democracy's Challenge* described its decision rule, while *Citizens in the Legislative Process* did not. Of the two Consensus Conferences, *Broadband for All?* briefly explained how participants settled on their recommendations, while *Just Food* made no mention of any aspect of the process of group decision making. This variation in reporting of similar kinds of forums leads us again to the conclusion that authorial choices about transparency are an independent variable quite apart from other elements of the forum.

Failing to explain the forum's decision rule is a serious loss for deliberative publicity. In Chapter 2, we discussed a range of research showing that the decision-making process can influence the substance of the group's decisions and whether participants can deliberate on equal terms. In particular, we reviewed recent experimental research that shows the difference between unanimity and majority rule can be especially important for disempowered groups, such as women. When women are the gender minority in a group, women are much more likely to close the gender gap in participation, to raise issues of distinctive concern to women, to experience more positive expressions of support from others in the group, and to be part of collective decisions that are more generous to the poor when unanimous rule is used.[47] Failure to mention decision rule in the reports of civic forums suggests an inattention to this important variable and the ways it can influence both the discussion and the group decision.

Organizers of deliberative forums can bring greater empirical precision to bear both by thinking carefully about the role of decision rule as they prepare for the forum and by offering more precise accounts of how those rules were used in the deliberative forums they sponsored. Even among those reports in our sample that mention decision rule, we sometimes see something less than a concrete explanation of how the rule was applied. For example, consensus itself is a contested ideal in deliberative theory, and given these disagreements, the burden is on organizers of civic forums to explain exactly what they asked participants to do.[48]

Given the lack of clarity about decision rules, it is perhaps not surprising that several reports also said little about the dynamics of deliberation.[49] A majority of reports (6 out of 10) met our minimal coding standards, which involved any revelation of information about the strength of agreement or disagreement among group members, or discussion of other qualities of the group discussion, such as how quickly the deliberators agreed (or failed to agree) about an issue, how easy or difficult it was for people to identify problems, reasons, and conclusions, or how intensely group members felt about the issues under discussion. A single mention of any of these qualities was enough to count as having reported the dynamics of the deliberation.

Our reports illuminated these dynamics in several ways. *Hard Times*, for example, described the "strong feelings" and "evident political differences" among the deliberators, supplementing those qualitative descriptions with post-forum survey data showing the strength of agreement or disagreement about a host of different issues. As we noted in Chapter 5, *Democracy's Challenge* included a long section on "tensions in the deliberations," which described major differences of opinion and how they shaped the participant's discussion. Other sections sketched the areas of "firm common ground." Some of these summary statements were bolstered with participants' survey responses on a few policy solutions and

---

[47] Karpowitz and Mendelberg 2014.

[48] See Thompson 2008 for a discussion of disagreements within deliberative theory about the role of consensus.

[49] Of the four reports that did not discuss dynamics, three of them did not mention decision rule either.

illustrated with partial transcripts from several deliberating groups. Providing these kinds of additional evidence of the group dynamics can help observers to judge whether authors' descriptions of the forum are partial (in both senses – incomplete and biased).

Perhaps most innovative in its approach to deliberative dynamics was *New GM Plants*, which we described in some detail earlier. Though the report did not offer any evidence of the give-and-take between the participants, by revealing the number of votes for each argument, condition, and recommendation, the report showed very specifically how strongly citizens were convinced by reasons and opposing views and how strongly people supported each recommendation. In fact, one of the initial questions put to the group was about which arguments about genetically modified agriculture should carry the most weight in policy making. Quantifying members' support for reasons, opposing views, and conclusions was a real strength of the process used here, but also of the way it was reported. This provided a strong contrast to our other reports, which did not reveal how strongly people ranked reasons for and against various policy alternatives.

All told, then, our sample exposed some innovative possibilities for reporting dynamics and decision rules, but also some clear shortcomings among many reports. These shortcomings ranged across civic forums of different designs, reminding us that authorial choice is a key factor that shapes deliberative publicity, which can be strengthened by reporting how participants were asked to arrive at conclusions and their experience of making up their minds as a group or individually.

Intended influence

In addition to the details of the decision-making process, transparency involves situating the civic forum within the larger democratic system, explaining why the forum is needed and who are the audiences for the group's efforts. Clarifying the forum's intended influence involves two aspects. First, it means specifying the *purposes* of the civic forum – the reason for convening the deliberative group and whether the group's views are intended to spark wider discussion, to influence decision makers, or simply to help participants come to greater clarity about their own views. Second, this aspect of publicity entails identifying the forum's *intended audience* – the participants only, the wider public (community, state, nation, or world), particular stakeholders, or officials or government agencies.

In our sample, every report stated the purpose of the forum, at least briefly, while six out of ten reports also specified their intended audiences. The reports that did not identify an audience included the two that were least attentive to many elements of transparency – *San Francisco Digital Inclusion* and *Just Food* – as well as the two National Issues Forums. While NIF results are shared annually at a briefing for congressional aides, these kinds of dialogic forums are sometimes critiqued for not offering clear policy direction to officials and other decision makers. The lack of clarity about audience in both *Democracy's Challenge* and *Citizens in the Legislative Process* supports these criticisms. Neither report identifies a well-defined audience and asks it to take specific actions, even just to continue the discussion begun in the forums. While dialogic forums like these can inspire participants to take further steps, the two NIF reports might have increased their chances of influencing the wider democratic system, even over the long term, if they had directed themselves to more clearly defined segments of the public or government. For example, the South Dakota forums presumably aimed in part to inform state legislators about how to engage their constituents better, but did not state this or contain any sections that spoke directly to lawmakers.

Other reports were clearer about revealing how their purposes were matched to influencing a specific audience. For example, *Global Warming* directly addressed itself to negotiators at the 2009 United Nations Climate Change Conference. The report asserted that deliberators "clearly expect their COP15 negotiators to settle on an agreement that will include a strong and effective financial mechanism," that "the participants mandate their politicians to take fast and strong action," and that "participants expect COP15 negotiators to ensure that new or stronger international institutions are put in place to advance the objectives of a new climate deal."[50] Reports such as this one tended to identify a live policy issue and think more strategically about speaking to decision-making bodies. This does not mean that deliberation should be restricted to the realm of short-term political debates. As our discussion of the NIF reports made clear, it is possible to set multiple goals for deliberation – some short-term and policy-focused, others longer-term and more diffuse. Yet it is also possible even for these kinds of reports to identify specific audiences for their short-term and long-term recommendations.

Finally, if being clear about the audience is one of many prerequisites not just for legitimacy but for wider public influence, what are we

---

[50] Danish Board of Technology 2009, 23, 11, 29.

to make of the lack of attention to this issue from *San Francisco Digital Inclusion*, which was organized by policy makers at city hall? As we have shown, this report was one of the least sensitive to transparency generally. It can be argued that reports of government-organized forums are obliged to speak to all publics and branches of government, so perhaps it is less worrisome that this report did not identify a more specific audience. But when we think about the current state of civic forums in a deliberative system, we are led to the conclusion that forums of all types ought to justify their role in the larger democratic structure, a role that is not always self-evident. Forums that incorporate citizens or stakeholders into government decision making are still fairly new and fragile institutions. Even in Denmark, where the Danish Board of Technology had a clear mandate to inform Parliament and the public, and a 25-year track record, the legislature voted to cut the agency's funding in 2012 and allocate it to other research programs.[51] Thus, even established agencies with clear mandates must attend regularly to justifying their legitimacy by explaining to others why they exist and who they hope to influence.

Evaluation

We now turn to the two final dimensions of transparency – evaluation and fidelity. In contrast to the previous elements, which tended to be found, at least at a minimal level, in the majority of our reports, evaluation and fidelity are mostly honored in the breach. These elements of legitimate publicity were the least developed among the reports we analyzed.

We looked for two aspects of evaluation: examinations *of the deliberation*, which includes participants' or others' assessments of the fairness or effectiveness of the process; and evaluation *of the participants*, which includes assessments of participants' changes in knowledge, attitudes, or dispositions during the deliberation. As we discussed in Chapter 4, the deliberative process should create conditions of political equality and public reasoning. A successful forum should also promote participants' civic capacities. Evaluation tells observers whether the forum met these goals. However, in our sample, only *Hard Times* and *Citizens in the Legislative Process* reported any evaluation data for both categories. *Democracy's Challenge* provided evaluation data on participants but not the deliberative process.

---

[51] For more information on these recent challenges, see Reardon 2011 and Jørgensen 2012.

These reports helped observers to assess several aspects of whether
the forums promoted equality, public reasoning, or civic capacities. *Hard
Times* provided survey results that revealed citizens' assessments of equal
participation in the forum. The report noted that 76 percent of participants agreed that "my group moderator provided the opportunity for
everyone to participate," though only 53 percent said that "my group
moderator tried to make sure that opposing arguments were considered,"
while 63 percent agreed that "members of my group participated relatively equally in the discussions." This report also offered specific evidence
of participants' gains in issue knowledge during the forum. Evaluation
of the deliberation in *Citizens in the Legislative Process* was somewhat less
thorough, but included self-reports from pre-forum and post-forum questionnaires showing gains in the percentage of participants who believed
they had a good grasp of how the legislative process works and knew
how to contact their representatives. Though direct tests of knowledge
in the pre- and post-forum questionnaires would have been even more
helpful, the report noted that 87 percent of participants believed that the
forum "provided them with good information about the legislative process." The report also summarized participants' comments about mutual
respect in the forum, such as that they "enjoyed hearing different opinions in an environment that was peaceful and non argumentative."[52] In
addition, organizers reported increased citizen intentions to participate
in civic activities and improved perceptions of their legislators (some of
whom participated in the forums).

Why did a majority of reports fail to include evaluation data? Several explanations are likely. First, expectations for conducting systematic evaluations of civic forums during this period were only starting
to emerge and many of the initial assessments were narrowly focused
on a handful of questions of interest to the sponsors or organizers.[53]
Even today, we see little tradition of carefully evaluating stakeholder and
activist forums. Second, evaluation can be perceived as demanding more
resources – including time, money, and expertise in gathering and analyzing data – than are available to many forums. Two of the three reports
that included assessment of the forum – *Hard Times* and *Democracy's
Challenge* – were especially well-funded projects. Third, some reports
may not have included evaluation data because of pressure to publish
by deadlines that would allow the forum to influence live policy issues.

---

[52] South Dakota Issues Forum 2009, 10.
[53] Gastil, Knobloch, and Kelly 2012; Rowe and Frewer 2004.

For example, the *Global Warming* report was finalized in only a few weeks after the worldwide forum, just in time for the Copenhagen climate summit.

Two other explanations are possible. Some of the authors may have assumed that civic forums are inherently legitimate and therefore do not need to include evaluation data in their publicity efforts. For example, while one of us gathered extensive assessment data on the *Broadband for All?* forum, which is reported in Chapter 3, the other, who co-organized the forum, confesses that a certain naïve enthusiasm for civic engagement helps explain why he did not think to include any of these data in the final report. Perhaps most worrisome, some authors might exclude evaluation data because they do not reflect well on the event, and therefore might be seen as for internal consumption by organizers and sponsors to learn how to improve their work, but too risky to share publicly. As we noted in the introduction and Chapter 4, the growth of a market for professional practitioners of civic forums may improve the field by promoting independent evaluation of forums. But professionalization may also lead practitioners to protect their reputations by practicing selective publicity, only divulging information that reflects well on the quality of their forums. Of the reports we analyzed that revealed evaluation data, none reported negative views of some aspect of the forum held by a majority of participants or observers. It may be that their impressions were, in fact, wholly favorable. Yet, while we do not assume that any of the authors of the reports in our sample concealed negative information or reported assessments selectively, this temptation is real.[54]

As examples of deliberative rhetoric, reports need to persuade decision makers and the public that forums were conducted fairly and that participants deliberated well. As in deliberation itself, authors should base their claims to legitimacy on reasons and evidence that can be widely accepted by others. Evaluation of the quality of the deliberative process and of participants offers important evidence in this regard. For these reasons, all reports should be able to provide some basic evaluation data. Lack of resources and time pressure can present barriers to conducting

---

[54] In their proposal for improving evaluation, based on reviewing many reports of forums, John Gastil and his colleagues find that many reports include "selective vignettes that usually showcase specific participants' positive experiences; particularly compelling moments in an uneven process; the favorable summary judgments of officials or witnesses with no training in ethnography or evaluation; and the optimistic and unsubstantiated attributions of policy or cultural impacts, as proclaimed by public agency staff, columnists, or event organizers" (Gastil, Knobloch, and Kelly 2012, 206).

evaluations, but it is not onerous to survey respondents on a few questions about their perceptions of the forum's fairness and what they gained from participating. Most forums include a small number of participants and organizers of larger forums typically have the resources to conduct evaluations easily.

Assuming that citizen deliberation will be seen as inherently legitimate is naïve, given the criticisms that forums with any power to influence policy making or public opinion are likely to face from some observers who disagree with their conclusions. It may be similarly naïve to assume that evaluations of deliberative events will be uniformly rosy, or even that wholly positive but selectively reported assessments will convince decision makers outside the forum. After all, these observers are often politically sophisticated people who are familiar with the kind of complex and mixed results produced by systematic policy analysis and evaluation, by public opinion polling, and in public hearings. If politicians and administrators are not aware that one cannot please everyone, who is? Therefore, divulging evaluative data about the forum, even when some of the results reveal shortcomings, is both in keeping with democratic deliberation and may be more persuasive than omitting or spinning evaluation data.

Fidelity

Some of the concerns we have articulated about the completeness and accuracy of the evaluation materials can be remedied through a commitment to our final dimension of transparency, fidelity. We have in mind here the extent to which publicity is true to the perspectives of the deliberators themselves. In our coding scheme, fidelity includes two dimensions: *authorization*, which involves disclosing the criteria used to decide how the group's arguments were included in the publicity materials, and *accountability*, or the extent to which the report explicitly discloses that most participants believe the publicity gives a full and accurate account of their deliberation or that it adheres to the authorization criteria.

As with evaluation, attention to fidelity is rare in our sample. *Broadband for All?* and *New GM Plants* are the only reports that addressed both categories, and they illustrate different ways in which authorization and accountability can be reported. In *Broadband for All?*, the traditional consensus conference format involved all participants reviewing and approving the language of policy recommendations, and the reasoning for them, prior to publication. The report briefly explains that "the community panelists reached consensus on policy recommendations," and more broadly, the report is introduced as comprising "the community panel's questions, evaluations of the issues, and recommendations." Thus, the authorizing criterion was complete agreement among participants, and the report addressed authorial accountability to deliberators by stating that its conclusions and reasoning emerged from a consensus drafting process.

In *New GM Plants*, the adapted Citizens' Jury, the report explained the authorizing criterion as inclusion of "all the arguments, conditions and recommendations formulated by the citizens, and the respective number of votes that the formulations were given." Accountability was established by a description of the panel's presentation of their work at a press conference attended by politicians from multiple parties, stakeholders, and journalists. At this public event, "the citizens presented the results of their votes and read their arguments, conditions and recommendations aloud for the audience." Outside Denmark, it is rare that citizen deliberators present their own reports as a group in a public meeting with others. Still, public presentation by the participants themselves is another form of evidence that a report reflects the deliberators' conclusions and views.

Together, *New GM Plants* and *Broadband for All?* demonstrate that reports can include authorizing criteria, even briefly, and that decision rules can facilitate authorization. The consensus drafting process used in Consensus Conferences and the innovative use of weighted-preference voting developed by the Danish Board of Technology helped each report anchor its recommendations and reasoning more clearly in the deliberation than other reports did. However, decision rules and deliberative formats do not themselves guarantee good reporting on authorization criteria. *Just Food*, also a Consensus Conference, never explicitly addressed how the final report reflected participants' reasoning or whether participants had reviewed it before publication. The extensive footnotes and citations to academic literature, which are rare in a report of civic deliberation, raise questions about the role of participants in drafting the report. Fidelity, like many other elements of transparency, depends on authors' decisions about what to reveal.

There are practical barriers to establishing fidelity in forums that do not employ clear decision rules for arriving at conclusions, such as consensus, voting, or polling on recommendations and arguments. In order to enhance fidelity, either the forum design or the authoring of reports may need to change. In particular, demonstrating participants' agreement that authors have reported the deliberation fully and accurately seems especially challenging for forums that involve many participants, such as Deliberative Polls, some NIFs, or the worldwide discussion of climate change disseminated in *Global Warming*. It would be prohibitively difficult to ask every participant to review a draft of the final report of such a forum and indicate their level of agreement with its faithfulness to the deliberation, especially because participants did not experience discussion in all of the small groups at the forum and do not have access to summary data. Nonetheless, in Chapter 7 we will present some ideas about how even these large, dispersed forums could improve fidelity.

Even if we simply take at face value authors' claims about how their work reflects the underlying deliberation, as we did in our coding scheme, such claims were rarely found in our sample. Without greater clarity about how authors make sense of deliberators' reasoning and conclusions, and some evidence that participants approve, the legitimacy of civic forums can be undermined. Establishing authorial fidelity seems especially important and challenging when decision rules used in forums do not facilitate clear reporting of conclusions and arguments, when forums involve deliberators in multiple groups at more than one site, and when participants themselves do not present their reports publicly or review them before publication. However, the fact that two reports explained their criteria for reporting participants' arguments and how authors were accountable to citizens for reporting their deliberation indicates that it is indeed possible for reports to accomplish these important tasks.

Internal and external legitimacy

Our argument has been that deliberative practitioners and researchers should pay more attention to transparency as a critical element of legitimate publicity. In our small but diverse sample of reports, we found considerable variation in the extent to which transparency was honored. While most reports divulged at least minimal information about the dimensions of control, design, and intended influence, when we examined the reports closely, we found that the coverage was often shallow. Most reports did not meet even minimal standards for reporting evaluation and fidelity. We see a patchwork quilt of commitments to different aspects of transparency in these reports.

This impression is reinforced even when we look at the results through a somewhat different lens. Perhaps some reports excel at reporting the quality of the deliberative process within a forum, while other reports are assiduous about revealing the web of connections to those outside the forum who shaped it or are its primary audience. The first kind of

Table 6.2 *Internal and external legitimacy*

		External legitimacy (control, intended influence, and fidelity)		
		High	*Medium*	*Low*
	High		HT	
Internal legitimacy (design and evaluation)	*Medium*	BBFA WB	DC GW NGMP	CLP
	Low		WT	JF

Note: BBFA = *Broadband for All?*; WB = *Wireless Broadband*; SF = *San Francisco Digital Inclusion*; NGMP = *New GM Plants*; DC = *Democracy's Challenge*; GW = *World Wide Views on Global Warming*; HT = *Hard Times, Hard Choices*; JF = *Just Foods*; CLP = *Citizens in the Legislative Process*; WT = *Working Together*

transparency speaks of the *internal legitimacy* of the forum by reporting on its design (including the representativeness of participants, the agenda, and so on) and evaluation (of whether the process was fair and effective, and whether participants engaged in public reasoning as equals). This tells us how well things went around the conference table. The second kind of transparency reveals the forum's *external legitimacy*, including its control (by funders, organizers, partners, and advisors) and its outputs (the publicity's intended influence and fidelity to the deliberation). This tells us about how well the people who shaped the deliberation did their work and how well the results were communicated to the political system.

Table 6.2 shows how successfully the reports established the internal and external legitimacy of the forums.[55] Once again, the results show an uneven pattern of commitments to transparency. None of the reports scored high on addressing both internal and external legitimacy. Even the reports that had the most impressive overall coverage of transparency categories fell short of full coverage on one or the other measure. *Hard Times*

[55] We divided the reports in our sample into high, medium, and low levels of internal and external legitimacy by computing the total number of transparency elements covered by the report in each of the categories associated with the two forms of legitimacy. For each legitimacy measure, we calculated the total proportion of categories covered by each document. The internal legitimacy measure comprises nine transparency sub-categories, and the external legitimacy measure comprises seven. Reports that were in the top quartile of coverage for each measure were counted as high, those in the middle two quartiles as medium, and those in the bottom quartile as low. Table 6.2 shows the interaction of these two measures.

scored high on addressing internal legitimacy, but was hampered by its absence of attention to fidelity. *New GM Plants* shows up in the middle category for both internal and external legitimacy because it slighted both control and evaluation. *Broadband for All?* and *Wireless Broadband* scored well on measures of external legitimacy, but neither included any information about evaluation.[56] Nearly one-third of reports fell in the middle range on both measures. All told, there is significant room for improvement in how each report accounted for both the internal quality of the deliberative process and the relationship of the forum to its conveners and audiences.

The scale problem of publicity

We have noted that the difficulty of accommodating large numbers of people in deliberation, which needs to occur in small groups, can lead to what John Parkinson has called the "scale problem" of deliberation. Because most people who are affected by the issues under consideration cannot participate directly, deliberators' decisions may "appear to be illegitimate for those left outside the forum, while bringing more than a few people in would seem to turn the event into speech-making, not deliberation."[57] We have argued that practicing deliberative publicity is the best solution to this problem because it holds civic forums accountable to other actors in a larger deliberative system. By revealing the details of participants' argumentation, forums can appeal to officials and the public to authorize the forum's judgments on their merits – the strongest form of authorization. Such publicity promulgates the reasons and conclusions discussed in the forum throughout the deliberative system. Knowledge that the conclusions and reasons of the participants will be communicated to the wider public can also affect the nature of the deliberation itself, encouraging participants to think broadly as citizens who should engage in a reciprocal give-and-take with their fellow citizens.

Beyond reasons and conclusions, the elements of publicity we have reviewed in this chapter can also strengthen the role of civic forums in the wider deliberative system. By divulging all aspects of how the forum was conducted, transparency allows non-participants to offer a weaker form of authorization, based on trust that the deliberative process was

---

[56] The comparatively high commitment of *Wireless Broadband* to many important elements of transparency is a reminder that it is possible for activist forums to practice legitimate publicity.

[57] Parkinson 2006a, 5.

sufficiently inclusive, autonomous from outside influence, and public-minded that it can be a proxy for public judgment, and its conclusions can be ratified even by observers who are unfamiliar with all the details of the issues discussed. Because civic forums are still relative newcomers to the political scene compared with more established institutions, they face a special obligation to develop the sort of trust that comes with full transparency. This obligation increases still further when – as will often be the case – civic forums are small and large portions of the public do not participate directly.

As we have seen, several forum designs try to mitigate the scale problem of deliberation by expanding the number of participants dramatically. These forums recruit large samples of people who are more or less representative of a larger population and have them deliberate in many small groups. However, these more inclusive mega-deliberations pose their own unique challenges for some aspects of deliberative publicity because it is much harder for participants or organizers to observe the entire forum, which is conducted in multiple groups and sometimes at many dispersed sites. Because of inevitable variance among each small group and the difficulty of any one person observing these differences it can be more challenging for large forums to report fully on the structure, facilitation, and dynamics of deliberation. For the same reasons, it is harder for larger forums to ensure that final reports are faithful to all participants' reasons and conclusions and to conduct evaluations of the forum. Thus, mega-forums especially face a scale problem of *publicity*: the larger the forum, the harder it is to report participants' arguments and practice full transparency about how the forum was conducted.

Democracy's Challenge and *Global Warming* are prime examples of multi-site deliberations that attempt to represent the considered views of a national and global community, respectively. Reliance on many local partners, with different missions and training in facilitation, likely resulted in rather different experiences in the small groups, which exacerbates the problem of fidelity. Basic evaluation data, including participants' self-reports about the perceived fairness and quality of the deliberation, could have helped to address these concerns somewhat. However, the large numbers of deliberators especially created challenges for establishing that these reports faithfully represented participants' conclusions and reasoning. A concern for legitimate publicity thus demands special attention to how the organizers of large-scale civic forums present themselves and their work to a wider audience in ways that can generate trust among both participants and non-participants.

However, as we have documented in this chapter, norms of deliberative publicity and of the proper relationship between transparency and argumentation are not yet as fully developed as they might be in *all* the reports we sampled. The key finding from our analysis is that no strong norms of attention to transparency were exhibited by the reports of either large or small civic forums; instead, uneven and often insufficient attention to these elements was the rule. Some important features of transparency – such as fidelity and evaluation – were barely mentioned at all, but even when authors included other aspects of transparency, they often failed to provide the sort of detail that would allow readers to put the information in context or facilitate the sort of trust that would strengthen civic forums' contribution to the deliberative system.

If publicity is to function effectively as the glue that binds various parts of the system together, then the present practices we found in our sample of reports are not likely to be sufficient. Having documented these problems, we turn in our final chapter to some potential solutions.

7

Strengthening deliberative civic forums

As relative newcomers to the political scene, most civic forums still need to demonstrate their legitimacy more fully than established institutions of democracy do. At their best, these forums can also make their case in ways that are true to the aims of democratic deliberation. Therefore, forums have both *political* and *deliberative* reasons to justify their role in the larger democratic system. We have argued that some forums can enhance their legitimacy by carefully incorporating enclave deliberation of the least powerful citizens, equalizing their participation and influence with more privileged citizens. We have contended that all forums can improve how they communicate their process and arguments to the political system. These advances should help forums to embed themselves more firmly within political routines; to build ongoing and trusted relationships with officials, the news media, advocates, and the public; and thereby to help establish a more deliberative democracy.

We conclude by offering practical suggestions for organizing enclave deliberations among the least powerful and incorporating them into cross-cutting civic forums or the larger deliberative system. We also suggest ways that forums can conduct more legitimate deliberative publicity. In each area, we suggest an accompanying agenda for scholarly and evaluation research, which can help guide practice.

We hope that these suggestions will prove valuable to each of the three audiences to whom this book is addressed: scholars of civic engagement and democratic reform, practitioners of deliberation and civic engagement, and organizations seeking to find more effective and legitimate ways to consult the public. For scholars, our aim is to offer some concrete suggestions for future research by drawing attention to early results, posing some hypotheses that need further testing, and identifying key questions that have yet to be addressed. For practitioners, the goal of this chapter is to raise important factors that organizers ought to consider as they develop new civic forums and make public their current and future efforts. Because practitioners are already committed to the success of civic forums, we offer some ideas for how to institutionalize forums in the wider decision-making system and to do so in ways that serve the causes of equality and publicity. Finally, public officials and other organizations that seek to consult the public will find suggestions for when and how civic forums can supplement existing institutions and how decision makers can demonstrate their accountability to the public.

Improving equality with enclaves

We have argued that enclaves of the disempowered can, and already do, make valuable contributions to advancing equality in civic forums. This kind of deliberation is especially valuable for democracy when it motivates the marginalized to participate in forums they would otherwise avoid. Enclave deliberation can encourage the least powerful to evaluate policy based on their perspectives, including their personal experiences, location within social structures, and local knowledge. It can mitigate extreme background inequalities among participants and perspectives. It can help address the challenges of small group discussion among people of unequal status. And it can help to overcome the constraints on associations of the politically weak and the ideas they espouse in the larger political system.

We suggested that these kinds of deliberating enclaves can be institutionalized in several ways: as one part of deliberation within cross-cutting civic forums, as part of a deliberative process that occurs between enclave forums and cross-cutting forums, or between enclave forums and officials who stand in for the larger public. Deliberative systems thinking should help us to appreciate enclave deliberation in forums as one step in a larger political process, rather than as an inferior or illegitimate form of microcosmic discussion among the whole polity. In a democracy, no single institution should be tasked with representing public opinion or the polity as a whole, including civic forums. Even the Athenian Assembly and the seventeenth-century New England Town Meeting were checked and balanced by other institutions of government. Indeed, enclave discussions are already a feature of many civic forums, as they are of most democratic institutions.

At the same time, forum organizers need to think carefully about how to structure the relationship of enclaves to other elements of the forum or deliberative system. In particular, we have not suggested that organizers or other citizens should assume that enclaves of the disempowered have a hotline to truth or justice, or that these enclaves alone should make or veto decisions that are binding on others. Nor do we have to assume that enclaves of the disempowered will necessarily make choices that advance all of the interests of the weakest. Indeed, enclave deliberation is valuable in part because the disempowered are likely to have various and sometimes conflicting interests, and enclaves can help identify, explore, and prioritize those interests. Employed judiciously, these groups can contribute to more legitimate political decisions in many forums.

When considering whether and how to form enclaves of the disempowered, organizers can ask themselves a series of questions:

- Whose interests or values are most affected by the issue? Of that group, who are the most politically disempowered, whose voices are least well-represented elsewhere in the political system? Is there anyone else who is situationally disempowered in relation to this particular issue? Is there anyone else who is likely to be disempowered by the act of deliberation itself? What sorts of enclaves might be formed to help them participate on more equal footing?
- Where does the forum fit in the political process, and what will it contribute to the larger deliberative system? Could enclaves of the marginalized help to clear a logjam elsewhere in the political system or prevent against a hasty decision that would harm their interests? Could such a group help to rank multiple options and better prioritize resources? Could the group help inform and generate solutions to emerging problems? Would enclave deliberation lend greater legitimacy to a choice because it most affects matters of distributional equality?
- Within larger civic forums, how can the perspectives of these disempowered groups be included in sufficient numbers so that they can talk among themselves as well as with others? How many of the marginalized need to be included to form a critical mass, so that they do not have to labor under the burden of being token representatives?
- With whom will enclave deliberators interact – citizens, officials, and so on? At what stage in the process will such interaction occur?
- Who will be the audience for the enclave's conclusions? How will these conclusions be communicated effectively and fairly? What will

the audience need to know about the aims and process of the enclave forum?

We think that enclave deliberation is especially *valuable for democracy* in several circumstances:

- To address issues in which the marginalized have few other avenues to empowerment elsewhere in the political system, such as issues on which associations and movements of the disempowered are weakest, least well-informed, or least democratic.
- To tackle emerging issues, when participants' interests, identities, and commitment to policy options are still in formation.
- When forums can help catalyze decision makers to take action, including co-governance arrangements between citizens and officials.
- By allowing disempowered participants to add their own proposals to the agenda rather than restricting discussion to a closed menu of policy options provided by others.
- When forums are more empowered to influence decisions that are binding on others. At present, many of the most empowered forums are popular assemblies where there is no clear, established role for enclaves or where self-selection may mean that the least empowered are significantly under-represented. Finding ways to include the voices of the weakest when decisions are binding is thus especially important for an inclusive vision of democracy.

To advance equality, we suspect that there are several ways in which civic forums can reap the benefits of enclave deliberation among the marginalized, while controlling for excessively sectarian thinking or group polarization for the wrong reasons:

- By offering marginalized citizens direct interaction with diverse policy elites and/or other citizens at some point in the forum. Opportunities for disempowered enclaves to exchange ideas with officials or more advantaged citizens, ask questions, and simply get to know people who are often inaccessible can help these enclaves avoid a narrow groupthink and increase democratic accountability for all involved.
- By giving enclave deliberators sufficient facilitation, information, and time to acknowledge the internal diversity of opinions *amongst themselves*. Enclave deliberation can result in the development of a common identity, but it can also involve a greater realization of how those with similar perspectives might come to different conclusions. Facilitators

should aim to help people consider their shared circumstances without prescribing a narrow range of answers to their predicament.

- By guaranteeing an audience of decision makers for the group's final proposals. The optimal situation is that enclave deliberation has clear institutional links to the political system or public sphere. Examples of institutional links include how the Brazilian Participatory Budget connects discussion in neighborhood groups with priority setting at larger levels of government, and how Chicago beat meetings hold police and citizens of poor neighborhoods accountable to one another. An example of a clear linkage between the public sphere and a civic forum, albeit not an enclave, is the Oregon Citizens' Initiative Review Board, which has guaranteed access to disseminate its voting recommendations on ballot initiatives in the state's voter pamphlet.

Figure 7.1 summarizes the questions that could help forum organizers decide whether and how to integrate enclave deliberation in ways that are likely to enhance equality and democratic legitimacy.

The evidence discussed in Chapters 2 and 3 also suggests the conditions in which enclaves of the weak are *most likely to be institutionalized*. These enclaves are most practical to establish when governments or other institutions that initiate or form the audience for civic forums are committed to sharing power over consequential decisions and open to considering redistribution of power and resources to the least privileged.[1] These are important motivations for overcoming the rational cynicism of the marginalized and convincing them to participate. While enclave deliberation can compensate for the weaknesses of voluntary associations on some issues, associations are often needed to mobilize popular participation in these forums and to monitor them to help maintain their independence from co-optation by sponsors. Ongoing and transparent evaluation of these forums' ability to deliver concrete improvements for the disempowered is also important for enticing them to continue participating over time. Because the least empowered are sometimes the least participatory, both targeted mobilization and the prospect of at least some practical change as a result of participation are key to the success of enclave forums.

---

[1] On the many conditions that explain when governments are more open to listening to civic forums, see the Introduction, as well as Baiocchi (2005) on Participatory Budgeting; Fung (2004) and Talpin (2012) on co-governance forums; Leighninger (2012) on local government forums; and Goodin and Dryzek (2006) and Smith (2009), especially Chapter 6, on a broad range of popular assemblies, co-governance forums, and mini-publics.

Publics
- What publics are most affected by the issue?

Enclaves
- Who is politically disempowered?
- Who is situationally disempowered?
- Who is deliberatively disempowered?

Forum Role
- How does the forum fit within the political process?
- What does the forum contribute to the process?

Inclusion
- How will the forum:
  - Attract a critical mass of disempowered perspectives?
  - Uncover diversity of opinion within the enclave?
  - Promote interaction with other citizens, officials, and experts?
  - Empower enclave participants' voices?

Audience
- Who are the audiences for the enclave?
- How will the enclave's conclusions and deliberative process be communicated?
- What institutional links will persuade the audience to listen?

Figure 7.1 Guiding questions for integrating enclave deliberation

Future research on enclaves

Given the great challenges of measuring equality of participation and influence in deliberation, they should be assessed using multiple measures, direct and indirect, in enclave and microcosmic forums. These studies should routinely disaggregate data to test whether less privileged participants think, talk, and form their views on equal footing with more advantaged citizens. Evaluators and scholars should especially continue to study whether citizens' opinions are based on mutual reasoning rather than status and which practices within forums contribute most to equality, particularly with regard to issue framing and facilitation. We should want to know whether initial issue framings and the range of policy options that are admitted into conversation allow the disadvantaged to arrive at their own authentic views or influence these participants to reduce their aspirations to fit their weaker position in society. We should design studies that begin with a clearer analysis of who is situationally disempowered by the issues under consideration, and ask how well forums help them to overcome their condition in deliberation. Instead of assuming that facilitators always solve the problem of equal participation, we encourage additional careful study of facilitation, with observational studies of existing forums and with lab and field experiments that vary not only the presence or absence of facilitators but also the type and frequency of their intervention.

With regard to group polarization, we need to know not only whether enclaves polarize but *why or why not*. We should study the role of exposure to competing arguments and facilitation in the forum on enclaves' ability to explore both their commonalities and their differences. Are there particular skills that facilitators need most in order to help enclaves of the marginalized to freely explore their shared and divergent interests? More remains to be done to understand how enclave groups can most effectively balance the agreements and commonalities that emerge from their shared perspectives with the need to create space for healthy differences of opinion as well. Research can tell us more about whether exposure to balanced arguments and information about an issue allows enclaves to elude undesirable forms of polarization, based on social coercion and inability to consider diverse views. In addition, are there particular issues that are more and less likely to induce polarization or autonomous deliberation in enclaves?

We should continue to test the effects of different decision rules on enclaves of the weak in civic forums. Are we right to hypothesize, in contrast with some group polarization research, that consensus decision making may best protect enclaves of the disempowered from unreflective polarization by protecting minority viewpoints within the group? To answer that question, effective research will incorporate sufficient numbers of groups and random assignment of groups to different decision rules.

What are the most effective ways to transition enclave deliberators to broader discussion with other citizens in the same forum? For example, are the voices of the disempowered most likely to keep resonating if they shift from enclaves to discussion groups in which they are the large majority or to groups in which they are no longer the majority but that use consensus decision making? The experimental research on gender and decision rules in groups suggests that when majority rule is used, peopling groups with majorities of the disempowered may be enough to promote their voice. Requiring consensus may also protect the marginalized enough that they can deliberate on equal terms with a majority of more powerful citizens.[2] Yet this research is limited to one kind of disadvantage, based on women's ongoing disempowerment by the *act of deliberation*. Do the same conditions hold for deliberators who are also *politically* disempowered with in the larger democratic system or *situationally* disadvantaged in relation to the topic of the forum?

Other group-level features of enclave forums, such as the norms of interaction that develop among those who share a perspective about the issue under discussion, also deserve additional attention. In that spirit, for example, research can also study the development of public-minded thinking in enclave forums, as participants move back and forth from considering their group interests to the interests of others. Observation, interviews, and other creative research designs can do more to uncover deliberators' *motives* for transforming their views, rather than imputing motives based on assumptions about why citizens made their policy choices, or about the relationship of their decisions to their pre-existing attitudes or beliefs.

Studies of deliberation can take a broader approach to assessing the role of knowledge in forums. While research still needs to ask how much citizens learn in order to assess how well-informed their opinions are, we should also want to know what officials and experts learn from their encounters with citizens. Do they become more or less open to civic deliberation? Under what conditions are they more likely to accept the conclusions of civic forums, especially enclave forums? What kinds of

---

[2] Karpowitz and Mendelberg 2014.

citizen knowledge do experts and officials value most and least, and what kinds should be valued more and less than they are?

When measuring what citizens learn in deliberation, research should go beyond both participants' subjective assessments of their knowledge gains and quizzing citizens on how much factual information they acquired. We need to ask how much participants learn about how the evidence that underpins their views was produced, and about how to evaluate interested knowledge. Studies should also routinely disaggregate participants' learning gains to show whether people who enter the forum with less issue knowledge achieve equitable levels of understanding with more knowledgeable citizens within the forum. The key question is not whether participants learn at the same rate, but whether their final policy preferences are equally well-informed. Comparative research should test our claims that enclaves of the disempowered are more likely than mixed groups to give a fair hearing to the situated knowledge of the marginalized, to assess expert knowledge and its origins more extensively from disempowered perspectives, and to offer their own considered local knowledge more fully.

Comparative studies on enclave deliberation could also tell us whether the many elements of forum design can be disentangled well enough to show which aspects most effectively foster equality. For example, are enclaves most likely to deliberate well and make valuable contributions to debate over issues that are more or less established, local, fact-driven or value-driven, and accessible to personal experience? At the same time, research needs to consider whether these many design factors – such as group composition, issue, the format of the forum, and its degree of empowerment over decision making – may interact to reinforce one another. The whole experience of a forum may be more than the sum of its parts.

In addition, comparative studies of enclave forums and other political opportunities for opinion formation and decision making – such as discussion in social networks, involvement in associations, traditional forms of public consultation, polls, and elections – could help illuminate when the disempowered are most wise to invest their energy in forums and in other venues. This research could examine the extent that deliberation in forums of disempowered people satisfies criteria of autonomous participation and influence compared with other political arenas. The most powerful way to address concerns about civic forums may be to publicize honest and independent evaluations that show whether participants can fulfill democracy's need for political equality and public judgment better than in established political arenas. More broadly, research can further illuminate the conditions under which the conclusions and reasons that emerge from enclave forums are taken up by other parts of the deliberative system.

Improving publicity

Our study of how a sample of forums disseminated citizens' conclusions shows that these statements – whether they are individual or consensus statements, the results of majority or plurality voting, or shifts in opinion polls – do not speak for themselves. Instead, authors must interpret, synthesize, and resolve citizens' many arguments and positions, often doing so after the forum. How can this publicity be authorized more legitimately by deliberators themselves, and therefore by observers of the forum? This conundrum requires authors to rethink the control and conduct of publicity in deliberative terms. Certainly, publicity must aim to persuade others across the political system that the forum and its conclusions are legitimate. But it is likely to do so only by showing greater respect for its audiences' autonomy than much political rhetoric does. A deliberative rhetoric should aim to help audiences make well-informed decisions about whether to accept the forum's process and argumentation.

We suggest several guiding principles. First, *more publicity is better,* unless its prospect would critically undermine conditions for deliberation in the forum. Fuller revelation of all elements of a group's argumentation and greater transparency about deliberative processes can and should be practiced. High-quality deliberation within the forum needs to be publicized in terms that respect the autonomy of those outside the forum. Second, *publicity should be presented in a coherent and comprehensible form* that allows audiences to understand participants' argumentation and assess the trustworthiness of the forum. The clearest reporting of a forum will employ argumentation that observers can grasp most easily and will be based on widely accepted measures of a forum's legitimacy, even if these measures are still being developed in the field at present. This kind of publicity is more desirable than reports that list many elements of participants' argumentation but fail to show how participants prioritized and connected reasons, evidence, values, and conclusions. Better publicity also organizes information about the elements of transparency we have identified to reveal the forum's democratic strengths and weaknesses, rather than dumping large amounts of data in ways that overwhelm observers with detail. Third, *the obligation to practice full publicity is proportional to the intended influence of the deliberation.* Decisional forums that enact policy directly or claim to represent public opinion to decision makers should meet the highest standards for divulging participants' argumentation and practicing transparency about how the forum was conducted. Fourth, *publicity should be authorized as directly as possible by deliberators.* Audiences should have good reason to be confident that reports reflect participants' views rather than authors' opinions or interpretations. We will suggest several ways in which publicity can meet these standards.

Argumentation

In our study of an illustrative sample of final reports of civic forums, we found several ways in which citizens' argumentation could be presented better. We suggested that authors' expectations of their audience and choice of genre for communicating deliberation can powerfully shape publicity. Especially in the way reports present evidence, deliberative publicity can be influenced by several dominant genres of political discourse: populist, policy analytic, academic, and activist. Choosing one of these genres exclusively can mean adopting a set of biases, such as emphasizing deliberators' cognitive and systematic reasoning, or their experiential and particular thinking about the issues. Ideally, forums need to develop new genres that capture the variety of citizens' reasoning, showing how they link the particular to the general, personal experience with systematic research, and individual or group interests to a vision of the public interest. We also found that the reports in our sample often omitted discussion of opposing views, which might have conveyed the range of arguments under deliberation and how participants resolved or avoided difficult trade-offs among policy options. Normative claims, which reveal how citizens prioritized competing values, were also scarce.

These findings have implications for different forum designs. In deliberations that are open to all who want to participate, such as many popular assemblies and co-governance forums, participants' reasons and evidence are often routinely recorded and made available to non-participants. But selective mini-publics especially need to be concerned about rethinking publicity because authorization of their recommendations within the political system depends so heavily on the quality of their arguments and on cultivating others' trust in their deliberative process. If mutual justification is the core act of democratic deliberation, some forums, such as

Deliberative Polls, need to preserve more systematic data on deliberators' reasoning.

The Danish Consensus Conference on GM foods that we analyzed provides one attractive solution. The organizers had participants rate each of the major arguments, conditions, and recommendations discussed during the forum, which are disseminated in the final report. The record of votes thus comprises a full catalogue of the main arguments and counterarguments considered during the forum. With admirable specificity and economy, this strategy also reveals how strongly participants were convinced by contending arguments and how strongly citizens supported each recommendation. Rating arguments and conclusions in this way could be supplemented by asking participants to *rank* reasons and preferences, especially to show how deliberators resolved difficult trade-offs, as participants in civic forums are often asked to do.

The statements issued by the Oregon Citizens Initiative Review panel offer a simpler model for disseminating citizens' reasoning, but it is well-suited to this forum's role in the political system. The panel issues brief assessments, which are printed in the official voter pamphlet, to advise other citizens on whether to support or oppose ballot initiatives. In its statements, the panel is required to list what it sees as the most germane reasons and evidence for and against a ballot initiative, after spending five days interviewing advocates and experts, fact checking their claims, and deliberating over the issue. The panel also reports its own major findings about the merits of the arguments. As a corrective to the manipulative rhetoric and dubious evidence often presented in political advertising, the panel's evaluation offers voters important information about which of the many arguments in public discourse were most plausible to the panel's 24 randomly selected voters who have studied the issue closely. Thus, one of the panel's main contributions is to distil the best possible arguments and evidence for each position on the initiative. The panel also reports its members' individual votes on the ballot initiative. A lopsided majority vote sends a clear signal to the electorate about how the panel resolved the arguments, while a split vote suggests that citizens need to investigate the issue more fully themselves and engage in further deliberation about it. The panel's assessments are written simply and limited by statute to 1250 words or less, which fits their purpose to give overwhelmed voters a convenient source of accessible, independent, and deliberative analysis of the issue, which citizens can use as a cue to guide their votes. In the panel's first three years, a majority of Oregonians became aware of its statements in the voter pamphlet and increasing numbers came to see the panel as a trusted proxy on whose authority they might base their votes.[3]

Our recommendations would help forums meet several of the principles of publicity we have suggested above more effectively. Fuller dissemination of citizens' arguments, especially the norms that motivated their conclusions and the opposing views they considered, would increase the forum's publicity and transparency. Developing more effective genres of publicity that include each of the elements of argumentation and transparency we have suggested would offer more coherent and understandable accounts of why forum participants arrived at their views and why others should listen to them. The *New GM Plants* and Oregon Citizens' Initiative Review panel statements show that deliberative publicity can reveal clearly and briefly how participants rate and connect reasons, evidence, values, and conclusions, without burying audiences in detail.

Transparency

In our sample, we found that all reports touched at least briefly on some elements of transparency but no report mentioned all aspects. Authors were much more likely to disclose information about the control, design, and intended influence of forums than to provide evaluation data or discuss how reports practiced fidelity to deliberators' views. But even when reports mentioned some aspects of these elements of transparency, contextual details that would help outsiders understand better the goals and potential biases of the forum were often absent.

Our recommendation here is not complicated: all reports of civic forums ought to be able to practice each of the elements of transparency we have defined. In a democracy, it is important to know who is trying to influence public opinion and political decision making. Of all political institutions, civic forums should be among the most committed to practicing transparency. As new institutions, they need to make a case for their own legitimacy. As deliberative institutions, they need to make arguments to others that respect similar expectations for good deliberation within the forum. Transparency allows citizens to develop trust in these new institutions, thus allowing them to play a more effective, meaningful role in public decision making. The ability to satisfy basic standards of transparency thus speaks to the overall value of the forum: a forum that aims to influence policy making, but that cannot demonstrate its legitimacy in some basic ways, might not be worth holding.

---

[3] Knobloch et al. 2013; Gastil and Richards 2013.

In particular, we encourage authors of deliberative publicity to practice the utmost transparency about the role and interests of sponsors, funders, and organizers of forums. As the "Our Budget, Our Economy" example with which we began the book showed, the first step of skeptics who fear that the forum will be biased is to follow the money and attribute citizens' opinions to its influence. (As the same example shows, critics may follow the money selectively, and claim that one partisan sponsor biases the forum.) Such criticisms, whether fair or not, can best be answered with increased publicity.

We also urge authors to be clearer about the ability of the forum to represent a larger population, which organizers are strongly tempted to oversimplify and overstate. Such oversimplification is especially tempting in small forums that are unlikely to be completely representative because no group of 10–20 citizens can possibly mirror the full range of interests and characteristics present in our large democracy. Broad assertions that the forum was "diverse" or included "different perspectives" are not sufficient. When the forum is larger and can more plausibly comprise a representative sample of some larger population, increased transparency can reveal a key strength of the forum. Whether the forum is large or small, authors should present as much detail about the characteristics of the participants as possible.

Given our view of the value of enclave deliberation, we do not claim that every forum need aspire to be statistically representative of the full polity. But where organizers choose not to assemble a random sample of a population, the need increases for clear justification of how the population and the sample were defined and how choices about the sample relate to the purposes of the forum. An example of a best practice comes from the Australian Deliberative Poll we discussed in Chapter 2. The report explained why the forum oversampled indigenous Australians (because the topic was the relationship between this small sector of society and the larger nation) and disclosed the views of the indigenous participants and of a representative sample of Australians so that readers could easily compare and contrast them.

Organizers also practice good publicity when they give full and precise disclosure of the agenda, initial framing of issues, and decision rules used in the forum, which can strongly influence citizens' conclusions. In addition to stating the intended audiences for the forum's conclusions, authors should consider communicating more specifically to these audiences, even if this requires issuing multiple reports or writing parts of reports addressed to each major target of the forum's influence. This is important for clarifying the intended contribution to the political system and making that contribution effectively.

In our data, we found that current publicity is especially likely to neglect fidelity and evaluation. Fidelity requires that publicity is faithful to citizens' discussion in the forum and that participants should be able to authorize or authenticate publicity materials. Consensus Conferences, at least as practiced by the Danish Board of Technology, offer a model for small, single-group forums. All participants typically review and approve the wording of each recommendation as a group, and participants often present the report publicly, giving them a strong incentive to take responsibility for the report's accuracy and inclusiveness of their views. In this way, participants exercise a right of review over how publicity resolves their opinions into conclusions, synthesizes their arguments, and interprets their meaning for audiences.

Other options are available to larger, multisite forums. One possibility, suggested by the *New GM Plants report* we analyzed in this book, is for all participants to rate (and even rank) the major reasons, evidence, and conclusions discussed at the forum. Keypad technology used forums such as 21st Century Town Meetings, or post-forum polling used in Deliberative Polls and some National Issues Forums, can be used for this purpose.

Another option is suggested by Planning Cells, a deliberative format we have not addressed in this book. In Planning Cells, multiple groups tackle policy issues at dispersed sites and a final report synthesizes the views expressed, without requiring individual participants to vote on conclusions or each group to come to consensus recommendations. Organizers check for the fidelity of the report by circulating drafts for approval by a committee comprised of citizen participants nominated by each Planning Cell. When the report is finalized, several weeks after the last cell is held, all participants reconvene at their separate sites to present the report to decision makers, including officials, presenters at the forum, and relevant associations.[4] The ongoing involvement of a committee of citizens in reviewing the report, and the prospect of all participants seeing the report before it is given to decision makers, is one way to hold authors accountable for fidelity. Like ethnographic researchers, Planning Cell organizers return to "the field" to share their interpretations with informants. This serves several purposes: checking for understanding,

---

[4] Hendriks 2005, 85–6.

checking the observer's individual biases, and sharing the power to synthesize and interpret results with informants. Other large mini-publics could do the same.

We suggested that forums ought to provide two kinds of evaluation data: evaluation *of the deliberation*, including citizens' or others' assessments of the fairness or effectiveness of the process; and evaluation *of the participants*, which includes assessments of participants' changes in knowledge, attitudes, or dispositions during the deliberation. Both are crucial for judging the quality of deliberation.

Systematic evaluation is central to increasing forums' legitimacy in the wider political system. Cherry-picking a few quotes from participants that testify to their inspiring experience of democratic discussion is unlikely to convince skeptics and may have already become a routinized cliché of many reports. As forums become a feature of the political landscape, persuading onlookers of a forum's legitimacy requires more than reporting selected epiphanies with no evidence of how common – or uncommon – such reactions might have been. And while we know from our own observations of forums that effective deliberation can be a satisfying experience, existing research tells us that it is not always so for all participants. Sometimes, working through differences of opinion and interest can be difficult, frustrating, or disappointing.[5] The field of civic forums is best served not by ignoring or hiding such reactions, but by discussing, analyzing, and learning from them. In fact, part of the purpose of deliberation is to bring those challenging disagreements into the open, including when they persist at the end of the forum. In addition, when deliberators leave with more positive reactions, it strikes us as far more important to understand whether that satisfaction comes as a result of real and civically broadening engagement with the differing views of fellow deliberators or something less democratically valuable, such as avoiding difficult choices or cheerleading for the abstract aims of the forum organizers.

As the new civic forums transition from experiments to recognized institutions, it is time to adopt some common standards and expectations for evaluation. Many academics and organizers of forums have developed expertise in assessing forums, but the field lacks shared expectations and

---

[5] Hibbing and Theiss-Morse 2002; Mansbridge 1983. Of course, frustration and disappointment with a forum can emerge because deliberation can be difficult in even a very well-organized forum or it can emerge because the forum itself is not well conceived or executed. Either way, systematic evaluation data, including data that would help nonparticipants identify the causes of any frustrations, is helpful.

instruments. Constructing them should help raise standards for evaluating forums, which should also improve how forums are conducted. Common standards would make it easier to compare the legitimacy of different forums. Shared evaluative criteria would also establish clearer expectations among sponsors, organizers, authors of publicity, and their audiences. In contrast, multiple evaluation systems based on distinct criteria that offer conflicting assessments are likely to confuse the audiences for forums.[6]

There is a need for some basic common instruments that can be administered to citizens, witnesses at hearings, advisory board members, facilitators, and others who participate in forums, as well as their intended audiences. As a first-time organizer and evaluator, we surveyed all of these groups for the research reported in Chapter 3 and did not find it overly burdensome. Our task would have been made even easier if a standard battery of evaluation questions existed, allowing us to better compare the experience of our participants with those of other civic forums. Armed with a good set of standard survey questions and additional measures, most evaluators should be able to understand the strengths and weaknesses of any forum fairly well.[7] Of course, these measures could be supplemented to track questions of interest to particular forums, based on their goals. Common assessment standards should set a floor, not a ceiling.

These shared standards are best created through deliberation among those who would be most immediately affected by them and who can offer valuable perspectives on how to construct them. Sponsors, organizers, evaluators, scholars, and typical audiences for forums (especially in government) should participate in hammering out common expectations and measures. John Gastil, Katie Knobloch, and Meghan Kelly have proposed an evaluation plan that is an especially good starting point for this

---

[6] A lesson from the proliferation of labeling and rating systems that have been developed to give consumers information about how to pursue their politics – by basing their purchasing decisions on whether products are organic, fair trade, energy efficient, and the like – is that people can be confused and paralyzed by the mixed signals that these disparate ratings send (Schor 2012). Although deciding whether a democratic forum is legitimate is not the same as choosing one brand of coffee over another, the problems of information overload and conflicting criteria are similar.

[7] These need not be created from scratch, but could draw productively on the growing academic literature that explores citizen responses to experiencing public institutions. For example, Tom Tyler's work on procedural justice, which began with an exploration of citizen experiences with police and courts (Lind and Tyler 1988), provides a series of useful questions about the fairness of institutions in which citizens participate.

discussion – one that is comprehensive, uses multiple methods, and distinguishes basic assessments that any forum should be able to perform from more advanced and expensive evaluations that especially empowered and well-funded deliberations should be expected to conduct.[8] Because organizers have a strong professional interest in appearing to be competent, independent evaluation by experienced evaluators free of conflicting interests would most enhance the legitimacy of civic forums. Evaluators should focus on assessing the quality of the deliberative process, not passing judgment on the substance of the proposals emerging from the civic forum.

But publicity extends beyond conducting good evaluations to how they are communicated. Evaluation tells us how well a forum achieved its aims. Publicity concerns how well a forum establishes its legitimacy in the larger democratic system. Therefore, publicity includes features not often considered in evaluations, such as the quality of argumentation, disclosure of how forums are conducted, and the fidelity of reports to the deliberation. Several lessons for civic forums can be drawn from research on transparency policies that allow the public to assess the performance and products of governments and markets. As Archon Fung, Mary Graham, and David Weil found in their study of multiple transparency policies, the most successful ones were crafted by "strong groups representing information users, offered benefits to at least some information disclosers, and provided comprehensible content."[9]

Embedding shared standards for publicity in the political system begins with incorporating audiences' expectations for argumentation and transparency. As Fung and his colleagues conclude, "the starting point for any transparency policy was an understanding of the priorities and capacities of diverse audiences who might use the new information. Effective policies did not simply increase information. They increased knowledge that informed choice."[10] Similarly, we have argued that informed choice ought to be a central goal of publicity. Effective publicity will allow non-participants to make better decisions about whether to embrace the arguments and conclusions of a forum on their merits (strong authorization) or whether to view the forum as a trustworthy proxy for public judgment because it was conducted legitimately (weak authorization).

Deliberation over establishing common standards could begin by considering how to implement the indicators of legitimate publicity we have suggested. We have compiled them into a "publicity checklist"

---

[8] Gastil, Knobloch, and Kelly 2012.   [9] Fung, Graham, and Weil 2007, xiv.
[10] Fung, Graham, and Weil 2007, xiv.

(see Figure 7.2). The checklist is based on the Legitimate Publicity Indicators (LPIs) we introduced in Chapter 4. It borrows from the LPI coding definitions we employed in Chapters 5 and 6, but it also incorporates lessons we have learned from the analysis we presented in those chapters. Therefore, it reflects a deeper understanding of the goals and purposes of deliberative publicity than we had at the time we began our study. We conceive of the checklist as a basic way for forum organizers and authors to remind themselves of important elements of transparency and for scholars and other interested observers to evaluate publicity efforts. Careful attention to the elements of the checklist can serve to remind report authors to incorporate the information needs of their audiences more fully into their work. The checklist can also be used as a tool for designing deliberation. For example, consulting the checklist at each stage of planning can prompt organizers to think carefully about the intended influence of the forum, to plan effective ways of gathering and preserving participants' arguments, to create thorough evaluations, and to ensure that publicity reflects participants' views and experience in the forum. Like the checklists increasingly used in many professional fields, including medicine and aviation, the publicity checklist can help organizers remember and manage a multitude of complex tasks, establish baseline expectations for competence in the field, and demonstrate accountability for their performance.[11]

As Fung and his colleagues indicate, a successful policy will also offer incentives to disclosers of information. A productive deliberation over shared standards should help sponsors, organizers, and authors understand the benefits of practicing better publicity. As we discussed in the Introduction, some of these organizations compete in a market for providing public consultation services. Effective transparency policies tend to reward market leaders who have the knowledge and commitment to implement disclosure, while increasing pressure on laggards to improve their practices in order to compete, or to leave the market. These policies also help governments to respond to public demand for competent and accountable public administration.

How might common standards for publicity help to provide more comprehensible information to the audiences for civic forums? The publicity checklist we offer here might be the basis for deliberation over whether and how to develop a certification system for forums, comparable to some of the better systems used to rate the sustainability of buildings, university campuses, and the like. For example, the Leadership

---

[11] Gawande 2010.

DELIBERATIVE PUBLICITY CHECKLIST

Legitimate publicity reveals all of the following elements of a civic forum

ARGUMENTATION

- □ **Conclusions:** Goals, strategies, solutions, or policies that deliberators endorsed.
- □ **Reasons:** Deliberators' rationale for their conclusions.
- □ **Evidence:** Facts on which deliberators based their conclusions, such as research, statistics, stories, testimony.
- □ **Norms:** Values that motivated deliberators' conclusions.
- □ **Opposing views:** Counter-arguments that were considered and rejected by deliberators.
- □ **Respect:** Whether deliberators saw opposing views as legitimate, illegitimate, or neutrally.
- □ **Coherence:** How deliberators linked their conclusions to relevant reasons, evidence, norms, and opposing views.

TRANSPARENCY

Control

- □ **Sponsors:** Funders of the forum and their missions.
- □ **Organizers:** Conveners of the forum and their missions.
- □ **Partners:** Other who helped design, conduct, advise, or monitor the forum; why they were chosen; their institutional affiliations: their roles in the forum.
- □ **Positions:** Sponsoring, convening, and partnering organizations' prior positions on issues discussed at the forum.

Design

- □ **Participant selection:** Criteria, process, and justification for choosing deliberators.
- □ **Representativeness:** Deliberators' characteristics and prior opinions that are salient to the issue and goals of the forum; how closely these characteristics and pre-forum opinions represent the public that would be most affected by the forum's conclusions.
- □ **Agenda:** Initial questions, issues, framings, range of views, tasks, and objectives presented to participants.
- □ **Structure and facilitation:** Times and places where the forum met and any major impacts they may have had on deliberation; role and training of moderators.
- □ **Format:** Process, strengths, and limitations of the deliberative format; why the format was chosen.
- □ **Decision rule:** How participants arrived at conclusions, individually or as a group.
- □ **Dynamics:** Strength, speed, or ease of deliberators' agreement; other qualities of group discussion that especially influenced deliberation.

Intended Influence

- □ **Purpose:** Reasons or goals for convening the forum and its intended impacts.
- □ **Intended audiences:** Organizations, politics, or publics to which the report is addressed.

Evaluation

- □ **Of deliberation:** Systematic assessment of the fairness and effectiveness of the deliberative process – especially the briefing materials, facilitation, and discussion – by participants and observers of the forum.
- □ **Of participants:** Systematic evaluation of the participants, especially the development of their knowledge, attitudes, or dispositions.

Fidelity

- □ **Authorization:** Criteria for including the major elements of argumentation in publicity and whether these criteria were agreed to by deliberators.
- □ **Accountability:** Whether deliberators thought the authorizing criteria were applied accurately in publicity.

Figure 7.2 Deliberative publicity checklist

in Energy and Environmental Design (LEED) system, developed by the US Green Building Council, has established accepted standards for green buildings that reflect how they are sited, designed, constructed, and operated. Like the publicity criteria we have applied in this book, the LEED standards encompass a very broad range of measures of environmental performance. Third-party evaluators certify a building's performance in one of four tiers of sustainability: platinum, gold, silver, and basic certification. Buildings earn points based on their ability to meet each standard, so that weaknesses in one area (such as energy efficiency) may be offset by strengths in another (such as reduced water usage). The system offers flexibility by setting different standards tailored to a building's use, such as health care facilities or homes. The LEED standards have spread in part because governments have required or rewarded builders for meeting them in new public buildings, and ability to meet these standards has become a selling point for some builders in the private real estate market.

A comparable system for certifying civic forums is worth discussing. Of course, no rating system, including LEED, is perfect. People within the field of civic deliberation and public consultation should be especially attentive to the dangers of creating perverse incentives to ignore some aspects of good publicity in order to pile up points for doing only a few things well, setting standards too low or high, creating costs of compliance that outweigh the benefits to forums, and failing to update the standards in ways that foster continued improvement. However, the conversation is worth having because if a good system can be devised, it would address several of the problems we have discussed in this book. A certification system created by representatives of the major actors in the field could establish a consensus about expectations for publicity, create incentives to improve the design and communication of forums, help sponsors understand the need to allocate sufficient funds to publicity, and offer audiences a clear and comprehensible indication of whether a forum meets accepted standards within the field. A workable rating system would provide flexibility, taking into account differences in the aims and budgets of different kinds of civic forums. It would allow audiences to compare the legitimacy of different forums without being overwhelmed by information overload about how they were conducted and publicized.

Future research on publicity

There is much more to be learned about how policymakers, activists, and the public view different types of argumentation and transparency. This work could illuminate how civic forums can maximize both their independence from external power and their policy impacts by communicating well to other actors in the deliberative system. This kind of research would begin by identifying the factors in the deliberative process that account for quality publicity. The main challenge for such research is that the outcomes of deliberation are overdetermined by myriad variables of control, design, intended influence, and issue selection.[12] Based on our observations in this study, it seems especially important to research the ways in which publicity is influenced by the organizers' goals and issue framings, intended audiences, the decision rule used in deliberation, and the authoring process. This research could expand its focus beyond final reports to consider all forms of external communication by deliberative policy bodies throughout their lifecycles. The response to these groups from attentive policy actors is likely shaped by whether they perceive such processes as legitimate and well-informed from the start.

There is also a need to study publicity's effects on the larger deliberative system. This research could identify which elements of publicity are most persuasive for policy actors, the news media, and the public. Work in this area might productively incorporate categories from the literature on policy making as rhetorical persuasion, such as the goodness of fit between reasons and the views of intended audiences for reports, or the credibility of sources of information cited for particular audiences.[13] This research could also deepen understanding of how publicity of deliberation is filtered through journalistic norms by exploring how to resolve potential tensions between journalists' economic imperatives and norms of newsworthiness, on the one hand, and the sort of transparency we have advocated, on the other.[14]

Is transparency more important than argumentation for persuading audiences, and if so, what kinds of disclosures? We have mentioned that in the popular referendum on the political redistricting proposal generated by the British Columbia Citizens' Assembly, citizens who lacked information about the details of the proposal based their vote on whether they saw elements of the Assembly's *process* as legitimate, such as including people like them, and whether they thought the Assembly members were well-informed about the issue.[15] Given our interest in both strong and weak forms of authorization, we see the need for much more research into the conditions under which citizens can legitimately use the verdicts of civic forums as trusted proxies for political judgment.

---

[12] Fung 2003.   [13] Majone 1989.   [14] Parkinson 2006b.   [15] Cutler et al. 2008.

Beyond ordinary citizens, what kinds of transparency are especially persuasive to officials, journalists, and interest advocates? Savvy about politics, these targets of deliberative publicity know that not everyone will agree on policy solutions or even about whether a political process was legitimate. They are very familiar with our contemporary professional culture of self-branding and impression management, including by non-profit organizations. Thus, they may be appropriately skeptical about – even irritated by – publicity that refuses to admit negative views of the forum. We should study whether these audiences find publicity that forthrightly admits of some limitations to the forum more convincing than publicity that presents only a happy picture of citizens and officials achieving deliberative nirvana.

Research on publicity's influences could also help address additional questions about the normative and practical performance of different components of the deliberative system, especially some trade-offs that are often seen as endemic to it. For example, there may be a tension between publicity and the internal legitimacy of deliberation. We have noted that when either deliberators or the surrounding political context are highly polarized, secrecy can build trust, encourage sincerity, and create empathy among participants. But the importance of publicity for democracy is greater when a forum has the power to enact policy directly (because publicity makes deliberators more accountable) and when there is a danger that some citizens who have reasonable claims to participate may be excluded (because publicity makes forum organizers more inclusive). Thus, we have maintained that even when deliberation in direct decision-making bodies is cloaked, the process and reasoning generally should be communicated afterward. Research could help answer whether and how the quality of communication about necessarily secret deliberations can boost their perceived legitimacy and influence among non-participants. In particular, we know little about how secrecy and publicity are handled in co-governance forums that elect citizen representatives to deliberate in smaller groups on other citizens' behalf.

Research could also address whether trade-offs between the influence and internal legitimacy of deliberation may be overcome in part through external communication. Mark Warren notes that deliberative democrats tend to assume that citizen deliberators with a stronger guarantee of influence on policy (often because they are convened by government) will be more committed to learning about the full scope and depth of issues and will offer more detailed conclusions, but that these deliberators may engage in excessively strategic reasoning and cede more independence in crafting their proposals to fit political expediency (compromising internal legitimacy).[16] This has long been a concern of social movement participants in state-sponsored forums. Is co-optation always the price of influence? Close study of how civic forums that maximize both their independence and impact communicate with the public, news media, stakeholders, and decision makers might help to identify optimal institutional designs and communicative practices for civic deliberation.

Clearly, there is much more to learn about civic forums and how they might strengthen citizens' voices in contemporary democracies. At another difficult time in the history of democracy, during the Great Depression and on the eve of World War II, the British novelist E. M. Forster raised "two cheers for Democracy: one because it admits variety and two because it permits criticism."[17] Given the limits to realizing democracy's promises then and now, who can blame him for reserving the third cheer? However, despite our many recommendations for improving civic forums, we see them as having already accomplished much to vitalize democracy at a time when its other institutions can seem weak, tired, and unable to resist capture by narrow and privileged interests. By continuing to strengthen how they practice equal and public deliberation, these new forums can fulfill their potential to help citizens realize their capacity to govern themselves.

[16] Warren 2007.   [17] Forster 1965, 70.

References

Abelson, Julia, and François-Pierre Gauvin. 2006. *Assessing the Impacts of Public Participation: Concepts, Evidence and Policy Implications*. Ottawa: Canadian Policy Research Networks.

Abers, Rebecca. 2000. *Inventing Local Democracy: Grassroots Politics in Brazil*. Boulder, CO: Lynne Rienner.

Abrams, Dominic, Margaret Wetherell, Sandra Cochrane, Michael A. Hogg, and John C. Turner. 1990. Knowing What to Think by Knowing Who You Are: Self-categorization and the Nature of Norm Formation, Conformity and Group Polarization. *British Journal of Social Psychology* 29: 97–119.

Ackerman, Bruce. 1991. *We the People*. Cambridge, MA: Belknap Press of Harvard University Press.

Ackerman, Bruce A., and James S. Fishkin. 2004. *Deliberation Day*. New Haven, CT: Yale University Press.

AmericaSpeaks, Everyday Democracy, Demos, and Ash Institute for Democratic Governance and Innovation. 2009. *Working Together to Strengthen Our Nation's Democracy*. Washington, DC: AmericaSpeaks, Everyday Democracy, Demos, and Ash Institute for Democratic Governance and Innovation.

Andries, Darcy. 2008. *American Idol* versus the Presidential Election Voter Turnout - Numbers Don't Lie. *Yahoo! Voices*. Available from voices.yahoo.com/american-idol-versus-presidential-election-voter-1396529.html, accessed 15 November 2013.

Arrow, Kenneth. 1963 [1951]. *Social Choice and Individual Values*. New Haven, CT: Yale University Press.

Bachrach, Peter, and Morton S. Baratz. 1962. The Two Faces of Power. *American Political Science Review* 56: 947–52.

Bächtiger, André, Simon Niemeyer, Michael Neblo, Marco R. Steenbergen, and Jürg Steiner. 2010. Disentangling Diversity in Deliberative Democracy: Competing Theories, Their Blind Spots and Complementarities. *Journal of Political Philosophy* 18: 32–63.

Baiochi, Gianpaolo. 2003. Participation, Activism, and Politics: The Porto Alegre experiment. Pp. 45–77 in *Deepening Democracy: Institutional Innovations in Empowered Participatory Governance*, edited by Archon Fung and Erik Olin Wright. London: Verso.

Baiocchi, Gianpaolo. 2005. *Militants and Citizens: The Politics of Participatory Democracy in Porto Alegre*. Stanford: Stanford University Press.

Baiocchi, Gianpaolo, Patrick Heller, and Marcelo K. Silva. 2011. *Bootstrapping Democracy: Transforming Local Governance and Civil Society in Brazil*. Stanford: Stanford University Press.

Baker, Dean. 2010. America Speaks Back: Derailing the Drive to Cut Social Security and Medicare. *HuffPost Business*. Available from www.huffingtonpost.com/dean-baker/america-speaks-back-derai_b_619465.html, accessed 5 September 2013.

Barabas, Jason. 2004. How Deliberation Affects Policy Opinions. *American Political Science Review* 98: 687–701.

Barber, Benjamin. 1984. *Strong Democracy: Participatory Politics for a New Age*. Berkeley: University of California Press.

Bardach, Eugene. 2009. *A Practical Guide for Policy Analysis (3rd ed.)* Washington, DC: CQ Press.

Barisione, Mauro. 2012. Framing a Deliberation. Deliberative Democracy and the Challenge of Framing Processes. *Journal of Public Deliberation* 8(1), Article 2. Available from www.publicdeliberation.net/cgi/viewcontent.cgi?article=1176&context=jpd, accessed 15 July 2013.

Baron, Robert S. 2005. So Right It's Wrong: Groupthink and the Ubiquitous Nature of Polarized Group Decision Making. *Advances in Experimental Social Psychology* 37: 219–53.

Barrett, Gregory, Miriam Wyman, and Vera Schattan P. Coelho. 2012. Assessing the Policy Impacts of Deliberative Civic Engagement: Comparing Engagement in the Health Policy Process of Brazil and Canada. Pp. 118–204 in *Democracy in Motion: Evaluating the Practice and Impact of Deliberative Civic Engagement*, edited by Tina Nabatchi, John Gastil, G. Michael Weiksner, and Matt Leighninger. Oxford University Press.

Bartels, Larry M. 2003. Democracy with Attitudes. Pp. 48–82 in *Electoral Democracy*, edited by Michael MacKuen and George Rabinowitz. Ann Arbor, MI: University of Michigan Press.

Bartels, Larry M. 2008. *Unequal Democracy: The Political Economy of the New Gilded Age.*: Princeton University Press.

Benhabib, Seyla. 1992. Models of Public Space: Hannah Arendt, the Liberal Tradition, and Jürgen Habermas. Pp. 73–98 in *Habermas and the Public Sphere*, edited by Craig Calhoun. Cambridge, MA: MIT Press.

Benhabib, Seyla. 1994. Deliberative Rationality and Models of Democratic Legitimacy. *Constellations* 1: 26–52.

Benhabib, Seyla. 1996. Toward a Deliberative Model of Democratic Legitimacy. Pp. 67–94 in *Democracy and Difference: Contesting Boundaries of the Political*, edited by Seyla Benhabib. Princeton University Press.

Bennett, W. Lance. 2008. Changing Citizenship in the Digital Age. Pp. 1–24 in *Civic Life Online: Learning How Digital Media Can Engage Youth*, edited by W. Lance Bennett. Cambridge, MA: MIT Press.

Berelson, Bernard R., Paul R. Lazarsfeld, and William N. McPhee. 1954. *Voting: A Study of Opinion Formation in a Presidential Campaign.* University of Chicago Press.

Bernthal, Philip R., and Chad A. Insko. 1993. Cohesiveness without Groupthink: The Interactive Effects of Social and Task Cohesion. *Group and Organization Management* 18: 66–87.

Berry, Jeffrey M., and Clyde Wilcox. 2009. *The Interest Group Society*, 5th ed. New York: Longman.

Bessette, Joseph M. 1994. *The Mild Voice of Reason: Deliberative Democracy and American National Government.* University of Chicago Press.

Birch, Anthony H. 1993. *The Concepts and Theories of Modern Democracy.* London: Routledge.

Bishop, George F. 2005. *The Illusion of Public Opinion: Fact and Artifact in American Public Opinion Polls.* Lanham, MD: Rowman and Littlefield.

Bjornlund, Eric. 2004. *Beyond Free and Fair: Monitoring Elections and Building Democracy.* Washington, DC: Woodrow Wilson Center Press.

Black, Laura W. 2003. Deliberation, Storytelling, and Dialogic Moments. *Communication Theory* 18: 93–116.

Black, Laura W. 2012. How People Communicate during Deliberative Events. Pp. 59–82 in *Democracy in Motion: Evaluating the Practice and Impact of Deliberative Civic Engagement*, edited by Tina Nabatchi, John Gastil, G. Michael Weiksner, and Matt Leighninger. Oxford University Press.

Blais, André. 2013. Evaluating U.S. Electoral Institutions in Comparative Perspective. Pp. 15–25 in *Representation: Elections and Beyond*, edited by Jack H. Nagel and Rogers M. Smith. Philadelphia: University of Pennsylvania Press.

Blake, John. 2012, January 23. Return of the "Welfare Queen." CNN U.S. Edition. Available from www.cnn.com/2012/01/23/politics/weflare-queen, accessed 15 August 2013.

Bohman James. 1995. Public Reason and Cultural Pluralism: Political Liberalism and the Problem of Moral Conflict. *Political Theory* 23: 253–79.

Bohman, James. 1996. *Public Deliberation: Pluralism, Complexity, and Democracy.* Cambridge, MA: MIT Press.

Bohman, James. 2012. Representation in the Deliberative System. Pp. 72–94 in *Deliberative Systems*, edited by John Parkinson and Jane Mansbridge. Cambridge University Press.

Bohman, James, and William Rehg. 1997. Introduction. Pp. ix–xxx in *Deliberative Democracy: Essays on Reason and Politics*, edited by James Bohman and William Rehg. Cambridge, MA: MIT Press.

Bohman, James, and Henry S. Richardson. 2009. Liberalism, Deliberative Democracy, and "Reasons that All Can Accept" *Journal of Political Philosophy* 17: 253–74.

Boldt, David. 1999. Through the Eyes of a True Believer. Pp. 87–103 in *The Poll with a Human Face: The National Issues Convention Experiment in Political Communication*, edited by Maxwell McCombs and Amy Reynolds. Mahwah, NJ: Lawrence Erlbaum Associates.

Bonham, Vence L., Toby Citrin, Stephen M. Modell, Tené Hamilton Franklin, Esther W.B. Bleicher, and Leonard M. Fleck. 2009. Community-Based

Dialogue: Engaging Communities of Color in the United States' Genetics Policy Conversation. *Journal of Health Politics, Policy and Law* 34: 325–59.

Borah, Porismita. 2011. Conceptual Issues in Framing Theory: A Systematic Examination of a Decade's Literature. *Journal of Communication*, 61: 246–63.

Bouas, Kelly S., and S. S. Komorita. 1996. Group Discussion and Cooperation in Social Dilemmas. *Personality and Social Psychology Bulletin* 22: 1144–50.

Bouie, Jamelle (2013, June 11). Could Some Democrats Vote Against Immigration Reform? *Washington Post*. Available from www.washingtonpost.com/blogs/plum-line/wp/2013/06/11/could-some-democrats-vote-against-immigration-reform/, accessed 12 July 2013.

Bowker, Geoffrey, Allen S. Hammond, and Chad Raphael. 2006, September 27. County Residents Can Help Shape the Future of Broadband. *San Jose Mercury News*.

Brady, David. 2003. The Politics of Poverty: Left Political Institutions, the Welfare State, and Poverty. *Social Forces* 82: 557–88.

Brown, Roger. 1986. *Social Psychology: The Second Edition*. New York: Free Press.

Browne, Mark B. 2006. Citizen Panels and the Concept of Representation, *Journal of Political Philosophy* 14: 203–25.

Bryan, Frank M. 2004. *Real Democracy: The New England Town Meeting and How It Works*. University of Chicago Press.

Button, Mark and Kevin Mattson. 1999. Deliberative Democracy in Practice: Challenges and Prospects for Civic Deliberation. *Polity* 31: 609–37.

Burkhalter, Stephanie, John Gastil, and Todd Kelshaw. 2002. A conceptual definition and theoretical model of public deliberation in small face-to-face groups. *Communication Theory* 12: 398–422.

Burnstein, Eugene, Amiram Vinokur, and Yaacov Trope. 1973. Interpersonal Comparison Versus Persuasive Argumentation: A More Direct Test of Alternative Explanations for Group-Induced Shifts in Individual Choice. *Journal of Experimental and Social Psychology* 9: 236–45.

Button, Mark, and Kevin Mattson. 1999. Deliberative Democracy in Practice: Challenges and Prospects for Civic Deliberation. *Polity* 31: 609–37.

Button, Mark, and David M. Ryfe. 2005. What Can We Learn from the Practice of Deliberative Democracy? Pp. 20–33 in *The Deliberative Democracy Handbook: Strategies for Effective Civic Engagement in the 21st Century*, edited by John Gastil and Peter Levine. San Francisco, CA: Jossey-Bass.

Callon, Michel, Pierre Lascoumes, and Yannick Barthe. 2009. *Acting in an Uncertain World: An Essay on Technical Democracy*. Cambridge, MA: MIT Press.

Caplan, Bryan. 2007. *The Myth of the Rational Voter: Why Democracies Choose Bad Policies*. Princeton University Press.

Cappella, Joseph N., Vincent Price, and Lilach Nir. 2002. Argument Repertoire as a Reliable and Valid Measure of Opinion Quality: Electronic Dialogue During Campaign 2000. *Political Communication* 19: 73–93.

Carcasson, Martín. 2009. Beginning with the End in Mind: A Call for Goal-Driven Deliberative Practice. Occasional Paper No. 2. Center for the Advancement of Public Engagement. Available from www.publicagendaarchives.org/files/pdf/PA_CAPE_Paper2_Beginning_SinglePgs_Rev.pdf, accessed 8 July 2013.

Carcasson, Martín. 2011. Reporting on Deliberative Forums: Current Practices and Future Developments. Research report prepared for the Kettering Foundation.

Carson, Lyn. 2001. Innovative Consultation Processes and the Changing Role of Activism. *Third Sector Review* 7: 7–22.

Carson, Lyn, and Brian Martin. 1999. *Random Selection in Politics*. Westport, CT: Praeger.

Chambers, Simone. 2003. Deliberative Democratic Theory. *Annual Review of Political Science* 6: 307–26.

Chambers, Simone. 2004. Behind Closed Doors: Publicity, Secrecy, and The Quality Of Deliberation. *Journal of Political Philosophy* 12: 389–410.

Chambers, Simone. 2005. Measuring Publicity's Effect. *Acta Politica* 40: 255–66.

Chambers, Simone. 2009. Rhetoric and the Public Sphere: Has Deliberative Democracy Abandoned Mass Democracy? *Political Theory* 37: 323–50.

Chambers, Simone. 2012. Deliberation and Mass Democracy. Pp. 52–71 in *Deliberative Systems*, edited by John Parkinson and Jane Mansbridge. Cambridge University Press.

Chandler, Daniel. 2000. An Introduction to Genre Theory. MCS Site, University of Wales, Aberystwyth. Available from www.aber.ac.uk/media/Documents/intgenre/intgenre1.html, accessed 12 May 2010.

Cheng, Antony S., and Janet D. Fiero. 2005. Collaborative Learning and the Public's Stewardship of its Forests. Pp. 164–73 in *The Deliberative Democracy Handbook: Strategies for Effective Civic Engagement in the 21st Century*, edited by John Gastil and Peter Levine. San Francisco, CA: Jossey-Bass.

Chong, Dennis, and James N. Druckman. 2007. Framing Public Opinion in Competitive Democracies. *American Political Science Review* 101: 637–55.

Christiano, Thomas. 2012. Rational Deliberation among Experts and Citizens. Pp. 27–51 in *Deliberative Systems*, edited by John Parkinson and Jane Mansbridge. Cambridge University Press.

CIRCLE. 2010. *Civic Skills and Federal Policy Fact Sheet*. Available from www.civicyouth.org/PopUps/FactSheets/FS_10_Civic_Skills_final.pdf, accessed 28 May 2013.

Clapp, Jennifer, and Peter Dauvergne. 2005. *Paths to a Green World: The Political Economy of the Environment*. Cambridge, MA: MIT Press.

Cohen, Geoffrey L. 2003. Party over Policy: The Dominating Impact of Group Influence on Political Beliefs. *Journal of Personality and Social Psychology* 85: 808–22.

Cohen, Joshua. 1989. Deliberation and Democratic Legitimacy. Pp. 17–34 in *The Good Polity: Normative Analysis of the State*, edited by Alan P. Hamlin and Philip Pettit. Oxford: Blackwell.

Cohen, Joshua. 1997. Procedure and Substance in Deliberative Democracy. Pp. 407–38 in *Deliberative Democracy: Essays on Reason and Politics*, edited by James Bohman and William Rehg. Cambridge, MA: MIT Press.

Cohen, Joshua. 2007. Deliberative Democracy. Pp. 219–36 in *Deliberation, Participation and Democracy: Can the People Govern?* edited by Shawn W. Rosenberg. New York: Palgrave Macmillan.

Cohen, Joshua, and Archon Fung. 2004. Radical Democracy. *Swiss Journal of Political Science* 10(4): 23–34.

Cohen, Joshua, and Joel Rogers. 1983. *On Democracy*. New York: Penguin Books.

Cohen, Joshua, and Joel Rogers. 1995. *Associations and Democracy*. London: Verso.

Colby, Anne, Elizabeth Beaumont, Thomas Ehrlich, and Josh Corngold. 2007. *Educating for Democracy: Preparing Undergraduates for Responsible Political Engagement*. San Francisco: Jossey-Bass.

Cole, Luke, and Sheila Foster. 2001. *From the Ground Up: Environmental Racism and the Rise of the Environmental Justice Movement*. New York University Press.

Collingwood, Loren, and Justin Reedy. 2012. Listening and Responding to Criticisms of Deliberative Civic Engagement. Pp. 233–60 in *Democracy in Motion: Evaluating the Practice and Impact of Deliberative Civic Engagement*, edited by Tina Nabatchi, John Gastil, G. Michael Weiksner, and Matt Leighninger. Oxford University Press.

Cooper, Emmeline, and Graham Smith. 2012. Organizing Deliberation: The Perspectives of Professional Participation Practitioners in Britain and Germany. *Journal of Public Deliberation* 8(1), Article 3: 1–39.

Corburn, Jason. 2003. Bringing Local Knowledge into Environmental Decision Making: Improving Urban Planning for Communities at Risk. *Journal of Planning Education and Research* 22: 420-433.

Cox, Gary W. and Mathew D. McCubbins. 2005. *Setting the Agenda: Responsible Party Government in the U.S. House of Representatives*. Cambridge University Press.

Craig, Jane M., and Carolyn W. Sherif. 1986. The Effectiveness of Men and Women in Problem-solving Groups as a Function of Gender Composition. *Sex Roles* 14: 453–66.

Crosby, Ned and Doug Nethercut. 2005. Citizens Juries: Creating a Trustworthy Voice of the People. Pp. 111–19 in *The Deliberative Democracy Handbook: Strategies for Effective Civic Engagement in the 21st Century*, edited by John Gastil and Peter Levine. San Francisco, CA: Jossey-Bass.

Cutler, Fred, Richard Johnston, R. Kenneth Carty, André Blais, and Patrick Fournier. 2008. Deliberation, Information and Trust: The BC Citizens' Assembly as Agenda-Setter. Pp. 166–91 in *Designing Deliberative Democracy: The British Columbia Citizens' Assembly*, edited by Mark E. Warren and Hilary Pearse. Cambridge: Cambridge University Press.

Dahl, Robert A. 1970. *After the Revolution? Authority in a Good Society*. New Haven, CT: Yale University Press.

Dahl, Robert A. 1989. *Democracy and its Critics*. New Haven, CT: Yale University Press.

Dalton, Russell J. 2004. *Democratic Challenges, Democratic Choices: The Erosion of Political Support in the Advanced Industrial Democracies*. Oxford University Press.

Danish Board of Technology. 2005. *New GM Plants – New Debate: The Final Document of the Citizens' Jury*. Copenhagen: Danish Board of Technology.

Danish Board of Technology. 2009. *World Wide Views on Global Warming: From the World's Citizens to the Climate Policy-Makers*. Copenhagen: Danish Board of Technology.

Davies, Todd, and Reid Chandler. 2012. Online Deliberation Design: Choices, Criteria, and Evidence. Pp. 103–31 in *Democracy in Motion: Evaluating the Practice and Impact of Deliberative Civic Engagement*, edited by Tina Nabatchi, John Gastil, G. Michael Weiksner, and Matt Leighninger. Oxford University Press.

della Porta, Donatella. 2006. *Globalization from Below: Transnational Activists and Protest Networks*. Minneapolis: University of Minnesota Press.

della Porta, Donatella. 2013. *Can Democracy be Saved? Participation, Deliberation and Social Movements*. Cambridge: Polity Press.

Delli Carpini, Michael X., Fay Lomax Cook, and Lawrence R. Jacobs. 2004. Public Deliberation, Discursive Participation, and Citizen Engagement: A Review of the Empirical Literature. *Annual Review of Political Science* 7: 315–44.

Democratic Party. 2012. 2012 Democratic National Platform: Moving America Forward. Available from www.democrats.org/democratic-national-platform, accessed 12 July 2013.

Devine, Dennis J., Laura Clayton, Benjamin B. Dunford, Rasmy Seying, and Jennifer Price. 2001. Jury Decision Making: 45 Years of Empirical Research on Deliberating Groups. *Psychology, Public Policy, and Law* 73: 622–727.

Dillard, Kara N. 2013. Envisioning the Role of Facilitation in Public Deliberation. *Journal of Applied Communication Research* 41: 217–35.

Doble Research Associates. 2006. *Democracy's Challenge: Reclaiming the Public's Role*. Dayton, OH: Kettering Foundation.

Druckman, James N. 2004. Political Preference Formation: Competition, Deliberation, and the (Ir)Relevance of Framing Effects. *American Political Science Review* 98: 671–86.

Druckman, James N., and Lawrence R. Jacobs. 2011. Segmented Representation: The Reagan White House and Disproportionate Responsiveness. Pp. 166–88 in *Who Gets Represented?*, edited by Peter K. Enns and Christopher Wlezien. New York: Russell Sage Foundation.

Druckman, James N., and Kjersten R. Nelson. 2003. Framing and Deliberation: How Citizens' Conversations Limit Elite Influence. *American Journal of Political Science* 47: 729–45.

Dryzek, John S. 1990. *Discursive Democracy: Politics, Policy, and Political Science*. Cambridge University Press.

Dryzek, John S. 1997. *The Politics of the Earth: Environmental Discourses*. Oxford University Press.

Dryzek, John S. 2000. *Deliberative Democracy and Beyond: Liberals, Critics, Contestations*. Oxford University Press.

Dryzek, John S. 2001. Legitimacy and Economy in Deliberative Democracy. *Political Theory* 29: 651–69.

Dryzek, John S. 2004. Legitimacy and Economy in Deliberative Democracy. Pp. 242–60 in *Contemporary Political Theory: A Reader*, edited by Colin Farrelly. London: Sage.

Dryzek, John S. 2007. Networks and Democratic Ideals: Equality, Freedom, and Communication. Pp. 262–73 in *Theories of Democratic Network Governance*, edited by Eva Sørensen and Jacob Torfing. New York: Palgrave Macmillan.

Dryzek, John. 2009. The Australian Citizens' Parliament: A World First. *Journal of Public Deliberation* 5(1), Article 9: 1–7.

Dryzek, John S. 2010. *Foundations and Frontiers of Deliberative Governance*. Oxford University Press.

Dryzek, John S. 2013. *The Politics of the Earth: Environmental Discourses*, 3rd ed. Oxford University Press.

Dryzek, John S., André Bächtiger, and Karolina Milewicz. 2011. Toward a Deliberative Global Citizens' Assembly. *Global Policy* 2: 33–42.

Dryzek, John S., Robert E. Goodin, Aviezer Tucker, and Bernard Reber. 2009. Promethean Elites Encounter Precautionary Publics: The Case of GM Foods. *Science, Technology & Human Values* 34: 263–88.

Dryzek, John S., and Simon Niemeyer. 2010. Pluralism and Meta-Consensus. Pp. 85–118 in *Foundations and Frontiers of Deliberative Governance*, by John S. Dryzek. Oxford University Press.

Dryzek, John S., and Aviezer Tucker. 2008. Deliberative Innovation to Different Effect: Consensus Conferences in Denmark, France, and the United States. *Public Administration Review* 68, 864–76.

Dutwin, David. 2003. The Character of Deliberation: Equality, Argument, and the Formation of Public Opinion. *International Journal of Public Opinion* 15: 239–64.

Eckersley, Robyn. 1992. *Environmentalism and Political Theory: Toward an Ecocentric Approach*. Albany: State University of New York Press.

Eliasoph, Nina. 1998. *Avoiding Politics: How Americans Produce Apathy in Everyday Life*. Cambridge University Press.

Elster, Jon. 1983. *Sour Grapes: Studies in the Subversion of Rationality*. Cambridge University Press.

Elster, Jon. 1998. Introduction. Pp. 1–18 in *Deliberative Democracy*, edited by Jon Elster. Cambridge University Press.

Elstub, Stephen. 2008. *Towards a Deliberative and Associational Democracy*. Edinburgh University Press.

Elstub, Stephen. 2010. Linking Micro Deliberative Democracy and Decision-Making: Trade-Offs between Theory and Practice in a Partisan Citizen Forum. *Representation* 46: 309–24.

Eskow, Richard. 2010. America "Speaks" on Saturday, but There's an Anti-Social Security Script. *HuffPost Politics*. Available from www.huffingtonpost.com/rj-eskow/america-speaks-on-saturda_b_622702.html, accessed 5 September 2013.

Esterling, Kevin, Archon Fung, and Taeku Lee. 2010. *The Difference Deliberation Makes: Evaluating the "Our Budget, Our Economy" Public Deliberation*. Washington, DC: America*Speaks*.

Estlund, David M. 1992. Who's Afraid of Deliberative Democracy? On the Strategic/Deliberative Dichotomy in Recent Constitutional Jurisprudence. *Texas Law Review* 71: 1437–77.

Estlund, David. 1997. Beyond Fairness and Deliberation: The Epistemic Dimension of Democratic Authority. Pp. 173–204 in *Deliberative Democracy: Essays on Reason and Politics*, edited by James Bohman and William Rehg. Cambridge, MA: MIT Press.

Evans, Sara M., and Harry C. Boyte. 1992. *Free Spaces: The Sources of Democratic Change in America*. University of Chicago Press.

Faden, Ruth R., Tom L. Beauchamp, and Nancy M. P. King. 1986. *A History and Theory of Informed Consent*. Oxford University Press.

Fagotto, Elena, and Archon Fung. 2006. *Embedded Deliberation: Entrepreneurs, Organizations, and Public Action*. William and Flora Hewlett Foundation. Available from www.wcgmf.org/pdf/publication_31.pdf, accessed July 22, 2013.

Farrar, Cynthia, Donald P. Green, Jennifer E. Green, David W. Nickerson, and Steven Shewfelt. 2009. Does Discussion Group Composition Affect Policy Preferences? Results from Three Randomized Experiments. *Political Psychology* 30: 615–47.

Fearon, James D. 1998. Deliberation as Discussion. Pp. 44–68 in *Deliberative Democracy*, edited by Jon Elster. Cambridge University Press.

Feldman, Lauren, Josh Pasek, Daniel Romer, and Kathleen Hall Jamieson. 2007. Identifying Best Practices in Civic Education: Lessons from the Student Voices Program. *American Journal of Education* 114: 75–100.

Ferejohn, John. 2008. Conclusion: The Citizens' Assembly Model. Pp. 192–213 in *Designing Deliberative Democracy: The British Columbia Citizens' Assembly*, edited by Mark E. Warren and Hilary Pearse. Cambridge University Press.

Festenstein, Matthew. 2002. Deliberation, Citizenship and Identity. Pp. 88–111 in *Democracy as Public Deliberation: New Perspectives*, edited by Maurizio Passerin d'Entrèves. Manchester University Press.

Festinger, Leon. 1957. *A Theory of Cognitive Dissonance*. Stanford University Press.

Fischer, Frank. 1995. *Evaluating Public Policy*. Chicago: Nelson-Hall Publishers.

Fishkin, James S. 1995. *The Voice of the People*. New Haven, CT: Yale University Press.

Fishkin, James S. 2009. *When the People Speak: Deliberative Democracy and Public Consultation*. Oxford University Press.

Fishkin, James S., and Peter Laslett, eds. 2003. *Debating Deliberative Democracy*. Oxford and Malden, MA: Blackwell Publishing.

Fishkin, James S., and Robert C. Luskin. 2005. Experimenting with a Democratic Ideal: Deliberative Polling and Public Opinion. *Acta Politica*, 40: 284–98.

Fishkin, James S., and Robert C. Luskin. 2006. Broadcasts of Deliberative Polls: Aspirations and Effects. *British Journal of Political Science* 36: 184–9.

Fiske, Susan T., and Shelley E. Taylor. 1991. *Social Cognition* (2nd ed.). New York, NY, England: Mcgraw-Hill Book Company.

Forster, E.M. 1965 [1938]. *Two Cheers for Democracy*. New York: Harcourt, Brace and World.

Fournier, Patrick, Henk van der Kolk, R. Kenneth Carty, André Blais and Jonathan Rose. 2011. *When Citizens Decide: Lessons from Citizens' Assemblies on Electoral Reform.* Oxford University Press.

Fraser, Nancy. 1992. Rethinking the Public Sphere: A Contribution to the Critique of Actually Existing Democracy. Pp. 109–42 in *Habermas and the Public Sphere*, edited by Craig Calhoun. Cambridge, MA: MIT Press.

Frey, Dieter. 1986. Recent Research on Selective Exposure to Information. *Advances in Experimental Social Psychology* 19: 41–80.

Fung, Archon. 2003. Recipes for Public Spheres: Eight Institutional Design Choices and Their Consequences. *Journal of Political Philosophy* 11: 338–67.

Fung, Archon. 2004. *Empowered Participation: Reinventing Urban Democracy.* Princeton University Press.

Fung, Archon. 2005. Deliberation before the Revolution: Toward an Ethics of Deliberative Democracy in an Unjust World. *Political Theory* 33: 397–419.

Fung, Archon. 2006. Varieties of Participation in Complex Governance. *Public Administration Review* 66: 66–75.

Fung, Archon. 2008. Citizen Participation in Government Innovations. Pp. 52–70 in *Innovations in Government*, edited by Sandford F. Borins. Washington, DC: Brookings Institution Press.

Fung, Archon. 2013. The Principle of Affected Interests: An Interpretation and Defense. Pp. 236–68 in *Representation: Elections and Beyond*, edited by Jack H. Nagel and Rogers M. Smith. Philadelphia: University of Pennsylvania Press.

Fung, Archon, Mary Graham, and David Weil. 2007. *Full Disclosure: The Perils and Promise of Transparency.* Cambridge University Press.

Fung, Archon, and Erik Olin Wright. 2003. Thinking about Empowered Participatory Governance. Pp. 3–44 in *Deepening Democracy: Institutional Innovations in Empowered Participatory Governance*, edited by Archon Fung and Erik Olin Wright. London: Verso.

Gastil, John. 1993. *Democracy in Small Groups: Participation, Decision Making, and Communication.* Philadelphia: New Society.

Gastil, John. 2008. *Political Communication and Deliberation.* Thousand Oaks, CA: Sage.

Gastil, John, and James P. Dillard. 1999. Increasing Political Sophistication through Public Deliberation. *Political Communication* 16: 3–23.

Gastil, John, Katie Knobloch, and Meghan Kelly. 2012. Evaluating Deliberative Public Events and Projects. Pp. 233–60 in *Democracy in Motion: Evaluating the Practice and Impact of Deliberative Civic Engagement*, edited by Tina Nabatchi, John Gastil, G. Michael Weiksner, and Matt Leighninger. Oxford University Press.

Gastil, John, and Peter Levine, eds. 2005. *The Deliberative Democracy Handbook.* San Francisco: Jossey-Bass.

Gastil, John, and Robert Richards. 2013. Making Direct Democracy Deliberative through Random Assemblies. *Politics & Society* 4: 253–81.

Gaventa, John. 1982. *Power and Powerlessness: Quiescence and Rebellion in an Appalachian Valley.* Urbana, IL: University of Illinois Press.

Gawande, Atul. 2010. *The Checklist Manifesto: How to Get Things Right.* New York: Metropolitan Books.

Geissel, Brigitte. 2012. Democratic Innovations: Theoretical and Empirical Challenges of Evaluation. Pp. 209–14 in *Evaluating Democratic Innovations: Curing the Democratic Malaise?*, edited by Brigitte Geissel and Kenneth Newton. London: Routledge.

Gibbs, Lois. 1994. Risk Assessment from a Community Perspective. *Environmental Impact Assessment Review* 14: 327–35.

Gibson, Christopher, and Michael Woolcock. 2008. Empowerment, Deliberative Development, and Local-Level Politics in Indonesia: Participatory Projects as a Source of Countervailing Power. *Studies in Comparative International Development* 43: 151–80.

Gibson, Cynthia, and Levine, Peter. 2003. *The Civic Mission of Schools.* New York: Carnegie Corporation of New York and the Center for Information and Research on Civic Learning.

Gilens, Martin. 2012. *Affluence and Influence: Economic Inequality and Political Power in America.* New York: Princeton University Press/Russell Sage Foundation.

Gimple, James G., and James R. Edwards. 1999. *The Congressional Politics of Immigration Reform.* Boston: Allyn & Bacon.

Goodin, Robert E. 2003. *Reflective Democracy.* Oxford University Press.

Goodin, Robert E. 2008. *Innovating Democracy: Democratic Theory and Practice after the Deliberative Turn.* Oxford University Press.

Goodin, Robert E. 2009. Rationalising Discursive Anomalies. *Theoria* 56(119): 1–13.

Goodin, Robert E., and John S. Dryzek. 2006. Deliberative Impacts: The Macro-Political Uptake of Mini-Publics. *Politics & Society* 34: 219–44.

Gould, Jonathan. 2011. *Guardian of Democracy: The Civic Mission of Schools.* Philadelphia: University of Pennsylvania Annenberg Public Policy Center.

Graber, Doris A. 1989. An Information Processing Approach to Public Opinion Analysis. Pp. 103–116 in *Rethinking Communication, Volume 2 Paradigm Exemplars*, edited by Brenda Dervin, Lawrence Grossberg, Barbara J. O'Keefe, and Ellen Wartella. Newbury Park, CA: Sage.

Grönlund, Kimmo, Maija Setälä, and Kaisa Herne. 2010. Deliberation and Civic Virtue: Lessons from a Citizen Deliberation Experiment. *European Political Science Review* 2: 95–117.

Grönlund, Kimmo, Kaisa Herne, and Maija Setälä. 2013. Deliberation within and across Enclaves – Opinion and Knowledge Change in an Experiment. Paper presented at public research seminar in Political Science, Åbo Akademi 4 April.

Gutmann, Amy, and Dennis F. Thompson. 1996. *Democracy and Disagreement.* Cambridge, MA: Harvard University Press.

Gutmann, Amy, and Dennis F. Thompson. 2004. *Why Deliberative Democracy?* Cambridge, MA: Belknap Press.

Gutmann, Amy, and Dennis Thompson. 2012. *The Spirit of Compromise: Why Governing Demands It and Campaigning Undermines It.* Princeton University Press.

Habermas, Jürgen. 1984. *The Theory of Communicative Action: Reason and Rationalization of Society, Vol. I.* Trans. Thomas McCarthy. Boston: Beacon Press.

Habermas, Jürgen. 1987. *The Theory of Communicative Action: The Critique of Functionalist Reason, Vol. II.* Trans. Thomas McCarthy. Boston: Beacon Press.

Habermas, Jürgen. 1989 [1962]. *The Structural Transformation of the Public Sphere: An Inquiry into a Category of Bourgeois Society.* Trans. Thomas Burger with Frederick Lawrence. Cambridge, MA: MIT Press.

Habermas, Jürgen. 1990. *Moral Consciousness and Communicative Action.* Trans. Christian Lenhardt and Shierry Weber Nicholsen. Cambridge, MA: MIT Press.

Habermas, Jürgen. 1996a. *Between Facts and Norms: Contributions to a Discourse Theory of Law and Democracy.* Trans. William Rehg. Cambridge, MA: MIT Press.

Habermas, Jürgen. 1996b. Reply to Symposium Participants. *Cardozo Law Review* 17: 1477–557.

Habermas, Jürgen. 1997. Popular Sovereignty as Procedure. Pp. 35–66 in *Deliberative Democracy: Essays on Reason and Politics*, edited by James Bohman and William Rehg. Cambridge, MA: MIT Press.

Habermas, Jürgen. 2001. Constitutional Democracy: A Paradoxical Union of Contradictory Principles? *Political Theory* 29: 766–81.

Habermas, Jürgen. 2005. Concluding Comments on Empirical Approaches to Deliberative Politics. *Acta Politica* 40: 384–92.

Habermas, Jürgen. 2006. *Time of Transitions*, edited and translated by Ciaran Cronin and Max Pensky. Cambridge: Polity Press.

Hansen, Mogens Herman. 2008. Direct Democracy, Ancient and Modern. Pp. 37–54 in *The Ashgate Research Companion to the Politics of Democratization in Europe: Concepts and Histories*, edited by Kari Palonen, Tuija I. Pulkkinen, and José María Rosales. Farnham, UK: Ashgate Publishing.

Hart, Stephen. 1992. *What Does the Lord Require?* Oxford University Press.

Hajnal, Zoltan. 2010. *America's Uneven Democracy: Race, Turnout, and Representation in City Politics.* Cambridge University Press.

Halle, David. 1984. *America's Working Man: Work, Home, and Politics among Blue Collar Property Owners.* University of Chicago Press.

Hamilton, Alexander, John Jay, and James Madison. 2000[1779]. *The Federalist Papers.* New York: Modern Library.

Hammond IV, Allen, and Chad Raphael. 2006. Municipal Broadband: A Background Briefing Paper. Broadband For All? Available from www.broadbandforall.org/app/briefing_paper.doc, accessed 10 September 2013. Hannaford-Agor, Paula, Valerie P. Hans, and G. Thomas Munsterman. 2000. Permitting Jury Discussions During Trial: Impact of the Arizona Reform. *Law and Human Behavior* 24: 359–81.

Hannigan, John A. 2006. *Environmental Sociology: A Social Constructionist Perspective, 2d Ed.* New York and London: Routledge.

Hansen, Allan Dreyer. 2007. Governance Networks and Participation. Pp. 247–61 in *Theories of Democratic Network Governance*, edited by Eva Sørensen and Jacob Torfing. New York: Palgrave Macmillan.

Hardin, Russell. 1995. *One for All: The Logic of Group Conflict*. Princeton University Press.

Haslam, S. Alexander, Penelope J. Oakes, Katharine J. Reynolds, and John C. Turner. 1999. Social Identity Salience and the Emergence of Stereotype Consensus. *Personality and Social Psychology Bulletin* 25: 809–18.

Haug, Christoph, and Simon Teune. 2008. Identifying Deliberation in Social Movement Assemblies: Challenges of Comparative Participant Observation. *Journal of Public Deliberation* 4(1), Article 8. Available from www.services. bepress.com/jpd/vol4/iss1/art8/, accessed 8 December 2008.

Hays, R. Allen. 2001. *Who Speaks for the Poor? National Interest Groups and Social Policy*. New York: Routledge.

Held David. 1996. *Models of Democracy*. Stanford University Press.

Heller, Patrick. 2005. Reinventing Public Power in the Age of Globalization: Decentralization and the Transformation of Movement Politics in Kerala. Pp. 79–106 in *Social Movements in India: Poverty, Power, and Politics*, edited by Raka Ray and Mary Katzenstein. New York: Rowman and Littlefield.

Hendriks, Carolyn M. 2005. Consensus Conferences and Planning Cells: Lay Citizen Deliberations. Pp. 80–110 in *The Deliberative Democracy Handbook: Strategies for Effective Civic Engagement in the 21st Century*, edited by John Gastil and Peter Levine. San Francisco, CA: Jossey-Bass.

Hendriks, Carolyn M. 2006a. Integrated Deliberation: Reconciling Civil Society's Dual Role in Deliberative Democracy. *Political Studies* 54: 486–508.

Hendriks, Carolyn M. 2006b. When the Forum Meets Interest Politics: Strategic Uses of Public Deliberation. *Politics and Society* 34: 571–602.

Hendriks, Carolyn M. 2011. *The Politics of Public Deliberation: Citizen Engagement and Interest Advocacy*. London: Palgrave Macmillan.

Hendriks, Carolyn M., and Carson, Lyn. 2008. Can the Market Help the Forum? Negotiating the Commercialization of Deliberative Democracy. *Policy Sciences*, 41: 293–313.

Hendriks, Carolyn M., John S. Dryzek, and Christian Hunold. 2007. Turning up the Heat: Partisanship in Deliberative Innovation. *Political Studies* 55: 362–83.

Hetherington, Marc J. 2005. *Why Trust Matters: Declining Political Trust and the Demise of American Liberalism*. Princeton University Press.

Hetherington, Marc J., and Jason A. Husser. 2012. How Trust Matters: The Changing Political Relevance of Political Trust. *American Journal of Political Science* 56: 312–25.

Hibbing, John R., and Elizabeth Theiss-Morse. 2002. *Stealth Democracy: Americans' Beliefs about How Government Should Work*. Cambridge University Press.

Hickey, Roger. 2010. In Deficit "Town Meetings," People Reject America Speaks' Stacked Deck. *HuffPost Business*. Available from www.huffingtonpost.com/roger-hickey/in-deficit-town-meetings_b_627030.html, accessed 5 September 2013.

Hill, Kim Quaile, and Jan E. Leighley. 1992. The Policy Consequences of Class Bias in State Electorates. *American Journal of Political Science* 36: 351–65.

Hill, Kim Quaile, Jan E. Leighley, and Angela Hinton-Andersson. 1995. Lower-Class Mobilization and Policy Linkage in the U.S. States. *American Journal of Political Science* 39: 75–86.

Hirst, Paul. 1994. *Associative Democracy: New Forms of Economic and Social Governance*. Amherst, MA: University of Massachusetts Press.

Hochschild, Jennifer. 1981. *What's fair?* Cambridge, MA: Harvard University Press.

Hoexter, Michael. 2010. The America Speaks Budget Deficit "Townhall" of June 26: Folk Economics In Action Pt. 1. Available from www.metaeconomics. wordpress.com/2010/07/04/deficittownhall/, accessed 26 September 2013.

Hogg, Michael A., and Sarah C. Hains. 1998. Friendship and Group Identification: A New Look at the Role of Cohesiveness in Groupthink. *European Journal of Social Psychology* 28: 323–41.

Hogg, Michael A., John C. Turner, and Barbara Davidson. 1990. Polarized Norms and Social Frames of Reference: A Test of the Self-Categorization Theory of Group Polarization. *Basic and Applied Social Psychology* 11: 77–100.

Horkheimer, Max. 1982. *Critical Theory: Selected Essays*. Trans. Matthew J. O'Connell. New York: Continuum.

Immigration Policy Center. 2012. Who and Where the DREAMers are, Revised Estimates. Available from www.immigrationpolicy.org/just-facts/who-and-where-dreamers-are-revised-estimates, accessed 9 July 2014.

Involve and National Consumer Council. 2008. *Deliberative Public Engagement: Nine Principles*. London, National Consumer Council.

International Association for Public Participation. ND. IAP2's Code of Ethics for Public Participation Practitioners. Available from www.iap2.affiniscape. com/displaycommon.cfm?an=1&subarticlenbr=8, accessed 11 September 2013.

Irwin, Alan. 2006. The Politics of Talk: Coming to Terms with the 'New' Scientific Governance. *Social Studies of Science* 36: 299–320.

Isaac, T.M. Thomas, and Patrick Heller. 2003. Democracy and Development: Decentralized Planning in Kerala. Pp. 77–110 in *Deepening Democracy*, edited by Archon Fung and Erik Olin Wright. London: Verso.

Issues Deliberation Australia, the Centre for Aboriginal Economic Policy Research at the Australian National University, the Hawke Research Institute at the University of South Australia, and the Centre for Australian Studies. 2001. *Australia Deliberates: Reconciliation – Where From Here?* Available from www.docstoc.com/docs/13120611/AUSTRALIA-DELIBERATES-RECONCILIATION – WHERE-FROM-HERE-FINAL-REPORT, accessed 12 August 2013.

Iyengar, Shanto, and Donald Kinder. 1987. *News that Matters*. University of Chicago Press.

Jackman, Simon, and Paul M. Sniderman. 2006. The Limits of Deliberative Discussion: A Model of Everyday Political Arguments. *Journal of Politics* 68: 272–83.

Jacobs, Lawrence R., and Theda Skocpol, eds. 2005. *Inequality and American Democracy: What We Know and What We Need to Learn.* New York: Russell Sage Foundation.

Jacobs, Lawrence, Fay Lomax Cook, and Michael X. Delli Carpini. 2009. *Talking Together: Public Deliberation and Political Participation in America.* University of Chicago Press.

Janis, Irving L. 1972. *Victims of Groupthink.* New York: Houghton Mifflin.

Janis, Irving L. 1982. *Groupthink: Psychological Studies of Policy Decisions and Fiascoes,* 2nd ed. Boston: Houghton Mifflin.

Johnson, Richard A., and Gary I. Schulman. 1989. Gender-role Composition and Role Entrapment in Decision-making Groups. *Gender and Society* 3: 355–72.

Joint Venture: Silicon Valley Network. 2005. A Vision of a Wireless Silicon Valley. Available from www.jointventure.org/images/stories/pdf/WirelessSiliconValleyVision.pdf, accessed 29 September 2013.

Jørgensen, Michael Søgaard. 2012. A Pioneer in Trouble: Danish Board of Technology Are Facing Problems. *European Association for the Study of Science and Tecnhology Review* 31(1). Available from easst.net/?page_id=883, accessed 2 December 2013.

Joss, Simon. 1998. Danish Consensus Conferences as a Model of Participatory Technology Assessment: An Impact Study of Consensus Conferences on Danish Parliament and Danish Public Debate. *Science and Public Policy* 25: 2–22.

Kadlec, Alison, and Will Friedman. 2007. Deliberative Democracy and the Problem of Power. *Journal of Public Deliberation* 3(1), Article 8. Available from www.services.bepress.com/jpd/vol3/iss1/art8/, accessed 17 July 2008.

Kahan, Dan M., Paul Slovic, Donald Braman, and John Gastil. 2006. Fear of Democracy: A Cultural Evaluation of Sunstein on Risk. *Harvard Law Review* 119: 1071–109.

Kahne, Joseph E., and Ellen Middaugh. 2008. *Democracy for Some: The Civic Opportunity Gap in High School.* Washington, DC: The Center for Information and Research on Civic Learning.

Kahne, Joseph E., and Susan E. Sporte. 2008. Developing Citizens: The Impact of Civic Learning Opportunities on Students' Commitment to Civic Participation. *American Educational Research Journal,* 45: 738–66.

Kameda, Tatsuya 1991. Procedural Influence in Small-group Decision Making: Deliberation Style and Assigned Decision Rule. *Journal of Personality and Social Psychology* 61: 245–56.

Kanter, Rosabeth Moss. 1977. *Men and Women of the Corporation.* New York: Basic Books.

Kaplan, Martin F., and Charles E. Miller. 1987. Group Decision-making and Normative versus Informational Influence: Effects of Type of Issue and Assigned Decision Rule. *Journal of Personality and Social Psychology* 53: 306–13.

Karpowitz, Christopher F. 2006. *Having a Say: Public Hearings, Deliberation, and Democracy in America*. Ph.D. diss., Department of Politics, Princeton University.

Karpowitz, Christopher F., and Jane Mansbridge. 2005. Disagreement and Consensus: The Importance of Dynamic Updating in Public Deliberation. Pp. 237–53 in *The Deliberative Democracy Handbook: Strategies for Effective Civic Engagement in the 21st Century*, edited by John Gastil and Peter Levine. San Francisco, CA: Jossey-Bass.

Karpowitz, Christopher F., and Tali Mendelberg. 2007. How People Deliberate about Justice: Groups, Gender, and Decision Rules. Pp. 101–29 in *Deliberation, Participation and Democracy: Can the People Govern?*, edited by Shawn W. Rosenberg. New York: Palgrave Macmillan.

Karpowitz, Christopher F., and Tali Mendelberg. 2008. Groups, Norms, and Gender: Initial Results from the Deliberative Justice Experiment. Paper Presented at the Annual Meeting of the American Political Science Association, Boston, MA, 28–31 August.

Karpowitz, Christopher F., and Tali Mendelberg. 2011. An Experimental Approach to Citizen Deliberation. Pp. 258–71 in *Cambridge Handbook of Experimental Political Science*, edited by James N. Druckman, Donald P. Green, James H. Kuklinski, and Arthur Lupia. Cambridge University Press.

Karpowitz, Christopher F., and Tali Mendelberg. 2014. *The Silent Sex: Gender, Deliberation, and Institutions*. Princeton University Press.

Karpowitz, Christopher F., Tali Mendelberg, and Lee Shaker. 2012. Gender Inequality in Deliberative Participation. *American Political Science Review* 106: 533–47.

Keeter, Scott, Cliff Zukin, Molly Andolina, and Krista Jenkins. 2002. *The Civic and Political Health of the Nation: A Generational Portrait*. Available from www.pollcats.net/downloads/civichealth.pdf, accessed 28 June 2013.

Kinder, Donald R., and Lynn M. Sanders. 1996. *Divided by Color: Racial Politics and Democratic Ideals*. University of Chicago Press.

Kinney, Bo. 2012. Deliberation's Contribution to Community Capacity Building. Pp. 163–80 in *Democracy in Motion: Evaluating the Practice and Impact of Deliberative Civic Engagement*, edited by Tina Nabatchi, John Gastil, G. Michael Weiksner, and Matt Leighninger. Oxford University Press.

Kleinman, Daniel Lee, Jason A. Delborne, and Ashley A. Anderson. 2011. Engaging Citizens: The High Cost of Citizen Participation In High Technology. *Public Understanding of Science* 20: 221–40.

Knight, Jack, and James Johnson. 1997. What Sort of Political Equality Does Deliberative Democracy Require? Pp. 279–319 in *Deliberative Democracy: Essays on Reason and Politics*, edited by James Bohman and William Rehg. Cambridge, MA: MIT Press.

Knobloch, Katherine R., John Gastil, Justin Reedy, and Katherine Cramer Walsh. 2013. Did They Deliberate? Applying an Evaluative Model of Democratic Deliberation to the Oregon Citizens' Initiative Review. *Journal of Applied Communication Research* 41: 105–25.

Kock, Christian. 2007. Norms of Legitimate Dissensus. *Informal Logic* 27: 179–96.

Kratochwil, Friedrich V. 1989. *Rules, Norms, and Decisions: On the Conditions of Practical and Legal Reasoning in International Relations and Domestic Affairs.* Cambridge University Press.

Kuklinski, James H., and Paul J. Quirk. 2000. Reconsidering the Rational Public: Cognition, Heuristics, and Mass Opinion. Pp. 153–82 in *Elements of Reason: Cognition, Choice, and the Bounds of Rationality*, edited by Arthur Lupia, Mathew D. McCubbins, and Samuel L. Popkin. Cambridge University Press.

Kunda, Ziva. 1990. The Case for Motivated Reasoning. *Psychological Bulletin* 108: 480–98.

Kuyper, Jonathan W. 2012. Deliberative Democracy and the Neglected Dimension of Leadership. *Journal of Public Deliberation* 8(1), Article 4, 1–32.

Lacy, Stephen, and Daniel Riffe. 1996. Sampling Error and Selecting Intercoder Reliability Samples for Nominal Content Categories: Sins of Omission and Commission in Mass Communication Quantitative Research. *Journalism and Mass Communication Quarterly* 73: 969–73.

Lang, Amy. 2008. Agenda-setting in Deliberative Forums: Expert Influence and Citizen Autonomy in the British Columbia Citizens' Assembly. Pp. 85–105 in *Designing Deliberative Democracy: The British Columbia Citizens' Assembly*, edited by Mark E. Warren and Hilary Pearse. Cambridge University Press.

Lau, Richard R., and David P. Redlawsk. 2001. Advantages and Disadvantages of Cognitive Heuristics in Political Decision Making. *American Journal of Political Science* 45: 951–71.

Lazarsfeld, Paul F., Bernard Berelson, and Hazel Gaudet. 1944. *The People's Choice.* New York: Columbia University Press.

Lee, Caroline W. 2011. Five Assumptions Academics Make about Public Deliberation, and Why They Deserve Rethinking. *Journal of Public Deliberation* 7(1), Article 7. Available from www.publicdeliberation.net/jpd/vol7/iss1/art7, accessed 10 July 2013.

Leib, Ethan J. 2004. *Deliberative Democracy in America: A Proposal for a Popular Branch of Government.* University Park, PA: Pennsylvania State Press.

Leighninger, Matt. 2012. Mapping Deliberative Civic Engagement: Pictures from a (R)evolution. Pp. 19–42 in *Democracy in Motion: Evaluating the Practice and Impact of Deliberative Civic Engagement*, edited by Tina Nabatchi, John Gastil, G. Michael Weiksner, and Matt Leighninger. Oxford University Press.

Levine, Peter, Archon Fung, and John Gastil. 2005. Future Directions for Public Deliberation. Pp. 271–88 in *The Deliberative Democracy Handbook: Strategies for Effective Civic Engagement in the 21st Century*, edited by John Gastil and Peter Levine. San Francisco, CA: Jossey-Bass.

Levine, Peter, and Rose Marie Nierras. 2007. Activists' views of deliberation. *Journal of Public Deliberation* 3(1), Article 4. Available from www.services. bepress.com/jpd/vol3/iss1/art4/, accessed 17 July 2008.

Lezaun, Javier, and Linda Soneryd. 2007. Consulting Citizens: Technologies of Elicitation and the Mobility of Publics. *Public Understanding of Science* 16: 279–97.

Lind, E. Allan, and Tom R. Tyler. 1988. *The Social Psychology of Procedural Justice*. New York: Plenum Press.

List, Christian, Robert C. Luskin, James S. Fishkin and Iain McLean. 2013. Deliberation, Single-Peakedness, and the Possibility of Meaningful Democracy: Evidence from Deliberative Polls. *The Journal of Politics* 75: 80–95.

Lowi, Theodore J. 1969. *The End of Liberalism: Ideology, Policy, and the Crisis of Public Authority*. New York: W.W. Norton & Company.

Lukensmeyer, Carolyn J. 2010. Written Testimony for the National Commission on Fiscal Responsibility and Reform. Available from www.usabudgetdiscussion.org/written-testimony-for-the-national-commission-on-fiscal-responsibility-and-reform/, accessed 5 September 2013.

Lukensmeyer, Carolyn J., Joe Goldman, and Steven Brigham. 2005. A Town Meeting for the Twenty-First Century. Pp. 154–63 in *The Deliberative Democracy Handbook: Strategies for Effective Civic Engagement in the 21st Century*, edited by John Gastil and Peter Levine. San Francisco, CA: Jossey-Bass.

Lupia, Arthur. 1994. Shortcuts versus Encyclopedias: Information and Voting Behavior in California Insurance Reform Elections. *American Political Science Review* 88: 63–76.

Lupia, Arthur, and Mathew D. McCubbins. 1994. *The Democratic Dilemma: Can Citizens Learn What They Need to Know?* Cambridge University Press.

Luskin, Robert C., and James S. Fishkin. 2002. Deliberation and "Better Citizens." Paper presented at the Annual Joint Sessions of Workshops of the European Consortium for Political Research, Turin, Italy, 22–27 March.

Luskin, Robert C., Fishkin, James S., and Jowell, Roger. 2002. Considered Opinions: Deliberative Polling in Britain. *British Journal of Political Science* 32: 455–87.

Lyu, Hyeon-Suk. 2008. Participative Deliberation and Policy Proposals on Government Websites in Korea: Analysis from a Habermasian Public Deliberation Model. *International Review of Public Administration* 12(2): 45–58.

Macedo, Stephen. 1999. Introduction. Pp. 3–16 in *Deliberative Politics: Essays on Democracy and Disagreement*, edited by Stephen Macedo. Oxford University Press.

Macedo, Stephen, Yvette M. Alex-Assensoh, Jeffrey M. Berry, Michael Brintnall, David E. Campbell, Luis Ricardo Fraga, Archon Fung, William A. Galston, Christopher F. Karpowitz, Margaret Levi, Meira Levinson, Keena Lipsitz, Richard G. Niemi, Robert D. Putnam, Wendy M. Rahn, Rob Reich, Robert R. Rodgers, Todd Swanstrom, and Katherine Cramer Walsh. 2005. *Democracy at Risk: How Political Choices Undermine Citizen Participation, and What We Can Do about It*. Washington, DC: Brookings.

Mackenzie, Michael K., and Mark E. Warren. 2012. Two trust-based uses of minipublics in democratic systems. Pp. 95–124 in *Deliberative Systems*, edited by John Parkinson and Jane Mansbridge. Cambridge University Press.

Mackie, Gerry. 2004. *Democracy Defended*. Cambridge University Press.

MacNeil/Lehrer Productions and Center for Deliberative Democracy. 2010. *By the People: Hard Times, Hard Choices*. Stanford, CA: Center for Deliberative Democracy.

Majone, Giandomenico. 1989. *Evidence, Argument, and Persuasion in The Policy Process*. New Haven, CT: Yale University Press.

Manaster, Kenneth. 2013. *The American Legal System and Civic Engagement: Why We All Should Think Like Lawyers*. New York: Palgrave Macmillan.

Manin, Bernard. 1987. On Legitimacy and Political Deliberation. *Political Theory* 15: 338–68.

Mansbridge, Jane. 1983. *Beyond Adversary Democracy*. University of Chicago Press.

Mansbridge, Jane. 1996. Using Power/Fighting Power: The Polity. Pp. 46–66 in *Democracy and Difference: Contesting the Boundaries of the Political*, edited by Seyla Benhabib. Princeton University Press.

Mansbridge, Jane. 1999. Everyday Talk in the Deliberative System. Pp. 211–39 in *Deliberative Politics: Essays on Democracy and Disagreement*, edited by Stephen Macedo. Oxford University Press.

Mansbridge, Jane. 2003. Practice-thought-practice. Pp. 175–99 in *Deepening Democracy: Institutional Innovations in Empowered Participatory Governance*, edited by Archon Fung and Erik Olin Wright. London: Verso.

Mansbridge, Jane. 2007. 'Deliberative Democracy' or 'Democratic Deliberation'? Pp. 251–71 in *Deliberation, Participation and Democracy: Can the People Govern?*, edited by Shawn W. Rosenberg. New York: Palgrave Macmillan.

Mansbridge, Jane, James Bohman, Simone Chambers, David Estlund, Andreas Føllesdal, Archon Fung, Cristina Lafont, and Bernard Manin. 2010. The Place of Self-Interest and the Role of Power in Deliberative Democracy. *Journal of Political Philosophy* 18: 64–100.

Mansbridge, Jane, James Bohman, Simone Chambers, Thomas Christiano, Archon Fung, John Parkinson, Dennis F. Thompson, and Mark E. Warren. 2012. A Systemic Approach to Deliberative Democracy. Pp. 1–27 in *Deliberative Systems*, edited by John Parkinson and Jane Mansbridge. Cambridge University Press.

Mansbridge, Jane, Janette Hartz-Karp, Matthew Amengual, and John Gastil. 2006. Norms of Deliberation: An Inductive Study. *Journal of Public Deliberation* 2(1), Article 7. Available from www.services.bepress.com/jpd/vol2/iss1/art7/, accessed 17 July 2008.

Mapes, Kathleen. 2009. *Sweet Tyranny: Migrant Labor, Industrial Agriculture, and Imperial Politics*. Urbana and Chicago: University of Illinois Press.

Martí, José Luis. 2006. The Epistemic Conception of Deliberative Democracy Defended. Pp. 27–56 in *Deliberative Democracy and its Discontents*, edited by Samantha Besson and José Luis Martí. Aldershot: Ashgate.

Mathis, Jerome. 2011. Deliberation with Evidence. *American Political Science Review* 105: 516–29.

Matthews, David. 1999. *Politics for the People: Finding a Responsible Public Voice*, 2d ed. Chicago: University of Illinois Press.

McCarty, Nolan, Ketih T. Poole, and Howard Rosenthal. 2006. *Polarized America: The Dance of Ideology and Unequal Riches*. Cambridge, MA: MIT Press.

McVeigh, Rory. 2009. *The Rise of the Ku Klux Klan: Right-Wing Movements and National Politics*. Minneapolis: University of Minnesota Press.

Melucci, Alberto. 1996. *Challenging Codes: Collective Action in the Information Age*. Cambridge University Press.

Melville, Keith, Taylor L. Willingham, and John R. Dedrick. 2005. National Issues Forums: A network of communities promoting public deliberation. Pp. 37–58 in *The Deliberative Democracy Handbook: Strategies for Effective Civic Engagement in the 21st Century*, edited by John Gastil and Peter Levine. San Francisco, CA: Jossey-Bass.

Mendelberg, Tali. 2002. The Deliberative Citizen: Theory and Evidence. *Political Decision Making, Deliberation and Participation* 6: 151–93.

Mendelberg, Tali, Christopher F. Karpowitz, and Nicholas Goedert. 2014. Does Descriptive Representation Facilitate Women's Distinctive Voice? How gender Composition and Decision Rules Affect Deliberation. *American Journal of Political Science* 58: 291–306.

Mendelberg, Tali, Christopher F. Karpowitz, and J. Baxter Oliphant. 2014. Gender Inequality in Deliberation: Unpacking the Black Box of Interaction. *Perspectives on Politics* 12: 18–44.

Mercier, Hugo, and Hélène Landemore. 2012. Reasoning is for Arguing: Understanding the Successes and Failures of Deliberation. *Political Psychology* 33: 243–58.

Mill, John Stuart. 1998 [1861]. *Utilitarianism*. Oxford University Press.

Miller, David. 1992. Deliberative Democracy and Social Choice. *Political Studies* 40 (special issue): 54–67.

Montague, Peter (1998, Feb. 18). The Precautionary Principle. *Rachel's Environment & Health News* 586: 1–2.

Moore, Alfred. 2011a. Expert Authority in a Deliberative System. Paper presented at the General Conference of the European Consortium for Political Research, Reykjavik, 25–27 August.

Moscovici, Serge, and Marisa Zavalloni. 1969. The Group as a Polarizer of Attitudes. *Journal of Personality and Social Psychology* 12: 125–35.

Mouffe, Chantal. 1999. Deliberative Democracy or Agonistic Pluralism? *Social Research* 66: 745–58.

Mutz, Diana C. 2006. *Hearing the Other Side: Deliberative versus Participatory Democracy*. Cambridge University Press, 2006.

Mutz, Diana C. 2008. Is Deliberative Democracy a Falsifiable Theory? *Annual Review of Political Science* 11:521–8.

Myers, David G., and Paul J. Bach. 1974. Discussion Effects on Militarism-Pacifism. *Journal of Personality and Social Psychology* 30: 741–7.

Nabatchi, Tina. 2012. An Introduction to Deliberative Civic Engagement. Pp. 59–82 in *Democracy in Motion: Evaluating the Practice and Impact of Deliberative Civic Engagement*, edited by Tina Nabatchi, John Gastil, G. Michael Weiksner, and Matt Leighninger. Oxford University Press.

Nabatchi, Tina, John Gastil, G. Michael Weiksner, and Matt Leighninger, eds. 2012. *Democracy in Motion: Evaluating the Practice and Impact of Deliberative Civic Engagement*. Oxford University Press.

National Coalition for Dialogue & Deliberation, International Association for Public Participation, and the Co-Intelligence Institute. 2009. Core Principles for Public Engagement. Available from www.ncdd.org/rc/item/3643, accessed 11 September 2013.

National Telecommunications and Information Administration. 2000. *Falling through the Net: Toward Digital Inclusion*. Washington, DC: U.S. Government Printing Office.

Neblo, Michael. 2010. Change for the Better? Linking the Mechanisms of Deliberative Opinion Change to Normative Theory. Working paper, Department of Political Science, Ohio State University.

Neblo, Michael A., Kevin M. Esterling, Ryan P. Kennedy, David M.J. Lazer, and Anand E. Sokhey. 2010. Who Wants To Deliberate – And Why? *American Political Science Review* 104: 566–83.

Neiheisel, Jacob R., Paul A. Djupe, and Anand E. Sokhey. 2009. Veni, Vidi, Disseri: Churches and the Promise of Democratic Deliberation. *American Politics Research* 37: 614–43.

Nemeth, Charlan J. 1977. Interactions between Jurors as a Function of Majority vs. Unanimity Decision Rules. *Journal of Applied Social Psychology* 7: 38–56.

Nemeth, Charlan J., and Jack A. Goncalo. 2011. Rogues and Heroes: Finding Value in Dissent. Pp. 17–35 in *Rebels in Groups: Dissent, Deviance, Difference and Defiance*, edited by Jolanda Jetten and Matthew. J. Hornsey. Hoboken, NJ: Wiley.

New America Foundation and Center for International Media Action. 2006. *Building Constituencies for Spectrum Policy Change. First Report: Wireless Broadband and Public Needs*. Washington, DC: New America Foundation.

Newton, Kenneth. 2012a. Making Better Citizens? Pp. 137–62 in *Evaluating Democratic Innovations: Curing the Democratic Malaise?*, edited by Brigitte Geissel and Kenneth Newton. London: Routledge.

Newton, Kenneth. 2012b. Curing the Democratic Malaise with Democratic Innovations. Pp. 3–20 in *Evaluating Democratic Innovations: Curing the Democratic Malaise?*, edited by Brigitte Geissel and Kenneth Newton. London: Routledge.

Nickerson, Raymond S. 1998. Confirmation Bias: A Ubiquitous Phenomenon in Many Guises. *Review of General Psychology* 2: 175–220.

Niemann, Yolanda Flores. 2003. The Psychology of Tokenism. Pp. 100–18 in the *Handbook of Racial and Ethnic Minority Psychology*, edited by Guillermo Bernal, Joseph E. Trimble, A. Kathleen Burlew, and Frederick T. L. Long. Thousand Oaks, CA: Sage Publications.

Niemeyer, Simon. 2004. Deliberation in the Wilderness: Displacing Symbolic Politics. *Environmental Politics* 13: 347–72.

Niemeyer, Simon John, Selen Ayirtman, and Janette HartzKarp. 2008. Achieving Success in Large Scale Deliberation: Analysis of the Fremantle Bridge Community Engagement Process. Working paper 2008/1, Australian National

University. Available from www.deliberativedemocracy.anu.edu.au/sites/default/files/documents/working_papers/FremBridgeNiemeyeretal2007.pdf, accessed 3 August 2013.

Nussbaum, Martha. 2000. *Women and Human Development: The Capabilities Approach*. Cambridge University Press.

Obama, Barack. 2007. Senator Barack Obama's Announcement for President. Available from www.docstoc.com/docs/110825658/Full-Text-of-Senator-Barack-Obamas-Announcement-for-President, accessed 15 August 2013.

Ober, Josiah. 1989. *Mass and Elite in Democratic Athens: Rhetoric, Ideology, and the Power of the People*. Princeton University Press.

O'Brien, Mary. 2000. *Making Better Environmental Decisions: An Alternative to Risk Assessment*. Cambridge, MA: MIT Press.

Olson, Jr., Mancur. 1965. *The Logic of Collective Action: Public Goods and the Theory of Groups*. Cambridge, MA: Harvard University Press.

Osberg, Lars, Timothy M. Smeeding, and Jonathan Schwabish. 2004. Income Distribution and Public Social Expenditure: Theories, Effects, and Evidence. Pp. 821–59 in *Social Inequality*, edited by Kathryn M. Neckerman. New York: Russell Sage Foundation.

Ostrom, Mary Anne. 2006, October 8. Wireless Network Concerns Get Venting. *San Jose Mercury News*.

Page, Benjamin I. 1996. *Who Deliberates? Mass Media in Modern Democracy*. University of Chicago Press.

Page, Benjamin I., and Lawrence R. Jacobs. 2010. Understanding Public Opinion on Deficits and Social Security. Roosevelt Institute Working Papers #2. Available from www.nextnewdeal.net/wp.../06/tuespage-and-jacobs-public-opinion.pdf, accessed 5 September 2013.

Papandrea, Marie-Rose. 2008. Student Speech Rights in the Digital Age. *Florida Law Review* 60: 1027–102.

Parker, Ashley and Jonathan Weisman (2013, July 10). G.O.P. in House Resists Overhaul for Immigration. *New York Times*, A1.

Parkinson, John. 2006a. *Deliberating in the Real World: Problems of Legitimacy in Deliberative Democracy*. Oxford University Press.

Parkinson, John. 2006b. Rickety Bridges: Using the Media in Deliberative Democracy. *British Journal of Political Science* 36: 175–84.

Parkinson, John. 2006c. Of Scale and Straw Men: A Reply to Fishkin and Luskin. *British Journal of Political Science* 36: 189–92.

Parkinson, John. 2012a. Democratizing Deliberative Systems. Pp. 151–72 in *Deliberative Systems*, edited by John Parkinson and Jane Mansbridge. Cambridge University Press.

Parkinson, John. 2012b. *Democracy and Public Space: The Physical Sites of Democratic Performance*. Oxford University Press.

Pennock, Roland. 1979. *Democratic Political Theory*. Princeton University Press.

Phillips, Anne. 1995. *The Politics of Presence*. Oxford University Press.Piketty, Thomas, and Emmanuel Saez. 2003. Income Inequality in the United States, 1913–1998. *Quarterly Journal of Economics* 118: 1–39.

Pincock, Heather. 2012. Does Deliberation Make Better Citizens? Pp. 135–62 in *Democracy in Motion: Evaluating the Practice and Impact of*

Deliberative Civic Engagement, edited by Tina Nabatchi, John Gastil, G. Michael Weiksner, and Matt Leighninger. Oxford University Press.

Pitkin, Hanna Fenichel. 1967. *The Concept of Representation*. Berkeley: University of California Press.

Polletta, Francesca. 2002. *Freedom is an Endless Meeting: Democracy in American Social Movements*. University of Chicago Press.

Polletta, Francesca, and James M. Jasper. 2001. Collective Identity and Social Movements. *Annual Review of Sociology* 27: 283–305.

Popkin, Samuel L. 1991. *The Reasoning Voter: Communication and Persuasion in Presidential Campaigns*. University of Chicago Press.

Public Policy Polling. 2013. Congress Somewhere Below Cockroaches, Traffic Jams, and Nickelback in Americans' Esteem. Available from www.publicpolicypolling.com/main/2013/01/congress-somewhere-below-cockroaches-traffic-jams-and-nickleback-in-americans-esteem.html, accessed 19 November 2013.

Putnam, Robert D. 2000. *Bowling Alone: The Collapse and Revival of American Community*. New York: Simon and Schuster, 2000.

Quattrone, George A., and Edward E. Jones. 1980. The Perception of Variability within In-Groups and Out-Groups: Implications for the Law of Small Numbers. *Journal of Personality & Social Psychology* 38: 141–52.

Raphael, Chad. 2005. *Investigated Reporting: Muckrakers, Regulators, and the Struggle over Television Documentary*. Urbana, IL: University of Illinois Press.

Rask, Mikko, and Richard K. Worthington. 2012. Prospects of Deliberative Global Governance. *Journal of Environmental Science and Engineering B* 1: 556–65.

Rawls, John. 1971. *A Theory of Justice*. Cambridge, MA: Belknap Press.

Rawls, John. 1993. *Political Liberalism*. New York: Columbia University Press.

Reardon, Sara. 2011. Budget Cuts Threaten Denmark's Science Assessment Body. *ScienceInsider* (November 22). Available from news.sciencemag.org/funding/2011/11/budget-cuts-threaten-denmarks-science-assessment-body, accessed 2 December 2013.

Regenwetter, Michel, Bernard Grofman, A. A. J. Marley, and Ilia M. Tsetlin. 2006. *Behavioral Social Choice: Probabilistic Models, Statistical Inference, and Applications*. Cambridge University Press.

Republican Party. 2012. Republican Platform: We Believe in America. Available from www.gop.com/2012-republican-platform_reforming/, accessed 12 July 2013.

Rhee, June Woong, and Joseph N. Cappella. 1997. The Role of Political Sophistication in Learning from News: Measuring Schema Development. *Communication Research* 24: 197–233.

Rigby, Elizabeth, and Gerald C. Wright. 2011. Whose Statehouse Democracy? Policy Responsiveness to Poor versus Rich Constituents in Poor versus Rich States. Pp. 189–222 in *Who Gets Represented?*, edited by Peter K. Enns and Christopher Wlezien. New York: Russell Sage Foundation.

Riker, William H. 1982. *Liberalism against Populism: A Confrontation between the Theory of Democracy and the Theory of Social Choice*. San Francisco: Freeman.

Rose, James D. 2011. Diverse Perspectives on the Groupthink Theory – A Literary Review. *Emerging Leadership Journeys* 4(1): 37– 57.

Rosenberg, Shawn W., ed. 2007. *Deliberation, Participation and Democracy: Can the People Govern?* New York: Palgrave Macmillan.

Rostbøll, Christian F. 2005. Preferences and Paternalism on Freedom and Deliberative Democracy. *Political Theory* 33: 370– 96.

Rostbøll, Christian F. 2008. *Deliberative Freedom: Deliberative Democracy as Critical Theory*. Albany, NY: State University of New York Press.

Rowe, Gene, and Lynn J. Frewer. 2004. Evaluating Public-Participation Exercises: A Research Agenda. *Science, Technology and Human Values* 29: 512–56.

Rucht, Dieter. 2012. Deliberation as an Ideal and Practice in Progressive Social Movements. Pp. 112–34 in *Evaluating Democratic Innovations: Curing the Democratic Malaise?*, edited by Brigitte Geissel and Kenneth Newton. London: Routledge.

Ryfe, David. 2005. Does Deliberative Democracy Work? *Annual Review of Political Science* 8: 49–71.

Ryfe, David M. 2006. Narrative and Deliberation In Small Group Forums. *Journal of Applied Communication Research* 34: 72–93.

Ryfe, David M., and Brittany Stalsburg. 2012. The Participation and Recruitment Challenge. Pp. 43–58 in *Democracy in Motion: Evaluating the Practice and Impact of Deliberative Civic Engagement*, edited by Tina Nabatchi, John Gastil, G. Michael Weiksner, and Matt Leighninger. Oxford University Press.

Saenz, Delia S. 1994. Token Status and Problem-Solving Deficits: Detrimental Effects of Distinctiveness and Performance Monitoring. *Social Cognition* 12: 61–74.

Sanders, Lynn. 1997. Against Deliberation. *Political Theory* 25: 347–76.

San Francisco Department of Telecommunications and Information Services. 2007. *San Francisco Digital Inclusion Strategy*. Available from www. sfgov.org/site/tech_connect_index.asp?id=47976, accessed 12 December 2008.

Santa Clara University Center for Science, Technology, and Society and Broadband Institute of California. 2006. *Broadband for All? A Consensus Conference on Municipal Broadband. Final Report and Recommendations*. Available from www.broadbandforall.org/MBCCFinalReport.doc, accessed 12 December 2008.

Saunders, Harold H. 2011. *Sustained Dialogue in Conflicts: Transformation and Change*. New York: Palgrave Macmillan.

Schattschneider, Elmer E. 1960. *Semi-Sovereign People*. New York: Holt, Rinehart and Winston.

Scheufele, Dietram A., Matthew C. Nisbet, and Dominique Brossard. 2003. Pathways to Participation? Religion, Communication Contexts, and Mass Media. *International Journal of Public Opinion Research* 15: 300–24.

Schlozman, Kay Lehman, Sidney Verba, and Henry E. Brady, *The Unheavenly Chorus: Unequal Political Voice and the Broken Promise of American Democracy.* Princeton University Press, 2012.

Schor, Juliet. 2012. Forum. Pp. 45–50 in *Shopping for Good*, edited by Dara O'Rourke. Cambridge, MA: MIT Press.

Schudson Michael. 1998. *The Good Citizen: A History of American Civic Life.* New York: Free Press.

Schumpeter, Joseph A. 1942. *Capitalism, Socialism, and Democracy.* New York: Harper.

Sclove, Richard. 1996. Town Meetings on Technology. *Technology Review* 99(5): 24–31.

Scott, Esther. 2008. "Broadmoor Lives": A New Orleans Neighborhood's Battle to Recover from Hurricane Katrina. Kennedy School of Government Case Program C14-08-1893.0. Cambridge, MA: Harvard University.

Sen, Amartya. 1999. *Development as Freedom.* New York: Knopf.

Setälä, Maija, Kimmo Grönlund, and Kaisa Herne. 2010. Citizen Deliberation on Nuclear Power: A Comparison of Two Decision-Making Methods. *Political Studies* 58: 688–714.

Simon, Adam F., and Tracy Sulkin. 2002. Discussion's Impact on Political Allocations: An Experimental Approach. *Political Analysis* 10: 403–12.

Sintomer, Yves, Carsten Herzberg, and Anja Röcke. 2008. Participatory Budgeting in Europe: Potentials and Challenges. *International Journal of Urban and Regional Research* 32: 164–78.

Siu, Alice. 2008. Look Who's Talking: Examining Social Influence, Opinion Change and Argument Quality in Deliberation. PhD diss., Stanford University.

Skocpol, Theda. 2003. *Diminished Democracy: From Membership to Management in American Civic Life.* Norman, OK: University of Oklahoma Press.

Skocpol, Theda, and Vanessa Williamson. 2011. *The Tea Party and the Remaking of Republican Conservatism.* New York: Oxford University Press.

Skogan, Wesley G., and Susan M. Hartnett. 1999. *Community Policing, Chicago Style.* Oxford University Press.

Smith, Eliot R., and Diane M. Mackie. 2000. *Social Psychology, 2d ed.* Philadelphia: Psychology Press.

Smith, Graham. 2005. *Beyond the Ballot: 57 Democratic Innovations from Around the World.* London: Power Inquiry.

Smith, Graham. 2009. *Democratic Innovations: Designing Institutions for Citizen Participation.* Cambridge University Press.

Smith, Graham, and Corinne Wales. 2000. Citizens' Juries and Deliberative Democracy. *Political Studies* 48: 51–65.

Smith, Ron F. 2008. *Ethics in Journalism*, 6th Ed. Malden, MA: Blackwell Publishing.

Snow, David A., E. Burke Rochford, Steven K. Worden, and Robert D. Benford. 1986. Frame Alignment Processes, Micromobilization, and Movement Participation. *American Sociological Review* 51: 464–81.

Sørensen, Eva, and Jacob Torfing. 2007. Introduction: Governance Network Research: Towards a Second Generation. Pp. 1–24 in *Theories of Democratic*

Network Governance, edited by Eva Sørensen and Jacob Torfing. New York: Palgrave Macmillan.

South Dakota Issues Forums. 2009. *The Role of Citizens in the Legislative Process*. Rapid City, SD: Chiesman Foundation for Democracy.

Spears, Russell, Martin Lea, and Stephen Lee. 1990. De-Individuation and Group Polarization in Computer-Mediated Communication. *British Journal of Social Psychology* 29: 121–34.

Spragens, Thomas A. 1990. *Reason and Democracy*. Durham, NC: Duke University Press.

Steiner, Jürg. 2012. *The Foundations of Deliberative Democracy: Empirical Research and Normative Implications*. Cambridge University Press.

Steiner, Jürg, André Bächtiger, Markus Spörndli, and Marco R. Steenbergen. 2004. *Deliberative Politics in Action: Analyzing Parliamentary Discourse*. Cambridge University Press.

Sturgis, Patrick, Caroline Roberts, and Nick Allum. 2005. A Different Take on the Deliberative Poll Information, Deliberation, and Attitude Constraint. *Public Opinion Quarterly* 69: 30–65.

Sunstein, Cass R. 1991. Preferences and Politics. *Philosophy and Public Affairs* 20: 3–34.

Sunstein, Cass R. 1993. *The Partial Constitution*. Cambridge, MA: Harvard University Press.

Sunstein, Cass R. 1997. Deliberation, Democracy, Disagreement. Pp. 93–117 in *Justice and Democracy: Cross-cultural Perspectives*, edited by Ron Bontekoe and Marietta Stepaniants. Honolulu: University of Hawaii Press.

Sunstein, Cass R. 1999. Agreement without Theory. Pp. 123–50 in *Deliberative Politics: Essays on Democracy and Disagreement*, edited by Stephen Macedo. Oxford University Press.

Sunstein, Cass R. 2000. Deliberative Trouble? Why Groups Go to Extremes. *Yale Law Journal* 110: 74.

Sunstein, Cass R. 2002. The Law of Group Polarization. *Journal of Political Philosophy* 10: 175–95.

Sunstein, Cass R. 2005. *Laws of Fear: Beyond the Precautionary Principle*. Cambridge University Press.

SunWolf. 2007. *Practical Jury Dynamics: From One Juror's Trial Perceptions to the Group's Decision-making Processes*, 2d ed. Charlottesville, VA: LexisNexis.

Taber, Charles S., and Milton Lodge. 2006. Motivated Skepticism in the Evaluation of Political Beliefs. *American Journal of Political Science* 50: 755–69.

Talpin, Julien. 2011. *Schools of Democracy: How Ordinary Citizens (Sometimes) Become Competent in Participatory Budgeting Institutions*. Colchester: ECPR Press.

Talpin, Julien. 2012. When Democratic Innovations Let the People Decide. Pp. 184–206 in *Evaluating Democratic Innovations: Curing the Democratic Malaise?*, edited by Brigitte Geissel and Kenneth Newton. London: Routledge.

Tepper, Steven J. 2004. Setting Agendas and Designing Alternatives: Policymaking and the Strategic Role of Meetings. *Review of Policy Research* 21, 523–42.

Tetlock, Philip E., Randall S. Peterson, Charles McGuire, Shi-jie Chang, and Peter Feld. 1992. Assessing Political Group Dynamics: The Test of the Groupthink Model. *Journal of Personality and Social Psychology* 63: 403–25.

Theodoulou, Stella Z., and Chris Kofinis. 2004. *The Art of the Game: Understanding American Public Policy Making*. Belmont, CA: Wadsworth.

Thompson, Dennis F. 1999. Democratic Theory and Global Society. *Journal of Political Philosophy* 7: 111–25.

Thompson, Dennis F. 2008. Deliberative Democratic Theory and Empirical Political Science. *Annual Review of Political Science* 11: 497–520.

Thompson, Dennis F. 2013. Are American Elections Sufficiently Democratic? Pp. 26–38 in *Representation: Elections and Beyond*, edited by Jack H. Nagel and Rogers M. Smith. Philadelphia: University of Pennsylvania Press.

Tickner, Joel. 2001. Democratic Participation: A Critical Element of Precautionary Public Health Decision-Making. *New Solutions* 11(2): 93–111.

Torney-Purta, Judith, and Britt S. Wilkenfeld. 2009. *Paths to 21st Century Competencies through Civic Education Classrooms: An Analysis of Survey Results from Ninth Graders*. Chicago, IL: American Bar Association Division for Public Education.

Toulmin, Stephen. 1958. *The Uses of Argument*. Cambridge University Press.

Tucker, Aviezer. 2008. Pre-emptive Democracy: Oligarchic Tendencies in Deliberative Democracy. *Political Studies* 56, 127–47.

Turner, John C., Michael A. Hogg, Penelope J. Oakes, Stephen D. Reicher, and Margaret S. Wetherell. 1987. *Rediscovering the Social Group: A Self-Categorization Theory*. Oxford: Basil Blackwell.

Turner, Marlene E., and Anthony R Pratkanis, eds. 1998. *Organizational Behavior and Human Decision Processes* 73: 103–374.

University of New Hampshire Office of Sustainability Programs and Cooperative Extension. 2002. *New Hampshire Just Food Citizen Panel Consensus Conference, February 7–9, 2002, Findings and Recommendations*. Durham, NH: University of New Hampshire Office of Sustainability Programs and Cooperative Extension.

Urbanati, Nadia, and Mark Warren. 2008. The Concept of Representation in Contemporary Democratic Theory. *Annual Review of Political Science* 11: 387–412.

US Congress. 2011, April 14. *Congressional Record: Daily Edition* 157 (55): S2472-S2474.

US Government Accountability Office. 2006. Telecommunications: Broadband Deployment Is Extensive Throughout the United States, but It Is Difficult to Assess the Extent of Deployment Gaps in Rural Areas. Washington, DC: US Government Accountability Office.

Verba, Sidney, Kay Lehman Schlozman, and Henry E. Brady. 1995. *Voice and Equality: Civic Voluntarism in American Politics*. Cambridge, MA: Harvard University Press.

Vinokur, Amiram, and Eugene Burnstein. 1978. Depolarization of Attitudes in Groups. *Journal of Personality and Social Psychology*, 36: 872–85.

Voltaire. 1949 [1759]. *The Portable Voltaire*. Edited by Ben Ray Redman. New York: Viking Press.

Walsh, Katherine Cramer. 2006. Communities, Race, and Talk: An Analysis of the Occurrence of Civic Intergroup Dialogue Programs. *Journal of Politics* 68: 22–33.

Walsh, Katherine Cramer. 2007. *Talking about Race: Community Dialogues and the Politics of Difference.* University of Chicago Press.

Walzer, Michael. 1991. Constitutional Rights and the Shape of Civil Society. Pp. 113–26 in *The Constitution of the People: Reflections on Citizens and Civil Society*, edited by Robert E. Calvert. University Press of Kansas.

Wampler, Brian. 2012. Participatory Budgeting: Core Principles and Key Impacts. *Journal of Public Deliberation* 8(2), Article 12: 1–13.

Wampler, Brian, and Janette Hartz-Karp. 2012. Participatory Budgeting: Diffusion and Outcomes across the World. *Journal of Public Deliberation* 8(2), Article 13: 1–4.

Warren, Mark E. 1992. Democratic Theory and Self-Transformation. *American Political Science Review* 86: 8–23.

Warren, Mark E. 2001. *Democracy and Association.* Princeton University Press.

Warren, Mark E. 2007. *Institutionalizing Deliberative Democracy.* Pp. 272–88 in *Deliberation, Participation and Democracy: Can the People Govern?*, edited by Shawn W. Rosenberg. New York: Palgrave Macmillan.

Warren, Mark E., and Hilary Pearse, eds. 2008. *Designing Deliberative Democracy: The British Columbia Citizens' Assembly.* Cambridge University Press.

Wesolowska, Elzbieta. 2007. Social Processes of Antagonism and Synergy in Deliberating Groups. *Swiss Political Science Review* 13: 663–80.

Williams, Melissa S. 1998. *Voice, Trust, and Memory: Marginalized Groups and the Failings of Liberal Representation.* Princeton University Press.

Williamson, Vanessa, Theda Skocpol, and John Coggin. 2011. The Tea Party and the Remaking of Republican Conservatism. *Perspectives on Politics* 9: 25–43.

Winston, Brian. 1988. The Tradition of the Victim in Griersonian Documentary. Pp. 269–86 in *New Challenges for Documentary*, edited by Alan Rosenthal. Berkeley: University of California Press.

Wolff, Edward N. 2009. *Poverty and Income Distribution*, 2d ed. Chichester, UK: Wiley Blackwell.

Wood, Lesley J. 2012. *Direct Action, Deliberation, and Diffusion: Collective Action after the WTO Protests in Seattle.* Cambridge University Press.

Yack, Bernard. 2006. Rhetoric and Public Reasoning: An Aristotelian Understanding of Political Deliberation. *Political Theory* 34: 417–38.

Yen, Hope. 2013. U.S. Poverty Rate Languishes at 15 Percent. *San Jose Mercury News*, 18 September, A10.

Young, Iris Marion. 1996. Communication and the Other: Beyond Deliberative Democracy. Pp. 120–36 in *Democracy and Difference: Contesting the Boundaries of the Political*, edited by Seyla Benhabib. Princeton University Press.

Young, Iris Marion. 2000. *Inclusion and Democracy.* Oxford University Press.

Young, Iris Marion. 2001. Activist Challenges to Deliberative Democracy. *Political Theory* 29: 670–90.

Zaller, John. 1992. *The Nature and Origins of Mass Opinion*. Cambridge University Press.

Zaller, John, and Stanley Feldman. 1992. A Simple Theory of the Survey Response. *American Journal of Political Science* 36: 579–616.

Zarefsky, David. 1986. *President Johnson's War on Poverty: Rhetoric and History*. Tuscaloosa, AL: University of Alabama Press.

Index